This is the first book to examine the literature of the Romantic period as a conscious attempt to influence the religious life of society. Robert Ryan argues that the political quarrel that preoccupied England during the Romantic period was in large part an argument about the religious character of the nation, and that the Romantics became active and conspicuous participants in this public debate. Where critics have traditionally viewed the Romantics as creative metaphysicians articulating private visions of a transcendent order in detachment from actual social conflict, Ryan shows instead how their religious prescriptions were formulated in response to specific historical and social circumstances. The writers of the time, driven by a dissatisfaction with the major religion of the day, devoted their talents to a subversion or revision of coercive systems of belief and assumed positions of leadership in a struggle for liberty of imagination in the religious sphere. This book shows how the careers of Blake, Wordsworth, Byron, Keats, and the Shelleys are radically reconfigured when viewed in the context of the period's passionate debate on religion, politics, and society.

CAMBRIDGE STUDIES IN ROMANTICISM

This series aims to foster the best new work in one of the most challenging fields within English literary studies. From the early 1780s to the early 1830s a formidable array of talented men and women took to literary composition, not just in poetry, which some of them famously transformed, but in many modes of writing. The expansion of publishing created new opportunities for writers, and the political stakes of what they wrote were raised again and again by what Wordsworth called those 'great national events' that were 'almost daily taking place': the French Revolution, the Napoleonic and American wars, urbanization, industrialization, religious revival, an expanded empire abroad and the reform movement at home. This was an enormous ambition, even when it pretended otherwise. The relations between science, philosophy, religion and literature were reworked in texts such as *Frankenstein* and *Biographia Literaria*; gender relations in *A Vindication of the Rights of Woman* and *Don Juan*; journalism by Cobbett and Hazlitt; poetic form, content and style by the Lake School and the Cockney School. Outside Shakespeare studies, probably no body of writing has produced such a wealth of response or done so much to shape the responses of modern criticism. This indeed is the period that saw the emergence of those notions of 'literature' and of literary history, especially national literary history, on which modern scholarship in English has been founded.

The categories produced by Romanticism have also been challenged by recent historicist arguments. The task of the series is to engage both with a challenging corpus of Romantic writings and with the changing field of criticism they have helped to shape. As with other literary series published by Cambridge, this one will represent the work of both younger and more established scholars, on either side of the Atlantic and elsewhere.

For a complete list of titles published see end of book

CAMBRIDGE STUDIES IN ROMANTICISM 24

THE ROMANTIC REFORMATION

Plate 18 of *Milton* by William Blake. Reproduced by permission of the Lessing J. Rosenwald Collection, Library of Congress

THE ROMANTIC REFORMATION

Religious politics in English literature, 1789–1824

ROBERT M. RYAN

Rutgers University

CAMBRIDGE
UNIVERSITY PRESS

PUBLISHED BY THE PRESS SYNDICATE OF THE UNIVERSITY OF CAMBRIDGE
The Pitt Building, Trumpington Street, Cambridge CB2 IRP, United Kingdom

CAMBRIDGE UNIVERSITY PRESS
The Edinburgh Building, Cambridge, CB2 2RU, United Kingdom
40 West 20th Street, New York, NY 10011–4211, USA
10 Stamford Road, Oakleigh, Melbourne 3166, Australia

First published 1997

Printed in the United Kingdom at the University Press, Cambridge

Typeset in Baskervilee 11/12.5pt

A catalogue record for this book is available from the British Library

ISBN 0 521 57008 5 hardback

For Brighid
and for Mark and Delia

Contents

Introduction

The political professions and evasions of British Romantic poetry have been a major preoccupation of literary studies for two decades. Yet amidst all the attention that has been given to the revolutionary agitation of the 1790s as the crucible in which Romanticism found its creative energy, and to the ensuing period of disillusion and reaction as the occasion of an apparent renunciation by poetry of its social commitments, one finds very little discussion of the religious milieu wherein English Romanticism acquired its distinctive character. This silence is surprising, since religion was a critically important dimension of the public life of the time and was itself a powerful generator of political and social change. Indeed, when one considers the far-reaching impact of the evangelical revival on the cultural life of Britain, the permanent alteration in the balance of political power caused by the struggle for religious liberty by Catholics and Dissenters, and the emergence of new strains of skepticism and secularism that contributed to the alienation and radicalization of the working classes, one might argue that the most significant stimuli for social change in the 1790s were generated in the religious rather than in the political sphere – if those two spheres can properly be spoken of as distinct from one another.

In recent years the Romantic poets have been reproached for withdrawing from engagement with political and economic realities and taking refuge in poetry that deliberately distanced itself from the social crises of the time. The most influential expression of this critique was Jerome McGann's *The Romantic Ideology*, but McGann himself credits M. H. Abrams for first noticing in Romantic poetry "a transcendental displacement of human desires from the political arena to the spiritual."[1] A more specifically Marxist formulation of the argument appeared in a history of modern criticism written by John Fekete:

The deformations of the French Revolution . . . and of the capitalist social relations being entrenched in urban-industrial England . . . led the romantics essentially to recoil from social and political aspiration . . . Their value-based notions of total social revitalization receded, as the values they represented came to be expressed in terms independent of the ongoing daily advance of the society. The cultural opposition they presented took the form increasingly of a value alternative or surrogate experience outside the dominant social practices rather than the critical edge of transformations within the frame of progress; more a means of evaluation than a means of orientation for social leverage."[2]

Fekete's analysis is reductive in its understanding of society's "dominant social practices" strictly in materialist terms. One important consequence of this limitation is inadequate attention to the central role religion was playing in the transformation of society during the period and the powerful "social leverage" it was able to exert. A more sophisticated materialist critic, Terence Hoagwood, conscious as he is of the "connection between mental structures and social institutions," has better understood the Romantics' concern with "the underlying and collective mental acts that constitute the human world in which politics and economic change take their place,"[3] and has interested himself accordingly in the poets' engagement with the "mental acts" that constituted the dominant religious ideology of the time. But generally the "new" historicist critics, although committed to examining literature within a broad network of contemporary discourses and social practices, have tended to overlook the practices and discourses of religion, that most conspicuous preoccupation of Britons at the time in their private and public lives.

Until recently, most social historians have tended in this way to underestimate the role of religion in political life. Hannah Arendt was expressing what was still a broad consensus when she remarked in 1963 that revivalist religion was "politically without consequences and historically futile."[4] One can see here the enduring influence of Enlightenment views of religion as a vestige of mankind's primitive past destined to disappear with the continued advance of knowledge, a conviction that was reinvigorated by Karl Marx's indictment of religion as intrinsically obscurantist and anti-progressive. But even if, as is still routinely argued, a major factor preventing revolution in England in the 1790s was the conservative counterforce exerted by religion, that counterforce, if such it can legitimately be called, should merit more scrutiny on the part of those concerned with investigating literature's political and social relations.

It is difficult to distinguish between the political and the religious aspects of the cultural transformation experienced by English society at the beginning of the nineteenth century. That no political revolution lacks a religious dimension is a generalization with special validity in Britain, where religion and politics have been involved in a particularly close relationship since the Reformation and where revolutionary agitation has had a tendency to begin on the religious front, as was manifestly the case in the great political upheavals of the seventeenth century. The crucial formative events of modern British history – the Elizabethan Settlement, the Civil War, the Revolution of 1688, and the Hanoverian Succession – were religious crises whose resolution contributed essential components of what is called the British Constitution in Church and State. During the Romantic period the religious identity of the British nation became once again a question in dispute as the result of intensified resistance by Dissenters to the Established Church's hegemony, the crusade-like character of the war against infidel France, and the millenarian consciousness that swept through all classes of society, giving eschatological resonance to current events, inspiring exaggerated hope or fear of social change, and generally adding a strong religious coloring to the debate on the national destiny that preoccupied liberals and conservatives during the Revolutionary and Napoleonic eras.[5]

The poets of the period were fully aware of the intimate connection between religion and government in Britain. When Richard Carlile was tried for blasphemous libel in 1819 after publishing Thomas Paine's *The Age of Reason*, Percy Bysshe Shelley came to his defence with an incisive analysis of the politics of religion as they operated in Carlile's case. In a striking anticipation of the anti-religious rhetoric of socialism, Shelley said of Carlile's accusers:

They know that the Established Church is based upon the belief in certain events of a supernatural character having occurred in Judaea eighteen centuries ago; that but for this belief the farmer would refuse to pay the tenth of the produce of his labours to maintain its numbers in idleness; that this class of persons if not maintained in idleness would have something else to do than to divert the attention of the people from obtaining a Reform in their oppressive government, & that consequently the government would be reformed, & that the people would receive a just price for their labours, a consummation incompatible with the luxurious idleness in which their rulers esteem it their interest to live.[6]

No one on the opposing side would have disputed Shelley's basic analysis, however they might have objected to his language. At Carlile's trial the Attorney General stated the government's position succinctly: "Christianity is, undoubtedly, a part of the common law of the land, and therefore a part of the constitution of the country; that it is so, cannot be disproved, and it has always been considered a crime to revile that religion, on which the proper administration of public justice depends."[7]

Perhaps because British history demonstrated that religion was not the antagonist of social change but rather its most potent stimulus, and perhaps because the Protestant tradition considered not religion *per se* but only corrupt, erroneous religion to be the enemy of progress, the Romantic poets accepted the role of religion as a dynamic ideology behind social and political action. To some degree they all shared Coleridge's insight that "Religion, true or false, is and ever has been the centre of gravity in a realm, to which all other things must and will accommodate themselves."[8] They knew that to adjust the "equilibrium between institutions and opinions" (Shelley's phrase) the religious principles cementing the social order would have to be reexamined critically and, when necessary, changed.

My primary thesis in this book is that all the poets committed themselves resolutely to this work of cultural critique and rehabilitation. It is not accurate to say, as Fekete does, that for the Romantics "aesthetic subjectivity was precluded from active participation in the construction of the social forms,"[9] or that the "cultural sphere" the poets represented became divorced from "the ongoing daily advance of the society." Religion was the crucial mediator between the cultural and the political-economic spheres in England,[10] and the Romantics directed their creative energies toward intervention in that arena. Their individual prescriptions varied, of course, with their political dispositions. While Wordsworth and Blake were able to reach an accommodation with orthodoxy, Shelley and Keats decisively repudiated the Christianity of their time as incorrigibly dishonest and pernicious. But they all adopted as a goal the spiritual and moral rehabilitation of their society, a renovation that presupposed an alteration in the national religious consciousness.

The fact that British Romanticism as a cultural movement addressed itself more consistently to broad questions of imaginative liberation than to specific issues of economic and social reform indicates something other than loss of political nerve or sedation of social conscience – derelictions that the poets shared with other ex-radicals whose revolutionary zeal was cooled by legal intimidation and the diminution of youthful ardor. Although the poets may have been frustrated by a repressive political environment, instead of "recoiling from social and political aspiration" they continued to dedicate their talents to the subversion or revision of coercive and obscurantist systems of belief, accepting as a primary cultural mission the articulation of alternative, more psychologically wholesome and socially beneficent conceptions of religion. M. H. Abrams has argued that in the Romantic consciousness revolutionary optimism gave way to "revolutionary disillusionment or despair,"[11] but the fact is that their optimism found a satisfying outlet in the sphere of religion. If the British Constitution in Church and State was resistant to change on its political side, the religious dimension of the power structure still seemed susceptible of correction. Instead of lamenting Romanticism as a political retreat, then, one may more usefully see it as a creative and effective engagement in the contemporary religious crisis, an engagement that was perceived as having far-reaching consequences in the political order.

In Britain after 1795 prophetic reformation became a more practicable agenda, and for poets a more appropriate one, than political agitation. Here, as in so much else, John Milton provided a model, his achievement offering consolation for the thwarted liberal aspirations of a post-revolutionary era. A repressive and perilous political environment had forced even the regicide Milton to withdraw from public life and turn his attention to the quieter enterprise of influencing the character of his country by appealing to its religious conscience. The cultural impact of *Paradise Lost* demonstrated that poetry possessed the power to adjust a society's understanding of itself. John Keats remarked that when *Paradise Lost* appeared after the Restoration, it "hit the new system of things a mighty mental blow – the exertion must have had or is yet to have some sequences."[12] Romantic poetry, then, may be more profitably considered as acts of Miltonic engagement in the religious culture of the time than as meditations in retirement from social realities. In fact, the Romantics were never more engaged in the public life of their society than when they addressed religious topics. Given the intense interest in things spiritual that increasingly preoccupied their countrymen in those years, one can say without paradox that their religious interests are what kept the poets in touch with the real world.

When religion became the primary arena in which the Romantics engaged the power structure of their society, their effective influence in that field was acknowledged by friend and foe alike. In the struggle for liberty of imagination in moral and spiritual matters they assumed positions of leadership of a kind not available to them in more purely political spheres of activity, and they embraced those leadership roles sometimes with remarkable boldness. As political activists the poets can seem ineffectual compounds of reckless eccentricity and practical timidity, but their authority in the religious sphere was widely acknowledged by their contemporaries (with varying admiration or reproach) and throughout the nineteenth century their major contribution was usually perceived more in religious than in political terms. Wordsworth, for example, never achieved the stature he longed for as political prophet or even pundit, but he became widely revered as a religious teacher and innovator – as admired for his influence in religion as Byron and Shelley were feared and excoriated for theirs. Shelley's claim to be an unacknowledged legislator could not be dismissed as gratuitous by those who saw a clear and present danger in his efforts to undermine the religious buttresses of the Constitution.

It was precisely their religious influence that enabled the Romantics to exert whatever political impact they had – an exercise of power that has too often been ignored in discussions of Romantic politics. "The life of Byron was of no political significance," observed a literary critic recently,[13] but this was not at all the perception of the poet's contemporaries, whose assessment of his political importance was given vivid expression in an 1822 pamphlet that identified Byron as the commandant of a monstrous regiment of infidels bent on destroying the soul of England – an army that included Richard Carlile as well as William Lawrence of the Royal College of Physicians, who had recently shocked the London medical community by delivering and publishing a series of skeptical lectures:

And though we have seen France revolutionized by the spread of Atheism which drew after it a spring-tide of blood, deluging the Continent, and this island seemed the only spot where the ark of salvation could find rest, yet even up to this hill of the Lord, the tide in its return has risen! Here the

same fiendish attempts are made to persuade the multitude there is no God
– to deprive them of hope here and bliss hereafter. Not only the despicable
bookseller vends his poison through the land, but the Anatomical Lecturer
joins the infidel troup . . . and the titled Poet takes command of the whole,
and with the gems of genius bestudding his sword and glittering on his helm
attracts myriads of our youth to his splendid standard, and soothes them
into voluptuous security, or rouses them to violence by the voice of the
Muses who follow in his train.[14]

The anonymous author went on to emphasize the political nature of
the threat posed by Byron's infidelity by equating the poet's influence
with that of Thomas Paine, warning of subversives "whose sentiments are written in the bloody characters of the Rights of Man, or
pictured off in the doggrel rhymes of ribaldry and revolution."[15] It is
noteworthy that a poet is here assigned a higher place in the order of
command than the political activist Carlile. That "despicable bookseller," by the way, also made a connection between *Don Juan* and
The Rights of Man when he associated the "Satanic School" of poetry
with "the school of Paine."[16] Carlile's pirated edition of Byron's *Cain*
(1822) was a calculated political act by a man who always understood
that to discredit Christianity was to contribute to the destabilization
of the British government.

In this book I will examine the literature of the Romantic period
as a conscious attempt by a group of writers to influence the religious
transformation that was taking place in their society. They all saw
that they could have an important cultural impact by altering the
character of the system of religion that was increasing its hold as the
dominant ideology and idealism of their time. I call what they
attempted a reformation because, after periods of youthful iconoclasm, they all finally became more interested in purifying or
redefining England's national religion than in attempting to eradicate it. Critics have always acknowledged and usually honored the
Romantics' tendencies toward skepticism, but I will argue here that
what made them important figures in our intellectual history was not
their skepticism but their belief – an exigent sense of religious
propriety that inspired radical dissatisfaction with the state of public
religion in their time. That some sort of national religion would exist
seemed to them inevitable; even Rousseau's *The Social Contract* understood the necessity of a "civil religion" that acknowledged the
existence of God and an afterlife as a means of encouraging and
enforcing "social sentiments without which no man can be either a

good citizen or a faithful subject."[17] The public religion envisioned by Rousseau excluded the specific doctrines and rites of Christianity, which in his eyes had disqualified itself from serving as a useful civil religion. In the English context, however, given the faith's historic role as a stimulus of political change, the reformation and liberalization of Christianity seemed to the Romantic poets not only a necessary but a practical political agenda.

When M. H. Abrams in *Natural Supernaturalism* examined the secularization of Biblical themes in Romantic poetry, his argument tended to obscure the reality and intensity of the poets' reformist engagement in the religious situation of their time. The poets would not so clearly have perceived their mission as the preservation of what was valuable in a dying belief system or the articulation of secular versions of a faith that was losing its cultural vitality. What in retrospect appears to us as the progressive secularization of Western culture since the Renaissance was in their time manifestly experiencing a period of retrograde motion; the Romantics found themselves confronting an increasingly militant religious ideology that seemed to be reasserting its dominance in the cultural order.

Insofar as modern critics have taken the poets seriously as religious thinkers, they have most commonly been treated as creative metaphysicians articulating private intuitions of a noumenal order rather than as active participants in the public religious life of their times.[18] But while they always insisted on the liberty and primacy of the individual imagination in religious speculation, they did so as Protestants have done from the beginning, conscious of historical and social circumstances that required a specific religious response. The dimension of Romantic religious thought I am examining here is not the denial of human limitations that T. E. Hulme called "spilt religion."[19] Religion as it operates in the political order participates in the art of the possible; although more visionary and optimistic than *realpolitik* tends to be, it finally has to acknowledge the limitations imposed by social circumstances. The Romantic religious agenda was a response to history, to politics, to economics; it took its character and sense of urgency from the atmosphere of crisis that prevailed in the public order. Blake, for example, who was the most theologically engaged of the writers to be discussed here, was primarily concerned with an historically situated community of believers as they faced the moral and political challenges of their time; everything he wrote was intended to change the national religious consciousness so that better moral and political effects would follow. It can be said of Blake as of the other poets that their interest in religion focused less on the internal consolations of belief than on its civil effects, its influence on behavior in society, its role as a blessing or a bane in human relationships. With the exception of Coleridge, they were all concerned much more with the politics of religion than with its metaphysics.

The career of each of the Romantic poets has a clearer outline when seen as an attempt to define a religious position in dialogue or conflict with the dominant belief system of their society. So Blake is more intelligible when read, not as an eccentric skeptic quoting scripture to achieve his own subversive ends, but as a believer who dedicated himself wholeheartedly to the correction and restoration of Christianity in order that it might become an effective weapon against the political and economic brutalities of his time. Likewise, Wordsworth's Christian poetry, most notably *The Excursion*, is more usefully seen not as a retreat from political engagement but as a purposeful contribution to public religious discourse, to a debate that Wordsworth perceived as having superseded the suppressed political arguments of the 1790s and that would significantly affect the nation's future character. Byron, too, seems less eccentric, less alienated from his society, when his lifelong, increasingly daring critique of the state religion is perceived as a purposeful campaign, inspired by belief as much as by skepticism, to force Christianity to live up to its self-representations. The anomaly of Shelley, the atheist who wrote splendid religious poetry, becomes less puzzling when he is understood as having cultivated a more exalted ideal of religion than any of the churches of his time had the vision or the courage to articulate, and when one sees that he too was finally less interested in destroying Christianity than in revising it to make it function more positively in society. The nature and extent of Keats's political engagement emerge with greater clarity when one appreciates the radical religio-political agenda that influenced some of his most crucial artistic decisions. His Greek themes, for example, were not a nostalgic retreat from contemporary reality, but were meant to help dislodge from his culture the Christian myth that cemented an inhumane social order. Even the Frankenstein monster's odd, confused Christian creed comes into clearer focus when it is understood as an expression of Mary Shelley's own religious politics, embodying a two-edged critique of the failures of Christians as well as of their Godwinian antagonists.

The absence of Samuel Taylor Coleridge from this otherwise conventional Romantic canon requires a word of explanation. While Coleridge's name appears in every chapter, I have included no extended discussion of him, partly because even a superficial discussion of his life-long effort to redefine Christianity would require disproportionate space, and partly because, unlike the other writers included here, Coleridge came to understand himself primarily as a theologian and only secondarily as a poet or a writer of fictions. His enormous contribution to what I call the Romantic Reformation deserves to be examined in detail, but such an enterprise would require at least another volume the size of this one.[20]

To fill in the social and historical context, I offer an introductory chapter developing my argument that British Romanticism's historical milieu was at least as intensely religious in character as it was political – or rather that the political and the religious dimensions were often indistinguishable in the agitated public life of the time. The chapter is not offered merely as background information or scene-setting. I hope to demonstrate the extent to which the national political quarrel that preoccupied England in the 1790s was initially and remained to an important degree an argument about religion – about individual autonomy in matters of the spirit and about the proper character and future tendency of the national faith. In order to establish that the Romantics' concern with religion was not a reactionary impulse, I will argue that religion was perceived at the time to function as an ideology of liberation rather than one of repression. Having developed those arguments, I will go on to examine the ways in which five poets and one novelist participated consciously, actively, and effectively in the life of their time as critics and reformers of the national religion of England.

I am aware that discussion of religion in literature creates rich opportunity for grinding personal axes; critics are never more likely to pursue their own hidden, even unconscious, agendas than when reading religion into their favorite poets. Evidence of this lies ready to hand in the history of Romantic criticism. Blake has been admired both as an atheist and as a Christian mystic. One critic found no Evangelicalism in Wordsworth's religious background and another has found little else. Byron's mind has been analyzed as quintessentially secular as well as uniquely Christian. And in two books published in the late 1970s, Keats emerged as both skeptical humanist and life-long theist.[21] In an attempt to avoid falling too often into special pleading I have tried to keep my object limited, examining the public articulation rather than speculating on the private content of the poets' creeds and showing how the Romantics' religious interests were politically conditioned and constituted an observable bond of connection between them and their society. As another means of controlling critical eccentricity I have tried always to test my generalizations on specific texts, organizing each chapter around one or two of them, e.g., *Jerusalem, The Excursion, Cain, Hellas, Frankenstein,* and Keats's "Hyperion" poems.

Looking beyond this focus on individual writers and their works, I offer the book as a contribution to the line of criticism that has attempted to understand the Romantic writers as participants in a single literary movement, a critical tradition that began with Shelley and Hazlitt and that has continued in the twentieth century with the work of D. G. James, Harold Bloom, Edward Bostetter, Carl Woodring, Marilyn Butler, and others.[22] Apart from inviting invidious comparisons with those accomplished scholars, to attempt a study of such broad scope brings other perils along with its rewards. Because I hope this book will interest a broader audience than one made up of specialists in Romantic studies, I will sometimes be guilty in the eyes of the specialist of overlooking or belaboring what any respectable scholar ought to take for granted. So I must ask Shelleyans to bear with this Keatsian while he reminds Wordsworthians of what Blake thought about Byron. We literary scholars must attempt more often to speak to each other across the borders of our specializations and do so in terms that make our writing accessible to readers who do not share our transient academic obsessions or our vested interests.

I owe an enormous debt to the scholars who have labored so well the minute particulars of Romantic studies; the extent of my debt to all those Blakeans, Wordsworthians, et al. will be apparent to them in the following pages. An older, broader indebtedness also accounts in part for the kind of book this is. From the faculty at Columbia University in the 1960s I learned to respect the formal integrity of poetic texts while investigating the matrix of historical relations in which they originated. My first teacher at Columbia was Marjorie Nicolson; my last was Carl Woodring. As I observed the former demonstrating the impact of astronomy on the Renaissance literary imagination and the latter investigating the politics of Romantic poetry, it became evident to me that there is no functional dichotomy between formal evaluation and historical analysis of literature. My colleagues in the English department at Rutgers University in Camden have for a quarter century provided a sane, congenial, and supportive intellectual community, helping, along with my students, to shape and clarify the ideas I have set down in this book. I am indebted to the library staffs of Rutgers University, the University of Pennsylvania, and the British Library, where most of the research was carried on. I am grateful also to the National Endowment for the Humanities for a fellowship that enabled me to begin work on the project, and to Rutgers University for its program of Faculty Academic Study Leaves that allowed the work to progress. Finally, I must thank my family for their affection and patience. This book grew up with my children and must at times have been the object of intense sibling rivalry. I take special pleasure in dedicating the book to them and to my wife, who orchestrated the harmonies that made its completion possible.

Part of chapter 4 and chapter 5 were originally delivered in the form of papers at the Wordsworth Summer Conference in Grasmere in 1987 and 1989; the papers were published in *The Wordsworth Circle*, vols. 19 (1988) and 21 (1990). Chapter 6 is an expansion of an article that first appeared in *Critical Essays on Keats*, ed. Hermione de Almeida (Boston: G. K. Hall, 1990).

CHAPTER I

"A sect of dissenters"

We owe the great writers of the golden age of our literature to
that fervid awakening of the public mind which shook to dust
the oldest and most oppressive form of the Christian Religion.
We owe Milton to the progress and development of the same
spirit; the sacred Milton was, let it ever be remembered, a
Republican, and a bold enquirer into morals and religion. The
great writers of our own age are, we have reason to suppose, the
companions and forerunners of some unimagined change in our
social condition or the opinions which cement it. The cloud of
mind is discharging its collected lightning, and the equilibrium
between institutions and opinions is now restoring or about to
be restored.

(Percy Bysshe Shelley, Preface to *Prometheus Unbound*) [1]

Shelley's perception of an intimate, necessary connection between
politics and religion as forces for social change and his assumption
that imaginative literature participated in the enterprise of political
and religious reformation were shared by other writers of the time,
even by those who did not sympathize with the radical politics that
colored Shelley's optimism. The special affinity he perceived between
his own time and that of the Protestant Reformation in England was
also noticed by the other Romantics. William Wordsworth remarked
on the resemblance between his own era and that of the first English
Protestants, who had lived, he wrote, in an age "conspicuous as our
own / For strife and ferment in the minds of men; / Whence
alteration in the forms of things / Various and vast."[2] And like
Shelley, John Keats saw the poets of his own time taking their rightful
place in the vanguard of "a grand march of intellect" that would
continue the liberalization of religion left unfinished by the Reformation. Keats honored Wordsworth, in particular, as the prophet of a
more enlightened faith, one more concordant with human nature
than Milton's Protestantism had been.[3]

Here I must think Wordsworth is deeper than Milton – though I think it has depended more upon the general and gregarious advance of intellect, than individual greatness of Mind . . . The Reformation produced such immediate and great benefits, that Protestantism was considered under the immediate eye of heaven, and its own remaining Dogmas and superstitions, then, as it were, regenerated, constituted those resting places and seeming sure points of Reasoning . . . Milton, whatever he may have thought in the sequel, appears to have been content with these by his writings – He did not think into the human heart, as Wordsworth has done – Yet Milton as a Philosopher, had sure as great powers as Wordsworth – What is then to be inferr'd? O many things – It proves there really is a grand march of intellect –, It proves that a mighty providence subdues the mightiest Minds to the service of the time being, whether it be in human Knowledge or Religion.[4]

Keats's Milton is rather different from Shelley's "bold enquirer into morals and religion," that impatient visionary who not only prophesied but actively abetted revolution in the religious and political orders. To Keats Milton seems a more passive product of the spirit of his age, one who remained content with a dogmatic, superstitious faith that he was incapable of seeing beyond. But both Keats and Shelley found in Milton an obvious illustration of their common conception of Britain's religious history as involving a progressive refinement of doctrine and morals, a liberalization in which poets in particular took positions of leadership not only as articulators of contemporary beliefs but as agents of continuing religious change. Shelley saw the great writers of his own age as driven by the same "spirit" that accomplished the Reformation; Keats understood Wordsworth to have been raised up by a "mighty providence" to help purify his countrymen's religious sense, illuminating a path that younger poets could follow.

It was not coincidental that Shelley and Keats arrived at similar visions of the English Reformation as a continuing process in which poets bore special responsibilities and in which Milton had played an exemplary role. This complex of ideas is not only suggested by the events of Milton's life; it is articulated frequently in that poet's writings. Church reform was a central issue in the quarrel between King and Parliament in which Milton participated so prominently. Although the English Reformation had reached a temporary resolution in the Elizabethan Settlement, the more radical Protestants never fully accepted the compromise with Catholic tradition that established the Church of England and they continued to demand a more complete reformation in doctrine, discipline, and liturgy of the kind John Calvin had effected at Geneva. The attempt of William Laud, Archbishop of Canterbury under Charles I, to increase episcopal power and revive Catholic traditions in liturgy and church furnishing made the need for a radical reformation even more urgent in the eyes of Charles's Puritan opposition. Milton articulated their position in his first published prose work, *Of Reformation Touching Church Discipline in England: And the Causes That Hitherto Have Hindered It* (1641), in which, after reviewing the reasons why the English Church had not been properly "rectified" by the reforms of Henry VIII, Edward VI, and Elizabeth I, he urged Englishmen to "cut away from the publick body the noysom, and diseased tumor of Prelacie, and come from Schisme to *unity* with our neighbour Reformed sister Churches."[5]

As the political crisis of the 1640s deepened, Milton's conception of reformation changed. After episcopal governance was legally abolished in 1643 it quickly became apparent that bishops had not been the only obstacles to religious progress in England. When the newly empowered Presbyterians issued an ordinance prohibiting the publication of books without the prior approval of a board of censors, it was clear that presbyters could be as obscurantist and coercive as prelates. Milton's response in *Areopagitica* (1644) was to argue that the English Reformation was a continuing process on which no one should try to impose a premature conclusion. The Reformation of the sixteenth century was only one phase in a movement that had begun in England two centuries earlier with John Wycliffe, at whose example the German and Swiss reformers "lighted their Tapers." Although Wycliffe was "the first Restorer of buried truth," his own country had not yet experienced the fullness of reformation enjoyed by other European states. Milton's objection to the Licensing Order was precisely that it denied the need and prevented the means for further reformation:

The light which we have gain'd, was giv'n us, not to be ever staring on, but by it to discover onward things more remote from our knowledge. It is not the unfrocking of a Priest, the unmitring of a Bishop, and the removing of him from off the *Presbyterian* shoulders that will make us a happy Nation, no, if other things as great in the Church, and in the rule of life both economicall and politicall be not lookt into and reform'd, we have lookt so long upon the blaze that *Zuinglius* and *Calvin* hath beacon'd up to us, that we are stark blind.[6]

Reformation involves more than ecclesiastical purgation; even the radical "rectifications" of Zwingli and Calvin are now perceived as involving too limited a conception of reform. Milton's Reformation has become a broader cultural process, one that has not only doctrinal but political and economic change in view: "For the property of Truth is, where she is publickly taught, to unyoke & set free the minds and spirits of a Nation first from the thraldom of sin and superstition, after which all honest and legal freedom of civil life cannot be long absent." In the ecclesiastical disturbances of his time Milton saw signs that "God is decreeing to begin some new and great period in his Church, ev'n to the reforming of Reformation it self."[7]

This work of national reformation was too important to be left to ordained ministers, whatever the cut of their cloth. *The Reason of Church Government*, an essay that has been widely read since its publication for its autobiographical content, recounts the mental process by which Milton determined that his own literary talent should be dedicated to the service of religious reform. Convincing himself that "the completion of England's reformation would bring with it the long-sought release of his poetical powers,"[8] Milton decided that his own God-given talent could be employed with equal justification in the arena of religious controversy as in the composition of poetry. Since literary genius is the gift of "that eternall Spirit who can enrich with all utterance and knowledge, and sends out his Seraphim with the hallowed fire of his Altar, to touch and purify the lips of whom he pleases," the divine calling of the poet provides credentials at least as legitimate as those bestowed by canonical ordination for addressing religious issues in the public forum: "These abilities, wheresoever they be found, are the inspired gift of God rarely bestow'd . . . and are of power beside the office of a pulpit, to imbreed and cherish in a great people the seeds of vertu and publick civility."[9]

Here is the Milton of Shelley and Keats (and Blake and Wordsworth also) illustrating in his own life the principle that religious reformation is a continuing process with consequences not only in the theological sphere but in politics and economics as well, and inviting and encouraging others to apply their talents to the ongoing work of reform. Keats, an admirer of Milton's "delectable prose,"[10] could have borrowed his concept of a grand march of intellect presided over by a mighty providence directly from *Areopagitica*:

When God shakes a Kingdome with strong and healthfull commotions to a generall reforming . . . God then raises to his own work men of rare abilities, and more then common industry not only to look back and revise what hath been taught heretofore, but to gain furder and goe on, some new enlightn'd steps in the discovery of truth. For such is the order of Gods enlightning his Church, to dispense and deal out by degrees his beam, so as our earthly eyes may best sustain it. Neither is God appointed and confin'd, where and out of what place these his chosen shall be first heard to speak.[11]

The Romantic poets had reason to believe that the same historical tendency, the same reformational spirit was working in their own time to bring some "unimagined change" in the religious opinions that cemented the social order. They saw in contemporary events signs that their own time might be as remarkable an era in English religious history as the ones that brought the Tudor Reformation and the Civil War. This expectation was not poetic fancy. The need and the opportunity for comprehensive religious reform were acknowledged by public figures representing a broad range of experience and theological opinion. Of course, the precise nature of this necessary reformation was understood differently according to the varying social agendas of those who expected it. The breadth of the spectrum is illustrated in two of the most influential books of the 1790s – Thomas Paine's *The Age of Reason* (1794) and William Wilberforce's *A Practical View of the Prevailing Religious Systems of Professed Christians* (1797). Paine, who had perceived that the social revolution outlined in *The Rights of Man* would require a fundamental change in the ideological underpinnings of the political order, and who identified organized Christianity as the chief abettor of repressive government, called for "a revolution in the system of religion [in which] human inventions and priestcraft would be detected; and man would return to the pure, unmixed, and unadulterated belief of one God, and no more."[12] Wilberforce's *A Practical View*, which was, after Burke's *Reflections*, the most influential book of the decade among the upper classes,[13] and was intended, in part, as a response to Paine, saw the national salvation as contingent on a return to orthodox, vital Christianity – as distinct from the "dry, unanimated religion . . . professed by nominal Christians."[14] Although Paine and Wilberforce were worlds apart in their vision of what a future society should look like, they resembled each other in their understanding of the need for a purification of the national religion of England and in the belief that their own time was ripe with opportunity for such a reformation.

Aside from the example of the French Revolution, which made all social structures seem vulnerable to change, two recent developments encouraged contemporary observers to expect or fear that a dramatic transformation might be occurring in the character of the national religion and in the political and social order it helped to sustain. Those events were the campaign for religious liberty being waged throughout the country by Protestant Dissenters and the remarkable nationwide rebirth of Christian faith and piety that became known as the Evangelical Revival.[15] Both phenomena involved resistance to coercion in the religious sphere and an insistence on the primary importance of authentic personal experience; both, therefore, tended toward subversion of traditional religious authority, with profound consequences for what Shelley called "the equilibrium between institutions and opinions." For a period of approximately three decades, the decades in which Romantic poetry flourished, religion in England seemed to abandon its character as a guarantor of social stability and to become, as it had during the sixteenth and seventeenth centuries, a force for potentially revolutionary change. In 1643 Milton had commended the "pious forwardness among men, to reassume the ill-deputed care of their Religion into their own hands again."[16] At the turn of the nineteenth century admirers and critics of such forwardness often commented on the similarities between Milton's time and their own.[17] Before continuing my account of how the Romantic poets participated in the reformational activity of their time, it will be useful to consider further the historical context that conditioned their thinking.

Throughout the Romantic period, the most clamorous political disputes in England were provoked by marginalized religious groups attempting to gain a larger share of political and economic power. Demands by Roman Catholics for relief from the severe political, economic, and cultural disabilities inflicted by the Penal Laws had been quiescent since an effort to moderate the laws provoked the Gordon Riots in 1780, but they were revived by the Act of Union with Ireland in 1800 and became the most explosive political issue in Britain in the early years of the century. Disputes over the "Catholic Claims" forced William Pitt's resignation in 1801, brought down the Whig ministry of "All the Talents" in 1807, and kept the Whigs out of power afterward until new pressure for Catholic Emancipation precipitated the political crisis that resulted in passage of the 1832

Reform Bill.[18] The Catholic Question, one might note in passing, embroiled Wordsworth in years of anti-popery campaigning, provoked Coleridge's *On the Constitution of Church and State*, and provided the subject of Byron's second speech in the House of Lords. However, it was not Catholics but Protestants who fomented most of the domestic agitation during the crucial decade of the 1790s in which British Romanticism first emerged as a cultural force. As the decade began, the most contentious political issue in England was the campaign to repeal the laws excluding Protestant Dissenters from full participation in the public life of England.

When the Interregnum following the death of Charles I ended in the accession of his son to the throne, those religious communities in England that refused to conform to the discipline and liturgy of the restored Church of England were subjected to punitive laws limiting their freedom of worship and imposing other civil and cultural disabilities. After the Revolution of 1688, an Act of Toleration permitted Protestant Nonconformists to worship as they desired but continued to restrict their civil rights. Throughout the eighteenth century the officially recognized Dissenting sects – Presbyterians, Baptists, Congregationalists, and Quakers – had been excluded by law from full participation in national and local government, as well as from various other educational and social opportunities.[19] Although the discriminatory laws were erratically enforced and the penalties were routinely abrogated, Dissenters officially remained second-class citizens, prevented from taking degrees at Oxford and Cambridge and from being legally married or buried by their own ministers, and sometimes subjected to petty, capricious tyranny by Anglican officials with whom they came in contact. This low-grade persecution kept alive the Dissenters' old heritage of intellectual resistance until it flared up again in the years 1787–1796, invigorated by a new wave of religious revivalism and inspired by events in France. Between 1787 and 1791, the Dissenting sects joined forces in three successive, increasingly militant attempts to win parliamentary repeal of the discriminatory laws under which they suffered. In what would now be called a national lobbying effort, the Dissenters organized themselves in towns and cities throughout the country, coordinating their local efforts through an interdenominational committee in London, to apply pressure in Parliament for repeal. Their ultimate aim – to change the religious character of the nation by breaking the legal monopoly of the Church – involved a dual effort to free religion from institutional control and to bring it into accord with a broadly liberal political program. This campaign for liberation from the tyrannies of prescription and privilege put religious freedom at the top of the national political agenda, impinging on the consciousness of people at every level of society.[20]

As the repeal campaign intensified, its object changed from a request for increased legal toleration to a demand for religious liberty as a natural right. The Dissenters had been appealing to abstract rights since the campaign began in 1787, but their vocabulary showed some new French seasoning when in January 1790 the central Repeal Committee resolved "that every test calculated to exclude [Dissenters] from civil and military offices on account of religious scruples is a violation of their rights as men and citizens of a free state, inconsistent with the principles of the constitution of this country and repugnant to the genuine spirit of true religion."[21] The echo of "*droits de l'homme et du citoyen*" was provocative, but not more so than the appeal to a truer religion than the one professed by the Established Church of England. The rhetoric of reformation was becoming more explicit, and criticism not only of the Church's privileges and revenues but even of its doctrines and liturgy was becoming part of the national debate.

While the majority of Dissenters involved in the campaign were orthodox, the most prominent spokesmen for the cause were "rational dissenters" (Joseph Priestley's term for anti-trinitarian nonconformists), particularly members of the newly distinct denomination of Unitarians. They had more at stake in the struggle than others, since their heterodox beliefs were not protected even under the terms of the Toleration Act of 1689 and were further penalized by the Blasphemy Act of 1698, which criminalized denial of the Trinity. Perhaps on that account they were the most audible in their demand for a continued Reformation and devoted much attention to preparing a new "correct" translation of the Bible as well as a revision of the Prayer Book. Even after the failure of the repeal campaign they were confident enough in their growing strength to petition Parliament again in 1792 for relief from their legal disabilities. Their persistent efforts finally bore fruit in 1813 with passage of the Trinity Act, which legalized Unitarian worship.[22]

The repeal campaign of the early nineties failed, largely because the Dissenters' organized pressure tactics provoked a hostile response from the Anglican community, a reaction that culminated in the

"Church and King" riots of 1791 in which the homes and chapels of Dissenters in many parts of England were destroyed. The agitation on both sides became so tumultuous that one historian of Dissent has called the repeal campaign "England's French Revolution."[23] It seemed to many that not since England's own revolution of the 1640s had religious disturbances posed such a threat to the stability of the social order. The Dissenters were challenging, as the Puritans before them had done, the legitimacy of the religious Establishment that made up an essential component of the British Constitution and a vital prop of the monarchy in particular. Religion, it bears repeating, had always been the most powerful solvent of political structures in Britain. Now, against the backdrop of the French Revolution, the old argument over "divine right" was being renewed in the ecclesiastical sphere, a more dangerous arena than the legislative forum because passions ran higher, certainties were more absolute, and consequences were, by definition, of greater moment, since they affected one's eternal life and not merely one's earthly pilgrimage. Faith and piety gave to political commitment the intimacy of a subject for meditative prayer and the urgency of a religious obligation – a situation that in Britain had always been pregnant with consequence for the order of power. Not surprisingly, the old association of "sectaries" with the regicide of 1649 was recalled frequently in the heated rhetoric of the day.

In purely political terms (setting aside the domestic effects of the war with France) the repeal controversy may be said to have had a more profound effect on public life in Britain than the French Revolution itself. The controversy dominated national politics for ten years years, from 1787 to 1796, and the issues and emotions raised by the campaign foreshadowed and in some ways shaped the debate over the French Revolution, creating ideological divisions that ran through British politics for decades afterward. The reactionary "Church and King" emotion provoked by the repeal campaign was easily redirected at "Jacobin" radicals when they succeeded the Dissenters as public critics of the Constitution. In fact, the national network that had agitated for repeal provided much of the infrastructure for later radical movements in politics.[24] In other words, the British counter-revolution may be said, paradoxically, to predate the French revolution, since it originated in a domestic religious dispute that began two years before the Estates General convened in Paris.

The repeal campaign generated the heated political climate in which, on November 4, 1789, the Presbyterian minister Richard Price delivered his provocative *Discourse on the Love of Our Country* at a meeting of a society founded to commemorate the English Revolution of 1688. Price, a "rational dissenter," was a leading spokesman for the cause of repeal and his address to the Revolution Society was primarily intended to rally enthusiasm for the campaign, including for that purpose a call for reformation of the national Church and elimination of "the defects (may I not say the absurdities?) in our established codes of faith and worship." In his celebrated "Nunc Dimittis" peroration, Price linked the repeal campaign in England with the political and religious changes then being effected in France: "And now, methinks, I see the ardour for liberty catching and spreading; a general amendment beginning in human affairs; the dominion of kings changed for the dominion of laws, and the dominion of priests giving way to the dominion of reason and conscience. Tremble all ye oppressors of the world! Take warning all ye supporters of slavish governments and slavish hierarchies! Call no more (absurdly and wickedly) REFORMATION, innovation."[25]

Literary historian H. N. Brailsford designated November 4, 1789 as the beginning of the French Revolution in England,[26] because it was Price's discourse that provoked Edmund Burke's *Reflections on the Revolution in France and on Proceedings in Certain Societies in London Relative to that Event*. The second part of Burke's title, often elided, indicates that the book was a response to domestic as well as foreign provocation, and his attack on Richard Price suggests that it was the religious content and tone of Price's reformational "sermon" that especially antagonized him. The *Reflections* characterize Price as a "political Divine," a "spiritual doctor of politics," and an "arch-pontiff of the *rights of men*" who along with other "apostolic missionaries" had been spreading a new "political gospel"; he is compared twice with the Reverend Hugh Peters, who was executed as a regicide in the seventeenth century. Burke was obviously evoking the 1640s when he expressed his fear of revolution, "the signals for which have so often been given from pulpits."[27]

Burke did his best to turn the debate on the French Revolution into a religious argument. He was astute enough to sense very early what historians now see clearly, that the Revolution's most serious tactical error was its attack on the Catholic Church, beginning with the confiscations and desecrations of ecclesiastical property in November 1789.[28]

Judging by the amount of space he gives to them in the *Reflections,* these depredations seem to have outraged him more than any other activity of the revolutionaries. They "rankled in his mind," a contemporary observer commented, "and tainted by infection the general current of his thoughts."[29] "Irreligious" and "unhallowed" became for him broad terms of political disapproval,[30] and he began to characterize the war against France as a crusade: "We cannot, if we would, delude ourselves about the true state of this dreadful contest," he said in 1793. *"It is a religious war.* It includes in its object every other interest of society as well as this; but this is the principal and leading feature. It is through the destruction of religion that our enemies propose the accomplishment of all their other views."[31] On the domestic front, Burke seldom missed a chance to associate the preservation of the political order in Britain with the welfare of the national Church. He said in *Reflections* that the people of England "know, and what is better we feel inwardly, that religion is the basis of civil society, and the source of all good and comfort." Englishmen "do not consider their church establishment as convenient, but as essential to their state . . . the foundation of their whole constitution, with which, and with every part of which, it holds an indissoluble union. Church and state are ideas inseparable in their minds, and scarcely is the one ever mentioned without mentioning the other."[32] Whether or not this assessment of the country's sentiments was accurate, Burke worked very hard to forge just such an identification between Church and State in the national consciousness and to defend the ecclesiastical establishment as an indispensable barrier against revolution.[33] The strategy was successful; religion became an increasingly important factor in the revolutionary debate, one that grew in significance as the prevailing revolutionary ideology in France became more militantly anti-Christian.

So the political argument that divided Britain in the 1790s was initially and remained in important senses a religious debate. Every prescription offered for the national welfare, whether radical or reactionary, had its religious ingredient. This fact has tended to be overlooked by some literary historians when they analyze Romanticism as an expression of the spirit of the age. The poets' increasing concern with religious matters was not a retreat from social activism; it was an energetic engagement in some of the central public policy debates of the era. The issues of religious authority and religious authenticity were at the heart of current events during the Romantic period, as they were close to the heart of the literary movement itself.

The repeal campaign generated throughout England an urgent reexamination of the nation's religious character, helping to create a national climate of intellectual unrest, of spiritual dissatisfaction and inquiry and desire. This mood of religious discontent and expectancy was reflected also in the evangelical revival that had been taking place in the country since the middle of the eighteenth century but which reached new levels of intensity in the 1790s, becoming what one historian called "the greatest revival of religious faith since the middle ages,"[34] and contributing to the sense of crisis in the public religious sphere. The connection between the repeal campaign and the revival is not often noted, because the best-known spokesmen for repeal, such as Richard Price and Joseph Priestley, were "rational dissenters" – liberal and even heterodox in their beliefs, while the revival was orthodox in tendency. But there was a remarkable spirit of ecumenical cooperation among Dissenters at this time, and much of the energy behind the repeal campaign, especially at the provincial level, came from orthodox Dissent.[35]

The revitalization of Christian faith and piety initiated by Wesley in the 1740s and its eventual spread to the middle and upper classes in the form of Church Evangelicalism is sufficiently well known that it does not need to be reviewed here.[36] What has not so often been discussed was the special political character given to the revival by the secession of the Methodists from the Church of England after Wesley's death in 1791 and the simultaneous quickening of religious fervor among the older Dissenting sects, especially the Independents and the Baptists, who suddenly rediscovered in the 1790s the duty of converting the rural population of England to a more vital Christian faith and piety. The new attention to domestic evangelism seems to have arisen partly as an afterthought to the fervor for foreign missions that emerged rather suddenly among the Dissenters in the early 1790s. As the Baptist minister Robert Hall recalled later, "A zeal for the conversion of pagans had occasioned a powerful reaction at home, by producing efforts, hitherto unexampled, toward carrying the Gospel into the darkest corners of the kingdom."[37] Imitating procedures that the Methodists had developed earlier in the century, the Dissenting revival of the 1790s was conducted mainly by itinerant preachers, many of them haphazardly educated laymen, who emphasized the experience of conversion to a saving faith more than doctrinal formulations or disciplinary codes.[38] At first the Methodists and other Dissenters concentrated on bringing religious ministry to places where the national Church provided none, but they eventually began challenging the regular clergy on their own ground, building alongside the parish structure and in opposition to it the alternative religious order suggested by the distinction still preserved in Britain between "chapel" and "church." The result was a suddenly expanded and increasingly homogeneous nonconformist religious culture that had in common primarily its sense of separation from the Established Church.

Cultural historians until recently have been inclined to describe the evangelical revival in Britain as a conservative force protecting Britain from radical political change.[39] While this may be an accurate enough description of the revival's final effect, in the 1790s and the years immediately following it was possible, indeed common, for contemporaries to see the revival as a dangerously destabilizing force in society and a threat to the established political order. The increase in the proselytizing activity of the older Dissenting communities called attention to what had been a previously unregarded aspect of the growth of Methodism – the massive disaffection from the Established Church that it had discovered and then stimulated, especially among the lower classes. When the spiritual revival spread to Dissent in the 1790s it added new intensity of religious fervor to the old heritage of political alienation; Anglican clergymen who had tended to ignore or deride the Methodists had to take more seriously a newly invigorated Dissent with its tradition of defiance of the established political and ecclesiastical order.

Christianity provided the central principle of cohesion in British society and the primary ideological rationale for submission to authority. It was within the sphere of religion, therefore, that class conflict might arise in the most dangerously destabilizing manner, as what ought to have been a common religious ideology became susceptible to radically differing political interpretations, driven by high intensities of zeal. Insofar as subservience had a religious sanction, insubordination that appealed to a higher religious rationale was the most dangerous kind of all. As the historian Theodore Maynard observed, "Religion, though it normally exerts a conservative influence on culture, also provides the most dynamic means of social change. Indeed one might almost go so far as to say that it is only by religion that a religious culture can be changed."[40] The millenarianism that tended to accompany religious revivals was, as J. F. C. Harrison has pointed out, an ideology of change: "it focused attention on the great changes which were currently taking place in these last days, and promised a vast transformation of the social order when all things would be made new. Men and women who were looking eagerly for a new heaven and a new earth could not but be consciously aware that the future would be utterly different from the present."[41] Such enthusiasm was truly dangerous because it induced a kind of recklessness that trusted Providence to pick up the pieces after apocalyptic events had run their course.

There was a more immediate threat to the social order in the revival's tendency to encourage disaffection from the Established Church, which in many parts of Britain was the most visible embodiment of the national government. Historian J. C. D. Clark has pointed out that the average person in England at the time had very little to do with the political power structure centered in London but had continual contact with the religious arm of the ruling order:

> The agency of the State which confronted him in his everyday life was not Parliament, reaching out as a machinery of representative democracy: elections were infrequent, contests less frequent still, the franchise restricted, and access to MPs minimal for most electors. The ubiquitous agency of the State was the Church, quartering the land not into a few hundred constituencies but into ten thousand parishes, impinging on the daily concerns of the great majority, supporting its black-coated army of a clerical intelligentsia, bidding for a monopoly of education, piety, and political acceptability.[42]

While it was routinely asserted that the Church of England lived under the protection of the State, in practice the reverse was true: the government depended on the Church to ensure the subservience, if not the loyalty, of the people. The Church created, more effectively than either the judiciary or the military could, a climate of respect for law and order. It was at the parish level that deference and obedience were taught as the standard of acceptable deportment and a manifestation of the divine order. In some areas the clergy and the criminal justice system were identical, since clergymen constituted a large proportion of the justices of the peace.[43] But even in their more routine priestly roles the clergy served a law-enforcement function. When the local landlord, whether nobleman or gentleman, took his pew in the parish church on Sunday morning and received the blessing of the parson, one could see in them a synecdoche of the national power structure – Church and State united for mutual advantage and protection in a hierarchical society where power derived from birth and educational privilege.

Infringement of the clergy's influence at this local level constituted, then, a potentially serious subversion of the political order. The rapid growth of alternative, nonconformist religious communities involved a radical alienation of the poor from the hegemonic systems into which they had been born. When the defections from the national Church began noticeably to increase during the French revolutionary period, the political danger became apparent to the more alert churchmen. As the Bishop of Chester complained, "Every addition [nonconformity] makes to the number of its supporters alters the proportion existing in the country between the monarchical and democratic spirit."[44] And Samuel Horsley, Bishop of Rochester and leader of the hierarchy's conservative wing, also suspected that the revival had a subversive political agenda:

In many parts of the kingdom new conventicles have opened in great numbers, and congregations formed of one knows not what denomination. The Pastor is often, in appearance at least, an illiterate peasant or mechanic . . . It is very remarkable, that these new congregations of non-descripts have been mostly formed, since the Jacobins have been laid under the restraint of those two most salutary statutes, commonly known by the names of the Sedition and Treason bills. A circumstance which gives much ground for suspicion, that sedition and atheism are the real objects of these institutions, rather than religion . . . The Jacobins of this country, I very much fear, are, at this moment, making a tool of Methodism.[45]

The notion that the "gagging acts" had redirected Jacobins into second careers as village preachers is comical but not entirely paranoid. Many Dissenting preachers, even quite orthodox ones, publically maintained "Jacobin" principles and allegiances right through the 1790s, and much of the radical agitation in the years that followed, such as that of the "Tolpuddle martyrs" and the Pentrich uprising, was led by Methodist activists.[46] Bishop Horsley's concern was justified in more general senses too. In a country whose Parliament each year still solemnly and penitentially commemorated the execution of Charles I, no one could predict confidently the direction a new revival of religious enthusiasm might take; improperly channeled religious passions created political hazards, as the Civil War had memorably demonstrated.

What made the widespread defections of the 1790s even more culturally remarkable was that these new conversions away from Anglicanism were individual assertions of religious independence, of personal choice in the spiritual realm. In the sixteenth century if uneducated people became Protestants it was usually a matter of enforced conformity with the religious policy of their political rulers. The disaffections from the Church that occurred in late eighteenth-century England had no such leadership from the top. Believers were converted one by one, usually by members of their own class who had been sent to them as lay preachers by the local Methodist connection or one of the older Dissenting sects. In this case, conversion away from the local parish church meant conversion into a temporary state of religious freedom, with liberty to choose from a range of sectarian options. The Methodists themselves soon after Wesley's death began to fragment into separate denominations, each appealing to a different set of political or theological predispositions. And this new kind of religious liberation could mean not only a transfer of allegiance from church to the chapel of one's choice; it could mean repudiation of all religious affiliation. For many, Methodism and the other revivalist sects provided a halfway house on the road to secularism or religious indifference, an increasingly common destination in those years for those who had been invited to think for themselves in matters of religion.[47]

To look upon the religious revival of the 1790s primarily as a counter-revolutionary force, then, is to underestimate its vitality as a destabilizing, liberating, and renovating cultural movement. Rather than encouraging political or intellectual subordination, the revival was, for a time, a potent force for intellectual liberation and political empowerment. A number of social historians have suggested that it was in their religious life that the British lower classes were first liberated, released from their previously determined place in the social order, and invited to assume positions of authority that made use of hitherto untried talents. For Alan Gilbert, the revival "offered particular social groups not just other-worldly salvation, but also a welcome escape from anomie and a more or less legitimate means of affirming social emancipation from old deferential relationships. But both these latter functions were of maximum significance only during the late-eighteenth-, early-nineteenth-century hiatus between the destruction of one cultural system and its replacement by another."[48]

This period of religious volatility did not endure very long; by the 1820s the various Dissenting denominations were reasserting doctrinal and disciplinary control over their numerous new converts, moving religious services from fields and barns into newly constructed chapels under the supervision of ministers who were more professional and conventional in demeanor than the earlier field preachers had been, and British Nonconformity began to take on that coercive, repressive character for which it was known later in the century. But during the time we call the Romantic period, public religion in England was in a transitional state that offered hope and apparent opportunity for genuine change in the spiritual temper of the country. This was the spirit of the age that conditioned British Romanticism, a spirit of religious spontaneity and innovation, and this destabilizing, liberalizing impulse was not confined to the sphere of religion only but had broad social, economic, and political implications as well.

The buoyant, optimistic temper of Nonconformist religion in the 1790s may be seen in the public expressions of sympathy with which Dissenters of all doctrinal persuasions greeted the French Revolution in its first years. The libertarian sentiments generated during the repeal campaign and the religious optimism that accompanied the revival encouraged a positive response to the outbreak of the Revolution, which was welcomed not only as striking a mortal blow against the Catholic Church and thus bringing apocalyptic cheer to the hearts of all good Protestants, but also as signifying a promising change for the better in human nature generally, a development that boded well for their newly invigorated missionary efforts at home and abroad. Millennial expectations generated by the revival greeted the Revolution as part of the shaking of the old order necessary for the construction of the new. Religious zeal and political optimism thus went hand in hand – a conjunction that Wordsworth illustrated in *The Excursion* when the Solitary was inspired by the good news from France to resume the clerical ministry he had earlier abandoned and, for a time, "from the Pulpit zealously maintained / The cause of Christ and civil liberty, / As one; and moving to one glorious end."[49] Such sympathies, it bears repeating, were expressed not only by "rational" Dissenters such as Priestley and Price but by orthodox Nonconformists as well. One of the most fearlessly outspoken of these, the Baptist preacher Robert Hall, repudiated Burke's efforts to sanctify the counter-revolution and demonstrated in his 1791 tract *Christianity Consistent with a Love of Freedom* that religious zeal could be recruited equally well on the radical side. Hall, like Richard Price, welcomed the Revolution as a work of God:

The empire of darkness and of despotism has been smitten with a stroke which has sounded through the universe. When we see whole kingdoms, after reposing for centuries in the lap of their rulers, start from their slumber, the dignity of man rising up from depression, and tyrants trembling on their thrones . . . these are a kind of throes and struggle of nature, to which it would be a sullenness to refuse our sympathy. Old foundations are breaking up; new edifices are rearing . . . That fond attachment to ancient institutions and blind submission to opinions already received, which has ever checked the growth of improvement . . . is giving way to a spirit of bold and fearless investigation. Man seems to be becoming more erect and independent. He leans more on himself, less on his fellow-creatures. He begins to feel a consciousness in a higher degree of personal dignity, and is less enamoured of artificial distinctions . . . The devout mind will behold in these momentous changes the finger of God, and, discerning in them the dawn of that glorious period, in which wars will cease, and antichristian tyranny shall fall, will adore that unerring wisdom, whose secret operation never fails to conduct all human affairs to their proper issue, and impels the great actors on that troubled theatre, to fulfill, when they least intend it, the counsels of heaven, and the prediction of its prophets.[50]

It is hard to distinguish religious from political exhilaration here. Biblical faith added an apocalyptic resonance, a heightened sublimity, to the politics of the day, representing them *sub specie aeternitatis* as a moment in the history of salvation.

One cannot help noticing the resemblance between the religious aspirations expressed by liberal preachers like Hall and the exalted vision of human potential that one finds in much Romantic poetry. Remove the more specific theological vocabulary and the passage above might have been written by Shelley or the younger Wordsworth. Like Hall, Wordsworth also discovered a higher degree of personal dignity in the commonest of people, a dignity that did not depend on artificial distinctions. The fall of the empire of darkness, the awakening of humanity from slumber, and the rearing of new social edifices constitute the central narrative of Blake's *Jerusalem*. In optimistic moments Byron, Shelley, and Keats thought they saw, or hoped they saw, blind submission giving way to bold investigation in the mental life of mankind. Whether by affinity or consanguinity, the ideology of Dissent and the Romantic ideology show signs of a close familial relationship. And however much they insisted on their unique visions and definitions of national salvation, poets who held out to their contemporaries the promise of "a new Earth and new Heaven, / Undreamt of by the sensual and the proud"[51] were working the same territory as the religious revivalists – who, for their part, could have described their mission in the terms that Wordsworth used to characterize his own effort: to "arouse the sensual from their sleep / Of Death, and win the vacant and the vain / To noble raptures."[52]

In 1802, in the first notice taken by a professional critic of what we now call the English Romantic movement, Francis Jeffrey sensed a connection between this new development in literature and the religious agitation being felt at that time. In a review of Robert Southey's *Thalaba*, he wrote,

The author who is now before us belongs to a *sect* of poets, that has established itself in this country within these ten or twelve years, and is looked upon, we believe, as one of its chief champions and apostles. The peculiar doctrines of this sect, it would not, perhaps, be very easy to explain; but, that they are *dissenters* from the established systems in poetry and criticism is admitted, and proved, indeed, by the whole tenor of their compositions. Though they lay claim, we believe, to a creed and a revelation of their own, there can be little doubt, that their doctrines are of *German* origin, and have been derived from some of the great modern reformers in that country. Some of their leading principles, indeed, are probably of an earlier date, and seem to have been borrowed from the great apostle of Geneva . . . The disciples of this school boast much of its originality, and seem to value themselves very highly, for having broken loose from the bondage of ancient authority, and re-asserted the independence of genius.[53]

In his attempt to characterize this new group of writers (Wordsworth, Coleridge, and Lamb are mentioned as well as Southey), Jeffrey chooses an analogy from the religious politics of his day. The poets are, he says, a *sect* of *dissenters* (the italics are his own) from established systems, who have liberated themselves from "the bondage of ancient authority." At one level the comparison is playful: writing at a time when a revival of religious enthusiasm among marginal groups was attracting national attention, Jeffrey is parodying the kind of theological scrutiny to which Nonconformists were being subjected when he finds the German origins of the new doctrines in "reformers" like Kotzebue and Schiller rather than in Martin Luther and cites Rousseau instead of Calvin as the Genevan inspiration. Beneath the jocularity, however, there are more serious reasons why Jeffrey would have associated the new poetry with religious dissent.

In one sense, the association was already established critical practice, one that began in 1798 when the *Anti-Jacobin Review* attacked Southey, Coleridge, and Lamb as "Jacobin poets" and lumped them together with Joseph Priestley and other liberal Dissenters.[54] Jeffrey had some knowledge of the poets' personal connections with the Dissenting communities in London, Bristol, and Cambridge. Coleridge's involvement in such circles, including his own brief career as a Unitarian preacher, was no secret, and Southey's relations with Dissenters in Bristol were also well known. But beyond what he knew of their personal backgrounds, Jeffrey thought he saw in these writers a complex of attitudes that had become associated with religious Nonconformity in England, especially as it was now being transformed by the religious revival. Having separated themselves from "the catholic poetical church," and abandoned "the establishments of language" this new "sect of dissenters" were affecting "simplicity and familiarity of language," translating, as the revivalists did, lofty conceptions into vulgar diction. The poets resembled Dissenters too in their "discontent with the present constitution of society." In all, Jeffrey's comparison of the Romantics with religious nonconformists was not so whimsical a conceit as it may appear to us, separated by two centuries from its cultural and political context. In 1802, Dissent provided the most familiar example on the domestic scene of rebellion against intellectual coercion, setting a pattern which any other movement for cultural innovation might be seen as imitating. By having "broken loose from the bondage of ancient authority, and re-asserted the independence of genius," the Romantics were repeating, consciously or not, the old radical Protestant insistence that in the most important aspects of life individual intuition, or private inspiration, was of more importance than doctrines defined by authority and sanctified by custom.

It was, then, perhaps not accidental that the birth of the Romantic movement in England coincided with a national struggle for religious freedom, the freedom to define the ultimate meaning of human life independent of traditional or legislated definitions. Just as the repeal campaign became a struggle for spiritual liberty against institutional coercion and the tyranny of prescription and privilege, the revival in

its earlier stage encouraged the rejection of older religious formulations and disciplinary codes. At the beginning of the repeal campaign
in 1787 Richard Price predicted, "The human mind must soon be
emancipated from the chains of Church authority and Church
establishments, for the liberality of the times has already loosened
their foundations."[55] Fifteen years later, this longing for spiritual
emancipation was being observed even among the most orthodox
Anglicans. In one of the earliest episcopal comments on the phenomenon of Church Evangelicalism, the Bishop of Oxford warned these
enthusiasts that "while they bring everything within private suggestion, they encourage in Religion the very principle, which in Politics
has proved so fatal to the peace and good government of states;
being no other than giving the reins to private opinion, in opposition
to public authority."[56] Consciously or not, the Romantic poets found
themselves adopting the agenda of the religious reformers of their
time when they themselves directed their energies toward creating a
climate of spiritual freedom that would liberate religion, at least,
from the control of repressive institutions.

Celebrating in his own time "this pious forwardness among men,
to reassume the ill-deputed care of their Religion into their own
hands again," Milton wrote in *Areopagitica*: "Now the time seems
come, wherein Moses the great prophet, may sit in heav'n rejoycing
to see that memorable and glorious wish of his fulfill'd, when not
only our sev'nty Elders, but all the Lords people are become
Prophets."[57] "Would to God that all the Lords people were
Prophets," echoed William Blake, as he began his remarkable
attempt to revise and rehabilitate Milton in the epic poem he
named for him. That Blake shared Milton's sense of the English
Reformation as unfinished business may be seen in Plate 11 of
Europe, which depicts King George III wearing the papal tiara – an
emblem not only of the pernicious union of Church and State
against which Blake waged relentless mental warfare but also of the
inadequacy of the Reformation in Britain. The English Church
under George III was still as corrupt and benighted, still as
repressive and as much in need of reform, as it had been under
papal domination.[58] In *Milton* one can find a less polemical, more
touching emblem of the Romantic reformation when Milton,
having joined himself to Blake, recants his own erroneous theology
and struggles to reshape in a more human form the image of
Urizen, the authoritarian, punishing Father he had portrayed in

Paradise Lost. Milton confronts his God at Peor, a place where the Israelites worshipped false divinities (Num.25):

> Urizen emerged from his Rocky Form & from his Snows . . .
> And met him on the shores of Arnon; & by the streams of the brooks
> Silent they met, and silent strove among the streams, of Arnon
> Even to Mahanaim, when with cold hand Urizen stoop'd down
> And took up water from the river Jordan: pouring on
> To Miltons brain the icy fluid from his broad cold palm.
> But Milton took of the red clay of Succoth, moulding it with care
> Between his palms: and filling up the furrows of many years
> Beginning at the feet of Urizen, and on the bones
> Creating new flesh on the Demon cold, and building him,
> As with new clay a Human form in the Valley of Beth Peor.[59]

This is not iconoclasm; it is reformation in a quite literal sense. Milton does not pull down and destroy the image of Urizen. Upon a hardened image of God he spreads fresh clay, susceptible to new representations of the Divine Vision. Meanwhile Urizen attempts to impose his control over the prophet in a parody of baptism, specifically the baptism at the Jordan in which God claimed paternal authority over Jesus (Matthew 3:13–17). Blake illustrates this confrontation between creative and ossified religious vision on Plate 18 of *Milton* (the plate I have used as frontispiece). In that richly ambiguous illumination one sees an image of the Romantic religious enterprise – a struggle which is almost an embrace, an assault that is an effort to support and rejuvenate the tottering victim, who must be revived and renewed because his decrepitude is dangerous and his death a threat to something valuable in human existence.

"Milton! thou shouldst be living at this hour," Wordsworth wrote, appealing to Milton as a standard against whom to measure the religious as well as the political and literary deficiencies of his own society at a time when "altar, sword, and pen . . . have forfeited their ancient English dower." His own most ambitious attempt to address his country's religious condition, *The Excursion*, was prefaced by an acknowledgement that he would need to surpass even Milton, "Holiest of Men," if he was to succeed in articulating a new religious vision adequate to the needs of his own contemporaries. He invokes Milton's muse:

> Urania, I shall need
> Thy guidance, or a greater Muse, if such
> Descend to earth or dwell in highest heaven!

For I must tread on shadowy ground, must sink
Deep – and aloft ascending, breathe in worlds
To which the heaven of heavens is but a veil.
All strength – all terror, single or in bands,
That ever was put forth in personal form –
Jehovah – with his thunder, and the choir
Of shouting Angels, and the empyreal thrones,
I pass them unalarmed. Not Chaos, not
The darkest pit of lowest Erebus,
Nor aught of blinder vacancy – scooped out
By help of dreams, can breed such fear and awe
As fall upon us often when we look
Into our Minds, into the Mind of Man –
My haunt, and the main region of my Song.[60]

This passage has been read as a proclamation of naturalistic humanism,[61] but such an interpretation requires decontextualizing the lines from their prefatory position in *The Excursion*, a poem that is usually lamented as a retreat from naturalistic humanism. But Wordsworth is more interested in mythopoesis here than in doctrine. He is not repudiating Milton's belief in a noumenal order, but only the "personal form" in which Milton clothed his conception of the Divine.

The challenge of finding an adequate language for religious expression is an important part of the "argument" of the poem that follows, an argument that is articulated most plainly in Book 4, which traces the history of humanity's attempts since the Fall to find an appropriate language for its religious insights. During the history of Israel, the Wanderer says, "Jehovah – shapeless Power above all Powers,/ Single and one, the omnipresent God" manifested his Presence unmistakably "By vocal utterance, or blaze of light,/Or cloud of darkness, localized in heaven."[62] In the absence of such direct perception of Divinity, fallen humanity's religious sense attempted in various ways to articulate its religious intuitions, and Wordsworth reports the results in his survey of ancient mythologies – that poetic *tour de force* which so impressed John Keats. Wordsworth's point is that human religious language, however sublime in power, must always be inadequate to express the inexpressible. A year after publishing *The Excursion* he wrote, "The religious man values what he sees chiefly as an 'imperfect shadowing forth' of what he is incapable of seeing. The concerns of religion refer to indefinite objects, and are too weighty for the mind to support them without relieving itself by resting a great part of the burden upon words and symbols." The more concrete these words and symbols, the less suitable they are to signify the Ineffable. "The anthropomorphitism of the Pagan religion subjected the minds of the greatest poets in those countries too much to the bondage of definite form; from which the Hebrews were preserved by their abhorrence of idolatry. This abhorrence was almost as strong in our great epic Poet, both from circumstances of his life, and from the constitution of his mind."[63] But even Milton had surrendered too much to "the bondage of definite form," and his successors were responsible for continuing the purification of religious language.

Enlightenment thinkers had argued persuasively that religion needed to be more philosophical than the kind of "vulgar superstition" which depended on concrete images and personages – e.g., the Biblical faith that had provided Milton with the material for his poem. Wordsworth's prospectus to *The Excursion* suggests that Milton's own concretions, his shouting angels, etc., now needed to be left behind by poetry. In his comparison of Milton and Wordsworth, Keats had criticized Milton for resting content with the dogmas and superstitions of Protestantism and praised Wordsworth for thinking more deeply into the human heart. Keats observed that humanity, having matured since the seventeenth century, now demanded a more sophisticated religion, one that had no need for palpable, named mediators or of the dogmas and superstitions associated with them.[64] Keats found in Wordsworth's "Prospectus" a forceful expression of the Romantic program of religious reformation through literature. Its bold balance of reverence and iconoclasm, dismissing Jehovah while submitting humbly to "the law supreme of that Intelligence which governs all," led Keats to conclude that Wordsworth was, in religious matters at least, "deeper" than Milton.

All the Romantic poets found *Paradise Lost* wanting in its attempt to answer definitively the great religious questions it raised. As Stuart Curran has observed, "Blake would never have written *Milton,* nor Shelley *Prometheus Unbound,* nor Byron *Cain,* nor Keats *Hyperion,* if *Paradise Lost* had been definitive. All these works are ultimately theodicies – justifications of the ways of God to man – and each attempts a new, more modern, more humane, or more inclusive vision than Milton's."[65] Each new generation of poets had to incorporate its vision of ultimate truth in new forms and fresh language. Religious poetry, like religious doctrine and discipline, must undergo continual revision to serve the changing needs of a maturing humanity.

And so, while all the Romantics struggled under "the burden of the past" and "the anxiety of influence," one major source of intimidation, the example of Milton, was also a source of encouragement.[66] The need for a continued reformation, which Milton himself had articulated, encouraged the hope that poetry still had new, historically important work to do under the direction of "a mighty providence" that reveals new truth to each generation. That hope contributed to Shelley's optimism about his own generation's literary opportunities: they would represent a new, critical phase in the ongoing reformation. The poets were consoled not only by the prospect of work to be done, but by the realization that such work was inevitably incomplete in any one generation.

As they undertook their mission of rehabilitating the religious imaginations of their countrymen, the writers of the period took considerable pains to demonstrate their qualifications for this work of national reformation. Wordsworth late in life articulated most clearly the Miltonic belief that poets could act as effectively in matters of the spirit as those who were canonically ordained to the work:

> Though Pulpits and the Desk may fail
> To reach the hearts of worldly men;
> Yet may the grace of God prevail
> And touch them through the Poet's pen.

That is the Wordsworth of 1841, but he was sounding the same note a quarter century earlier when he claimed in the Appendix to his 1815 *Poems*, "Poetry is most just to its own divine origin when it administers the comforts and breathes the spirit of religion."[67] And ten years before that, reminiscing about his life in a still earlier period, he was already presenting himself in the character of a kind of field preacher:

> To the open fields I told
> A prophecy; poetic numbers came
> Spontaneously, and clothed in priestly robe
> My spirit, thus singled out, as it might seem,
> For holy services.[68]

One has little difficulty accumulating evidence of this tendency of the Romantic poets to ordain themselves ministers of the word, charged with the task of bringing the means of redemption to a community that had lost its way morally and spiritually. They all repeated in one form or another what the Bard proclaimed in *Milton*: "Mark well my words! they are of your eternal salvation."[69] Each of them found the public religion of his country to be deficient – a partial vision, at best, of a larger truth – and took it as his mission to chastise, to purify, or to redefine Christianity so that it might better reflect its own authentic ideals and serve more effectively as an instrument of social reform. From Blake's "Bible of Hell" in 1794 to Byron's *Cain* and Shelley's *Hellas* in 1821, all grappled with the national religion in a broad-scale attempt at changing its character.

Among the Romantics, Byron was the least comfortable about laying claim to any sort of religious magisterium, but such authority was nevertheless generally conceded to him, if only in negative terms. John Wilson of *Blackwood's* was not being simply perverse when he said of Byron, "the chief power of his poetry is its religion."[70] In 1823 the Evangelical minister James Kennedy said to the author of *Cain*, "whatever you do or say is of infinite importance to the church."[71] Byron's theological pronouncements were taken seriously enough to be considered a political as well as a religious danger. Fear of his destabilizing views can be observed even in a liberal periodical like the *Edinburgh Review*, when it suggested that *Cain* should be banned because of its undisciplined theological speculations:

We think . . . that poets ought fairly to be confined to the established creed and morality of their country, or to the *actual* passions and sentiments of mankind; and that poetical dreamers and sophists who pretend to *theorize* according to their feverish fancies, without a warrant from authority or reason, ought to be banished the commonwealth of letters.[72]

The concluding allusion to Plato's *Republic* is revealing. In a political order dominated by a religious ideology, those who challenged the official national creed were a menace to society. It was just this insistence on proclaiming religious doctrine "without a warrant from authority" – their tendency, in short, to behave like a sect of dissenters – that made the Romantics most worrisome politically. While none of the other Romantics defied orthodox opinion with the public audacity of Byron and Shelley, or the private audacity of Blake, even partisans of the national Church like the older Words-worth and Coleridge refused totally to surrender their religious independence. Even they could endorse the sentiment if not the rhetorical style of Leigh Hunt when he wrote: "I declare that I do not believe one single dogma, which the reason that God has put in our heads, or the heart that he has put in our bosoms, revolts at."[73]

Hunt, who devoted much of his energy through a long life to the struggle for religious liberty, left one of the clearest statements of the Romantic understanding of literature as a crucial arena for this struggle in the preface to his 1818 volume, *Foliage*, which surveyed the history of English poetry as a record of conflict between superstition and enlightenment, coercion and freedom. A central element in Hunt's program for modern poetry was resistance to the darkening shadow of Evangelical religion, which the *Examiner* had been combatting since its founding in 1808.[74] The same theme appears later in the volume in the poem "To Percy Shelley, on the Degrading Notions of Deity." For Hunt, bad religion perverts the aesthetic sense as well as the moral sense:

> What wonder, Percy, that with jealous rage
> Men should defame the kindly and the wise,
> When in the midst of the all-beautiful skies,
> And all this lovely world, that should engage
> Their mutual search for the old golden age,
> They seat a phantom, swelled into grim size
> Out of their own passions and bigotries,
> And then, for fear, proclaim it meek and sage!
> And this they call a light and a revealing![75]

The Romantics all saw themselves as charged with a mission not only to continue the liberalization of religion that began in modern times with the Reformation, but also to fight against any counter-reformational tendencies that appeared in their own society. The Romantic conception of literature as the organ of reformation made them especially alert to any attempt to use literary art in an effort to reverse the progress of religious liberalization. In *The Spirit of the Age* William Hazlitt accused the conservative *Quarterly Review* of an intention "to pervert literature, from being the natural ally of freedom and humanity, into an engine of priestcraft and despotism."[76] Like Shelley and Keats, Hazlitt saw an intimate relationship between the spirit of reformation and that which inspired great literature and he was always on the alert when literature was employed for reactionary purposes. He detected, for example, in

Coleridge's 1816 "Lay Sermon" just such a counter-reformational tendency:

The whole of this Sermon is written to sanction the principle of Catholic dictation, and to reprobate that diffusion of free inquiry – that difference of private, and ascendancy of public opinion, which has been the necessary consequence, and the great benefit of the Reformation . . . [Coleridge], or at least those whom he writes to please . . . would give us back all the abuses of former times, without any of their advantages; and impose upon us, by force or fraud, a complete system of superstition without faith, of despotism without loyalty, of error without enthusiasm, and all the evils, without any of the blessings, of ignorance.[77]

To conclude this preliminary overview I return to Shelley, who poses the severest challenge to my thesis since he is the most ostensibly irreligious of all the Romantics. But although he contemptuously rejected the Christian faith of his contemporaries he never willingly surrendered the religious arena to those more conventional in their beliefs than he. On the contrary, he persistently claimed for himself as poet a privileged status as an articulator of eternal truth and an instrument of moral good.[78] Like Wordsworth he gave the poet not only the title of prophet but even that of priest; poets, he said, were "priests of an unapprehended inspiration" whose verse "participates in the eternal, the infinite, the One."[79] Poets are "teachers, who draw into a certain propinquity with the beautiful and the true that partial apprehension of the agencies of the invisible world which is called religion" (p. 482). All great poetry provides a record of authentic religious revelation: "What were our consolations on this side of the grave – and what were our aspirations beyond it – if Poetry did not ascend to bring light and fire from those eternal regions where the owl-winged faculty of calculation dare not ever soar?" (p. 503) And Shelley went so far as to assert that "the office and character of a poet participates in the divine nature as regards providence, no less than as regards creation" (p. 492). Poets serve in every generation as teachers, guardians, and protectors, assisting mankind to see the truth and pointing out the way (or ways) to salvation.

By the time he wrote the *Defence* Shelley had outgrown many of his cruder prejudices against religion; he had come to see Christianity not as the source of despotism and superstition so much as the victim of those tendencies that conspire in every age to extinguish the "poetical principle" from which religion derives whatever value it may possess (pp. 495–6). It is the responsibility of poets to help restore that vital principle so that religion may become a more beneficent force in society. Of all the Romantics, Shelley had the clearest vision of the relationship connecting literature and religious reform. I began this chapter by quoting one of his remarks on the subject. He makes a similar observation in *A Philosophical View of Reform* when he speaks of the English Reformation as a time when

the exposition of a certain portion of religious imposture drew with it an inquiry into political imposture and was attended with an extraordinary exertion of the energies of intellectual power. Shakespeare and Lord Bacon and the great writers of the age of Elizabeth and James the 1st were at once the effects of the new spirit in men's minds and the causes of its more complete development.[80]

What is noteworthy here is not only the priority Shelley gives to religious reform as a stimulus for political change but also the mutually invigorating relationship he perceives between reformation and literary achievement. Great literature is inspired by change in the religious order and then goes on to become itself an impetus for continuing religious reform.

As "hierophants of an unapprehended inspiration" (p. 508), poets are often better qualified to undertake the work of reformation than those who are professionally committed to the religious enterprise. Shelley relegated even the father of Protestantism to a subordinate role in the history of religious reform when comparing his achievement with that of one great poet in particular: "Dante was the first religious reformer," Shelley wrote, "and Luther surpassed him rather in the rudeness and acrimony, than in the boldness of his censures of papal usurpation" (p. 499). The line of poet-reformers runs from Plato through Dante and Milton to the poets of Shelley's own day:

We live among such philosophers and poets as surpass beyond comparison any who have appeared since the last national struggle for civil and religious liberty. The most unfailing herald, companion, and follower of the awakening of a great people to work a beneficial change in opinion or institution, is Poetry (p. 508).

The poet-philosophers of the Romantic period, Shelley believed, were committed to finding the right answers to "those obscure questions which under the name of religious truths have been the watch-words of contention and the symbols of unjust power ever since they were distorted by the narrow passions of the immediate followers of Jesus from that meaning to which philosophers are even now restoring them."[81] In that sentence, its quick progress from denial to affirmation so typical of Shelley's range of response in this matter, one finds a summary of the Romantic determination to reform the religious life of the time by penetrating the corruptions and distortions of the national religion so that a better order of belief might be discerned and restored.

CHAPTER 2

Blake's orthodoxy

I stood among the valleys of the south
And saw a flame of fire, even as a Wheel
Of fire surrounding all the heavens: it went
From west to east against the current of
Creation and devoured all things in its loud
Fury & thundering course round heaven & earth . . .
And I asked a Watcher & a Holy-One
Its Name? he answered. It is the Wheel of Religion
I wept & said. Is this the law of Jesus
This terrible devouring sword turning every way?
He answered; Jesus died because he strove
Against the current of this Wheel: its Name
Is Caiaphas, the dark Preacher of Death
Of sin, of sorrow, & of punishment,
Opposing Nature! It is Natural Religion
But Jesus is the bright Preacher of Life
Creating Nature from this fiery Law,
By self-denial & forgiveness of Sin.   (*Jerusalem* 77)

The spirit of reform and revival that transformed religious life in Britain during the Romantic period found an inevitable object of criticism in the Established Church, which was then experiencing what historians agree was the most disreputable period of its modern history.[1] The Church's privileged status and the political docility that insured that status, its intellectual and spiritual lassitude, its apparent indifference to the social maladies generated by war and industrialization, as well as the canonical abuses and irregularities that were the inheritance of centuries, all became objects of increasingly vocal criticism from Evangelicals within the Establishment and Dissenters outside it, as well as from growing numbers of unbelievers at every level of society. Of all those, believing and unbelieving, who protested the condition of the Church in those years, no one elaborated a critique so profound or so imaginative as the one to be found in the writings of William Blake.

This self-proclaimed inheritor of Milton's prophetic mantle had as little use for priests and prelates as his seventeenth-century predecessor, but his indictment of the Established Church was far more radical than the protest against ritualism and episcopal governance that Milton articulated as a spokesman for the Puritan cause. Blake objected to the Church's most fundamental conceptions of the relationship between God and humanity; he condemned its very Christianity as vitally flawed and mistaken. The Establishment was, in his view, an apostate church, one that preached, instead of the religion of Jesus, a system of belief and conduct not essentially different from the paganism that had existed in Britain before the Christian missionaries came. Druidism, as Blake understood it,[2] had been a religion of human sacrifice, and the state religion of his time countenanced, even encouraged human sacrifice on a much larger scale with its outspoken endorsement of warfare, its complacence regarding poverty and misery among the lower classes, and its complicity in the government's suppression of attempts at social reform. Blake called state religion "the Abomination that maketh desolate"[3] – an allusion to the Book of Daniel (11:31) suggesting that to his apocalyptic imagination the Church of England was a tool, if not an embodiment, of Anti-Christ, the ancient arch-enemy of Christ's church. Blake took it as his primary poetic mission to combat the corrupt, deformed Christianity that served as the state religion of Britain and to articulate an alternative, more authentic, radically reformed and purified version of the religion of Jesus.

Blake's broad anathema was directed not only at the Establishment, but at most other forms of organized Christianity that sanctioned or participated in the social iniquities of his time. In his eyes all had apostasized, all had repudiated the true Christian faith in favor of what he called natural religion or deism. Politically, he was one with the Dissenters in his determination to free the Christian faith from control by the state Church. Theologically, in the belief that fallen humanity would finally be saved only through the redemptive intervention of Jesus, Blake's thought was in harmony with that of all orthodox believers. But his projected reformation of the national religion of England was so radical in its political and theological rhetoric that it would have been shocking if not incomprehensible to most Christians of his time, and it has caused careful and sympathetic readers down to our own day to deny him the right to be called a Christian or even a theist in any disciplined use of those words.

Despite the admirable collaborative efforts of critics and historians which have made Blake's difficult composite art increasingly more accessible, the religious vision that provided the unifying principle for all his imaginative endeavors remains a question in dispute. In 1947 (still relatively early in the modern history of Blake criticism), J. G. Davies noted the radical disagreement already prevailing among critics on the matter of Blake's religion, observing that "a collation of their estimates of his beliefs is bewildering in the extreme."[4] The confusion has not been resolved in the decades that followed. To name only Blake's two most influential modern interpreters, Harold Bloom and Northrop Frye came to strikingly different conclusions on the matter. For Frye Blake was "a Bible-soaked English Protestant," "the bulk of [whose] mysterious and esoteric doctrines come straight out of the New Testament."[5] Bloom, on the other hand, has always insisted that Blake was never in any theological sense a Christian, or even a theist. "If the theologians of the different Christian orthodoxies are true Christians," he wrote, "then Blake is not, and it seems more accurate to name him an apocalyptic humanist than a Christian, little as he would have liked such a classification."[6]

In recent years there has developed a critical consensus acknowledging Blake's Christianity – but surrounding that word with so many qualifications that it is deprived of much of its historical and theological meaning. Almost every scholar who has written on Blake's religion has denied his orthodoxy, including many of those who have examined most carefully the Christian content of the later prophecies.[7] Almost all concur with Gerard Bentley's typical judgment that Blake's Christianity "was, of course, only related by marriage to any other known example." The "of course" indicates how widely accepted is the view that Blake's religion is a unique species of the genus Christian, so idiosyncratic as to fall outside the pale of orthodoxy.[8]

In much of the criticism one detects an underlying sentiment that to admit Blake's orthodoxy would be to deny or diminish his radicalism or his modernity. For example, Jean Hagstrum asks, "What does the return of Christ to Blake's poetry and art imply? Certainly not orthodox or dogmatic Christianity, for that kind of

Christianity Blake continued to fight in the full panoply of intellectual battle."[9] Note how "orthodox" slides into "dogmatic" with all its connotations of illiberality and coercion. Yet when one recalls that historically the most dangerous opponents of government in England were Christians of the most dogmatic stripe – those Calvinists who since the sixteenth century were always quicker than others to strike at the established order in church and state and who were still actively engaged in radical reform movements in Blake's time – it becomes apparent that a commitment to orthodoxy is compatible not only with political insubordination but with religious radicalism as well.[10] I will argue here that Blake's critique of the national religion of England was a reformist's attempt to purify and restore the Christian faith, which he saw as offering a revolutionary alternative, the most readily available one, to the existing political and economic order, and that his poetry as a whole makes more sense when seen in this light than when it is interpreted as a skeptical or atheistic attempt to subvert and destroy the Christian faith itself. In suggesting that Blake's radical Christianity was only an extreme form of Protestantism, I am conscious of Edmund Burke's ironic remark: "A man is certainly the most perfect Protestant who protests against the whole Christian religion,"[11] but that statement comes close to describing the poet's stance. While Blake's Protestantism had the appearance at times of apostasy, my argument is that he rejected what he judged to be a corrupt and spurious Christianity and that the alternative faith he articulated was itself authentically Christian by the theological standards of the time. In short I take seriously and will examine critically Blake's own claim to the title of Christian, as expressed for example in a letter to his friend Butts in 1802: "I still & shall to Eternity Embrace Christianity and Adore him who is the Express image of God."[12]

Because Blake's orthodoxy has been and remains a central issue in literary criticism, and because some who have disputed his orthodoxy have done so by appealing to a stricter standard of doctrinal purity and precision than the poet's contemporaries would have required, it will be useful here (and for the larger purposes of this study) to recall the contemporary standards of orthodoxy by which his works would have been judged. This is not merely an academic exercise: Blake's critique of Christianity is at the heart of his work; it was a matter of central importance to him to demonstrate what was wrong with the national religion and to show how it might be corrected. All of Blake's poetry can be read as an attempt to express his understanding of correct belief (the literal meaning of "orthodoxy"), an attempt that culminated in his epic poem *Jerusalem* – itself an extended definition of Christianity as he understood it. Blake once confided to a friend: "The Thing I have most at Heart! more than life or all that seems to make life comfortable without. Is the Interest of True Religion & Science & whenever anything appears to affect that Interest (Especially if I myself omit any duty to my Station as a Soldier of Christ) It gives me the greatest of torments."[13] One may ask, then, what was generally accepted as "True Religion" among the orthodox in England at the beginning of the nineteenth century, and why, compared with other Christian Soldiers of his time, Blake seemed to march, not only to the beat of a different drummer, but to an entirely different war, one apparently requiring relentless mental fight against Christianity itself.

Since Blake was baptized into the Church of England,[14] one could simplify the problem by pointing out that for him the standard of orthodoxy would have been the Church's Thirty-nine Articles of Religion. But subscription to the Thirty-nine Articles in Blake's time was a complicated matter, much more a political than a theological act, as Dissenters demonstrated by their refusal to accept an imposed formulation of doctrines whose intrinsic truth they did not deny. Even a wary Anglican like the older Robert Southey conceded the orthodoxy of most Dissenters: "The Methodists of every description, the Presbyterians, the Independents, and the Baptists, differ not in doctrine from the Church of England."[15] Indeed, despite their insistence on religious liberty, Dissenting congregations tended to be more doctrinally scrupulous than the Church itself, which was, in Basil Willey's suggestive phrase, only "nominally orthodox."[16] Among the Anglican bishops in Blake's time, consensus rather than precision seemed the primary desideratum in theological matters – perhaps an inevitable requirement for the peace of any comprehensive national Church.

There was, nonetheless, a fairly clear consensus about the most basic doctrines of the faith, those that had to be accepted by anyone who would claim the name of Christian. While there were different shadings of emphasis, most British Christians would have agreed with Charles Blomfield, Bishop of Chester and later of London, when he stated in 1825 that "the fundamental and vital doctrines of Christianity" as espoused by the Church of England along with "the great body of protestant dissenters" were two: "the doctrines of our Saviour's divinity, and of the atonement which he has made for our sins."[17] The one doctrinal deviation that no orthodox Christian was able to countenance was Socinianism or, in its new denominational identity, Unitarianism – a heresy that was, in fact, a criminal offense in Britain until 1813. This denial of Christ's divinity and consequently of the redemptive efficacy of his death clearly separated Unitarians from all others who called themselves Christians. Despite his broad-church principles, Thomas Arnold of Rugby informed the Unitarian parents of one of his students: "I feel bound to teach the essentials of Christianity to all those committed to my care – and with these the tenets of the Unitarians alone, among all the Dissenters in the kingdom, are in my judgment irreconcilable."[18] Most British Christians, then, whether Romanist, Anglican, or Protestant Dissenter, would have been able to accept Samuel Taylor Coleridge's succinct description of Christians as those "who receive Christ as the Son of the Living God who submitted to become Man in the flesh in order to redeem mankind."[19]

Applying Ockham's razor to the question of Blake's creed, one can inquire whether his beliefs concerning the divinity and the redemptive mission of Jesus Christ accorded with those of contemporary Christians as articulated by spokesmen like Coleridge and Bishop Blomfield. Most modern scholars, as I have suggested, have found Blake's doctrine in these areas to deviate from orthodoxy. Leopold Damrosch's thoughtful, comprehensive analysis of the question is typical in its conclusion that "Blake's religion was never that of the orthodox, and to the end of his life he continued to assert the humanity of Jesus as the only God."[20] Focusing here on the most persistent of Blake's doctrinal peculiarities, Damrosch intended the second clause in his sentence to support the first, but the fact is that it was possible in Blake's time to assert the humanity of Jesus as the only God and still be well inside the vaguely drawn boundaries of Protestant orthodoxy. What Damrosch was objecting to is a Swedenborgian formulation of the doctrine of Christ's divine nature. Among the 32 resolutions approved and signed by "W. Blake" and "C. Blake" at the First General Conference of the New Jerusalem Church in 1789 was an assertion "that all Faith and Worship directed to any other, than to the One God Jesus Christ in his Divine Humanity, being directed to a God invisible and incomprehensible, have a direct tendency to overturn the Holy Word, and to destroy every thing spiritual in the Church."[21] Or, as Swedenborg himself wrote, "unless God is thought of and approached as a Man, all idea of Him perishes; for then the thought is either lost in the contemplation of empty space, or directed to nature and its objects."[22] Part of the attraction for Blake of Swedenborg's emphasis on the humanity of God was that it stood in radical opposition to the deistic conception of God as a remote First Cause. Blake rejected as pernicious any belief that "God in the dreary Void / Dwells from Eternity, wide separated from the Human Soul" (*J* 23:29–30; E168).

Blake's orthodoxy has been challenged also in regard to the doctrine of the redemption because he repudiated the notion of Christ's atonement as a sacrificial ransom. ("Must the Wise die for an Atonement? does Mercy endure Atonement? / No! It is Moral Severity, & destroys Mercy in its Victim" (*J* 35 (39): 25–26; E 181).) This too is a Swedenborgian conviction, but the orthodox doctrine of the Atonement was obscure enough and controversial enough to permit considerable latitude of interpretation. Blake denies one conception of the Atonement – that the Father demanded Jesus's death as satisfaction of a debt and appeasement of his anger at humanity – in favor of another traditional formulation, the one expressed, for example in John 3:16: "For God so loved the world, that he gave his only begotten Son, that whosoever believeth in him should not perish, but have everlasting life." In *Jerusalem* Jesus gives his life out of love – to save Albion and to demonstrate the need for liberation from the Selfhood. What is important is Blake's consistent assertion of the need for the intervention of Jesus to effect human salvation, a salvation that mankind is powerless to achieve on its own. Near the end of *Jerusalem* Jesus enunciates a quite orthodox formulation of this doctrine of redemption:

Fear not Albion unless I die thou canst not live But if I die I shall arise again & thou with me . . . And if God dieth not for Man & giveth not himself Eternally for Man Man could not exist. (*J* 96: 14–15, 25–26; E 255)

This identification of Jesus as God and the unqualified insistence that only the intervention of Jesus can save the fallen human race is about as clear an expression of the central doctrines of Christianity as one could ask from a poet.

It would seem evident that, while the specific notion of a ransoming sacrifice was not acceptable to Blake, the broader concept of a necessary redemption by a Divine Savior was central in his understanding of mankind's destiny. Indeed Blake comes very close to Calvinism in his insistence that "all our righteousness is filthy rags" and that we are saved only by a gratuitous act of divine mercy. In *Milton* the inspired Bard prophesies:

> And the Elect shall say to the Redeemd. We behold it is of
> Divine Mercy alone! of Free Gift and Election that we live.
> Our Virtues & Cruel Goodnesses, have deserv'd Eternal Death.
>
> (*M* 13: 28–34; E 107)

Here the "elect" came close to versifying the Church of England's Eleventh Article of Faith: "We are accounted righteous before God, only for the merits of our Lord and Saviour Jesus Christ, by faith, and not for our own works or deservings." They are also, by the way, restating the teaching of the Tenth Article:

The condition of man after the fall of Adam is such, that he cannot turn and prepare himself by his own natural strength and good works to faith and calling upon God. Wherefore we have no power to do good works pleasant and acceptable to God, without the grace of God by Christ preventing us, that we may have a good will, and working with us when we have that good will.

That statement could serve as a summary of the theological doctrine of *Jerusalem*.

In recent years scholars have been giving increased attention to the antinomian tradition in British Christianity that flourished during the 1640s and 1650s and survived into the nineteenth century, trying to find a home for Blake among the religious fringe groups that were active in the London of his day. E. P. Thompson, for example, has situated him socially and doctrinally among the Muggletonians. Morton Paley has more persuasively demonstrated the central influence of Swedenborg on Blake's thinking throughout his life, "sometimes as a source of ideas and of subject matter, sometimes as a promulgator of ideas to be opposed, but in either respect as a powerful intellectual force."[23] Reading Swedenborg or his English disciples, one is continually struck by the similarities between the Baron's theology and Blake's characteristic religious formulations. Although his annotations to Swedenborg repudiate certain specific teachings on predestination and eternal punishment, Blake's Christology retained its essentially Swedenborgian character until the end of his life, or at least until he completed *Jerusalem*.

Were Swedenborg's ideas on the divinity of Christ and the

Atonement, which so closely resemble Blake's, concordant with Christian orthodoxy? The first English Swedenborgians insisted that their doctrines did not conflict with those of the Church of England, and the "Theosophical Society" they formed to discuss the Baron's writings considered its activities a supplement rather than an alternative to regular church attendance. It was only in 1787 that the London community decided to open its own place of public worship and ordain its own ministers.[24] Thereafter there were two strains in English Swedenborgianism, resembling the eventual division of Wesley's disciples into Methodist Dissenters and Evangelical Anglicans. The division is represented in the careers of two men, Robert Hindmarsh of London and the Reverend John Clowes of Manchester.[25] Both were tireless propagandists of the new faith, but while Hindmarsh led the London community into schism and thereafter became increasingly antagonistic toward the Church of England, Clowes remained as rector of St. John's parish in Manchester, preaching the new doctrine from its pulpit and insisting that there was no conflict between being a Swedenborgian and being a priest of the Church. When some of the faithful complained about the content of his sermons, Clowes was visited by the local bishop and, after an examination of his beliefs, was declared free of heresy. Clowes left an account of his interview with the bishop, which provides us with clear formulations of the doctrines in dispute and shows their resemblance to Blake's own characteristic beliefs. Defending his views on the Trinity, for example, Clowes told the Bishop:

My idea is that the whole Trinity of Father, Son, and Holy Ghost is contained in the one divine and glorious Person of our Lord and Saviour Jesus Christ, who, as to His inmost, hidden essence or soul, is Jehovah the Eternal Father; as to His outward existence or body, is the Son of God; and as to His divine operation, is the Holy Spirit. Thus there is only one God in the Church, and Jesus Christ is that one God, in whom is a Divine Trinity, being Creator from eternity, Redeemer in time, and Sanctifier or Regenerator to eternity.

Blake was not so concerned with preserving the doctrine of the Trinity, but Clowes's language helps to account for the poet's continual use of the name Jehovah in a theological context where Jesus acts as the only Divine Being.

Clowes also shared Blake's objection to definitions of the Atonement as a sacrificial ransom, espousing an alternate view close to the poet's vision of Jesus as a redeemer who saves humanity from Satan's power by his love and example. Clowes argued as follows:

Jesus Christ came into the world, not for the purpose of offering Himself as a vicarious sacrifice for the sins of the world, or as some express it to satisfy the offended justice of the Father, (for Jesus Christ, as to His divine nature, was Himself the Father, and required no satisfaction, except the salvation of His children,) but He came into the world to make His children wise, and good, and happy, by turning them from the power of sin and Satan unto Himself.[26]

Clowes reported that the bishop had "no particular objection" to these ideas, agreed with many of them, and declared himself "perfectly well satisfied" with the rector's explanation of his beliefs. Although the bishop, Beilby Porteus, had a reputation for tolerance in religious matters,[27] he later became, when Bishop of London, a favorite of the Evangelicals and a persecutor of political and religious heterodoxy, which suggests that Clowes's doctrines would have received careful scrutiny. Swedenborgian Christianity was evidently good enough for Porteus, whose watchdog orthodoxy was good enough later on for the most dogmatic Churchmen of the day.

Swedenborgian doctrine was also good enough for Samuel Taylor Coleridge, whose theological orthodoxy is not usually called into question.[28] Coleridge gave his own unsolicited testimony to Clowes's version of orthodoxy when he described his friend Charles Augustus Tulk as "a Partizan and Admirer of the Honorable Emanuel Swedenborg; but of the genuine School, with the Revd J. Clewes, [sic] Rector of St John's, Manchester, who oppose strenuously all sectarian feeling and remain sincere and affectionate Members of the Established Church." Coleridge told Tulk that he could find very little difference of opinion between himself and Swedenborg, and went so far as to say that the Baron's ideas on the Redemption, the Divinity of Christ and the Trinity, are "perhaps the purest form of the Gospel Truth." Coleridge's annotations to Swedenborg's *True Christian Religion* show no significant objection to the doctrines expressed; on the contrary, Coleridge places Swedenborg securely in the Protestant mainstream, suggesting that the Baron tended to exaggerate his own differences with Luther and Calvin: "He mis-states their opinions, which, in substance at least, he might have found reconcilable with his own, & with little other difference than arises almost inevitably when the same Object is contemplated by several persons from several different points of view."[29]

While employing Coleridge as a touchstone of orthodoxy, I might point out that his opinions resembled Blake's also in regard to some of the less essential doctrines of the Christian faith. On the virginity of Mary, for instance, and the existence of a particular being called Satan, both poets expressed views that were not concordant with the orthodoxy of their time, although the opinions have become more common among Christians in the twentieth century.[30] Indeed, Coleridge's list of "the characteristic and peculiar doctrines of Christianity" in *Aids to Reflection* contains none that doesn't appear in some form in Blake's later prophecies.[31]

In summary, by the standard of his time Blake seems to have been quite adequately orthodox in regard to the essential core of the faith – the divine humanity of Jesus Christ and his redemption of the fallen human race. All of which raises the central question of this chapter: if according to the standards of his time Blake was an orthodox Christian, why has his expression of his faith persuaded so many thoughtful, informed readers that he was not at all orthodox, and even that he was an atheist?

One primary source of the difficulty confronting those who interpret Blake's religion is his dialectical mode of argument, in which different dramatic voices express conflicting theological views, so that the poetry can be quoted convincingly on both sides of any important religious dispute.[32] To a peculiar degree, then, Blake encourages the tendency of literary critics to select from an author's work only what suits their preunderstanding of his meaning.[33] In his book *Blake's Humanism*, whose title suggests its argument concerning the poet's religious position, John Beer has described the critical problem succinctly: "Where a poet is so loath to declare his central principles, the reader is presented with a set of statements, from which the central ones have to be extracted . . . It is not surprising that individual sentences have been picked up and regarded as central, simply because they give a clear statement, while others more obscure but more telling, are disregarded." Ironically, Beer proceeds immediately to disregard his own warning and provides an exemplary instance of selective misreading when he writes: "Blake's fashioning of God in the image of man could never be regarded as orthodox by the Christian churches.

> Thou art a Man God is no more
> Thy own humanity learn to adore

No theologian in the orthodox tradition of Christianity could accept so uncompromising a statement." It is correct that no orthodox Christian could accept that statement. But Blake did not accept it either. As Margaret Bottrall pointed out more than forty years ago, the advice here is Satanic, spoken by "the God of this world," and is clearly meant to be repudiated by Jesus, to whom the words are addressed.[34]

Even when explicitly invited to think dialectically in *The Marriage of Heaven & Hell*, normally careful critics tend to hear the voice of the Devil as Blake's own voice and not as one "contrary" that needs to be balanced with an opposing view. In the concluding dialogue between the devil and the angel on plates 22 and 23 of *Marriage*, the devil proclaims, "The worship of God is. Honouring his gifts in other men each according to his genius. and loving the greatest men best, those who envy or calumniate great men hate God, for there is no other God." Readers have accepted that diabolic viewpoint as Blake's own, dismissing as irrelevant the angel's response: "Thou Idolater, is not God One? & is he not visible in Jesus Christ? and has not Jesus Christ given his sanction to the law of ten commandments and are not all other men fools, sinners, & nothings?" [E 43] One doesn't have to like the doctrine or the rhetorical style to acknowledge that this angelic emphasis on the unique identity of Jesus as the incarnate God who calls humanity from its sinful ways is merely an overheated expression of the orthodox Christian position. Blake is underwriting neither the ten commandments nor the comically strained attempts of the devil to prove that Jesus broke all of them; he is indicating that morality may involve negotiation between Biblical prescription and individual freedom. The unifying embrace that concludes the dialogue between angel and devil suggests that the truth is to be looked for in the marriage of, or dialectic between, their uncompromising theistic and humanistic viewpoints.

Blake's *Jerusalem* engages on an epic scale in this dialectical mode of religious discourse. For example, the Preface to Chapter Four states: "I know of no other Christianity and of no other Gospel than the liberty both of body & mind to exercise the Divine Arts of Imagination." (*J* 77; E 231) This apparent equation of Christianity with imaginative freedom would seem to rob the faith of all transcendent reference and theological content. But, as I have indicated, the narrative itself goes on to present a quite traditional vision of humanity as a fallen race that can be saved only by the intervention of a transcendent Savior. Blake has contributed to the theological confusion by calling Jesus "the Divine Imagination." A more common appellation for God at the time was "the Divine Intelligence," but for Blake imagination was the supreme mental faculty and therefore provided a worthier metaphor for Divinity.

Critics unwilling to recognize the unique transcendent status of Jesus have tended to identify him with Los, the Zoa of Imagination, splicing the two with a hyphen as when Thomas Frosch says that "Los-Jesus" is "the sole agent of regeneration, for Blake seems convinced that no mode of consciousness other than artistic can free itself sufficiently from the restrictions of the spectre to experience a Divine Vision."[35] Terence Hoagwood's insistence on the "absolute humanism" of *Jerusalem* leads him to say that "Jesus – another name for human imagination – is 'in' men because he is a mental faculty."[36] But as Leonard Deen has pointed out, in *Jerusalem* the identification of Los with Jesus "is never quite complete or allowed to stand."[37] The central theme of *Jerusalem*, and of *The Four Zoas* before it, is that mankind's best efforts, as represented in the creative activity of Los, cannot bring about human regeneration without the continuous encouragement and the periodic assistance of Jesus. Los is revealed as ultimately defenceless without the Savior, who must intervene from a transcendent realm of existence to rescue mankind when the highest human gifts prove inadequate to the effort. Indeed, at one point of crisis we are told that Los "must have died, but the Divine Saviour descended" (*J* 42: 5–6; E 189). If Los resembles Jesus more closely than any other of the Zoas ("And the Divine Appearance was the likeness & similitude of Los" *J* 96:7), it is because both are in the line of the prophets and because Jesus serves as Los's model in his struggle to save humanity.

E. P. Thompson has asserted that if Blake had become truly orthodox after the 1790s, he would not have needed to invent Los and the rest of his complicated mythological scheme.[38] The orthodoxy of Dante, Spenser, and Milton might be challenged on similar grounds. The manner in which Blake in his later prophecies wraps his Zoa myth around the gospel message defamiliarizes the doctrines of the faith, but does not change their essential meaning, any more than the medieval mystery plays changed the creed with their daring recontextualizations of doctrine. Blake's articulation of Christian doctrine was unconventional, but in religion eccentricity is not the same as heterodoxy, as a cursory glance at the Roman Martyrology or Butler's *Lives of the Saints* will demonstrate. M. H. Abrams has written of "the symbolic obliquities by which [Blake] veiled the unorthodoxy of his religious and moral opinions."[39] But symbolic obliquities can be used just as readily to veil orthodoxy. Blake deliberately defamiliarized doctrines for political and religious effects, not only for the purpose of "giving the interest of novelty by the modifying colours of imagination," as Coleridge said in another context, but to "rouze the faculties to act." Like all reformers, he saw the need for rearticulating Christian truth in a manner radical enough to unsettle the religious complacency of his contemporaries.

Criticism and conflict were essential for the health, indeed for the survival of Christianity as Blake understood it. In the *Marriage*, Swedenborg is belittled as a religious thinker because "He conversed with Angels who are all religious, & conversed not with Devils who all hate religion, for he was incapable thro' his conceited notions" (E 43). The idea that religion itself may be the enemy of the true faith, and that a religious visionary must be able to balance belief and disbelief in a dialectic that most religions would not dare to encourage, lies at the heart of Blake's reformist vision and of his central myth as it is embodied in his prophetic books.[40] Any effective reformation of the national religion would require a critique so radical that it might look like atheism to those against whom it was directed. To penetrate the centuries-old corruption of Christianity would involve an appeal to an orthodoxy that would look like apostasy to those who had forgotten what the religion of Jesus truly was.

Theology is a crucial theater in the mental conflict among the Zoas that represent for Blake different aspects of humanity's intellectual and emotional life, especially those three most powerful forces he calls Los, Urizen, and Luvah. Los, who becomes the hero of Blake's story of fall and redemption, represents imaginative power, especially as it is employed in artistry and prophecy. Urizen is associated with reason, the human propensity toward analysis, organization, and control. And Luvah may be described simply as the energy that resists rational analysis, organization, and control. (I request the reader's patience with this reductive allegorizing; it is a way to begin.) There has been a tendency among Blake critics to identify organized religion as the province of Urizen, but this is a careless or a deliberate misreading of Blake. When Harold Bloom wrote, "the doctrine of Urizen *is* the Christianity of all the churches, of every institutional and historical form of Christianity, so far as

Blake is concerned,"[41] he was oversimplifying for his own purposes what is in Blake a much more complex and subtle set of interactions.

To begin with, any "historical form of Christianity" must, as a cultural construct, be ascribed to Los, who presides over the evolution of human civilization and who is associated in a unique way with religion as the counterpart in the fallen world of what poetry is in Eternity (*M* 27 [29]: 55–63; E 125). Blake describes Judaism, for example, as an imaginative achievement of Los (*J* 85: 2–6; E 243), and the cathedral cities of Britain act as Los's allies in the attempt to save Albion's life. Indeed, the four primatial dioceses of Britain – Verulam, London, York, and Edinburgh – are called sons of Los (*J* 74: 1–3). Like everything else of value in the fallen world, like sexuality or technology or artistic genius, religion takes a positive or a negative form depending on whether it is fashioned in the furnaces of Los or the mills of Satan, but because this is a fallen world, even the best manifestations of religion on earth are inevitably imperfect. Just as any artistic or cultural achievement results from the struggle of creative energy with resistant materials, Los's attempt to create a salutary religion is complicated and undermined by the necessity of mediating between the conflicting tendencies, coercive and disruptive, of Urizen and Luvah, or, in other words, between the authoritarian and the antinomian impulses in religion. If Urizen, the "primeval priest" (E 70), represents religion's tendency to ritualism, dogma, and coercion, Luvah stands for that instinct in humanity that has resisted and repudiated the priestly control of doctrine, worship, and morality. Religion must be associated with Luvah, if only because of the fierce energies it releases and justifies in the form of iconoclasm, persecution, and religious warfare.

When Luvah makes his dramatic debut in the role of Orc in *America*, he introduces himself in Biblical imagery of resurrection and apocalypse, but the threat he poses to organized religion is recognized at once by Albion's Angel, who excoriates him as "Blasphemous Demon, Antichrist, hater of Dignities; / Lover of wild rebellion, and transgressor of Gods Law" (7: 5–6). Orc's reply escalates the rhetoric of irreverence as he proclaims his anti-religious mission:

> I am Orc, wreath'd round the accursed tree:
> The times are ended; shadows pass the morning gins to break;
> The fiery joy, that Urizen perverted to ten commands,
> What night he led the starry hosts thro' the wide wilderness:

That stony law I stamp to dust: and scatter religion abroad
To the four winds as a torn book, & none shall gather the leaves.

(8:1–6; E 54)

"Wreath'd round the accursed tree," Orc recalls the serpent of
Genesis, and Albion's angel does not fail to notice the resemblance to
Satan, the "rebel form that rent the ancient / Heavens; Eternal
Viper self-renew'd" (9: 14–15). But the wreathed serpent is also the
healing brazen image of Numbers 21: 6–9, which is traditionally
interpreted as a type of Christ, and the accursed tree is also,
obviously, the cross of Calvary. Here and throughout Blake's
prophetic books Orc/Luvah is identified with Jesus as well as with
forces antagonistic to religion. The ambiguity has been troublesome
for some critics,[42] but it is not difficult to account for. The history of
most religions is the story of a continuing conflict between a
conservative priestly tendency and a radical prophetic impulse. The
prophetic impulse is itself ambiguous, having destructive as well as
constructive tendencies. The iconoclastic tendency may effect a
purifying reformation of religion, of the kind that all the prophets
including Jesus have urged, but it can also mean desecration,
violence, and murder; it can be inspired by denial of the spiritual
dimension of human life and thereby reveal itself to be Satanic in
motivation and effect.

The reactionary Urizen, who has little tolerance for ambiguity,
cannot understand how Jesus and Orc/Luvah can possibly be
connected with each other:

> When Urizen saw the lamb of God clothed in Luvahs robes
> Perplexd & terrified he Stood tho well he knew that Orc
> Was Luvah But he now beheld a new Luvah. Or One
> Who assumd Luvahs form & stood before him opposite.

(*FZ*, p. 101; E 373)

Urizen understands the Christian religion in authoritarian terms, as
a structure of prescribed dogmas, hierarchies, and rituals; he cannot
imagine how "the lamb of God" can stand in opposition to this kind
of religion, or how godliness can be associated in any way with
Luvah, just as the speaker in *Songs of Experience* is unable to conceive
how the Lamb's creator and the Tyger's could be the same divine
being (E 24).

In the fallen world Los is Orc's father, perhaps because all
innovation requires imagination, and so one might expect that Los

would be identified primarily with the iconoclastic impulse in religion. But the artist-prophet is also joined in a special relationship with Urizen, the principle of organization.[43] As an artist Blake had no tolerance for the indefinite or indistinct. He wrote in *A Descriptive Catalogue*: "The great and golden rule of art, as well as of life, is this: That the more distinct, sharp, and wiry the bounding line, the more perfect the work of art" (E 550). If "everything in Art is Definite and Determinate" (E 646), and if religion is one of the arts of Los, definition and clarity and organization are necessary elements in theological thinking too. In the effort to define and preserve "true belief," the hard line of precision and certitude must be an essential component. It is Los's function in history to define and preserve a correct Christian religion. During the moments when his prophetic vision weakens, he seems to fear that faith in Jesus will not survive if not properly guarded and protected, and then he is tempted to find in Urizenic certainties a refuge from Luvah's relentless attempts to destabilize every established religious system.

Los's task is that of any Christian theology, to comprehend the meaning of Jesus, to explain as precisely as possible his identity and his doctrine. But a final definition of true Christianity cannot be formulated while Jesus as Luvah intrudes in the process. It was perhaps the first article of Blake's faith that the fact of Jesus, the Divine Humanity, radically challenges and disrupts all religion in the fallen world. Luvah's positive function is to represent that aspect of Jesus that frustrates religious assumptions, evades definitions, and breaks down systematic theologies, subverting all the legalistic and repressive forms of Christianity that have been fostered by Urizen. More negatively, from Blake's viewpoint, Luvah inspires skeptical denial of all beliefs, even belief in the reality of Jesus as Savior. The ultimate paradox with which we must learn to live, Blake suggests, is that while certitude can be dangerous in religion, doubt also is destructive. The challenge to Los, as fallen imagination, is to define "correct belief" without ossifying the faith in the Urizenic manner or surrendering entirely to the radical iconoclasm and antinomianism of Luvah.[44] Neither Urizen nor Luvah can be allowed to dominate mankind's religious sense. Mediating between the conflicting demands of the other two Zoas, Los struggles to clarify the definition and character of true Christianity.

So orthodoxy for Blake is not dogmatic or complacent; it is an active search, a dynamic investigation. In the manner of Los, each individual must mediate with difficulty between Urizenic assurance and Luvah-esque freedom, with imagination as the only dependable guide. In *Milton* we are told that we must be "just & true to our own Imaginations, those Worlds of Eternity in which we shall live for ever; in Jesus our Lord." And in *Jerusalem* Christianity is defined as imaginative liberation: "I know of no other Christianity and of no other Gospel than the liberty both of body & mind to exercise the Divine Arts of Imagination" (*J* 77 E 231). In the epic narrative itself, that liberty is represented by the female figure who is named Jerusalem after the bride and dwelling-place of the Lamb of God in Revelation 21, and the poem becomes a narrative of the difficulty humanity has in finding and preserving the accurate vision of Jesus on which its salvation depends. The epic is also a prophecy that once true Christian orthodoxy is ascertained, the discovery will have revolutionary implications in the social and political order.

Jerusalem tells the story of the fall and redemption of mankind, or Albion, after he has forsaken the "Divine Vision," the spiritual and imaginative liberty that is his by right, and resigned himself to an existence limited by the perspectives and values of the natural world. This limited vision of human life is personified as Vala, a beautiful female who has alienated Albion's affections from Jerusalem, their proper object.[45]

Among the things Jerusalem represents is fallen mankind's memory or understanding of Jesus, the Divine Humanity, who is a paradigm of the godlike freedom and power we have all lost in the fall of Albion. At the top of Plate 4 of *Jerusalem*, in a picture that David Erdman says "adumbrates the full plot of the poem,"[46] the character Jerusalem points toward a Greek motto, *Monos o Iesous*, "Only Jesus," while another female form, evidently Vala, attempts to prevent Albion from seeing Jerusalem or the name to which she points. The narrative of *Jerusalem* suggests that our image of Jesus, like all perception in the fallen world, is inevitably subject to distortion. Even Jerusalem herself, the Bride of the Lamb, cannot always keep her vision of Him free from misperception. The Christian vision as found and cherished by the liberated imagination is nevertheless subject to destructive delusions, if only because any true freedom of imagination must allow the possibility of error. Jerusalem seems at times a helpless victim, continually misled and abused by other forces who are momentarily stronger than she. Los's responsibility in the poem is to protect and guide her, to perfect humanity's religious vision insofar as that is possible in the fallen world.

During the centuries following the Savior's death the memory of Jesus became institutionalized in the doctrines and rituals of historical Christianity and corrupted by the distorted values of earthly religion:

> Jerusalem wept over the Sepulchre two thousand Years
> Rahab triumphs over all she took Jerusalem
> Captive A Willing Captive by delusive arts impelld
> To worship Urizens Dragon form to offer her own Children
> Upon the bloody Altar.   (*FZ* VIII, 114: 33–115: 1–4; E 385)

Rahab is identified as Mystery as well as "the System of Moral Virtue" (*J* 35 (39): 10; E 181), but she might more generally be understood as the kind of organized religion to which the Christian gospel became captive nearly from the start. One could press the allegory and call her Roman Catholicism, the Scarlet Whore of Protestant polemic, were it not that Urizen's Dragon form has been worshipped as devoutly in Geneva as in Rome, inspiring among Protestants their own quota of arrogance and persecution, along with the sexual repression that feeds cruelty and violence. And the fact that Rahab is also identified as the muse of Voltaire, Rousseau, and Gibbon is an indication that the fallen, bewildered religious imagination is not tempted only in the direction of superstition and bigotry; it can react in the direction of rationalistic skepticism as well. Rahab is an alternative identity of Vala, who is the daughter of Luvah, so iconoclasm is also part of her nature. Vala speaks for that skeptical tradition when she tells Jerusalem of her determination "That Man may be purified by the death of thy delusions" (*J* 45: 64; E 195). For a time, apparently spellbound by Vala, Jerusalem herself is persuaded that repudiating Jesus is an act of imaginative liberation or enlightenment. But when she is most true to herself she is able to resist the delusions of both superstition and skepticism, as one hears in the lovely confession of faith she utters during her imprisonment by Vala in the dungeons of Babylon:

> O Lord & Saviour, have the Gods of the Heathen pierced thee?
> Or hast thou been pierced in the House of thy Friends?
> Art thou alive! & livest thou for-evermore? or art thou
> Not: but a delusive shadow, a thought that liveth not.
> Babel mocks saying, there is no God nor Son of God
> That thou O Human Imagination, O Divine Body art all
> A delusion. but I know thee O Lord when thou arisest upon

> My weary eyes even in this dungeon & this iron mill . . .
> And although I sin & blaspheme thy holy name, thou pitiest me;
> Because thou knowest I am deluded by the turning mills
> And by these visions of pity & love because of Albions death.
>
> (*J* 60: 52–64; E 211)

The turning mills that confuse Jerusalem's vision of Jesus may include the "Wheel of Natural Religion" (*J* 77) or any theological or philosophical system that has obscured or distorted Christianity during its passage through history. To say that Jerusalem is held captive by Vala in Babylon is to say that she has come under the influence of erroneous, destructive beliefs and ideals.

Throughout *Jerusalem* a disturbing relationship exists between the two female figures, who almost seem to amalgamate at times when Vala becomes the shadow of Jerusalem (e.g., *J* 11: 24–25, 12: 19, and 19: 41). This consolidation suggests that earthly, natural religion and the vision of Jesus can look confusingly alike, even though they should be radically opposed to each other. In his own time, Blake felt, it had become especially difficult to distinguish true Christianity from the false form of it practiced in the churches of Europe, a system of belief that was not Christianity at all but its direct opposite and mortal enemy – the creed he called natural religion or deism.

Blake's "deism" was a subtler and more pervasive system of error than the rationalist, critical religious movement that emerged in England at the end of the seventeenth century, associated with names like Herbert of Cherbury, John Toland, and Anthony Collins.[47] Blake was not nearly so concerned about skeptical assaults on Christianity from without as he was about the debilitating incursions that rational religion had made within Christianity itself during the eighteenth century, to the point that he now could see little difference between the Church and its deist critics. In *Jerusalem* Los cries out against those "calling themselves Deists" and then goes on to speak of them as though they were priests of the Church:

> Go to these Fiends of Righteousness
> Tell them to obey their Humanities, & not pretend Holiness;
> When they are murderers . . .
> Go tell them this & overthrow their cup,
> Their bread, their altar-table, their incense & their oath:
> Their marriage & their baptism, their burial & consecration . . .
>
> (*J* 91: 4–6, 12–14; E 251)

No deist worthy of the name would acknowledge a connection with the rites and paraphernalia of priestcraft alluded to here, but to Blake's mind the Fiends of Righteousness were operating inside the Christian churches as actively as outside. He gave the name Urizen to the God worshipped by the generality of Christians as well as to the Supreme Being of rational religion, since the first, like the second, was a man-made divinity projected out of human fear and desire, an authoritarian God antithetical to humanity's best interests and repressive of its best energies.

To understand how rational or "natural" religion came so to dominate the Christianity of Blake's time, some historical background is necessary. The Church of England survived the political upheavals of the seventeenth century in a weakened state, beset by critics on every side, including increasing numbers of freethinkers, various groups of inner-light fanatics left over from the Interregnum, and the more respectable Dissenters who had gained new stature and influence from their support of King William in the Revolution of 1688. Among the more able and articulate champions of the Church in that difficult environment were a group of churchmen called Latitudinarians because of their interest in encouraging doctrinal consensus among Christians and their tolerance for diversity in modes of worship and church discipline. The designation "latitude-men" also reflected critically on their willingness to make the political and intellectual accommodations necessary for survival during the Interregnum, when less flexible clergymen went into exile. The Latitudinarians became increasingly influential after the Revolution; within five years of William's accession they controlled the majority of episcopal sees, although in numbers they still represented a minority opinion in the Church.[48] Their success stemmed not only from their talents but also from their pragmatic ability to adjust to changing political circumstances.

The Latitudinarians set out to restore the stability and respectability of the Established Church by combatting irreligious skepticism on one side and sectarian fanaticism on the other with a new apologetics emphasizing the intrinsic reasonableness of the Christian faith. Attempting to articulate a theology whose basic tenets were clear and indisputable, they tended to refine Christian doctrine into a set of self-evident theological and moral principles, emphasizing those beliefs that were most likely to be agreed upon by all Christians and most readily defensible against atheists – the basic principles of natural religion.[49] John Tillotson, the Latitudinarian Archbishop of

Canterbury, observed: "As for the *revealed religion*, the only design of that is, to revive and improve the natural notions which we have of God."[50] Natural religion involves the assumption that, without any need for special revelation, by observing the physical creation and consulting one's internal dispositions, any individual can discern certain fundamental truths about the existence of a Supreme Being and about humanity's relationship with that Being. One can conclude, for example, that the universe was designed by a benevolent Creator who apparently desires the happiness of his creatures, who infuses in every human being a moral sense that can distinguish good from evil, and who sanctions the moral order by rewards and punishments in this world and probably in an afterlife. Natural theology is an old tradition within Christian doctrine, but it received impressive new corroboration at the end of the seventeenth century from Isaac Newton's demonstration of the sublime order of the cosmos, which seemed to make it a matter of common sense to conclude that a benevolent deity had been responsible for constructing the universe. No other hypothesis seemed scientifically respectable at the time.

The historians James and Margaret Jacob have recently called attention to the curious conjunction between Newtonian science and Church politics in England after the Restoration, and in particular to the manner in which a series of lectures endowed by Robert Boyle "for proving the Christian Religion against notorious Infidels, *viz.* Atheists, Theists, Pagans, Jews, and Mahometans, not descending lower to any Controversies, that are among Christians themselves" employed Newton's discoveries to help consolidate the established order in Church and State.[51] The lecture series were organized and controlled by Latitudinarians, who, in their effort to restore the intellectual respectability of the Church and "free religion from scorn and contempt," had closely associated themselves, at Cambridge and in the Royal Society, with the latest scientific knowledge and with the work of Newton in particular.[52]

Because those invited to present the first series of Boyle Lectures were associates of Newton and because it seemed to them that the new astronomy detailed in his *Principia* demonstrated the existence of God more conclusively than any other mode of argument, the initial series of lectures were devoted largely to explaining Newtonian science in a simplified style for large, fashionable congregations of people involved in business, trade, communications, and politics.

Eight lectures were delivered and published each year, and the annual series were periodically collected in comprehensive editions, which, translated into Latin, German, French, Dutch, and Swedish, became more widely read than Newton's own treatises ever were. In this way Newtonian science penetrated the culture of Europe, but it was science that had been coopted in the service of a religious and political agenda that had little to do with Newton directly.

Beyond refuting atheists and pacifying dissenters, Newtonian science was discovered by churchmen to have other practical uses as well. To guarantee its own survival and prosperity along with that of the monarchy it depended on, the Church needed to recruit the good will of the increasingly important class of merchants and financiers who constituted the new Whig establishment. Church leaders were pragmatic enough to understand that economic ambition and self-interest were an increasingly pervasive motivation in good society, and while idealists might hope that the new capitalists would be guided by religion, realists understood that at any rate they should not be antagonized by it.[53] Searching for ways to harmonize the economic and religious orders, Latitudinarian churchmen discovered that Newton's divinely ordered cosmos provided a model of social and political relations that was concordant with the needs and structures of a new economic order. In Margaret Jacob's analysis, "the most historically significant contribution of the latitudinarians lies in their ability to synthesize the operations of a market society and the workings of nature in such a way as to render the market society natural."[54] If there was inevitable harmony and balance in the workings of the universe at large, similar qualities might be looked for in the economic order also, which, like the cosmos, could be assumed to operate by certain fixed natural laws. These laws, if left unimpeded, would govern economic affairs for the ultimate benefit of all; a free market, concordant with God's overall design, would "gravitate" toward a "natural balance" of prices, profits, and wages.

So Newtonian science, with its "almost obsessive concern for design, order, and harmony as the primary manifestations of God's role in the universe,"[55] was recruited in the service of the Whig establishment in Church and State. The order and stability that were evident divine priorities offered a standard by which the oligarchy could encourage submission to authority. Emphasis on the sublime transcendence of the Prime Mover had the effect of sacralizing the political and economic status quo that had evolved under the laissez-faire providence of an absentee Creator. The extent to which these religious economics came to pervade the consciousness of Blake's society can be seen, to choose one example from many, in Edmund Burke's "Thoughts and Details on Scarcity" (1795), in which Burke reacts to a succession of bad harvests by advising parliament to resist any attempt

to supply to the poor, those necessaries which it has pleased the Divine Providence for a while to with-hold from them. We, the people, ought to be made sensible, that it is not in breaking the laws of commerce, which are the laws of nature, and consequently the laws of God, that we are to place our hope of softening the divine displeasure to remove any calamity under which we suffer, or which hangs over us.[56]

The easy equation of the laws of commerce, nature, and God is a Latitudinarian legacy. And one detects even more clearly the Newtonian flavor in a letter sent to Burke in 1791 by an Oxford don, which also demonstrates how routinely religion was used in those days to sanctify existing social structures:

In the subordination and gradation of persons and rights, consists the very life and health of every well constituted state. In this political arrangement, made not by the wisdom or the will of man, but by the invisible hand of Providence, every man moves in that sphere of life, whether higher or lower, in which that Providence, not his own choice, has placed him at his birth.[57]

The echo of Adam Smith's "invisible hand," the metaphor used in *Wealth of Nations* to convey Smith's idea of the economy as a self-ordering system,[58] and the casual acceptance of a social order organized in a hierarchy of predetermined orbits, remind one why Blake considered Newton's influence in his own time to be as pervasive as it was baneful. "Natural religion" had been made to coincide with "natural economics," making the self-interest of the prosperous appear to be as compatible with virtue as with the mechanism of the universe. The desire for profit and power became part of the providential order, an order given geopolitical dimensions and additional religious rationale by the imperialist wars waged by Protestant Britain against Catholic France and Spain throughout the eighteenth century.

The exoneration of avarice was facilitated by the decreased attention to Christian revelation that came as an inevitable entailment of natural religion. The Bible had suffered some political discredit for having fueled seditious conduct among Puritans and worse radicals during the Civil War and Commonwealth. Now its teachings on social justice were found to be not entirely compatible with the new social order that the Latitudinarians were committed to sanctifying. Wealthier churchgoers might have been made uncomfortable by the kind of sentiments that prophets like Isaiah and Amos attributed to the Supreme Being:

The Lord will enter into judgment with the ancients of his people, and the princes thereof: for ye have eaten up the vineyard; the spoil of the poor is in your houses. What mean ye that ye beat my people to pieces, and grind the faces of the poor? saith the Lord God of hosts. (Is. 3: 14–15)

The same congregation would feel no more enthusiastic about the searing denunciation in the Epistle of James of the rich who do not pay their laborers a just wage (5: 1–6) or the vision of social revolution in Luke's gospel, which rejoices in a God who "hath put down the mighty from their seats, and exalted them of low degree. He hath filled the hungry with good things; and the rich he hath sent empty away" (1: 52–53). The Bible's insistence on social justice was found to be as discordant with rational religion as with the new economics. Enlightened believers prided themselves on worshipping a Cosmic Architect that was more transcendent in His perspective, and therefore less attentive to life among the lower orders, than was the watchful, demanding God of Israel. As Abraham Heschel remarked, "It is a thought staggering and hardly compatible with any rational approach to the understanding of God, that the Creator of heaven and earth should care about how an obscure individual man behaves toward poor widows and orphans."[59] Blake saw the dominant social ethics of his society as predicated on just such an idea of a distant deity. "Moral Virtue," he said, is "the Law / Of God who dwells in Chaos hidden from the human sight" (*J* 28: 15–16; E 174).

Blake could look around and see how the Church of his day continued to accommodate itself to the values of an acquisitive and economically stratified society by accepting its inequalities as divinely ordained and inevitable, resolutely ignoring the strict Biblical injunctions to social justice. It was casually accepted among the clergy that the social order required inequality for its proper functioning, and that therefore inequality must be God's will.[60] One can find a typically brutal example of Church economics in Richard Watson's sermon *The Wisdom and Goodness of God in having made both Rich and Poor*, delivered in 1785 and published in 1793 with a new appendix directed against the French Republic – an attack that provoked Wordsworth to write the angry response known as the *Letter to the Bishop of Llandaff*. Blake himself, judging Watson's sermon only by its title, concluded that it "must be a most wicked & blasphemous book" (E 612). He would have had his suspicions amply confirmed if he had read the sermon, which asserted, for example, that "the unequal distribution of the world's goods" is not only "a great spur to industry and frugality in the lower classes" but also "a state most admirably fitted for the producing in mankind the great Christian virtues of content, patience, meekness, of universal benevolence, compassion, and good will, without which, though we should possess the whole world, we shall certainly lose our own souls."[61] When Blake wrote

> Pity could be no more
> If we did not make somebody poor,
> And virtue no more could be
> If all were as happy as we,

he might have had Watson's sermon in mind, but the bishop's mode of reasoning was only too typical. Indeed Watson represented the clerical green wood: he was generally considered the most liberal of all the bishops of the Church.

An even clearer indication to Blake that the Church of his day had abandoned the vision of Jesus for the worship of strange gods ("the detestable Gods of Priam," he called them) was the enthusiastic support it was giving to the war against France. Blake called Deism "religion hid in war" (*J* 89: 53), and perhaps only religious enthusiasm could have inspired the righteous vindictiveness one finds in the clergy's war sermons of 1803, delivered in response to Napoleon's threat of invasion after the breakdown of the Peace of Amiens. Even the more thoughtful and scholarly clergymen were caught up in the war fever; a sermon by Archdeacon Charles Daubeny, one of the few real intellectuals among Church leaders, illustrates the fashionable ferocity:

When the arm of an infidel, a blaspheming, a merciless oppressor, speaking vain swelling words, is lifted up against a nation which hath the Lord for its God; when irreligion, anarchy, and lawless tyranny, are placed in array against religion, order, and constitutional freedom; our cause in such case being, in a word, the cause of God against that of the devil; the ministers of that God ... become ministers of war, and sound the trumpet, as the priests of the temple heretofore did round the wall of Jericho.[62]

To this Blake might have replied as he did to Bishop Watson five years earlier: "To me who believe the Bible & profess myself a Christian a defence of the Wickedness of the Israelites in murdering so many thousands under pretence of a command from God is altogether Abominable & Blasphemous" (Annotations to Watson, E 614). The crusading spirit was for Blake among the clearest indications that the Church had abandoned the Christianity of the gospels. In his address "To the Deists" in *Jerusalem*, he says:

the Religion of Jesus, Forgiveness of Sin, can never be the cause of a War nor of a single Martyrdom. Those who martyr others or who cause War are Deists, but never can be Forgivers of Sin. The Glory of Christianity is, To Conquer by Forgiveness. All the Destruction therefore, in Christian Europe has arisen from Deism, which is Natural Religion. (*J* 52; E 201)

Natural religion was as old as humanity, but its modern English manifestation originated in the particular system of errors that the Church of England had embraced more than a century before. The root error lay in the theory of natural religion itself – the belief that one could find in humanity's instinctive religious insights and impulses a positive foundation for a satisfactory theology. For Blake, on the contrary, fallen mankind's religious sense was radically corrupt, so that religion, which ought to indicate the path to redemption, became a nearly insuperable stumbling block to it. Human religiosity was most likely to be self-serving devotion to the God of this world, a God invented to give moral legitimacy to "the selfish virtues of the natural heart." In natural religion as Blake understood it we make the tendencies of the selfhood to conformity and covetousness the moral norm, and we devise a God who will justify that morality and sanctify the inequalities it generates in society. The chief evil of "deism" is that it advocates acceptance of our defective human condition as final, discouraging us from imagining anything better. Human nature as it now is, and the political and economic order in which we feel most at home, are final, inevitable. Realization of the extent to which Christianity had been corrupted and drained of life by the heresies of natural religion drove Blake's sense of the urgent need for a radical reformation, so that the authentic religion of Jesus, a religion of justice and mercy, could be reimagined and restored.

The all-pervasiveness of deism in his own country, its impact on every aspect of British life, is expressed throughout *Jerusalem*, most impressively in the wonderful Plate 65, in which the influence of Vala is shown to be at work in the exploitation of labor in the new industrial revolution (specifically in an early version of the assembly line) as well as in the prosecution of the war against Napoleon, in which unwilling recruits were being conscripted in unprecedented numbers. It is in extended passages like this that Blake reveals, along with his tremendous power, the sophistication and scope of his prophetic vision of a society driven by a combination of cynicism and false idealizations into dehumanizing beliefs about military glory and technological progress. At the heart of this system of self-destructive values stands Vala, turning the flywheel of the great military-industrial machine. The center of her power is Stonehenge, site of the sacrificial religion of ancient Britain, which now, in its new guise as deistic Christianity, still maintains its hold as the national religion.

> They build a stupendous Building on the Plain of Salisbury . . .
> Labour unparallelld! a wondrous rocky world of cruel destiny,
> Rocks piled on rocks reaching the stars, stretching from pole to pole.
> The building is Natural Religion, & its altars Natural Morality,
> A building of eternal death, whose proportions are eternal despair.
> Here Vala stood turning the iron spindle of destruction
> From heaven to earth, howling, invisible!   (*J* 66: 2, 6–11; E 218)

In his annotations to Watson's *Apology for the Bible* Blake wrote, "To defend the Bible in this year 1798 would cost a man his life. The Beast & Whore rule without controls" (E 611). Vala is one of the names Blake gave to the Whore of Babylon, of whom it is said "the kings of the earth have committed fornication with her, and the merchants of the earth are waxed rich through the abundance of her delicacies" (Rev. 18:3). In the crisis of *Jerusalem*, as the Whore and the Beast gather their power to bring about the death of Albion, the only hope for humanity's salvation is Los, guided by his vision of Jesus.

> Los prayed and said. O Divine Saviour arise
> Upon the mountains of Albion as in ancient time. Behold!
> The Cities of Albion seek thy face, London groans in pain
> From Hill to Hill & the Thames laments along the Valleys
> The little Villages of Middlesex & Surrey hunger & thirst
> The Twenty-eight Cities of Albion stretch their hands to thee:
> Because of the Opressors of Albion in every City & Village:

They mock at the Labourers limbs! they mock at his starvd Children!
They buy his Daughters that they may have power to sell his Sons:
They compell the Poor to live upon a crust of bread by soft mild arts:
They reduce the Man to want: then give with pomp & ceremony.
The praise of Jehovah is chaunted from lips of hunger & thirst!

(*J* 44: 21–32)

Against this cynical, manipulative travesty, Los works to forge an authentic Christianity of "Mercy, Pity, Peace, and Love" – the Divine Image of the *Songs of Innocence*. So entrenched were the politics and religion of deism in the Church and in society that to invoke against them what Blake understood to be the principles of Jesus was nothing less than a call to revolution. That the teachings of Jesus offered a revolutionary program was an understanding that Blake shared with many radicals of his time, Christian and anti-Christian. John Wade in *The Black Book* (1820) described Jesus as "the great Radical Reformer of Israel – waging fearless war with the bloated hypocrites, who, under the mask of religion and holiness, devoured in idleness the rewards of virtuous industry."[63] It was a judgment in which even a professed atheist like Shelley could concur. If we read the life of Jesus critically, Shelley said, penetrating the distortions of those who wrote the gospels, "we discover that he is the enemy of oppression and of falsehood, that he is the advocate of equal justice, that he is neither disposed to sanction bloodshed or deceit under whatsoever pretences their practice may be vindicated." For Shelley, the political vision of Jesus was more radical than that of any other social reformer: "Doctrines of reform were never carried to so great a length as by Jesus Christ. The *Republic* of Plato and the *Political Justice* of Godwin are probable and practical systems in the comparison."[64]

The primary difference between Blake and Shelley in this matter was belief. It made a difference to believe that Jesus was not only another persecuted radical but the eternal living God, who would Himself, in the fullness of time, accomplish the social revolution he had projected. It explains why Blake remained an optimist and why Shelley's final statement was *The Triumph of Life*. Religious faith could espouse the most radical of revolutionary programs precisely because its trust in a superintending Providence permitted disregard of *realpolitik*, encouraging believers to conceive and then demand a social order drastically different from one that presently existed – the "new heaven and new earth" imagined in the Book of Revelation

(21:1). Realistically, the revolutions of the time merely transferred power from one oligarchy to another, having the primary effect of increasing the economic opportunity and power of the commercial middle class at the expense of the landed aristocracy, a minor adjustment in the distribution of wealth rather than a radical reconstruction of the social order. In France, the counter-terror of Thermidor in 1795 had brought power firmly into the hands of the *bourgeoisie* and *nouveaux riches*, strengthened the royalist faction, and gave increased influence to the military, an influence that would triumph with the coup of Napoleon Bonaparte. As for the British "Jacobins" – a number of the radicals of the 1790s were by 1815 on their way to becoming prosperous capitalists.[65]

Blake understood that only by invoking an ideal that transcended the possibilities inherent in secular orders of power could a true transformation of society even be imagined. One needed to look beyond the prisonhouse of modern history and appeal to a transcendent order, an order that could not compromise or coexist with the existing economic systems. Among the social programs available in the culture of the day, only the Bible articulated a truly radical yet broadly familiar ideal of social justice – but it was an ideal that since the Restoration had been suppressed and nullified by those who were the official custodians and monitors of Biblical religion. To enunciate such an ideal clearly, to espouse a truly orthodox Christianity concordant with the Bible's teachings on social justice, brought one into radical conflict with the Church religion of his day. "In a Christian commonwealth," Burke said in 1792, "the Church and the State are one and the same thing, being different integral parts of the same whole."[66] Blake saw this union of Church and State in England as lying at the root of the public evils of his time. Not only did the Church anoint the nation's kings and consecrate its regimental banners and help enforce its inequitable laws, in Parliament the Bench of Bishops gave an aura of religious respectability to all proceedings of government, however brutal or repressive. Worst of all was the complicity of the Church in the conspiracy of the ruling classes to exploit and degrade the powerless poor, its encouragement of the pernicious codependency of poverty and charity that was still being blessed even by liberal prelates like Richard Watson. Los cries out indignantly,

They compell the Poor to live upon a crust of bread by soft mild arts:

They reduce the Man to want: then give with pomp & ceremony.
The praise of Jehovah is chaunted from lips of hunger & thirst!

No one else in his time – not Godwin, not Paine, not Thelwall –
exposed with such sustained, withering accuracy the collusion
between religion and the established political and economic systems.
Those "soft mild arts" are what Karl Marx had in mind later on
when he called religion the opiate of the people.

Bonded to the State in an unholy hypostasis, the Church of
England could not bring itself to acknowledge that the social
program outlined in the gospels condemned the present social order,
that to put the social teachings of Jesus into effect would mean
political and economic revolution. More effectively than any other
agency of power, the Church had taken upon itself the task of muting
the radical teachings of the Old and New Testaments and was
prepared to fight determinedly alongside the State to keep that
message from being heard clearly. The indignation that inspired
Blake's religious protest came from his sense that the Church's
conduct was a blasphemous perversion of what Christianity truly
meant. Against this "pretence of religion to destroy religion" (*J* 38
[43]: 36; E 185), Blake appealed to what he understood as authentic
Christianity. Against an image of God projected by the fear and
selfishness of mankind, against the heresies of materialism and
militarism, against the hallowed degradation of the poor and helpless, he proclaimed the true religion of the gospels, calling upon Jesus
to return and redeem England from the Christian Church and its
ally the Christian State.

Can one repudiate what most people, including all the official
leaders and spokesmen of the national Church, call Christianity –
even what they call religion – and still legitimately claim the title of
Christian? One finds in our own time a parallel case that may
provide an answer. Blake's indictment of the Church anticipates in
striking ways the radical critique of historical Christianity that was
articulated by the Swiss theologian Karl Barth (1886–1968), founder
of the school known as Neo-Orthodoxy and undoubtedly the most
influential Christian theologian of the twentieth century. Barth also
attacked the Christianity of his day for its corruption by natural
religion, which he called, more simply, "religion" and defined as

"man's attempts to justify and sanctify himself before a capricious and arbitrary picture of God."[67]

Karl Barth's critique of religion was inspired by his recognition of the social and political failures of Christianity, particularly of the Liberal Protestant tradition that dominated religious thinking in Europe in the nineteenth century. The inadequacies of this religious vision first became apparent to him when the national Christian churches enthusiastically endorsed their various governments' war policies in 1914, and they became even clearer when a majority of German Lutherans subscribed to Hitler's new order in 1933, displaying the swastika and singing "Deutschland über Alles" in their churches. Barth led the clerical opposition to what was then called "German Christianity" and was primarily responsible for the text of the Barmen Declaration of 1934, the manifesto of the anti-Nazi "Confessing Church" and one of the few public protests against the new order in Germany after it came to power. The Barmen statement invoked Christian doctrine against the heresies of the "German Christians" and denounced National Socialism as a false religion in conflict with the teachings of Christ.[68]

Barth, like Blake before him, saw natural religion as the primary cause of the "embourgeoisement" of Christianity that had debased its character in the modern era. The religious degeneration that culminated in the cult of Hitler began with what Barth called "the catastrophe" – the movement of rational religion in Germany at the beginning of the eighteenth century which, paralleling the tendency of Latitudinarian theology in Britain, established natural religion as the norm by which all belief was to be judged (*CD* 1/2, 285–86). Barth characterized such religion as "unbelief." Historian William Nicholls offers a succinct summary of Barth's analysis:

As unbelief, religion is man's constant attempt to do for himself what only God can do for him, i.e., to form a concept of God, and to justify and sanctify himself in relation to it. Thus religion is idolatry, because its concept of God is man-made and based on man's arbitrary choice of what he will worship, and it is self-righteousness, because man uses his religious activities as a means of justifying and sanctifying himself instead of letting God do it by grace.[69]

Against this "religion" Barth appealed to God's revelation in scripture. The Bible, as he read it, was anti-religious in tendency, directing its most vehement criticism "not against the godless world but against the *religious* world, whether it worships under the auspices of Baal or Jehovah."[70] The gospels present the life of Jesus as a series of confrontations with the religious establishment, ending predictably in his condemnation to death by priests acting in collusion with the civil authorities. In Barth's view the independence of Jesus from his own religious milieu provided a pattern that Christians ought to follow. But the faith Jesus himself articulated was as susceptible of degeneration into "religion" as any other. Barth did not hesitate to condemn Christianity insofar as it had succumbed to religious self-assurance and arrogance. In *Church Dogmatics* he wrote, "Christianity itself as an historical and cultural form is simply one among the human religions, as liable to God's judgment on unbelief as any of them" (*CD* 1/2, 352).

Barth was frequently criticized for his leftist politics, but his religious orthodoxy was never questioned, except as being too rigidly traditional. Yet his orthodoxy did not prevent him from denying Christianity's absolute claim to be the only true religion. Barth's stance helps to clarify the similar position adopted by Blake – in the Annotations to Watson for instance: "That the Jews assumed a right Exclusively to the benefits of God will be a lasting witness against them & the same will it be against Christians." The tendency of Christianity to degenerate into religion creates a continual need for reformation of a radical kind. And so Blake can assert the prophetic role even of those who deny the faith when he says that the Holy Ghost in Tom Paine "strives with Christianity as in Christ he strove with the Jews" (Annotation to Watson).

Christianity's worst enemies were not its antagonists but its own adherents, those with defective visions of its character. In *Jerusalem* the cathedral cities of Britain are a beneficent force, but they acknowledge the dangers inherent in their own Christianity:

> Alas! The time will come, when a mans worst enemies
> Shall be those of his own house and family: in a Religion
> Of Generation, to destroy by Sin and Atonement, happy Jerusalem,
> The Bride and Wife of the Lamb. (*J* 41 (46): 25–28)

"Generation" is Blake's name for the fallen world of experience. A religion of Generation is one fashioned in and adapted to the world, subscribing to its values and sanctifying its ideals, even while apparently chastizing its immorality. In the passage just quoted the "Religion of Generation" might signify the Evangelicalism that had become the most vital form of Christianity in Blake's time. Its

emphasis on sin and atonement and its increasing insistence on
moral conformity were at odds with the spirit of forgiveness and the
imaginative freedom that Blake understood as essential elements of
true Christianity.

Another passage in *Jerusalem* expresses, in Blake's dialectical
manner, a different viewpoint on "the religion of generation," the
fallen and corrupt Christianity of his time. Although tending toward
the destruction of Jerusalem (since all institutional religion inhibits
intellectual and spiritual freedom), Christianity can also serve to
protect Jerusalem against even worse enemies. Los proclaims:

> Pity must join together those whom wrath has torn in sunder,
> And the Religion of Generation which was meant for the destruction
> Of Jerusalem, become her covering, till the time of the End.
> O holy Generation [*Image*] of regeneration!
> O point of mutual forgiveness between Enemies!
> Birthplace of the Lamb of God incomprehensible!
> The Dead despise and scorn thee, & cast thee out as accursed:
> Seeing the Lamb of God in thy gardens & thy palaces:
> Where they desire to place the Abomination of Desolation.
> Hand sits before his furnace: scorn of others & furious pride!
> Freeze round him to bars of steel & to iron rocks beneath
> 　　His feet.　　　　　　　　　　　　　　　　　(*J* 7: 62–73; E 150)

The "Religion of Generation" may not much resemble the true faith
of Jesus; only with difficulty can the Lamb of God be discerned
amidst palaces and gardens (like the Archbishop's park and palace at
Lambeth, where Blake lived in the 1790s[71]). But it still preserves the
Christian gospel and defends the Bible against attacks by skeptics.
Scorn for this Religion of Generation, which shelters while it
disguises Jerusalem, is here associated specifically with Hand, the
"Reasoning Spectre" who stands "between the Vegetative Man &
his Immortal Imagination" (*J* 36:38–41) Hand has been identified as
Leigh Hunt, or perhaps all three of the Hunt brothers who were
involved in publishing the weekly *Examiner*. David Erdman has
traced Blake's hostility to Hunt to the *Examiner*'s derisive review of
his private exhibition in 1809, but if Erdman's dating of the passage
is correct it may have been a more recently issue of the periodical
that troubled the poet now.[72] Hunt's lead editorial for May 3, 1812
(two months after the libel on the Regent that put him behind those
"bars of steel and iron") was a bold attack on Christianity as a dying
religion, of no further service to humanity, which was being replaced

by a more rational and natural religion. Hunt stated as "a fact easily ascertainable by general readers and observers, that the Christian faith itself is on the decline and has been so these hundred and fifty years past." "The well-informed classes," he was pleased to report, "begin to suspect that a system of philosophic morals, – a love of the general good, founded on a well-educated conscience and a trust in the wisdom of Deity, is a much more useful as well as noble principle of conduct than any which involves a dereliction of reason and a shock to humanity . . . We are not Christians ourselves: we believe in nothing but God and the beauty of virtue." Coming upon such an editorial in the journal that had despised his visionary art, at the very time when he was engaged upon his epic narrative of the war between true Christianity and deism, Blake might well have been moved to sympathy with the discredited faith that was being repudiated by his old enemy in favor of a rationalist religion devoted to cultivating the selfish virtues of the natural heart. Later in *Jerusalem* even monks and Methodists are praised for having championed Christianity against the likes of Voltaire, Rousseau, Hume, Gibbon, and Bolingbroke, who are called in *Milton* "the destroyers of Jerusalem, . . . the murderers of Jesus, who deny the Faith & mock at Eternal Life" (*M* 41: 21–22; E 142).

Evidently some institutional incarnation of the vision of Jesus, however defective or inadequate, is better than none. It was essential that the memory of Jesus be preserved, and the Christian churches were useful if only for that purpose. Even Shelley later would come to concede the value of historical Christianity as the imperfect symbol of an unrealizable ideal. So it is too much to say, with Harold Bloom for example, that Blake never was sympathetic to any form of organized Christianity. Although he saw more clearly than most the corrupt condition of the public religion of his time, he granted it a useful emblematic function, as it pointed beyond itself toward a better possibility. Karl Barth also saw the positive semiotic value of a corrupt religion: "Even though Christianity is a religion like others, it is significant and eloquent, a sign, a proclamation" (*CD* 1/2, 358). Despite the "embourgeoisement" of the faith, despite the reactionary role it had long played in society, Christianity carried through history the revolutionary teaching of Jesus, insistently preaching the gospel that it consistently betrayed. For Blake, insofar as contemporary Christianity was even a shadow of the vision of Jesus, it was to be valued as a symbol of hope and as a necessary counterforce to an otherwise triumphant natural religion. For that reason, compassion and hope must balance indignation as appropriate responses to the damaged, dangerous, indispensable Christianity of the fallen world. That mingling of attitudes, finally, explains the paradox of Blake the anti-Christian Christian, the religious reformer who has been mistaken for an atheist by so many careful readers.

It was vitally important for Blake not to relinquish a claim to orthodoxy and thus countenance the State Church's arrogation of the title of sole arbiter and custodian of God's truth. It was essential for him to insist that there was a true belief from which the churches of his time had deviated, with disastrous consequences for themselves and for the society they influenced. In this insistence he was one with the Dissenters, with whom he rejected imposed orthodoxy on principle, but he went far beyond denominational Dissent in the religious individualism that proclaimed: "One law for the lion & ox is oppression" (*MHH* 24; E 44). Yet even that antinomian position has its dialectical contrary in the value Blake placed on the religious unity subsisting within the diversity of mankind. At the very beginning of his career he wrote: "As all men are alike (tho' infinitely various) So all Religions . . . have one source. The true Man is the source he being the Poetic Genius" (E 3). In the address "To the Jews" that prefaces Book 2 of *Jerusalem* he makes the point more specifically: "Ye are united O ye Inhabitants of Earth in One Religion. The Religion of Jesus: the most Ancient, the Eternal: & the Everlasting Gospel – The Wicked will turn it to Wickedness, the Righteous to Righteousness." So while Blake can say, "The Vision of Christ that thou dost see Is my Visions Greatest Enemy," he understands that there is only one Jesus, whom all mankind will perceive clearly in eternity:

> Lo the Eternal Great Humanity
> To Whom be Glory & Dominion Evermore Amen
> Walks among all his awful Family seen in every face
> As the breath of the Almighty.

Even in Eternity, however (in Blake's dialectical theology there is always a "however"), in a situation where one might assume that the question of orthodoxy would be settled by an unobscured vision of the Divine Humanity, even then the possibility of heterodoxy remains open:

But every Man returned & went still going forward thro'
The Bosom of the Father in Eternity on Eternity
Neither did any lack or fall into Error without
A Shadow to repose in all the Days of happy Eternity

(M 30: 15–18, 31: 4–7; E 129–30)

The inability to err would diminish one's imaginative freedom. It would stop or stultify thinking to have the important questions finally settled. Eternity is the opposite of finality.

Blake is buried in Bunhill Fields, the Dissenters' cemetery, not far from the resting places of George Fox and John Wesley. On his deathbed the poet requested an Anglican service for his funeral but also specified the place of burial.[73] It seems fitting that Blake lies among those whose protest against the Established Church carried on the Reformation tradition in his own time. The ambiguity of a Church burial in a Dissenters' cemetery also seems appropriate to this poet, one of those who, in Francis Jeffrey's words, "having broken loose from the bondage of ancient authority, . . . re-asserted the independence of genius." Blake's grave has not been located and so is unmarked. If a tomb ever should be raised to his memory, there among the advocates of religious liberty, a fitting epitaph might be selected from the following statements found among his writings:

He who is out of the Church & opposes it is no less an Agent of Religion than he who is in it. to be an Error & to be Cast out is a part of Gods design.

The strong Man acts from conscious superiority, and marches on in fearless dependance on the divine decrees, raging with the inspiration of a prophetic mind.[74]

CHAPTER 3

Nature's priest

When John Keble, Professor of Poetry at Oxford from 1832 to 1842, published his collected lectures, he dedicated them "TO WILLIAM WORDSWORTH, true philosopher and inspired poet, who by the special gift and calling of Almighty God, whether he sang of man or of nature, failed not to lift up men's hearts to holy things, nor ever ceased to champion the cause of the poor and simple, and so in perilous times was raised up to be a chief minister not only of sweetest poetry but also of high and sacred truth."[1] In that same year but from a point considerably to the left of Keble on the Church's theological and political spectrum, Charles Kingsley wrote to his wife: "I have been reading Wordsworth's 'Excursion,' with many tears and prayers too. To me he is not only poet, but preacher and prophet of God's new and divine philosophy – a man raised up as a light in a dark time, and rewarded by an honoured age, for the simple faith in man and God with which he delivered his message."[2] It was a remarkable moment when those two eminent Victorian churchmen, one a conservative Anglican who shared with John Henry Newman the leadership of the Oxford Movement, the other a Low-church activist and future spokesman for the Christian Socialist movement (and the most celebrated public antagonist of Tractarianism) joined in celebrating and, in effect, ordaining a living poet as "preacher and prophet of God's new and divine philosophy," one who had been "raised up" at a critical moment in history to proclaim sacred truth.

What seems to me most significant about the judgment of those two Church leaders on Wordsworth was their perception of the poet's career as having had primarily a religious importance. Kingsley's reference to *The Excursion* reminds us why it was inevitable that the poet's life would have had that appearance in 1844. *The Prelude* had not yet been published, and *The Excursion* stood as Wordsworth's most impressive and most representative accomplishment in poetry, the work that had finally brought him, beginning in the 1820s, the widespread popularity he had hoped for.[3]   In the preface to that work Wordsworth had actually invited his readers to understand his poetic mission as having a religious character when he described his life's work as a sacred structure resembling a church, in which *The Excursion* (as part of *The Recluse*) represented the nave, while all his other poems, including the unpublished *Prelude*, were assigned subordinate positions as antechapel and oratories.

That we no longer see Wordsworth's poetry as centrally religious in character has much to do with the suppression of *The Excursion* within the canon through the efforts of Matthew Arnold and later critics who have disliked it for various good and bad reasons,[4] and the substitution in the twentieth century of *The Prelude* as the main focus of critical attention. The elision of *The Excursion* has also had the effect, since criticism feeds on itself as much as on the literature that justifies it, of creating the distorted image of a writer alienated from history and the social realities of his day.[5] In disregarding *The Excursion*, modern criticism of Wordsworth began by ignoring the poet's history and ended in condemning him for having ignored history. We call him apolitical now mainly because we have repudiated, partly for political reasons of our own, his most ambitious political poem. Apart from some of the sonnets, *The Excursion* was the poem in which Wordsworth most directly addressed the social and economic condition of his country. If one looks again at *The Excursion*, not as a kind of embarrassing appendix to the canon, but as the actual climax, for better or worse, of Wordsworth's career as a man of letters, one sees the poet not as a fugitive from history but as a man intensely engaged in the public life of his time. *The Excursion* was not a withdrawal from social realities into a religious refuge; it was an energetic contribution to public religious and political discourse, on topics that Wordsworth perceived as being vitally connected with the welfare and destiny of the nation. Nor did the poem sound a retreat from Wordsworth's earlier radical interests, either in politics or in poetry; in the attempt to subsume those interests into a coherent synthesis, *The Excursion* involved a more thorough investigation of the question raised by "Tintern Abbey" – how the "still sad music of humanity" and "the Presence that rolls through all things" are related to each other and to the social order.

It was a work like *The Excursion* that Wordsworth must have had in mind when he concluded the 1805 *Prelude* with a proclamation of his and Coleridge's prophetic mission to a generation that was in danger of failing a crucial test of its spiritual character:

> Then, though, too weak to tread the ways of truth,
> This Age fall back to old idolatry,
> Though men return to servitude as fast
> As the tide ebbs, to ignominy and shame
> By Nations sink together, we shall still
> Find solace in the knowledge which we have,
> Blessed with true happiness if we may be
> United helpers forward of a day
> Of firmer trust, joint labourers in the work
> (Should Providence such grace to us vouchsafe)
> Of their redemption, surely yet to come.
> Prophets of Nature, we to them will speak
> A lasting inspiration, sanctified
> By reason and by truth. (*Prelude* 13: 431–44)[6]

Like Biblical prophets sent to an idolatrous people who, once freed from bondage, had turned again to the worship of idols, a new generation of visionaries here announce their sacred mission to bring another opportunity for redemption to the post-revolutionary society of Britain.

Taking Wordsworth's word for it and looking at his career as essentially that of a religious teacher, one finds that his life takes on a more symmetrical appearance than it has had in the eyes of many of his critics. One sees that his religious interests were connected from the start with the social vision that shaped his politics, and those interests constituted a strong bond of relationship between his early radicalism and his later conservatism. It becomes apparent that Wordsworth's idiosyncratic metaphysical opinions "on Man, on Nature, and on Human Life" did not change as drastically as critics have followed one another in asserting.

Misperception of the nature and tendency of Wordsworth's life-long religious commitment has contributed not only to recent indictments for political dereliction and "displacement" but to the older charge of apostasy that has played such an important role in Wordsworth criticism at least since 1813. The word is generally used to denote a shift to the right in the poet's political and religious thinking, a shift that precipitated or, at any rate, coincided with a decline in his creative powers. Since those who use the term have tended to disapprove of the direction of this political and religious shift, an element of moral judgment has been added to literary judgment, creating an image of a poet who betrayed his best instincts for unworthy motives and as a consequence damaged his imagination. In E. P. Thompson's assessment, for example, Wordsworth's apostasy involved "a mutilation of the writer's own previous existential being."[7] Thompson, like most of those who repeat the charge of apostasy, was not especially precise in demonstrating the connection between political or religious opinion and poetic talent or in determining the effective date of this reactionary, debilitating movement of Wordsworth's mind.[8] I will try to clarify some of these issues by looking closely at the religious component of what is generally thought of as a twofold political and religious apostasy. It is to the sphere of religion, of course, that the word apostasy properly belongs, where it signifies a repudiation of a creed previously held. In an odd reversal, criticism has used "apostasy" to denote Wordsworth's return to the religion in which he was brought up, a return that repudiated an apostasy that more truly deserved the name – the one that took place in 1793 when Wordsworth abandoned his affiliation with the national Church and the Christian faith in which he had been baptized. This defection, I will argue, represented a true mental crisis, a psychic deracination that had major consequences in shaping Wordsworth's unique character as a poet.

Wordsworth's religious alienation seems to have begun somewhat later than his political radicalization, and to have been for him a rather more traumatic process. His conversion to revolutionary politics during his residence in France in 1792 did not, it seems, entail any notable change in his religious disposition. He went to France a candidate for Holy Orders and when he returned to England he was still considering the priesthood as his likely vocation. While living in Blois with Annette Vallon, who was already pregnant with his child, he wrote to his friend Mathews on May 17, 1792, "It is at present my intention to take orders, in the approaching winter or spring. My uncle the clergyman will furnish me with a title." And as late as February 1793 his sister Dorothy was still fondly anticipating her future life with William in a parsonage.[9] Wordsworth does not seem to have abandoned his ecclesiastical allegiances even while being catechized in revolutionary ideology by his friend Michel Beaupuis. When he witnessed the first spoliations of Church property in France, his sympathies were with the victims:

> And sometimes
> When to a convent in a meadow green
> By a brook-side we came – a roofless pile,
> And not by reverential touch of time
> Dismantled, but by violence abrupt . . .
> I could not but bewail a wrong so harsh,
> And for the matin-bell – to sound no more –
> Grieved, and the evening taper, and the cross
> High on the topmost pinnacle, a sign
> Admonitory to the traveller,   (*Prelude* 9: 468–72, 476–80)[10]

In 1792 there was nothing anomalous in the prospect of combining revolutionary ardor with a career in religion. The French Constitutional Church was still playing an essential public role in consecrating and domesticating the Revolution, and Wordsworth had watched with interest the political activity of the Abbé Siéyès and Bishop Gregoire of Blois, the latter of whom the poet may have met. Years later he recalled that while in France "he had known many of the abbés and other ecclesiastics, and thought highly of them as a class: they were earnest, faithful men."[11] In England, as we have seen, liberally-inclined Christians were interpreting events in France as providential, indeed as the fulfillment of Biblical prophecies of the Millennium. The figure of the Solitary in *The Excursion*, who resembles the radical Wordsworth in so many ways, was inspired by the Revolution to a renewal of religious ardor and a resumption of his priestly office (*Excursion* 2: 220–22).

By the beginning of 1794, however, one notices a change in Wordsworth's vocational ambitions and in his general religious demeanor when he remarks to a friend, "I cannot bow down my mind to take orders"[12] – a statement suggesting intellectual rebellion against the doctrine as well as the discipline of the Church. The change in attitude seems to have been part of a larger mental crisis precipitated by the outbreak of war between Britain and France. His mind, Wordsworth later recalled, underwent "change and subversion from this hour." Nothing that had happened before, even during his unsettling year in France, had affected him so profoundly as this war:

> No shock
> Given to my moral nature had I known
> Down to that very moment – neither lapse
> Nor turn of sentiment – that might be named

A revolution, save at this one time:
All else was progress on the self-same path
On which with a diversity of pace
I had been travelling; this, a stride at once
Into another region.   (*Prelude* 10: 233–41)

What is striking about Wordsworth's analysis of this moral shock is his persistent tendency to describe it in religious terms. His devotion to England gave way to a higher allegiance, he says, in the way that John the Baptist's mission was subsumed in the ministry of Jesus Christ – although in Wordsworth's case the shift in religious disposition was more radical, a mental event for which the word apostasy was appropriate. It was a time, the *Prelude* recalls,

when patriotic love
Did of itself in modesty give way
Like the precursor when the deity
Is come, whose harbinger he is – a time
In which apostasy from ancient faith
Seemed but conversion to a higher creed.   (10: 280–85)

The ironic distance expressed by "seemed" is the distance between 1793 and 1804, when Wordsworth was looking back as a practicing Christian upon the political defection that separated him from his earlier beliefs.

Thus strangely did I war against myself,
A Bigot to a new Idolatry,
Did like a Monk who hath forsworn the world
Zealously labor to cut off my heart
From all the sources of her former strength.   (11: 74–78)

To epitomize the conflicts by which he was then torn, he selects from all others a religious memory, a spot of time that gives us one of the most evocative images we have of the alienation of young radicals in those divisive times.

It was a grief –
Grief call it not, 'twas anything but that –
A conflict of sensations without name,
Of which he only who may love the sight
Of a village steeple as I do can judge,
When in the congregation, bending all
To their great Father, prayers were offered up
Or praises for our country's victories,
And, 'mid the simple worshippers perchance

I only, like an uninvited guest
Whom no one owned, sate silent – shall I add,
Fed on the day of vengeance yet to come!   (10: 263–74)

In all the literature of the time one can find few more vivid
expressions of the conflict of transcendent ideals, the clashing of rival
sublimities, religious and revolutionary, that troubled this period
when English society was divided by religious politics. Only a few
months earlier Wordsworth had concluded *Descriptive Sketches* with a
prayer invoking divine assistance for the revolutionary cause:

> Oh give, great God, to Freedom's waves to ride
> Sublime o'er Conquest, Avarice, and Pride . . .
> And grant that every sceptred child of clay,
> Who cries, presumptuous, "here their tides shall stay,"
> Swept in their anger from the affrighted shore,
> With all his creatures sink – to rise no more.[13]

When in 1793 such prayers for the Revolution's success came into
conflict with the Church's petitions for the King's victory, Wordsworth's religious disaffection became acute.

It ought not to be surprising, then, that the young radical whose
apostasy from ancient faith seemed conversion to a higher creed
should have decided to nail his protest on the door of a cathedral –
or rather, following a more contemporary polemical fashion, to
express his remonstrance in a public letter to an official of the
Church. I refer to the poet's unpublished (and unposted) *Letter to the
Bishop of Llandaff*. Essentially a political document defending the new
French Republic, the *Letter* is also at its heart an expression of
indignation that a prelate of the Church should have publically
expressed an opposing view – especially a prelate from whom better
things might have been expected.

Richard Watson of Llandaff had been the most articulate liberal on
the Bench of Bishops since the 1780s. He had welcomed the French
Revolution and defended it consistently even in the dark days of 1792,
earning a special commendation from Thomas Paine in the second
part of *The Rights of Man*.[14] In his *Letter* Wordsworth acknowledges
Watson's almost unique liberal role among the hierarchy during the
Repeal campaign and the ensuing debate on the French Revolution:

While, with a servility which has prejudiced many people against religion
itself, the ministers of the Church of England have appeared as writers
upon public measures only to be the advocates of slavery civil and religious,

your Lordship stood almost alone as the defender of truth and political charity. The names of levelling prelate, bishop of the dissenters, which were intended as a dishonour to your character were looked upon by your friends, perhaps by yourself, as an acknowledgment of your possessing an enlarged and philosophical mind.[15]

It is not clear whether Wordsworth had considered himself among Watson's "friends," but since the Bishop was one of the Lake District's most celebrated residents (he preferred the society of Windermere to that of his poor Welsh diocese), the young poet would have been especially aware of his career. He may indeed have been one of those admirers who, he claims, were bitterly disappointed when in his recent publication Watson condemned the new French Republic for having executed Louis XVI. Wordsworth speaks as if the defection of Watson from the liberal cause was the last blow to his hope for the utility and probity of the national Church, to whose service he had until recently intended to devote himself. Wordsworth wrote his letter just a month or two before he reached the canonical age for Holy Orders, at which time he would have been expected to express formally his desire for ordination to a bishop who could offer him employment in a diocese. Whether conscious of the irony or not, Wordsworth here reversed the canonical procedure, announcing to the "bishop of the dissenters" his repudiation of the Church and what it had come to represent in the political and social order.

Wordsworth could hardly have boasted of his republican principles to a bishop without being conscious of Rousseau's words in *The Social Contract* (from which his *Letter* elsewhere borrows freely):

I am guilty of error in speaking of a Christian Republic, for the words are mutually exclusive. Christianity preaches only servitude and dependence. Its spirit is over-favourable to tyranny, and the latter always draws its profit from that fact. True Christians are made to be slaves! They know it, and care little, for, in their eyes, this brief life counts for nothing.[16]

For Wordsworth, who could not "bow down" his mind to take orders, Watson's defection served to confirm Rousseau's accusation. There seemed no reason to expect any enlightened or liberal conduct from the national Church.

In repudiating Christianity in that year Wordsworth was following, perhaps only coincidently, the French revolutionary party line. The initial good favor in which the Constitutional Church was held in France dissipated at this time when émigré bishops began helping to organize a foreign invasion and when a rebellion of Catholics broke out in the Vendée. Wordsworth believed that his friend Beaupuis had been killed in the attempt to quell this uprising. In the paranoia created by the foreign and domestic threat, in which non-Constitutional clergy emerged as mortal enemies of the Republic, churches were closed and pillaged, and large numbers of suspect priests and nuns were imprisoned and executed. When a new calendar was proclaimed in October 1793, abolishing Sundays and all other religious feast days and dating the future from the birth of the Republic rather than that of Jesus Christ, it was, in the words of one historian, "sensational proof that the government regarded revolutionary France as a post-Christian country."[17]

After 1793 Wordsworth seems to have moved quickly in the direction of religious radicalism, following a common enough pattern in that angry year when the country became increasingly polarized and moderate positions more difficult to maintain. "My mind," said Wordsworth, "was both let loose, Let loose and goaded" (*Prelude* 10: 863–64). What evidence we have suggests a period of four or five years when, insofar as he thought about religion at all, Wordsworth considered it either irrelevant or pernicious. Certainly the influence of Godwin, which most biographers assume to have been operative in these years, might have had such an effect. Wordsworth could well have been among those radicals described in the *Excursion* as sharing a

> confidence in social man,
> By the unexpected transports of our age
> Carried so high, that every thought, which looked
> Beyond the temporal destiny of the Kind,
> To many seemed superfluous.[18]

Superfluous at best, and at worst a delusionary distraction from mankind's temporal interests. Wordsworth's reaction against established religion as a political menace can be seen in the rhetorical flourish that concludes his 1793 poem *Salisbury Plain*:

> Heroes of Truth pursue your march, uptear
> Th'Oppressor's dungeon from its deepest base;
> High o'er the towers of Pride undaunted rear
> Resistless in your might the herculean mace
> Of Reason; let foul Error's monstrous race
> Dragged from their dens start at the light with pain
> And die; pursue your toils, till not a trace
> Be left on earth of Superstition's reign.

In the rationalist rhetorical arsenal from which Wordsworth drew his personifications, Superstition meant orthodox Christianity, seen as the inveterate foe of intellectual and political emancipation. This critical attitude toward religion appears again three years later in "The Convict":

> From the mighty destroyers, the plagues of their kind
> What corner of earth is at rest,
> While Fame with great joy blows her trumpet behind,
> And the work by Religion is blest.

And one finds similar sentiments expressed in the *Imitation of Juvenal* that Wordsworth worked on sporadically in 1795–96, which criticized the Church hierarchy and accused religion of conspiring to have "her creeds by war restored."[19] This is the Wordsworth whom Coleridge identified in 1796 as "a republican and at least a *semi-atheist*."[20]

The religious moods of Wordsworth's mind between 1793 and 1798, those five years whose significance is both insisted on and concealed in "Tintern Abbey," are sufficiently difficult to reconstruct that they have provided abundant labor for scholars.[21] What the poem tells us fairly explicitly is that, while in 1793 Wordsworth had loved nature primarily for its physical beauty, by 1798 he had come to perceive in the natural world a "Presence" that resembled what others called God; that this intuition came accompanied by a new perception of "the still sad music of humanity" heard within the harmony of nature; and finally that he had learned

> to recognize
> In nature and the language of the sense,
> The anchor of my purest thoughts, the nurse,
> The guide, the guardian of my heart, and soul
> Of all my moral being.

In "Tintern Abbey," Jerome McGann has remarked, Wordsworth "declares himself to be a 'worshipper of Nature' rather than a communicant in a visible church. Whereas these fade and fall to ruin, the abbey of the mind suffers no decay."[22] The ruined abbeys of Britain were visible emblems of religious reformation, and it seems not entirely coincidental that Wordsworth chose to locate his poem in the vicinity of such a relic, since he is here enunciating a radically purified religious faith, a substitution of the uncontaminated religion of nature for a politically discredited Christianity. The poetry of the late 1790s consistently expresses, in the words of Paul Sheats, "a hope that looks not to the invisible heaven of an orthodox Christian dualism but to a substantial order of truth and grace, nature"[23] – a nature that had its own power to instruct the mind and sanctify the soul, not as the manifestation or the agent of God but as all the divinity we need on earth. The assertion that nature and sensation are enough for spiritual sustenance, pointedly excluding the need for any additional revelation or redemption, is the clearest suggestion that Wordsworth did not consider himself a Christian in 1798 – a conclusion verified for us by Coleridge, who understood his metaphysical dispositions better than anyone else at this time.[24] Belief in the sufficiency of natural religion was the truly unorthodox element in Wordsworth's nature poetry between 1797 and 1800, and this belief is what disappeared afterward, as Wordsworth began to define in more traditionally theological terms the source of the truth and grace he felt being mediated through nature.

In resorting to the religion of nature as an alternative to Christianity, Wordsworth was in one sense following a well beaten path. Natural religion was an old tradition in England, as I have pointed out in the preceding chapter, but it had been given new currency and vitality by the French Revolution, in which dedication to the religion of nature took on special political significance. When the revolutionary government of France launched its dechristianization campaign in 1793, what was offered in the place of Catholic ritual was the cult of nature, exemplified in the new calendar whose months took their names from the agricultural cycle. New secularist liturgies were conducted, like the one that Jacques Louis David choreographed in August 1793 celebrating a new Constitution, a ceremony that featured "a colossal statue of the Goddess Nature, spurting water from her breasts into an ornamental pool, on the site of the Bastille."[25] In England, fellow travelers took their cue from the French. A contemporary critic said of the British radicals, "They fondly imagined the time, for the explosion of the whole fabric of Christianity, had at length arrived; and that, to convert all sects from the absurdity of Christian notions, nothing was wanting but the opportunity which then presented itself, for proclaiming the *beauties of nature*, and *unassisted reason* to the world at large."[26] The new bible of these natural religionists was Thomas Paine's *The Age of Reason* (1794), which insisted that "the Creation we behold is the real and ever existing word of God, in which we cannot be deceived. It proclaimeth his power, it demonstrates his wisdom, it manifests his goodness and beneficence." "It is in *this word*, which no human invention can counterfit or alter, that God speaketh universally to man."[27]

But what Wordsworth experienced in 1797–98 and celebrated in "Tintern Abbey" was not only a pragmatic shift in political or rhetorical strategy; it was, by all appearances, a heartfelt religious conversion. Other young radicals seem to have had similar experiences at about this time. In 1796 in Dublin, Daniel O'Connell read *The Age of Reason* and was inspired by it to abandon his Catholic faith: "To the God of nature do I turn my heart," he wrote in his journal; "to the meditation of His works I turn my thoughts. In Him do I find my soul saturated."[28] Wordsworth and the Liberator did not share many political or religious opinions later in life, but their early "dechristianization" involved substituting an intense natural piety for the politically discredited religion of Christ. For O'Connell as for Wordsworth, "apostasy from ancient faith seemed but conversion to a higher creed."

It was once thought that after 1793 Wordsworth moved very quickly to the nature mysticism that inspires the poetry of the late 1790s. In a book that was influential in its day, H. W. Piper argued that Wordsworth acquired his belief in the "active principle alive in all things," the "one life" pervading Nature, from the French Materialists and English Dissenters with whom he associated in 1792–93, but the text that provided the primary evidence for this conclusion, the Windy Brow revisions of *An Evening Walk*, has recently been shown to have a much later date than 1794.[29] This evidence has further validated Jonathan Wordsworth's persuasive argument that Coleridge was the primary influence on Wordsworth's doctrine of the "one life" that mankind shares with the rest of nature, and that this influence was brought to bear most effectively at Alfoxden in 1797 and early 1798.[30] What Coleridge presided over was something that had all the characteristics, emotional as well as intellectual, of a religious conversion. One catches the intensity, the totality of the experience in the following passage from *The Pedlar*, written early in 1798.

> Oh! then what soul was his when on the tops
> Of the high mountains he beheld the sun
> Rise up, and bathe the world in light. He look'd;
> The ocean and the earth beneath him lay

In gladness and deep joy. The clouds were touch'd,
And in their silent faces did he read
Unutterable love. . .
In such access of mind, in such high hour
Of visitation from the living God,
Thought was not. In enjoyment it expir'd.
Such hour by prayer or praise was unprofan'd;
He neither pray'd, nor offer'd thanks or praise;
His mind was a thanksgiving to the Power
That made him: It was blessedness and love.[31]

That the Pedlar's experience was to some degree Wordsworth's is suggested by the transfer of several passages like this one to the autobiographical *Prelude*. Jonathan Wordsworth finds in these lines the same recollection that, somewhat muted and couched in a more deliberately literary style, is more familiar as the luminous account of the moment of Wordsworth's own consecration reported in *The Prelude* 4: 330–45:

Ah, need I say, dear friend, that to the brim
My heart was full? I made no vows, but vows
Were then made for me: bond unknown to me
Was given, that I should be – else sinning greatly –
A dedicated spirit. On I walked
In blessedness, which even yet remains.

Wordsworth seems to have experienced something like the joy, peace, and "refreshment" that was being reported throughout the country by those touched by the religious revival of the 1790s. His language on more than one occasion curiously, or perhaps deliberately, recalls the language of the revival, as though he found in the experience of conversion an appropriate metaphor for his new interaction with the natural world. He felt, he said, "the deep enthusiastic joy, / The rapture of the hallelujah sent / From all that breathes and is" (*Prelude* 13: 61–63). Another passage is even more reminiscent of the psychology of conversion:

Gently did my soul
Put off her veil, and, self-transmuted, stood
Naked as in the presence of her God.
As on I walked, a comfort seemed to touch
A heart that had not been disconsolate,
Strength came where weakness was not known to be,
At least not felt; and restoration came
Like an intruder knocking at the door

Of unacknowledged weariness. I took
The balance in my hand and weighed myself.   (*Prelude* 4: 140–49)

In the most ambitious poem of this period, *Peter Bell*, the hero
experiences psychic healing through a return to nature that is,
simultaneously, a religious conversion, a response to a Methodist
preacher's call to repentance. Peter's change of heart outside the
Methodist chapel is accompanied with a change in his attitude
toward and relationship with nature, as well as his relationship with
his community.

> And now does Peter deeply feel
> The heart of man's a holy thing;
> And nature, through a world of death,
> Breathes into him a second breath
> Just like the breath of spring.   (1251–55)[32]

Wordsworth's conversion was not a retreat into a solitary form of
nature mysticism. The Methodist analogy points to a socializing
experience, perhaps one of identification with the poor and disen-
franchised. "Tintern Abbey" attributes his new nature religion to the
same process of mental evolution that brought him an intensified
concern for suffering humanity. The poem states that awareness of
the divine "Presence" in all things came accompanied by a heightened consciousness of the "still sad music of humanity" and that
nature, the soul of all his moral being, influenced his acts of kindness
and of love, inspiring deep sorrow at what man has made of man.
Jerome McGann has remarked, aiming for the moment at wit rather
than truth, "Between 1793 and 1798 Wordsworth lost the world
merely to gain his own immortal soul."[33] But when Wordsworth
discovered in those years that his real genius was for poetry and not
for political action, it does not seem to have occurred to him that the
natural religion he embraced so fervently meant an escape from
social or political concerns. The Pedlar's raptures on the mountain-
tops did not make him less conscious of "such misrule / Among the
unthinking masters of the earth / As makes the nations groan."[34]
Wordsworth was interested from the first in the public ramifications,
the political and social consequences, of the new faith he had found.
He wanted to believe that if society were ordered according to
"Nature's holy plan," true religion, better morality, and a more
equitable social order would follow.
Some of the most eminent Wordsworth scholars of our time –

Jonathan Wordsworth prominent among them – are able to perceive a clear distinction between the "pantheist" poet of the 1790s and the Anglican one that succeeded him, and, with an evident preference for the younger poet's metaphysics, suggest that the authentic Wordsworth was the one whose beliefs tended in the direction of pantheism.[35] But in reality this unsystematic metaphysician seems from the start not to have noticed any important theological discrepancy – whatever the political difference – between his own natural religion and Christianity. It is too much to say, as Jonathan Wordsworth does, "In his hands the One Life lost any connection with formal Christianity."[36] The poet does not in fact seem to have acknowledged any need to dissociate the two. In *The Pedlar* of 1798, which for Jonathan Wordsworth expresses Wordsworth's pantheism at its purest, a few lines after the "consecration" passage quoted earlier and shortly before the passage on the "One Life" that is often presented as a *locus classicus* of pantheistic belief, one finds these lines:

> A Herdsman on the lonely mountain-tops
> Such intercourse was his; and in this sort
> Was his existence oftentimes possess'd.
> Oh! then, how beautiful, how bright appear'd
> The written promise! He had early learned
> To reverence the volume which displays
> The mystery, the life which cannot die:
> But in the mountains did he *feel* his faith:
> There did he see the writing.[37]

The Pedlar evidently detected no conflict between the "One Life" and the transcendent Creator whose works he read about in "the volume which displays the mystery, the life which cannot die."

If there were metaphysical inconsistencies and contradictions in Wordsworth's "system" they did not seem to worry the poet, nor did they trouble in later years his growing numbers of Christian readers. To accommodate orthodox Christians, all Wordsworth needed to do was adjust his claim to rely solely on nature for revelation and grace by assigning to nature an auxiliary function as conduit of a higher power. And so it was not necessary for Wordsworth to leave his "pantheism" at the door when he resumed his pew in the Church. Although a number of scholars tend to agree with James Boulger that "Wordsworth did not, and could not, leap immediately from his nature-mysticism to Anglican orthodoxy" without a "period of transition,"[38] it seems to me that the poet's return to Christian practice and belief required no significant recantation of his earlier metaphysics, but rather involved a quiet personal reintegration into the local and national religious community from which he had kept his distance for a decade, a return in which he brought his "nature religion" with him almost intact.

The point is worth making, since Wordsworth's return to the Church of England is so often condemned as either a calculated or a panicky repudiation of the nature metaphysics – whether called animism, or pantheism, or panentheism, or panpsychism – that characterized his greatest poetry, and the substitution for it of an Anglican orthodoxy which inspired inferior composition and damaging revisions of earlier, better work. In reality the two religious visions went on existing side by side. Wordsworth continued to indulge in his favorite speculations about God's presence in the physical world, perhaps choosing his words more carefully and pruning lines from earlier poems whose orthodoxy might be problematic for others, while he wrote new poems of specifically Christian content, such as the *Ecclesiastical Sketches* (1822).

Wordsworth's metaphysical inconsistencies were apparent to some careful readers, most notably his old mentor Samuel Taylor Coleridge. That more systematic theologian went so far as to accuse Wordsworth of intellectual dishonesty, or at best irresponsibility:

The vague misty, rather than mystic, Confusion of God with the World & the accompanying Nature-worship . . . is the Trait in Wordsworth's poetic Works that I most dislike, as unhealthful, & denounce as contagious: while the odd occasional introduction of the popular, almost the vulgar, Religion in his later publications (the popping in, as Hartley says, of the old man with a beard) suggests the painful suspicion of worldly prudence (at best a justification of *masking* truth (which in fact is a falsehood substituted for a truth withheld) on plea of Expediency) carried into *Religion*. At least, it conjures up to *my* fancy a sort of *Janus*-head of Spinoza and Dr. Watts, or "I and my Brother, the Dean!"[39]

"My Brother, the Dean" was Christopher Wordsworth, whose successful career in the Church was bringing a kind of extraneous religious respectability to his brother the poet, who dedicated the *Ecclesiastical Sketches* to him. Coleridge's intolerance of Wordsworth's ability to hold Spinoza and Isaac Watts in loose solution can be seen repeated in the efforts of modern critics who carefully monitor the poet's changing attitude toward nature in an attempt to see exactly where pantheism gives way to orthodox dualism. But the change in

Wordsworth was not the product of a train of subtle, complex philosophical speculations; it was much more political than metaphysical in character; much more a public gesture than an internal conversion.

If one were forced to name a single date that marked Wordsworth's renewed commitment to the Christian religion in his public and private life, one might be justified in selecting July 15, 1803, the day when his first child was baptized and his wife "churched" – brought before a clergyman in order to give thanks publically "for safe Delivery from Childbirth's perilous throes," as Wordsworth put it later in a sonnet celebrating the ritual.[40] The fact that John Wordsworth was baptized less than a month after his birth becomes more significant when one recalls that Coleridge, with his supposedly stronger commitment to orthodoxy at this time, had not yet gotten around to baptizing any of his own children, the eldest of whom was then approaching his eighth birthday.[41] I am not suggesting that Wordsworth's participation in these rites was itself a crucial event in his own intellectual history, but it served to announce publically his reintegration into the religious life of his community as it was centered in Grasmere church. In a sense, Wordsworth and all his family were "churched" on that day.

It may be questioned whether religion is more essentially something that is believed or something that is practiced. Many people, perhaps most, go to church for reasons that are more social than theological, more related to family life and community values than to credal formulations. In an 1811 letter Dorothy Wordsworth touched on some of these non-theological motives for religious behavior: "I assure you we are become regular church-goers (we take it in turn) for the sake of the children, and indeed Mr Johnson, our present curate, appears to be so much in earnest, and is so unassuming and amiable a man that I think we should often go even if we had not the children, who seem to make it a duty to us."[42] Wordsworth's own mature opinion was that religious commitment might have little to do with intellectual persuasion. Commenting on the *Excursion*, he speculated that the Solitary (who so much resembles himself as a skeptical young radical), having resisted the exhortations of both Wanderer and Pastor, might finally be converted without theological argument:

he might witness, in the society of the Wanderer, some religious ceremony –

a sacrament, say, in the open fields, or a preaching among the mountains – which, by recalling to his mind the days of his early childhood, when he had been present on such occasions in company with his parents and nearest kindred, might have dissolved his heart into tenderness, and so have done more toward restoring the Christian faith in which he had been educated, and, with that, contentedness and even cheerfulness of mind, than all that the Wanderer and the Pastor, by their several effusions and addresses, had been able to effect.[43]

In Books 11–13 of *The Prelude* Wordsworth recalls that his own psychic and imaginative health was likewise restored through the renovating virtue of childhood memories and through reintegration into a community rooted in tradition, including religious tradition. Since Wordsworth's earlier political radicalization had an important religious dimension, reintegration with his pre-revolutionary self would have had to entail some accommodation with the religious beliefs and practices that were part of his childhood and early manhood. Having learned from the Revolution, and perhaps from Edmund Burke's interpretation of it, that the insight of an individual – whether political or religious – should not be allowed to outweigh the accumulated tradition of the past and that the individual life to be healthy must be rooted in community ("independent intellects," he had concluded, were dangerously volatile – *Prelude* 10: 805–29), he would have been more ready to surrender to the national religion, which was a product of national consensus and, in a sense, of nature too in its historical development.

And so when in *The Prelude* he dedicates his poetic art to celebrating the dignity of the poor and simple, he finds in an ecclesiastical figure an appropriate beginning:

> How oft high service is performed within
> When all the external man is rude in shew,
> Not like a temple rich with pomp and gold,
> But a mere mountain-chapel such as shields
> Its simple worshippers from sun and shower.
> 'Of these,' said I, 'shall be my song. Of these,
> If future years mature me for the task,
> Will I record the praises, making verse
> Deal boldly with substantial things – in truth
> And sanctity of passion speak of these,
> That justice may be done, obeisance paid
> Where it is due. Thus haply shall I teach,
> Inspire, through unadulterated ears

> Pour rapture, tenderness, and hope, my theme
> No other than the very heart of man
> As found among the best of those who live
> Not unexalted by religious hope,
> Nor uninformed by books (good books, though few).
> In Nature's presence.   (*Prelude* 12: 226–44)

I suspect that we have here a conscious recollection of that other congregation of "simple worshippers" (10: 258–74) whose prayers for a British victory the alienated radical had scorned in 1793. The mountain chapel, as much a part of the English landscape as it is of the lives of believers, represents the vision that Wordsworth came to have of the Church of England, a national religion naturalized by time to become an integral part of English life, a broad church providing space for a variety of spiritual and political viewpoints.[44]

Wordsworth's decision to "rejoin" the Church of England, then, was closer to a pledge of allegiance than to a confession of faith. It is important to emphasize that he resumed the practice of Christianity while his theological convictions were still unsettled – before, for example, having arrived at a steady belief in the immortality of the soul. As late as 1805 he still seems to have been struggling toward a confident assurance of an afterlife.[45] In the spiritual crisis that followed the death of his brother John in that year, Christian doctrine gave him a comfort that his own religious instincts could not provide. When the *Elegiac Stanzas* affirmed: "Not without hope we suffer and we mourn," the grudging double negative betrayed a struggle of belief in which faith, or perhaps only hope, held a very narrow margin of victory.

His appearance at Grasmere church was only one, local aspect of Wordsworth's entrance into the public religious life of his society at this time. The political sonnets that he submitted to the newspapers in 1802 and 1803 indicate a shift in Wordsworth's sense of his poetic vocation, an acknowledgement of the public dimension and responsibilities of the literary career he had chosen. This new consciousness of a social role he expressed in 1802 to John Wilson:

You have given me praise for having reflected faithfully in my poems the feelings of human nature I would fain hope that I have done so. But a great Poet ought to do more than this he ought to a certain degree to rectify men's feelings, to give them new compositions of feeling, to render their feelings more sane pure and permanent, in short more consonant to nature, that is to eternal nature, and the great moving spirit of things. He ought to travel before men occasionally as well as at their sides.[46]

Public pronouncements necessitate the use of an intelligible language; rhetoric becomes an essential part of religion as it functions in the marketplace. For an isolated poet the vaguest nature mysticism may suffice for spiritual sustenance; a social borderer can allow his metaphysical ruminations free range. But to participate in public discourse in an attempt to influence the religious sentiments of his countrymen requires articulating an accessible, identifiable set of beliefs. It was in 1802 that Wordsworth first gave his Pedlar a connection with the Scottish Kirk, as though he suddenly saw the need to ground him in a recognizable tradition.[47] In that regard one of the most significant moments in the 1805 *Prelude* comes in Book 6 when Wordsworth finally names the Presence that presided over his youth,

> the one
> Surpassing life, which – out of space and time,
> Nor touched by welterings of passion – is,
> And hath the name of, God.   (6: 154–57)

This willingness specifically to identify what elsewhere he calls Spirit, Life, Presence, etc. with what others call God is a major concession to the requirements of public religious discourse, a surrender to history.[48] Wordsworth made a similar accommodation in an 1803 letter to the Beaumonts: "I use the word 'Nature' partly to avoid the too frequent use of a more awful name, & partly to indulge the sense of the *motherliness* of general Providence – when the Heart is not strong enough to lift itself up to a distinct contemplation of the Father of all things."[49]

In adopting a new stance of prophetic leadership, as he took the Miltonic sonnet as his medium he took Milton himself as his model – the national religious poet who had been shaped, like himself, by experience of radical politics and who had gone on to become the moral conscience of his generation, championing ideals that Wordsworth now felt needed to be reaffirmed in his own time. In the sonnet entitled "Written in London, September, 1802" – one of a series invoking or alluding to Milton – Wordsworth lamented the absence in his idolatrous society of those older values:

> Plain living and high thinking are no more:
> The homely beauty of the good old cause

Is gone; our peace, our fearful innocence,
And pure religion breathing household laws.

The pure religion was, of course, Reformation Christianity, a faith
that was not, in Milton's case, a conservative or counter-revolutionary ideology. As Milton's religion was a force for radical change,
a revival of that "pure religion" or an even purer one, might help
bring about the national reformation that England needed. Wordsworth seems to have shared Shelley's perception that cultural
renaissance, religious reformation, and political progress tended to
coincide in English history. "The sacred Milton was," Shelley reminded his contemporaries, "a Republican, and a bold enquirer into
morals and religion." In his own *Letter to the Bishop of Llandaff* Wordsworth set himself up as a teacher and reformer as Milton had done in
his anti-prelatical tracts, admonishing the hierarchy from an
assumed position of superior insight and experience.

The sonnets are public poetry, but still only at the level of
occasional verse. Milton had spoken to the nation in loftier forms,
and Wordsworth's ambition was no less epic in scope. It was in *The
Excursion*, as I have said, that Wordsworth definitively assumed the
role he projected for himself at the end of *The Prelude*, that of a
prophet sent by Providence to effect the work of his countrymen's
redemption. He himself would be the new Milton of which England
had need in the present historical crisis, and he laid claim to his
Miltonic inheritance forthrightly in the "Prospectus" to the new
poem (which may have been written in this year 1802) when he
invoked Milton's muse, or a higher one, because he was attempting
more difficult things than Milton had achieved. When he was about
to publish *The Excursion* he once again invited comparison with
Milton: "I have at last resolved to send to the Press a portion of a
Poem which, if I live to finish it, I hope future times will not 'willingly
let die'. These you know are the words of my great Predecessor, and
the depth of my feelings upon some subjects seems to justify me in
the act of applying them to myself."[50] Proclaiming his new identity
as a religious teacher, a consecrated prophet embarking on a public
religious mission, Wordsworth set out in *The Excursion* to share with
his countrymen what his own religious and political experience had
taught him.

He presents the poem as the culminating achievement of a life
devoted to poetry; in the preface the structure of a gothic church is

used to illustrate the subordinate and preliminary character of all his other work to date. And the poem makes an admirable effort to be true to the entirety of his experience, to the radical humanism and the natural religion he had espoused earlier in his life as well as the Christian faith he had more recently embraced. There still exists among literary scholars an impression that *The Excursion* is an unequivocal exposition of orthodox Christian belief, even though careful readers at the time and others since then have found the Christianity of the poem to be superficial and at times heterodox. One very attentive reader, John Keats, saw the poem as a rejection of Milton's faith in favor of a more liberal and enlightened one, an exploration of the "dark passages" of human experience rather than the enunciation of a settled creed.[51] It is true that *The British Critic*, the Church of England's own review, was apparently satisfied with the poem's orthodoxy and that the Bishop of London was reported to be "in raptures" with the poem,[52] but if those churchmen had read the work more attentively or with more concern for doctrinal precision they might have noticed, as the Evangelical poet James Montgomery did, that most of the religion propounded in *The Excursion* was not especially Christian at all:

The pastor of "the church among the mountains" indeed, touches delightfully on the Christian's hopes on each side of the grave; but this is only in character, and *his* sentiments are *not* vitally connected with the system of *natural religion*, if we may call it so, which is developed in this poem. The sentiments of the Author, when he speaks in his own person, and of the Wanderer, who is his oracle, *are* connected with it; yet in the fourth book, where a misanthrope and sceptic is to be reclaimed, when there was not only an opportunity, but a necessity for believers in the Gospel to glorify its truths, by sending them home with conviction to the conscience of a sinner, they are rather tacitly admitted, than either avowed or urged; while the soul's own energy to restore itself to moral sanity, by meliorating intercourse with the visible creation, is set forth in strains of the most fervid eloquence, and the theme adorned with the most enchanting illustrations.[53]

Montgomery's reference to the Pastor's acting "in character" shows an awareness of the dramatic quality of the poem that many later critics have not shared (although even Montgomery falls into the error of identifying the Poet-narrator with the author). Most misinterpretation of the poem's religious meaning has resulted from refusal to take seriously Wordsworth's attempt, however awkwardly executed, to compose a true drama of conflicting character and idea, rather than the kind of "interlocutions between Lucius and Caius" that are common in philosophical dialogues, which Hazlitt dismissed as "impertinent babbling."[54] Dorothy Wordsworth, who usually spoke her brother's mind in such matters, objected strongly to Hazlitt's suggestion that the Solitary, the Pedlar, and the Pastor were "three persons in one poet": "His opinion that all the Characters are but one character, I cannot but think utterly false – there seems to me to be an astonishing difference considering that the primary elements are the same – fine Talents and strong imagination."[55] Dorothy's astonishment may have been genuine surprise at the intellectual independence and candor her brother had allowed his characters. The three strong voices in the poem represent three distinct religious opinions that conflict radically. No one of them adequately represents Wordsworth's own voice, although the biographies of the two dominant figures, the Wanderer and the Solitary, bear unquestionable similarities to Wordsworth's own life. Insofar as the figures do represent three sides of Wordsworth, there is genuine conflict among them, an unresolved conflict that tells us much about Wordsworth's mind at the time of composition. When he read the poem, Charles Lamb asked the right question: "Are you a Xtian? or is it the Pedlar & the Priest that are?"[56]

Those who assume the poem's orthodoxy can point to the praise of the Church that opens Book 6.

> Hail to the State of England! and conjoin
> With this a salutation as devout,
> Made to the spiritual Fabric of her Church;
> Founded in truth; by blood of Martyrdom
> Cemented; by the hands of Wisdom reared
> In beauty of Holiness, with ordered pomp,
> Decent and unreproved.   (6: 6–12)

But it is worth considering that this tribute is uttered by the Poet-narrator, who is the least substantial, least realized of the poem's four main characters, as well as the most conventional and unsophisticated in his reactions; it is a voice whose callowness at some moments suggests that Wordsworth intended him to be what we have learned to call an unreliable narrator (see, for example, 7: 821–31). Indeed, "moderator" may be a more precise term for his function than "narrator," since his primary role is to introduce and arbitrate the remarks of the three more impressive characters.

The speech that begins with that ardent praise of the Church of England quickly deconstructs itself with expressions of longing for a reality worthy of the ideal he is celebrating. The praise is gracious in the presence of the Anglican Pastor, who has just joined the group, but although the Poet's lament about the rarity of worthy ministers makes an exception of present company, it nevertheless casts a searching light on the Pastor, who, with all his civility and sensitivity, hardly bears close comparison with the reformation martyrs the Poet invokes as his standard of clerical worth. In an age whose resemblance to the Reformation is noticed in the poem, an age "conspicuous as our own / For strife and ferment in the minds of men; / Whence alteration in the forms of things / Various and vast" (7: 1009–12), an age when, it is said, the Church needs a return to the "pure religion" of the Reformers, one would not look to this man for bold intellectual or moral leadership. The Wanderer calls the priesthood a "sublime vocation" (7: 335), but sublimity does not seem easily within the reach of this "philosophic Priest" (5: 983), who resembles most Anglican clergymen of the time in being more comfortable in ethical than in theological discourse. He does not seem entirely competent to deal with the hard religious questions raised by the Solitary, even though he listens to them with respectful attention. When the Solitary speaks with passionate indignation of the desperate lives of the poor, of "the dread strife / Of poor humanity's afflicted will / Struggling in vain with ruthless destiny," the Pastor (of aristocratic lineage himself) objects to such intemperate language and takes refuge in clerical platitudes about "mysteries" and the value of suffering as a test of faith (6: 538–66, 1133–39).

The conflict here acquires added interest from the fact that the Solitary is himself an ordained minister of the Church, one who has abandoned his vocation out of political disillusionment. In fact we are presented with three priests in all, since the Wanderer also lays claim to the sacerdotal character on the basis of an uncanonical ordination by God himself in the great cathedral of nature:

> Me didst Thou constitute a Priest of Thine,
> In such a Temple as we now behold
> Reared for Thy presence: therefore, am I bound
> To worship, here, and everywhere. (4: 43–46)

The central drama of *The Excursion*, then, somewhat muffled in the sonority of Wordsworth's blank verse, is a debate among three divines over what true religion should be – on what one must do to be saved. The Pastor's position as a spokesman for the Church and the Wanderer's insistence on an alternative religion of nature can both be said to represent Wordsworth's thinking in 1814. But the Wordsworth who could not entirely avoid political disquietude by turning to church services or to communion with nature is also represented here in the figure of the Solitary, whose spiritual "despondency" challenges his interlocutors to articulate a convincing defence of their own religious positions – rather in the way that Job's dejection required from his friends a justification of the ways of God to men. That the justification in this case, as in Job's, is unpersuasive, that the denouement of the intellectual power struggle is a stand-off, is itself an indication that Wordsworth's own position in the matter reflects no clear-cut or complacent orthodoxy.

The Wanderer is, as James Montgomery saw, a more formidable character than the Pastor, so forceful as a spokesman for religion that he emerges as less an ally than a rival of the clergyman. In the fervor of his religious language, the unembarrassed intensity of his vocal piety, he far outreaches the Pastor, who does not attempt to compete with the older man's religious effusions, at least not until the end of the poem. In purely secular terms, the Wanderer's force of person-ality makes him more impressive, as his experience of life makes him more interesting, than the ordained minister. By the evidence of the poem the Wanderer has experienced God more immediately and profoundly than the Pastor ever has. He claims to have received special revelations which have given him not only religious insight but religious authority, a unique magisterium derived not from canonical orders but from the order of nature. He is "One whom time and nature had made wise / Gracing his doctrine with authority" (4: 1288–99). And as though he had actually been ordained to the ministry, he serves as moral counselor and spiritual director to the people he visits on his rounds throughout the country (2: 62–80). His very mobility makes him a more effective minister than the resident rector of a country parish could be.

While it often seems that the Pastor and Wanderer are collabor-ating in the work of the Solitary's spiritual rehabilitation, they do not much agree in matters of doctrine. The Wanderer is introduced as a lapsed Christian, one who has shaken off the orthodox faith of his youth. He had been brought up in the Scottish Kirk, the Poet tells us,

But by the native vigour of his mind,
By his habitual wanderings out of doors,
By loneliness, and goodness, and kind works,
Whate'er, in docile childhood or in youth
He had imbibed of fear or darker thought
Was melted all away; so true was this,
That sometimes his religion seemed to me
Self-taught, as of a dreamer in the woods;
Who to the model of his own pure heart
Shaped his belief, as grace divine inspired,
Or human reason dictated with awe.   (3: 403–13)

The religion the Wanderer taught himself and now teaches others is an idiosyncratic version of natural religion that sounds at times like traditional deism with its emphasis on a transcendent "Divine Artificer" (4: 557), but more frequently like a panentheistic worship of a Divine Being who is immersed in nature as the "active Principle" and "Soul of all the worlds" (9: 1–15).[57]

When an acquaintance criticized the Wanderer's heterodoxy, Wordsworth protested that the character was simply "preparing the way for more distinct conceptions of the Deity by reminding the Solitary of such religious feelings as cannot but exist in the minds of those who affect atheism."[58] But the Wanderer himself expresses a conception of God no more distinct than a natural monotheism that concorded with but did not require Biblical revelation. The Wanderer is willing to allow the value of "holy Writ" in ensuring the belief in human immortality that nature and reason promise, but his great speeches in Book 4 use the history of primitive religions to demonstrate that God reveals an adequate faith to the human imagination, one that does not require further revelation. His history of religion begins with a Miltonic account of the fall from Edenic happiness (4: 631–48) but does not end, as Milton's does, with the promise of Redemption. With all his affection for and deference to the Pastor, the Wanderer clearly gives a moral priority and a higher value to his own self-taught religion. Despite his expressed admiration for Christianity, he comes close to what Christians would have called the sin of indifference in his insistence that Christ's religion is not the only path to salvation (4: 1106–16). His own personal experience of God had been so intense and his self-reliance so complete that he now seems not to require the assistance of a tradition and community of belief. He has become, in Jung's term, "spiritually autonomous."[59] Judson Lyon concluded that "Words-worth could not bring himself to abandon that cardinal principle of empiricism which says that sensory experience of nature is the ultimate source of all our finest thoughts."[60] One part of him was always "pleased to recognise / In nature and the language of the sense, / The anchor of my purest thoughts, the nurse, / The guide, the guardian of my heart, and soul / Of all my moral being."

The Pastor was not present when the Wanderer (in Book 4) was reducing Christianity to a level not much above pagan myths in theological value, but, as though in reply, at the end of the poem he levels a surprisingly pointed attack on the Wanderer's cherished natural piety and his notion that all human beings have intuitions of benevolent deities. In a quite orthodox, even Calvinistic prayer, he invokes the Eternal Spirit as a "Power inaccessible to human thought, / Save by degrees and steps which thou hast deigned / To furnish . . . to the infirmity of mortal sense" (9: 615–18). And he undercuts the religious optimism of Book 4 with his account of the inhuman and brutal religion of the Celts, whose natural piety found malignant gods and devised terrible ways to worship them. John Keats was especially impressed by Wordsworth's praise of the intuitive religion of pre-Christian peoples such as the Greeks, "whose fancy fetched, / Even from the blazing chariot of the sun, / A beardless Youth, who touched a golden lute, / And filled the illumined groves with ravishment" (4: 857–60). But the Pastor here points out that there were less attractive manifestations of natural religion, such as those that practiced human sacrifice.

> Once, while the Name, Jehovah, was a sound
> Within the circuit of this sea-girt isle
> Unheard, the savage Nations bowed the head
> To Gods delighting in remorseless deeds;
> Gods which themselves had fashioned, to promote
> Ill purposes, and flatter foul desires.   (9: 682–87)

Like Blake, Wordsworth believed that human sacrifice had been an important part of the religious rites conducted at Stonehenge and other stone circles. The cruelties of "Druidism," the Pastor observes, were just as natural as the beauties of Greek mythology, and they filled the illumined groves not with ravishment but with horror.

Another defect of natural religion, as Blake also understood, was its tendency to dissolve religious communities, isolating individuals in

solitary devotion to privately conceived divinities and encouraging a
morality based not on community values or common scriptures but
on "the selfish virtues of the natural heart" – the kind of religion that
the leaders of England's commercial capitalism had found so congenial in the eighteenth century. Spiritual autonomy, Blake would
have suggested, is an ambiguous condition, one that might be
claimed by Napoleon as readily as by Wordsworth's philosophical
Pedlar. It is the failure of religion as a cohesive force binding society
together in justice and charity that the Solitary will articulate as his
primary objection to the beliefs of both Pastor and Pedlar.

Whatever theological differences separate them, the Pastor and
the Wanderer generally tend to subordinate them in their common
effort to rescue the Solitary from his despondency and skepticism. In
making this reclusive figure the special object of their priestly
attentions, they have taken on a formidable antagonist. If the Solitary
seems at times to be at a rhetorical disadvantage in the debate that
occupies most of the poem, it is due partly to his initial reluctance to
be drawn into religious argument and partly to the prejudicial
account of him given by the Poet-narrator, who seems to have
disliked the despondent Solitary from the start (e.g., 2: 593–95). His
own speeches show him to be, not the cynical trifler and misanthrope
of the Poet's description, but a passionate and profound social critic
whose moral indignation in the face of injustice makes all the other
characters seem superficial and complacent by comparison.[61] That
the Solitary's virtues are somewhat ambiguously represented in the
poem may be attributed to the fact that he embodies aspects of
Wordsworth's own personality and history that the author himself
disliked and feared ("a dangerous part of the poet's mind," as
Geoffrey Hartman called him[62]) even as he recognized their importance and the validity of the claims they made on him.

If the Solitary finally shows himself to be more than a match for
the Wanderer's rhetorical strategies, perhaps that is because he is as
much Wordsworth's alter-ego as the Wanderer is and because, even
as fictional characters, the two are so much alike. The Solitary was
also brought up in the Scottish Kirk, but he has not shed its influence
nearly so easily or thoroughly as the other apostate has done.
Because of his skepticism and his attack on the value of religion in
general, it is not often noticed that the Solitary's religious imagination remains so colored by his early experience that he sounds, in
spite of his skepticism, more orthodox in his theological language

than anyone else in the poem. The God that he rejects is a much
more traditional divinity than the Wanderer's Active Principle, a
transcendent personal God of distinctly Biblical character:

> an Authority enthroned above
> The reach of sight; from whom, as from their source,
> Proceed all visible ministers of good
> That walk the earth – Father of heaven and earth,
> Father and king, and judge, adored and feared!   (3: 569–73)

In an early draft, it is the Solitary who articulates in uncompromising
terms the doctrine of original sin – the belief "that Man by nature
lies / Bedded for good and evil in a gulf / Fearfully low" (5: 292–4).
Moreover, the poem offers evidence that his skeptical stance masks a
longing for religious consolation of a quite specifically Christian
kind. Brooding in a classic Protestant fashion on the nature of
justification, he says,

> Religion tells of amity sublime
> Which no condition can preclude; of One
> Who sees all Suffering, comprehends all wants,
> All weakness fathoms, can supply all needs:
> But is that bounty absolute? – His gifts,
> Are they not, still, in some degree, rewards
> For acts of service? Can His love extend
> To hearts that own not Him? Will showers of grace,
> When in the sky no promise may be seen,
> Fall to refresh a parched and withered land?
> Or shall the groaning Spirit cast her load
> At the Redeemer's feet?   (4: 1089–100)

Yearning for the amazing grace that comes unpurchased by good
works, the gratuitous mercy of Calvin's unappeasable God, he is
unable to find within himself any assurance of divine love or mercy.
Like Cowper's Castaway, he sees himself as excluded from the
number of the saved. In the account of his voyage to America he
recalls:

> Within the cabin stood
> That Volume – as a compass for the soul –
> Revered among the Nations. I implored
> Its guidance; but the infallible support
> Of faith was wanting. Tell me, why refused
> To One by storms annoyed and adverse winds;
> Perplexed with currents; of his weakness sick;

> Of vain endeavours tired; and by his own,
> And by his Nature's, ignorance, dismayed! (3: 861–69)

One is reminded here of the younger Wordsworth, the disillusioned radical who, "Sick, wearied out with contrarieties, Yielded up moral questions in despair (*Prelude* 10: 899–900). And when the Solitary recalls the death of his two children, one thinks of the older poet who in a similar bereavement found religion to be a less than adequate comfort.

Despite his yearning for faith, the Solitary remains disconsolate. Like Job he resists the arguments of his three comforters, determined to work out his religious difficulties for himself. Part of the problem the three advocates of religion have is that the Solitary's objections are not fundamentally metaphysical; they are moral and political, involving a demand that religion show its relevance to the social crisis of the time. His central objection to religion is that it does not make human life any better – a critique that he illustrates convincingly from the state of the lower classes in England. He points to religion's social and political failures as the key indicator of its lack of absolute value, much as Wordsworth did to the Bishop of Llandaff in 1793. If there was any power for good in religion, he says, it ought to have made society more equitable, more just, more merciful. His indignation at the misery of the poor rises occasionally to heights of passion that make one think of the bitter social protest in *Jerusalem* or the sardonic indignation of Dickens in *Bleak House*.

> By what Power
> Of language shall a feeling Heart express
> Her sorrow for that multitude in whom
> We look for health from seeds that have been sown
> In sickness and for increase in a power
> That works but by extinction? On themselves
> They cannot lean, nor turn to their own hearts
> To know what they must do; their wisdom is
> To look into the eyes of others, thence
> To be instructed what they must avoid:
> Or rather let us say, how least observed,
> How with most quiet and most silent death,
> With the least taint and injury to the air
> The Oppressor breathes, their human Form divine,
> And their immortal Soul, may waste away. (9: 138–52)

The religious language is typical of the Solitary in impassioned moods and points again to the discrepancy between what religion says and what it does, between its high claims and its deplorable failures. Earlier, in Book 8, the Solitary scorns the churches along with other institutions whose rhetoric is not matched by action. Pointing to Britain's degraded laborer, he asks:

> his country's name,
> Her equal rights, her churches and her schools,
> What have they done for him? And, let me ask,
> For tens of thousands uninformed as he?　　　　　(8: 429–32)

In one of the more dramatic silences of *The Excursion*, this critique is not answered by any other character. Wordsworth left this indictment of Church and State, of England's political and religious complacency, ringing in the air, unqualified, unchallenged, unrefuted.

The Solitary is not the only one who is troubled by the discrepancy between religion's claims and its civil effects. Even the Poet, who had praised the Church so fulsomely in Book 6, is moved to ask,

> Who can reflect, unmoved, upon the round
> Of smooth and solemnized complacencies,
> By which, on Christian Lands, from age to age
> Profession mocks Performance? Earth is sick,
> And Heaven is weary, of the hollow words
> Which States and Kingdoms utter when they talk
> Of truth and justice.　　　　　(5: 375–81)

And the Solitary's passionate social critique succeeds in abridging even the Wanderer's optimism, forcing him to acknowledge that in Britain the minds of the poor are "starved by absolute neglect" and their bodies "crushed by unremitting toil" (9: 97–98) – as they see before them in "the rustic Boy, who walks the fields untaught; The slave of ignorance, and oft of want, And miserable hunger" (9: 162–64).

The Solitary thus forces contemporary political concerns into the generally timeless and displaced frame of reference that would otherwise dominate the poem's discourse. His angry remarks on the misery and desperation of the poor serve as a delayed rejoinder to the Wanderer's tranquil acceptance of Margaret's death in Book 1, when he rejected sorrow and pity as inappropriate and unphilosophical. The Wanderer was able to find solace in nature for the ills that flesh is heir to, much in the way that Wordsworth himself had turned to nature for comfort amidst the bewilderment and alienation brought on by disenchantment with the Revolution (*Prelude* 11: 96–102). The Solitary seems to represent the part of Wordsworth's mind that could not entirely evade political distress through communion with nature. In Books 8 and 9 he challenges the Wanderer to demonstrate the fruits by which his natural religion may be judged – to do, in other words, what Kenneth Johnston says Wordsworth failed to do in 1798 – "satisfactorily establish the connection between landscape viewing and social responsibility."[63]

Responding to the challenge, the Wanderer appeals to the "violated rights" of Nature as his moral standard when he utters his indignant protest against the degradation of workers in the early phase of industrial capitalism. Those who accuse Wordsworth of ignoring the social problems of his time have forgotten passages like the one that protests "the outrage done to nature" in a textile mill with its "multitude of dizzy wheels" – that refinement of human sacrifice demanded by England's new national religion:

> Men, maidens, youths,
> Mother and little children, boys and girls,
> Enter, and each the wonted task resumes
> Within this temple, where is offered up
> To Gain, the master idol of the realm,
> Perpetual sacrifice.   (8: 180–85)

It was at this time that Blake also expressed his horror at the "intricate wheels invented . . . to bind to labours in Albion / Of day and night the myriads of eternity . . . that they might spend the days of wisdom / In sorrowful drudgery, to obtain a scanty pittance of bread" (*Jerusalem* 65: 21–26; E 216) – a condition that he too saw as a consequence of bad religion. The Wanderer's lament over the exploitation of human beings continues with a prescient critique of the new kinds of social injustice brought by industrialism, when the ruling classes responded to new kinds of moral degradation with sterner demands for law and order:

> Our life is turned
> Out of her course, wherever Man is made
> An offering, or a sacrifice, a tool
> Or implement, a passive Thing employed
> As a brute mean, without acknowledgement
> Of common right or interest in the end;
> Used or abused, as selfishness may prompt;

Say, what can follow for a rational Soul
Perverted thus, but weakness in all good,
And strength in evil? Hence an after-call
For chastisement, and custody, and bonds,
And oft-times Death, avenger of the past,
And the sole guardian in whose hands we dare
Entrust the future.   (9: 113–26)

The religious metaphors employed in the Wanderer's condemnation of this new economic order, "industrious to destroy," tacitly acknowledge what the Solitary has asserted, that the national religion has failed, is failing, to prevent the brutalization of the new working class. The blame for these evils, the poem suggests, must be shared by the national clergy who have failed in their duty of admonishment, indeed have collaborated in the iniquity by accepting it as part of the natural order of things.

In *The Excursion* 9: 363–68, the Wanderer indicates his familiarity with and his disapproval of Thomas Malthus's *Essay on Population*. When he first learned of Malthus' grim forecasts, Wordsworth may have been struck by the ironic coincidence that in 1798, when "Tintern Abbey" was noticing "the still sad music of humanity" interfused in nature while celebrating a "cheerful faith that all which behold is full of blessings," in that same year Malthus, also having listened intently to what nature was saying about humanity, proclaimed in his *Essay* the immedicable social misery that is determined by natural laws. Constructing a religious foundation for his economic theory, Malthus urged his readers to consult "the book of nature, where alone we can read God as he is."[64] The fact that "Parson Malthus" (as William Cobbett liked to call him) was a priest of the Church was a reminder that Pastors were no less likely than natural religionists to go wrong in these matters, a suspicion that would be verified by the widespread, almost eager acceptance of Malthus' theory among the Anglican clergy.[65] But Wordsworth, who had once responded indignantly to Bishop Watson's praise of "The Wisdom of God in Having Made Both Rich and Poor," would hardly have been surprised at additional evidence of the clergy's social insensitivity. In fairness one should point out that not all believers accepted Malthus's ideas: "For some decades devoted Christians vociferously opposed them, for Malthus had not only dismissed as futile the charity that the Church enjoined, but envisioned a providential system more cruel and pitiless than eighteenth- and nineteenth-century Anglicans cared to assign to the Creator."[66]

This climactic discussion of religion's social failures occupies the space between two invocations to the Divine Spirit that begin and end the last book of *The Excursion*. The opening prayer is the Wanderer's final articulation of his idiosyncratic natural religion, and the other is a Christian prayer spoken by the Pastor. Neither of these pious rhapsodies appears to impress the Solitary or qualify his repudiation of religion. He remains impervious to their eloquence. "As the plow follows words," he might have said, repeating Blake's Proverb, "so God rewards prayers." He cannot, it seems, be converted to any faith that does not accommodate the objections of his social conscience, and neither of the two faiths represented here has succeeded in doing so. Christians and natural religionists alike have cultivated "the selfish virtues of the natural heart," participating with equal enthusiasm in the worship of Gain, "the master idol of the realm." Neither the Pastor nor the Wanderer appears to sense the inadequacy of his own religious rhetoric to correct the Solitary's despondency.

One is left at the end of *The Excursion* with a complex of discordant impressions arising from the conflict of three different conceptions of ultimate value, three contradictory prescriptions for national salvation. The poem reminds one of the beauty and consolations of the religion of nature as well as of its inadequacies and dangers; it tells of the dignity and the comfort of organized Christianity, but also of the established complacency that compares so poorly with the disaffiliated integrity and fervor of both Wanderer and Solitary. Finally there is the frustrated religious yearning of that isolated figure whose vision of the dark side of human experience distracts him from his interest in a transcendent order. To him, as to his radical comrades in earlier days, "every thought, which looked / Beyond the temporal destiny of the Kind . . . seemed superfluous" (4: 261–65). To say that only the theistic viewpoints expressed in the poem accurately reflect Wordsworth's thinking in 1814 is to ignore the impressive stature and force of personality he gave to the Solitary, who is, after all, the central dynamic character in the drama, the one who creates the conflict that the others must attempt to resolve. It is true that the conflict arises from the Solitary's refusal to accept what seems to be the poem's central thesis – the wisdom of humble submission to divine control, an attitude that Wordsworth had concluded was the most satisfactory response a thoughtful man could make to the hardships of life. But it is also true that the poem comes to no theological resolution.

Some critics have suggested that this failure to win over the Solitary to religious conviction and consolation was a kind of artistic error on Wordsworth's part, a combination of ineptness and confusion. Edward Bostetter, for example, remarks: "But the somber figure of the Solitary remains to give the lie to the wishful thinking of the Pastor *and of Wordsworth*. So long as he is unconverted, nothing has been resolved" (my italics).[67] Bostetter found it easier to believe that Wordsworth lost an argument with a character who was smarter or more tough-minded than the author who created him, rather than to accept the more likely proposition that the inconclusive denouement was Wordsworth's deliberate choice. I would argue that leaving the Solitary in that uncertain state, standing irresolute and disconsolate as the poem ends, was an act of admirable poetic integrity and of calculated boldness.

The lack of closure is a reflection of Wordsworth's mental state in 1814, that of a man who had returned to the practice of the religion of his family and his community but to whom belief had not come easily or in full measure. With all his serenity, even the Wanderer's optimistic religion could not be described as complacent:

> Here then we rest; not fearing to be left
> In undisturbed possession of our creed,
> For aught that human reasoning can achieve
> To unsettle or perplex us: yet with pain
> Acknowledging, and grievous self-reproach,
> That, though immovably convinced, we want
> Zeal, and the virtue to exist by faith
> As Soldiers live by courage; as, by strength
> Of heart, the Sailor fights with roaring seas.   (4: 197–204)

In those last lines one hears the memory of Wordsworth's brother's death in 1805, the shipwreck that sank forever the "cheerful faith" of "Tintern Abbey". Any optimism that remained did not survive the loss of two of the poet's children in 1812. Although it has been said that Wordsworth, at the time of his children's death, possessed the "faith absolute in God" needed for consolation, "the contemporary letters suggest otherwise.[68]

The Excursion stands as a progress report on Wordsworth's religious faith in 1814, a summary of his metaphysical investigations to date.

Each of the main characters resembles Wordsworth at one phase in his personal religious history. The Solitary is the alienated revolutionary who, having rejected a clerical career, never found an alternative professional calling and lived his life as a recluse from society. The Wanderer is the natural religionist whose soothing faith brought real consolation to a troubled mind but seemed increasingly inadequate as a guide to life in the urban, industrial nineteenth century and was already being subverted by intimations of Darwinism, such as those to be found in the work of Malthus. The Wanderer's visions, as the Pastor's wife observes, "cannot be lasting in a world like ours" (9: 469). The Pastor represents the Church that offered Wordsworth a refuge from the disturbing realities of modern life, a refuge whose best claims were its antiquity and its lack of doctrinal rigidity. But the institution's age and its genial, hospitable tolerance were not inconsiderable credentials.[69]   Of the Pastor's country church and churchyard one might say what Philip Larkin later said of a similar edifice:

> A serious house on serious earth it is,
> In whose blent air all our compulsions meet,
> Are recognised, and robed as destinies.
> And that much never can be obsolete,
> Since someone will forever be surprising
> A hunger in himself to be more serious,
> And gravitating with it to this ground,
> Which, he once heard, was proper to grow wise in,
> If only that so many dead lie round.[70]

That *The Excursion*'s four debaters arrive at a state of social harmony or equanimity in the Pastor's congenial parsonage suggests something about Wordsworth's understanding of the role of a national Church. That final tea party on an island in the lake could serve as an emblem of a religious community presided over by the clergy but making room for eccentrics and heretics and even for radical skeptics. That would not be an inaccurate description of the Church of England in Wordsworth's time or in our own. The Pastor officiates here as host – not hierophant, not theologian, not even catechist. Neither of the two apostates, Wanderer or Solitary, is brought any closer to Christian orthodoxy by his instruction; to the Pastor's final assertion that the social renovation desired by the other two will come only by increase of Christian faith and with the help of God's grace (9: 639–78), they return only a respectful silence. But the tolerant Pastor appears to feel no sense of urgency about their conversion. He simply invites them to continue their participation in a community of common concern and in a dialogue that may be fruitful even if not conclusive.

Rather than expounding Christian orthodoxy, *The Excursion* argues the importance to society of a tolerant, humane religion which might serve as a bulwark against worse forms of belief, "profaner rites" reflecting mankind's inveterate tendency to worship idols, whether of stone or of gold, that require tributes of human sacrifice. Natural religion was clearly inadequate for this purpose. If the book of nature could be read so differently by different inquirers, if "the anchor of my purest thoughts, the nurse, / The guide, the guardian of my heart, and soul / Of all my moral being" could be invoked by Robespierre to sanctify the Terror and by Malthus to rationalize social injustice and discredit public charity, something beyond "Tintern Abbey"'s cheerful faith was needed, something beyond the sway of impulse and caprice and the uncharted freedom that had wearied the poet of the "Ode to Duty." "A ceremonial fence," wrote Wordsworth in the *Ecclesiastical Sonnets,* "was needful round men thirsting to transgress."[71] And yet natural religion's emphasis on what was simple and essential in religion had two important uses: it might help free a person from radical skepticism and the religious bigotry that Wordsworth saw as both cause and consequence of skepticism, and it also could serve to remind the Church of what all human beings have in common and thus discourage rigidity and fanaticism of the kind Wordsworth saw increasing in his time. He was suspicious of the Evangelicals' zeal for orthodoxy, and included in the *Ecclesiastical Sonnets* a warning against Puritan fanaticism as a return to Druid religion, the worship of "Gods delighting in remorseless deeds" (*Excursion* 9: 685).

Wordsworth wanted the individual mind left free in matters of religion, as his had been free to find his own way. He was not in Blake's way striving with systems to deliver individuals from those systems, but he wished to make the systems broad enough and flexible enough to accommodate a community of independent, imaginative religious thinkers. Since he himself had found a refuge in the Church he concluded that others could likewise harbor there, even Catholics and Dissenters if they lay aside their specific doctrinal rigidities.[72] Regina Hewitt has argued that Wordsworth's didactic aim from the start was not to impose his own metaphysics on others but to encourage the individual reader's freedom of inquiry. Even in a work devoted to eulogizing the Church of England, the *Ecclesiastical Sonnets*, Hewitt finds that

from the beginning, individual judgment is privileged. The view of church history that the persona presents through the poem focuses on the struggle of individual belief against group-imposed substitutes. The Church of England represents the former; pagan rites, Papal abuses, and Protestant extremisms variously represent the latter. The poem does not endorse a set of beliefs so much as it holds up the individual act of faith as a good, celebrates the benefits of exercising it, and shows the consequences of surrendering it.[73]

This perception of an anti-sectarian, liberationist tendency in Wordsworth's religious poetry is not a new critical insight. In 1828, Frederick Denison Maurice, who at the age of twenty-three was just embarking on the career that would win him recognition as the most prestigious theologian of Victorian England and the father of the Broad Church Movement, published in the *Athenaeum* his 'Sketches of Contemporary Authors", a series of essays on Wordsworth, Byron, Shelley, Scott, Southey, and others, that, taken together, constitute the first comprehensive critical assessment of the English Romantic movement after it was seen to have come to an end. The essay on Wordsworth honored the poet especially for his acceptance of the primacy of individual perception in religion. While Robert Southey, by contrast, was condemned as "a mournful example of the ruin which may be wrought upon the fairest minds by attaching an universal feeling to particular institutions, and by professing to find all truth in the creed of one establishment," Maurice praised the "catholic religion so conspicuous throughout [Wordsworth's] writings."[74] Even taking *The Excursion* and the *Ecclesiastical Sketches* into consideration, it was

one of the highest and most glorious of the merits for which that mighty poet will receive the gratitude of his own age, and of all future ones, that, by expressing the purest and divinest religion, divested of its usual associations, he has furnished the very best test for trying the religious feelings of a community, far too much given up to the dogmas of the understanding and the catch-words of the memory.[75]

The absence of dogmas and catchwords made Wordsworth's poetry appealing to readers as diverse as Newman and Keble, leaders of the Oxford Movement, the Low-Church Maurice and Kingsley, and Unitarians like Henry Crabb Robinson, Harriet Martineau, and the editors of the *Monthly Repository*. It was a tribute to Wordsworth's unique religious manner that he could appeal across such a broad spectrum of opinion. Robinson observed, "It is remarkable that the most zealous of Wordsworth's admirers have been the Unitarians and High Church."[76] Wordsworth himself noticed the phenomenon; he wrote to his publisher in 1844: "Within the last week I have had three letters, one from an eminent High Churchman and most popular poet [probably Keble], another from a Quaker, and the third from a Scottish Free Churchman, which together prove how widely the poems interest different classes of men."[77] Although an unfriendly reader like Shelley could see this imprecision as blameworthy ("No Deist and no Christian he;/ He got so subtle that to be / Nothing, was all his glory")[78] the older Wordsworth evidently took as much satisfaction in the way his religious appeal transcended sectarian divisions as he did in his stature as a widely admired religious teacher.

Wordsworth seems always to have perceived his career as a religious mission, even in its most radical phases. His repudiation of Christianity in the early 1790s and his resumption of Anglican religious practice ten years later represented different styles of engagement in the public life of his society, both inspired by awareness that religion would be a critical factor in determining the kind of society England would become. Rather than a retreat from politics and history, Wordsworth's religious evolution suggests a continuing, determined ambition to adjust the spiritual consciousness of his contemporaries in the hope that a more authentic and tolerant national religion would foster a more benign social order and a more nourishing cultural life for all.

CHAPTER 4

The ironies of belief

Four years after Byron's death, his friends began raising funds for a memorial to be placed in the "poets' corner" of Westminster Abbey. When news of the plan reached the ecclesiastical authorities (the Dean and Chapter of Westminster), they objected that a man such as Byron had no right to a memorial in the sacred edifice. In the controversy that ensued,[1] one of those who defended Byron's claim to a place in the Abbey was Frederick Denison Maurice, editor of the *Athenaeum*. Six months earlier, in one of his "Sketches of Contemporary Authors," Maurice had concluded that Byron was not a first-rate poet, mainly because of his ability to give adequate expression to "a comparatively small and superficial class of feelings."[2] Reconsidering the question of Byron's stature in the context of the memorial dispute, Maurice decided that Byron had indeed earned a place among the great writers of England because his had been the most characteristic poetic voice of his generation, and, more to the point, that he had made a significant contribution to the religious life of his country. Works like *Cain* and *Don Juan*, Maurice insisted, had produced a beneficial spiritual effect in their power to disturb intellectual complacency, in their having challenged readers to confront difficult religious questions they might otherwise have evaded.

The most important task facing Christian ministers in those days, Maurice believed, was not to bring reassurance and consolation to the doubting, but to unsettle the apathy of the unreflecting.

The most pious and thinking part of the English clergy know that the sin of the age is indifference: they well know that the great glory of that Reformation which they, and we, think the greatest event (except the introduction of Christianity) the world has ever witnessed, was its letting loose the human mind from indifference; and they will feel that those who wish to shake this evil from the minds of themselves and their brethren, are the truest friends to religion. They will feel that he who releases the soul from this bondage, if he does nothing more, does yet an incalculable benefit.[3]

If the great achievement of the Protestant Reformation was "its letting loose the human mind from indifference," then Byron deserved a place with Wordsworth among those contemporary poets who were continuing the work of the Reformation by fostering a spirit of religious dissatisfaction and inquiry. It is paradoxical that what Maurice found valuable in Byron as a "true friend of religion" was precisely what provoked the condemnation of most of his religious critics – his talent for generating spiritual discomfort.

It may be surprising to hear Byron's critique of the national religion described as reformist rather than abolitionist in intent, but in fact that was the poet's own assessment of his motivation. Not long before his death, he said of Jesus Christ, "If ever God was Man – or Man God – he was *both*. I never arraigned his creed, but the use – or abuse – made of it."[4] We have the testimony of Shelley that Byron maintained some approximation of Christian belief during the years when he was generally considered a bitter enemy of the faith. When Shelley was blamed for encouraging the impieties in *Cain*, he responded: "I have not the smallest influence over Lord Byron in this particular; if I had I certainly should employ it to eradicate from his great mind the delusions of Christianity, which in spite of his reason, seem perpetually to recur."[5] Even while he was routinely being accused of a design "against the creed and morals of the land," Byron always insisted that his criticism was inspired by respect for religion and indignation at the abuses that discredited the faith. His primary objection to Christianity was that the religion practiced or at least preached by the majority of the faithful was insincere, self-serving, and compromised by its subservience to a corrupt political order. He adopted as his goal the reformation of the national religion through exposure of the discrepancies between its self-representations and the actuality of its performance in society, and he discovered that he achieved this object most effectively when he adopted the public stance of an advocate of true religion.

The controversy over erecting a monument to his memory in Westminster Abbey illustrates a peculiar difficulty that Byron had always caused his countrymen. At a time when poets were still conventionally spoken of as divinely inspired, and when the nation took pride in a poetic tradition that ran in a line of piety from

Spenser through Milton to Thomson and Cowper, it was an acute cultural embarrassment that Britain's most celebrated modern poet was a persistent, mischievous critic of the national religion. In those years when society was becoming ever more convinced of the need for a broad-scale reformation of religion and morals, Byron's bad eminence could be measured in the hypersensitivity of the religious community's response to him. One popular Methodist preacher, John Styles, thought Byron "the most dangerous abettor of the infidel cause it has ever had to boast,"[6] and the *British Critic*, a periodical sponsored by the Church of England, was complaining even before the publication of *Cain* that irreligion had become the keynote of Byron's career as a poet: "He has now for many years past never published any work in which he has not directly or indirectly denounced Christianity, 'the religion of the country,' as a system of delusion and superstition, and as the fruitful source of innumerable ills." After his death, the same periodical remembered him as a "rebel to God and slanderer of God's creatures – infesting the world with the outpourings of blasphemy and vice, and courting immortal infamy in the cantos of Don Juan."[7]

The heated rhetoric suggests that Byron had succeeded in antagonizing the orthodox in an especially disturbing manner, had found their most sensitive vulnerabilities and probed them deeply. During the eighteenth century, defenders of the national faith had become accustomed to attacks from skeptics and radicals and had prepared books of "answers," such as Charles Leslie's *A Short and Easy Method with the Deists*, a 1698 book that was republished in 1799, evidently in response to *The Age of Reason*. Byron had a gift for posing questions for which there were no short and easy answers, raising the kind of objections that believers are most persistently troubled by. Indeed, what discomforted his religious readers most were not Byron's skeptical pronouncements but rather his recurrent assertions of belief. While his Satanic colleague Shelley was obliging enough to enunciate his atheism distinctly and thus allow himself to be shuddered at and marginalized, Byron annoyed his critics most by his very resistance to exclusion from the community of believers. While he went on elaborating his derisive critique of the religious establishment in all its works and pomps, he perversely insisted on maintaining his pew in the very temple of belief, where, like a disreputable intruder at a Sunday service, he could be heard proclaiming at irregular intervals that he was just as religious as

anybody else. And so in 1821, when *Cain* provoked the nearest thing
to a formal excommunication that the Church allowed itself in those
days, and anathemas were being hurled at Byron from pulpits
throughout England and even in Italy, there was detectable in the
rush to judgment an element of triumphant vindication, along with a
sense of relief, that Byron had at last revealed his true character and
emerged clear of perplexing ambiguities. Amidst the angry accusations of heresy and blasphemy, few readers seemed able or willing to
see that *Cain* owed its disturbing power not to an abandonment but
to a refinement of its author's characteristic religious ambivalence.

To illustrate the kind of metaphysical versatility that made Byron's
contemporaries uneasy, consider two passages from *Childe Harold*,
each an account of the pilgrim's visit to a celebrated shrine.
Moralizing at the Parthenon early in Canto 2, the narrator reflects:

> Look on this spot – a nation's sepulchre!
> Abode of gods, whose shrines no longer burn.
> Even gods must yield – religions take their turn:
> 'Twas Jove's – 'tis Mahomet's – and other creeds
> Will rise with other years, till man shall learn
> Vainly his incense soars, his victim bleeds;
> Poor child of Doubt and Death, whose hope is built on reeds.

> Bound to the earth, he lifts his eyes to heaven –
> Is't not enough, unhappy thing! to know
> Thou art? Is this a boon so kindly given,
> That being, thou wouldst be again, and go,
> Thou know'st not, reck'st not to what region, so
> On earth no more, but mingled with the skies?
> Still wilt thou dream on future joy and woe?
> Regard and weigh yon dust before it flies:
> That little urn saith more than thousand homilies.[8]

The religious relativism and the contemptuous dismissal of belief in
immortality brought shocked protests from pre-publication readers,
and Byron was persuaded to make some equivocating revisions. His
critics were no doubt surprised, if not edified, to find that by the time
the Byronic narrator had arrived at St. Peter's Basilica in Canto 4,
his religious disposition had evidently undergone a striking change in
the direction of piety:

> But thou, of temples old, or altars new,
> Standest alone – with nothing like to thee –
> Worthiest of God, the holy and the true.

Since Zion's desolation, when that He
Forsook his former city, what could be,
Of earthly structures, in his honour piled,
Of a sublimer aspect? Majesty,
Power, Glory, Strength, and Beauty, all are aisled
In this eternal ark of worship undefiled.

Enter: its grandeur overwhelms thee not;
And why? it is not lessened; but thy mind,
Expanded by the genius of the spot,
Has grown colossal, and can only find
A fit abode wherein appear enshrined
Thy hopes of immortality; and thou
Shalt one day, if found worthy, so defined,
See thy God face to face, as thou dost now
His Holy of Holies, nor be blasted by his brow.　　　(4: 154–55)

The mocker of all religions and of man's desire for immortality now stands graciously welcoming us into the Holy of Holies and confidently assuring us of an equally friendly welcome before the judgment seat of God. One must ask, as contemporary readers did, what these expressions of religious denial and affirmation are doing in the same poem, even so disjointed a poem as *Childe Harold*. Since they were composed six or seven years apart, one might be tempted to see the later stanzas as a repudiation of the earlier. But if chronology matters, we must read the second passage in the corrective light of the still later *Don Juan* and *Cain*, which to many readers offered conclusive evidence of Byron's infidelity and even atheism.

What we see vividly illustrated in these stanzas are the two impulses, to doubt and to believe, that alternated in Byron's religious consciousness throughout his adult life and left his works filled with what Frederick Garber has called "canonic ironies" – contrasting passages that "speak to each other in a way that uneases them both."[9] The skeptical impulse apparently never took him as far as denying the existence of God. John Cam Hobhouse, who knew him better than most, observed in 1816 that Byron seemed immune to atheism: "His *sens intime* of a divinity, although he could not account for it, was as certain a proof to him that there was a cause for it as the influence upon the compass was a sign there was some cause for the direction of the magnetic needle to the pole."[10] That this kind of instinctive theism was not merely a sentimental or irrational impulse

Byron would have been reassured by the writings of his favorite philosopher, David Hume.[11] Nevertheless, the poet's skeptical tendency was vigorous enough in his early years to allow recurrent doubts about the immortality of the soul, and it persisted throughout his life as a tendency to dismiss as inadequate and futile almost all traditional forms of religious expression.

Byron's religious ambivalence has been widely discussed, and the critical consensus that has emerged is that, in the words of E. W. Marjarum, "his vacillation between the acceptance and rejection of traditional doctrines cost a *bitter inner struggle* of doubt with belief . . . Byron is unlike either [Wordsworth or Shelley] in his *inability* to arrive either at firm belief or at utter rejection of the doctrine of Christianity. It remained for him a personal *difficulty* of consummate importance."[12] My italics are meant to show how Marjarum reflects a common tendency among Byron scholars to speak as if the poet lived in a continual state of metaphysical anxiety, and as if, in regard to this topic at least, he was not entirely in control of his art or even of his mind, which is commonly depicted as the arena of a violent psychomachia pitting a dark, atavistic sense of sin and damnation against a modern, enlightened, humanistic skepticism. This highly colored account seems to be a relic of an old critical tendency to identify the poet with the troubled heroes of his Romantic tales, as though Byron were not also the author of *Don Juan* and the letters, a man to whom religious speculation seemed to occasion as much amusement as discomfort.

Although he may have struggled privately with a sense of guilt and a fear of eternal punishment, when addressing the public Byron generally handled religious themes adroitly, with apparent equanimity, and often with good humor. It seems to me that what has been called religious vacillation might in his case be more precisely termed oscillation, a regular, predictable, harmonic motion between two opposing intellectual tendencies whose mutual correction resulted in something much closer to equipoise than to turmoil. Since neither skepticism nor uncritical belief seemed to him an adequate response to the condition of the universe, he deliberately adopted a strategic position between the two alternatives.

Ernest Lovell's thoughtful and painstaking examination of Byron's religious ambivalence found the poet wavering "between the contradictory ideas of a Calvinistic Creator of a universe indifferent or even harmful to man and the benevolently inclined Creator and creation of the deists."[13] "Deism" and "Calvinism" are historically slippery terms, having been used from the beginning with more polemic energy than precision. But the two words can usefully be employed as a kind of shorthand to denote Byron's conflicting or complementary impulses toward religious rationalism in one direction and toward unquestioning belief in the other. They may stand as synecdoches for more universal and recurrent religious tendencies, one insisting on reason as the surest guide in any effort to comprehend God's nature or purpose, the other surrendering to a sense of the mysterious and terrible in contemplating a God who is totally other – the *mysterium tremendum et augustum* that Rudolf Otto has associated with the idea of the holy.[14] To call this latter tendency Calvinism is only to say that Calvin accentuated the Bible's insistence on the awful omnipotence of an all-seeing God. The idea of predestination that Byron apparently entertained presupposes belief in such an all-powerful, mysterious divinity, one on whom a human being has no natural claim for mercy or even justice, since divine justice is only another name for God's arbitrary will.[15]

Evidence pointing to deism as Byron's most characteristic, most frequently articulated religious stance can be found in every period of his adult life, in his own writing and the testimony of others, most convincingly in the late assessment by Colonel Stanhope in Greece.[16] Byron's Calvinism, on the other hand, is more often asserted than documented. The primary testimony comes from his wife, who recalled in 1855,

Not merely from casual expressions, but from the whole tenour of Lord Byron's feelings, I could not but conclude he was a believer in the inspiration of the Bible, and had the gloomiest Calvinistic tenets. To that unhappy view of the relation of the creature to the Creator, I have always ascribed the misery of his life . . . Judge, then, how I must hate the Creed which made him see God as an Avenger, not a Father . . . I, like all connected with him, was broken against the rock of Predestination.[17]

In Lady Byron's account, it is not easy to sort out her husband's domestic histrionics from her own religious politics. She was, as Byron observed, "a great one among [the Socinians], and much looked up to."[18] She had grown up in a family of Unitarians, and her childhood tutor and lifelong confidant was William Frend, who had helped convert Coleridge to Unitarianism at Cambridge.[19] At the time when Lady Byron was writing, her fellow Unitarians had been carrying on a bitter feud with Evangelicals over control of dissenting chapels and tended to use "Calvinist" as a term of abuse designating their orthodox antagonists. When a Unitarian journal spoke of Byron as "driven . . . by the revolting absurdities of Calvinism, to the reception of infidelity," it included the Trinity among the "doctrines of Calvinism" that tormented the poet.[20] Lady Byron's remarks on Calvinism were written to another Unitarian; she may have been imposing on her late husband a polemic caricature of what he (perhaps for his own polemic purposes) had claimed to believe.

Generations of critics have followed one another in assuming that Byron never outgrew his early exposure to Calvinist doctrines, but it is not clear upon what solid evidence this assertion is based. Leslie Marchand provides little documentation for his suggestion that Byron had been terrified as a boy by Calvinist doctrine.[21] The poet's own recollection was that he had been "early disgusted with a Calvinistic Scotch School where I was cudgelled to Church for the first ten years of my life,"[22] but he also recalled having been "bred a moderate presbyterian" and having loved the Old Testament, which he enjoyed reading with his Calvinist nurse. The widespread critical assumption of Byron's lifelong "gloomy" Calvinist tendencies may be another relic of the confusion of Byron with the Byronic hero, who seemed to find hereditary corruption and predestined damnation essential constituents of his public image. Claire Clairmont sensed the theatrical, factitious quality of this religious posture: "He turns [religion] into a demon; the fit companion of his savage heroes, bending to all their purposes."[23]

Calvinism and deism represent two radically conflicting religious tendencies in modern European thought, one liberal, rationalist, anthropocentric, the other fundamentalist, fideist, and theocentric – two versions of Western culture's attempt to understand what is by definition intellectually inaccessible. For the Calvinist, there is no legitimate mental movement "upward" from mankind to God, no relationship at all except "downward" by divine initiative. Humanity's fallen condition renders us incompetent and error-prone in all religious investigation. This sense of God's absolute transcendence and total otherness conflicts radically with the primary premise of deism that human reason is sufficient in itself to discover what is necessary or useful to know about the Divine Creator. For the deist writer Matthew Tindall, "natural and revealed religion can't differ, because what reason shows to be worthy of having God for its author must belong to natural religion, and whatever reason tells us is unworthy of having God for its author can never belong to true revealed religion."[24] For the deist, then, no God exists who does not meet human standards of rational and moral behavior, while for the Calvinist human reason unassisted is radically incompetent to form any correct conception of God. Paradoxically, the two tendencies join in a common suspicion of all religions as potential obstacles to a correct understanding of and relationship with the Supreme Being. And yet each accepted the premise that there must be one form of faith that is purer and more correct than all others – one true, appropriate religion of God.

Any attempt to balance a deistic confidence in the rationality of the Supreme Being with a Calvinist sense of God as a mysterious omnipotence that is under no obligation to conform to human expectations must inevitably engender a peculiar metaphysical ambivalence. Rationalist assumptions about God's identity and purpose are continually subverted by the suspicion that human conceptions may be irrelevant. One finds evidence throughout Byron's works of this kind of insecure, equivocating rationalism. Even in moods of religious insubordination like the one that characterized his work in 1816, for example in Manfred's and Prometheus's defiance of higher powers, even then Byron manifested some uncertainty about the value or efficacy of such intellectual bravado. The admiration of Gibbon and Voltaire expressed in Canto 3 of *Childe Harold* is qualified by the suggestion that both of them overestimated their ability to penetrate the Divine Mystery:

> They were gigantic minds, and their steep aim,
> Was, Titan-like, on daring doubts to pile
> Thoughts which should call down thunder, and the flame
> Of Heaven, again assail'd, if Heaven the while
> On man and man's research could deign do more than smile.
>
> (3: 105)

Gazing serenely down on his titanic assailants is a Supreme Ironist, conscious of humanity's radical incompetence to do or say anything of importance in the sphere of religion. Coming at the end of that swelling Promethean language, the word "research" is a withering reduction of the whole enterprise of militant skepticism. Byron seems to have been more consistently aware than either of the celebrated ironists he names that anyone who speaks with assurance on religion is himself likely to become an object of irony. He was closer than either Voltaire or Gibbon to that intellectual condition we have learned to call general or cosmic irony, defined as an awareness of "those contradictions, apparently fundamental and irremediable, that confront men when they speculate upon such topics as the origin and purpose of the universe."[25]

Scholars have disagreed on the nature of the irony that Byron employed so effectively in works like *Don Juan* and *Cain*. Earlier critics like George Ridenour and Andrew Rutherford understood his irony as rhetorical rather than constitutional, to use Wayne Booth's useful distinction; in other words, Byron directed his irony against human folly and iniquity from a relatively secure moral or political position situated in an identifiable hierarchy of values.[26] More recent readers, most prominently Anne Mellor, have identified Byron as an exemplar of "Romantic irony," an attitude that was first named by Friedrich Schlegel and that Mellor defines as positing "a universe founded in chaos and incomprehensibility rather than in a divinely ordained teleology." Rather than operating from a stable set of values, the Romantic ironist "sees the world as fundamentally chaotic. No order, no far goal of time, ordained by God or right reason, determines the progression of human or natural events."[27] While Mellor's account of the stylistic qualities of Romantic irony may suit Byron's self-conscious, self-mocking tendency to revise and contradict himself as he went along, her account of the ideological basis of artistic irony does not seem especially relevant to him, since he was not fundamentally irreligious in his consciousness. For Byron the universe was not ultimately absurd or chaotic, only puzzling and unpredictable. The Creator was not absent but mysterious, resisting conceptualization by philosophical and theological systems, including skeptical and materialistic systems. This does not mean that Byron espoused what theorists of irony call "a closed-world ideology," belief in a predictable, hierarchically structured order established by God. On the contrary he accepted the premise that God is free to devise an order that is incomprehensible, evading and frustrating all theological and philosophical "research." Tilottama Rajan has criticized the absence in the first generation Romantics of "that radical irony which makes it impossible to turn back to illusion."[28] But a truly radical irony would have to allow for the possible truth of apparent "illusion" – and the possibility that irony itself might not be the most appropriate response to the condition of the world. This I think was Byron's position. For him the chief irony of religion lay in the confident assertions of believers and unbelievers alike that they had found out the truth and spoken the definitive word on the subject. Byron's idea of God ironizes the claims of religion's critics as well as those of its defenders. As often as faith is subverted by doubt in *Don Juan*, doubt is qualified by expressions of faith. When he insists on proclaiming "the nothingness of life," he points out that the inanity of our existence has also been confessed by saint, sage, and preacher, appealing for support to the authority of the Bible, Martin Luther, and John Wesley (7: 3–6). The absurdity of human life has provided some modern thinkers with a rationale for atheism, but Byron was aware that in the Judaeo-Christian tradition, irony and even comedy are considered more appropriate responses to absurdity than despair or indifference.

Byron was a consistent skeptic in the manner of David Hume, acknowledging the limitations of skepticism as well as those of belief. The double-edged irony that resulted, involving what Friedrich Schlegel called "the constantly self-generating alternation of two contesting thoughts,"[29] has posed critical problems from the beginning for readers who are less flexible than Byron in such matters, who have preferred the clarity of a predominantly skeptical poet to the complexity of one who believed and disbelieved in more equal measure. The tendency to underestimate the believing side of Byron has impaired criticism because it was precisely his belief that made his denials so incisive, offered as they were as the reluctant conclusions of a frustrated seeker of religious truth.

It was in the character of a disappointed pilgrim that Byron first became known to the world. The word pilgrim was used with some irony when it was first applied to the disreputable Childe Harold, who, having found nothing at home to satisfy his hungry heart, sailed off to the Eastern Mediterranean to drink from the fountains of European art, philosophy, and religion. But the title of pilgrim was one that Byron claimed more and more as his right as he redefined its meaning for a culture just beginning to articulate the modern conception of alienation. When Shelley wanted a phrase that would readily identify Byron for readers of *Adonais* he called him the "Pilgrim of Eternity," taking his cue from Byron's own assessment of his life's mission in *Childe Harold* (3: 70):

on the sea
The boldest steer but where their ports invite,
But there are wanderers o'er Eternity
Whose bark drives on and on, and anchor'd ne'er shall be.

The ocean is an appropriate milieu for a Pilgrim of Eternity, an open pathway for the seeker whose itinerary is uncertain. At the end of the poem's final canto, when Byron leads his reader out of the Vatican and back onto the sea for the last time, the progression has a religious significance that he seems just then to have clarified for himself. Although St. Peter's Basilica had seemed for the moment an adequate objective correlative for mankind's idea of divine power and immensity, its limitations as a symbol were soon apparent. The sublimity of the Catholic baroque is given its due respect, but then a radical Protestantism reasserts itself. No architectural structure, and no credal construct or religious organization, however comprehensive, adequately reflects a proper conception of Divinity. Enter even the largest church in Europe, one that calls itself "catholic," and you are in an enclosed, defined, monopolized space. Climb a mountain in search of religious experience as Wordsworth did in imitation of various Biblical personages, and the narrowing terrain leaves inadequate room to maneuver.[30] Only the sea provides sufficient freedom and opportunity for the pilgrim who would avoid confinement. Its very formlessness, its resistance to stabilization or control, seemed an important ingredient of its symbolic efficiency for Byron's rhetorical purpose. Water is continually suggesting and canceling significant meaning. It can mean dissolution or regeneration, affirmation or negation, death or life.[31]

The celebrated sequence of stanzas on the sea that concludes *Childe Harold's Pilgrimage* expresses what Byron had at last discovered to be the theme of his poem – that amidst the disillusionment brought by knowledge of society and history there remains an ideal that is untouched by human corruption and ambition, something unruinable and in that sense eternal. Man's steps, he says to the ocean,

are not upon thy paths, – thy fields
Are not a spoil for him, – thou dost arise
And shake him from thee; the vile strength he wields
For earth's destruction thou dost all despise,
Spurning him from thy bosom to the skies,
And send'st him, shivering in thy playful spray

> And howling, to his Gods, where haply lies
> His petty hope in some near port or bay,
> And dashest him again to earth: – there let him lay. (4: 180)

The contempt for the petty hope humanity invests in its local, dry-docked gods recalls the earlier stanzas on the temple of Athena deriding mankind's devotion and hope, but as those stanzas were qualified by the St. Peter's passage, so this one is qualified immediately by a prayerlike verse apostrophizing the sea as a mighty emblem of Divinity.[32]

> Thou glorious mirror, where the Almighty's form
> Glasses itself in tempests; in all time,
> Calm or convulsed – in breeze, or gale, or storm,
> Icing the pole, or in the torrid clime
> Dark-heaving; – boundless, endless, and sublime –
> The image of Eternity – the throne
> Of the Invisible; even from out thy slime
> The monsters of the deep are made; each zone
> Obeys thee; thou goest forth, dread, fathomless, alone. (4: 183)

The imagery recalls Job's encounter with the Whirlwind (chapters 38–41), but what seems at first reading an unambiguous expression of reverence for God as the *mysterium tremendum et augustum* soon shows the subtlety and complexity that increasingly characterized Byron's religious rhetoric as he grew older. Insofar as the ocean can act as a mirror, what it reflects is the terrible power of almighty God. But it is difficult to see how a turbulent ocean can "glass" any "form." The mirror metaphor is given additional complexity by conflicting associations with the eternal "sea of glass" in Revelation 4: 6 and the contemporary use of "glass" as a synonym for barometer. Byron is suggesting here that our most sublime analogies can give only an inadequate account of divinity. But this deconstruction is not a denial; it is a self-conscious and carefully qualified expression of faith, with the kind of precise ambiguity poetry can achieve more effectively, or at any rate more economically, than theology. Byron is displaying more metaphysical subtlety here than we usually give him credit for.

Peter Thorslev has recently written, "For the Romantic ironist nature . . . is supremely indifferent."[33] Byron goes one step farther into irony by maintaining that nature is supremely ambiguous. This ambiguity – that stormy seas may reflect either an all-powerful Divinity or the absence of any controlling power at all – is one that figures again in the notorious shipwreck passage in *Don Juan*, the harrowing narrative of panic, madness, cannibalism, and death that brought widespread negative criticism from readers and gave Byron a foretaste of the response *Cain* would provoke later on. The reactions of Keats and Shelley were, for once, representative of Byron's general readership. Coming upon the passage while he was himself on an ocean voyage shadowed by the threat of his own death, Keats was repelled: "This gives me the most horrid idea of human nature, that a man like Byron should . . . laugh & gloat over the most solemn & heart rending {scenes} of human misery this storm of his is one of the most diabolical attempts ever made upon our sympathies."[34] Shelley too, although impressed by the Dantesque power of the "strange and terrible storm," regretted "the bitter mockery of our common nature" as unworthy of Byron's genius.[35]

The ground of much of the negative response to the shipwreck scene was the suspicion that Byron was using his formidable descriptive and dramatic power to say something pernicious and blasphemous about God and about mankind's relationship with God. That the disastrous events have some religious meaning is continually hinted at from the moment Juan and the others set sail on a ship named "the most holy *Trinidada*" to the final sardonic remark that "by God's grace" there had been many shipwrecks in the vicinity (2: 132). A continuous thread of scriptural allusion, particularly to the story of Noah's ark, along with a number of other references to Divine Providence, nudge the reader toward the notion that God has glassed himself in this tempest too and that its victims are objects of his detached attention throughout their agony. The hints of divine involvement are ambiguous enough, however, to have the effect of simultaneously intimating and denying metaphysical significance in the events being narrated, and Byron's tone achieves a strange balance, or imbalance, of solemnity and frivolity.

> There's nought, no doubt, so much the spirit calms
>   As rum and true religion; thus it was,
> Some plunder'd, some drank spirits, some sung psalms,
>   The high wind made the treble, and as bass
> The hoarse harsh waves kept time; fright cured the qualms
>   Of all the luckless landsmen's sea-sick maws:
> Strange sounds of wailing, blasphemy, devotion
> Clamour'd in chorus to the roaring ocean.   (2: 34)

Some went to prayers again, and made a vow
  Of candles to their saints – but there were none
To pay them with; . . . and there was one
That begg'd Pedrillo for an absolution,
Who told him to be damn'd – in his confusion.   (2: 44)

All the rest perish'd; near two hundred souls
  Had left their bodies; and what's worse, alas!
When over Catholics the Ocean rolls,
  They must wait several weeks before a mass
Takes off one peck of purgatorial coals,
  Because, till people know what's come to pass,
They won't lay out their money on the dead –
It costs three francs for every mass that's said.   (2: 55)

The continual joking about the doomed mariners' religious conduct seemed to most readers oddly out of place amidst the awful sublimity of the storm. Beneath the superficial profanity and anti-clericalism, readers thought they sensed a deeper kind of nihilistic mockery of common beliefs about human nature and divine providence. But while Byron may have lost control of the tone of his narrative at this point, one might also discern a serious purpose behind the joking. What sounds like horselaughter seems to have been meant as an expression of contempt for mankind's petty attempts in times of crisis to control, even to comprehend, the ways of the Almighty. Priests and sacramentals are useless in most circumstances, Byron seems to say; they become laughable here because they fail to observe the kind of religious decorum appropriate in this fearful liminal situation. The *mysterium tremendum* eludes the easy domestication attempted by the likes of the priest Pedrillo; a God who glasses himself in tempests is not to be bargained with on such cheap terms. The tough gospel being proclaimed here is that all efforts to impose our limited and limiting definitions on Divinity are absurd. Byron's Divinity, like Job's, rebuffs all such presumption as impertinent.

    A similar kind of religious critique, subtler than the burlesque anti-clericalism, is suggested in the pattern of allusion the narrative makes to *The Rime of the Ancient Mariner* – another poem in which a ship's agony is played out under the eye of controlling supernatural powers who intervene arbitrarily to save only one of hundreds of sailors, as Juan is here uniquely saved from drowning when an oar is washed his way "providentially" (2: 107). The stanza quoted above, with its reference to nearly two hundred souls leaving their bodies, is followed by an even more specific allusion that comes in the context of a series of "good omens" encouraging delusive hope among the mariners.

> About this time a beautiful white bird,
>   Webfooted, not unlike a dove in size
> And plumage, (probably it might have err'd
>   Upon its course), pass'd oft before their eyes,
> And tried to perch, although it saw and heard
>   The men within the boat, and in this guise
> It came and went and flutter'd round them till
> Night fell: – this seem'd a better omen still.

In *The Ancient Mariner* a mysterious divinity frustrates human efforts to understand him in traditional religious terms (the terms are Roman Catholic ones, as they are in Byron's sea story), but Coleridge's supernatural spirit does in fact demonstrably intervene. No such intrusive Power operates in Byron's poem, which says blandly of the doomed voyagers, "Their preservation would have been a miracle" (stanza 50). Byron's naturalistic account offers his readers, whether believers or non-believers, little grounds for hope in miracles. The omens prove false – a rainbow fades into darkness, the white bird flies away, and the rest of the voyagers drown even in sight of land. Only Juan is saved to bring love and death to Haidee, the innocent islander who provides for him a haven from the pitiless sea.

Byron's provocative negations seem inspired by something more than simple malice. He appears to be challenging the easy refuge offered by conventional religion from the pain and mystery of human existence – as he did earlier in the skeptical stanzas at the Parthenon in Canto 2 of *Childe Harold* and afterward in *Manfred* when the dying Count refuses the last rites and other spiritual ministrations offered by the concerned Abbot, consolations that are made to seem irrelevant to a man of Manfred's character, as though to accept such comforts and props would involve a failure of metaphysical nerve. The threat posed to religious integrity by easy religious consolation is addressed again in *Don Juan* in yet another series of nautical stanzas, the first of which was written shortly after Shelley was drowned in the Gulf of Spezia. Shelley is not mentioned by name (his name never appears in *Don Juan*) but the memory of his death is clearly felt in a stanza that contrasts his skepticism with the piety of Isaac Newton who, as the poem recalled earlier, once said that he felt "like a youth / Picking up shells by the great Ocean – Truth" (7: 5).

It is a pleasant voyage perhaps to float
  Like Pyrrho on a sea of speculation;
But what if carrying sail capsize the boat?
  Your wise men don't know much of navigation;
And swimming long in the abyss of thought
  Is apt to tire; A calm and shallow station
Well nigh the shore, where one stoops down and gathers
Some pretty shell, is best for moderate bathers.

"But Heaven," as Cassio says, "is above all, –
  No more of this then, – let us pray!" We have
Souls to save, since Eve's slip and Adam's fall,
  Which tumbled all mankind into the grave,
Besides fish, beasts, and birds.   (9: 18–19)

The Biblical understanding of human nature and human history provides an intellectual harbor, however shallow, from a wide sea of turbulent speculation, and Byron here recognizes the attractions of the mental refuge that has comforted so many. A very few weeks later, however, a renewed commitment to his pilgrim's mission leads him to separate once more from the moderate bathers who cling to the shore. Alluding again to Newton, and thinking again of the drowned Shelley's shattered sailboat and perhaps also of the *Trinidada*, he writes:

In the Wind's Eye I have sailed, and sail; but for
  The stars, I own my telescope is dim;
But at the least I have shunned the common shore,
  And leaving land far out of sight, would skim
The Ocean of Eternity: the roar
  Of breakers has not daunted my slight, trim,
But *still* seaworthy skiff, and she may float
Where ships have foundered, as doth many a boat.   (10: 4)

The intrepid navigator never ventured farther from the common shore in religious speculation than he did in *Cain: A Mystery*, whose theological boldness astonished even Shelley, and the indignant outrage that the play provoked in pious readers indicated that it had disturbed their complacency in unusual ways. Less than full justice is done to Byron's achievement by critics who see the drama only as an attack on orthodoxy written from an essentially skeptical viewpoint – critics like Edward Bostetter, for instance, who read the play as "a sustained effort to expose the absurdity of the Judaeo-Christian conception of the relation of God and man."[36] On the contrary, what makes *Cain* unusual, what puts it in a different class of religious polemic from the derisive travesties of Bible stories one finds, for example, in Voltaire's *Dictionnaire Philosophique*, is that it was written from a viewpoint sympathetic to belief. In *Cain* Byron dramatizes his own dilemma as a skeptical and disconsolate believer, imprisoned in a cosmic order that is finally, to borrow a word from his drama's title, a mystery.

The tendency to underestimate the believing side of Byron seriously impaired criticism of *Cain* until our own time. Readers have been either so shocked or so attracted by its rhetoric of defiance that they have ignored what is a basic *donnée* of the play – the climate of belief that invigorates and intensifies that rhetoric. With the exception of a few independent readers in every generation, Byron would until recently have been justified in saying, as he said to James Kennedy in 1823, "They have all mistaken my object in writing Cain."[37]

Beyond his own defensive claims concerning *Cain*'s orthodoxy, Byron left other clues as to how the ideological disposition of the play should be understood. One may be found in a passage from *Don Juan* written a year earlier, in which he speaks of Lucifer's sin of pride,

> which leads the mind to soar too far,
> Till our own weakness shows us what we are.

> But Time, which brings all beings to their level,
> And sharp Adversity will teach at last
> Man, – and, as we would hope, – perhaps the devil,
> That neither of their intellects are vast.   (4: 1–2)

A more compelling hint that Byron intended Lucifer's rhetoric and Cain's response to it to be scrutinized critically may be found in another work that was conceived at precisely the same time as *Cain* – the *Letter to [John Murray] on the Rev. W. L. Bowles' Strictures on the Life and Writings of Pope*. In this essay Byron called Pope "the moral poet of all Civilization" and gave as grounds for this assessment the fact that "without canting, and yet without neglecting, Religion, he has assembled all that a good and great man can gather together of moral wisdom cloathed in consummate beauty."[38] The *locus classicus* of Pope's "moral wisdom" is *The Essay on Man*, whose theme, as Maynard Mack sums it up, is "the clash of irreligious pride with religious resignation."[39] That this clash is precisely the theme of *Cain* makes more significant the fact that the ideas for the play and the essay on Pope apparently came to Byron in the same week in late January and early February 1821.[40] The moral wisdom employed in Pope's effort to "vindicate the ways of God to Man" (*Essay* 1: 16) casts a searching critical light on the indictment of the divine order articulated in Byron's drama by Lucifer and Cain. Indeed the most original invention in the play, Cain's exploration of the cosmos under Lucifer's guidance, could easily have been suggested by Pope:

> Go, wondrous creature! mount where science guides,
> Go, measure earth, weigh air, and state the tides; . . .
> Go, soar with Plato to th'empyreal sphere,
> To the first good, first perfect, and first fair;
> Or tread the mazy round his followers trod,
> And quitting sense call imitating God; . . .
> Go, teach Eternal Wisdom how to rule –
> Then drop into thyself, and be a fool.

That Cain behaves like a dramatic representation of Pope's discontented fool suggests that we have in these two contemporary works, the play and the *Letters* on Pope, another of Byron's canonic ironies. The *Letters* inevitably ironize the drama, since it would be difficult simultaneously to admire Pope's moral wisdom and sympathize with a character who so completely rejects that wisdom. What Byron described as Cain's "rage and fury against the inadequacy of his state to his conceptions"[41] is exactly the kind of self-indulgent discontent that Pope derides:

> Presumptuous man! the reason wouldst thou find,
> Why formed so weak, so little, and so blind?
> First, if thou canst, the harder reason guess,
> Why formed no weaker, blinder, and no less!   (1: 35–38)

> Then say not man's imperfect, Heaven in fault;
> Say rather, man's as perfect as he ought:
> His knowledge measured to his state and place,
> His time a moment, and a point his space.   (1: 69–72)

The viewpoint of Pope's *Essay* is actually adopted in the play by one of the main characters – Adah, Cain's sister-wife. Although its impact is muted by the character's diffidence, Adah's continued advice that Cain submit himself to the divine order and to the fallen world as his proper sphere makes her Lucifer's primary antagonist in the drama.

Although he may have mismanaged the dramatic conflict, Byron evidently thought he had presented a balanced argument between faith and skepticism, resignation and rebellion, and was, it seems, sincerely taken aback by the almost universal assumption among his contemporaries that Lucifer and Cain were mere mouthpieces for the author's own skeptical and blasphemous views. He wrote to Thomas Moore in March 1822,

With respect to "Religion," can I never convince you that *I* have no such opinions as the characters in that drama, which seems to have frightened every body? . . . I am no enemy to religion, but the contrary . . . I incline, myself, very much to the Catholic doctrines, but if I am to write a drama, I must make my characters speak as I conceive them likely to argue . . . This war of "Church and State" has astonished me more than it disturbs; for I really thought "Cain" a speculative and hardy, but still a harmless production.[42]

The "harmless," at least, is disingenuous; he must have known how offensive the play would be to most believers. But he seems honestly to have assumed that most readers would understand, what most readers have not, that Lucifer and Cain have to behave and speak like rebels against the sovereignty of Jehovah; that Lucifer's indictment of God and the divine order must be plausible enough to impress the smart, skeptical young man who is to be seduced from his proper allegiance; that, despite his experiments in humanistic rhetoric, Lucifer's position in the play, morally, is that of an accessory to murder; and that Cain, ill-natured from the start, continually demonstrates the inherited corruption he continually denies until finally it drives him to commit the worst sin of which he is capable.

The murder of Abel is, of course, the climax of the drama, the catastrophe in every sense, the point when its values suddenly clarify in a terrible sense of irremediable loss. Byron so effectively stage-manages the murder to highlight Cain's horror and remorse that one may be justified in suspecting that he was deliberately setting a kind of moral trap for his readers of the kind that Stanley Fish found Milton employing in *Paradise Lost*. In Fish's reading, Milton lured his audience into admiration of Satan's rhetoric and sympathy with Adam's sin in order to impress upon them an awareness of their own fallen perceptions and corrupt instincts.[43] In a similar way Byron tempts us to admire Cain's and Lucifer's rebelliousness and then embarrasses us with the consequences of our irreligious thinking. To the extent that we have sympathized with Cain's antinomianism, we must share the guilt of its bloody consequences. I am not arguing that Byron had his readers' salvation at heart exactly in the way that Milton did, but only that the play is, as Byron claimed, more orthodox in its disposition than most critics have allowed it to be.

"The reader who falls before the lures of Satanic rhetoric displays again the weakness of Adam," wrote Fish.[44] The same might be said of those of Byron's readers who have found Lucifer to be, in Leslie Marchand's words, "a champion of humanity against an authoritarian and arbitrary deity." Jerome McGann, for example, speaks of that character's final speech as "a stirring rhetorical plea for one of Byron's deepest convictions: intellectual freedom."[45] It is a tribute to Byron that his Lucifer still has the ability to seduce such discerning listeners, but his rhetoric will not really bear very close scrutiny:

> *One good* gift has the fatal apple given –
> Your *reason*: – let it not be over-sway'd
> By tyrannous threats to force you into faith
> 'Gainst all external sense and inward feeling:
> Think and endure, – and form an inner world
> In your own bosom – where the outward fails;
> So shall you nearer be the spiritual
> Nature, and war triumphant with your own.[46]

A careful reader might detect the prophecy of fratricide in that last line and realize that the invitation to form an inner world like Satan's was intended to isolate Cain even further from the human community to which he belonged. The mind that is its own place, we recall from *Paradise Lost* (1: 254–55), can make a Hell of Heaven, and Cain's mind is from the start too much its own place, a cul-de-sac of resentful egotism that increasingly estranges him from the values and sentiments of ordinary human life as they are represented by Adah.

Uncritical admiration of Cain has created a pernicious casuistry, to borrow a Shelleyan phrase,[47] in regard to the murder. Seeking a moral justification for Cain's act, scholars have shown a tendency to blame the victim. Edward Bostetter wrote, "It is the violent rejection of his appeal to reason that arouses Cain to frustrated rage against the obsequious Abel, whose speech and actions are almost a parody of the behavior of the self-righteous, well-intentioned people who by their blind submission encourage the perpetuation of social tyranny and evil."[48] In other words, Abel was asking for it. But such an interpretation is simply not supported by the evidence of the text.

Abel is certainly no more self-righteous than Cain is, and his submission to the divine order seems to be a thoughtful, deliberate choice rather than a blind act. He is a decent enough man, if not a colorful one, beloved by his entire family, deferential to his elder brother and usually tolerant of, if puzzled by, Cain's irreligion. The prayer he delivers over his sacrifice has a dignity in its reverence that serves as a dramatic foil to Cain's impiety. In short, Abel's conduct and character do nothing to mitigate Cain's crime or relieve the terrible irony that makes him the executioner of God's sentence of death on humanity.

Critics have also not perceived clearly that Lucifer's and Cain's indictment of the Almighty as malevolent and punitive is supported by very little evidence in the play. Apart from the tumbling of Cain's altar, the only action that can with assurance be credited to Jehovah is the merciful intervention that protects the murderer from violent retribution at the end of the play.[49] In Genesis, God curses Cain for his crime and curses the earth with him, but Byron does not include those divine maledictions in his drama; all the serious cursing is left to Cain's mother. But instead of the death penalty that Eve insists would be suitable punishment for the fratricide, God guarantees Cain's life – a convincing refutation of the murderer's generalization that God does nothing but evil (II, ii, 20). Describing Cain's exemption from the chain of murder he himself has begun as "a miracle of divine grace," Peter Manning observed: "*Cain* is the saddest of Byron's works, for Cain's obtuse inability to comprehend the absolution awarded him is his most tragic example of human rigidity . . . Cain continues to envision himself as the victim of an implacable God, and his self-pity is the final note of the play."[50]

It is important to remember, too, that the only crime for which Cain is punished is the murder of his brother; there is no divine retribution for his discontent or his irreverence. Through most of the play, to his relentless litany of recrimination against the divine order, Jehovah apparently turns either a deaf ear or, perhaps, that ironic smile with which in *Childe Harold* God hears the criticism of Gibbon and Voltaire. Only in the last act, after a speech filled with the kind of insolent impiety that in a Greek tragedy would bring swift and terrible retribution, only then does Jehovah finally respond by sending a whirlwind to scatter Cain's altar. The whirlwind, one should note, does not appear in Genesis; it comes from another book of the Old Testament that Byron knew well and admired, the one wherein God answers Job out of the whirlwind, rejecting his attempt to impose upon a Divine Being his inadequate human conceptions of justice and evil. In Byron's drama, when the whirlwind similarly repudiates Cain's effort at self-justification, one realizes that from the beginning Cain has been asking questions very like Job's: why are we born to suffer? what kind of God allows so much pain for no comprehensible reason?[51] Job was given no satisfactory response to his protests, except to be reminded that his intellect and experience were limited and that, whether he approved of the order of things or not, he must acknowledge God's sovereignty and submit to the divine will. Although Cain's complaints are more characteristically modern in emphasis and language, embodying the scientific and philosophic "research" of Byron's day, they are shown to be just as impertinent and futile as Job's when confronted by the mysterious omnipotence of God.

But if Byron maintains a large measure of ironic detachment from his despondent hero, he also makes obvious his sympathy with Cain, trapped as he is in an intellectual milieu where dissatisfaction, curiosity, and even honesty are condemned, if only by the human apologists for the divine order. If the *Essay on Man* ironizes *Cain*, the play offers its own rebuttal to the Augustan complacency that asserted "in erring reason's spite, One truth is clear, whatever is, is right." In *Cain*'s universe much of what is, is terribly wrong, and Cain's discomfort expresses Byron's own response to a cosmic order that is imperfect and irrational, but which, nevertheless, is unquestionably the creation of a Divine Being. It is a major part of Cain's frustration that he is unable to deny the existence of the God he holds responsible for his misery. Even if he was inclined to doubt his parents' report of their interactions with Jehovah, he cannot ignore the evidence of his own senses: he himself hears the seraphs singing God's praises and sees the gates of Eden "guarded by fi'ry-sworded Cherubim" (I: 133, 171–74). Cain questions and rebels within an undeniable, inescapable religious order, knowing that, while God may be defied, he cannot be discounted. His existence is an inexorable fact in the light of which everything else must be explained. The origin of evil, for example, the primary intellectual dilemma with which Cain wrestles, would present no philosophical puzzle to an atheist; only the believer in a benevolent God must account for the unmerited sufferings of living creatures. Having articulated his angry protest against what is fundamentally and immedicably wrong with the natural order and with the condition of humanity as created by God, at the end of the play Cain might have said, as Byron once said to his wife, "The worst of it is, I *do* believe."[52]

And so, although its goal and its effect was to enrage and embarrass Christian believers, *Cain*'s primary motivation can be more precisely described as heuristic rather than merely iconoclastic. "The forcefulness of Byron's question," as Wolf Z. Hirst remarked, "must not be interpreted as a blasphemous answer."[53] Cain's remonstrances against the order of things are not denials but protests, and, expressed within the context of belief, many are legitimate criticisms of a defective cosmos and a problematic theological order. Cain's most irreverent act, the destruction of Abel's altar, is done out of indignation at God's apparent "high pleasure in / The fumes of scorching flesh and smoking blood" (III, i, 298–99). But even this protest takes on positive significance when considered in the context of a reformational tradition that runs through the Bible itself.

Pity for suffering animals is one of Cain's most attractive qualities throughout the play. This sympathy intensifies his resentment of God's apparent approval of Abel's blood sacrifice and generates the asperity of the grudging invocation he delivers over his own sacrifice – that uniquely Byronic syncretism of rationalism and resignation which begins with echoes of Pope's "Universal Prayer" and ends with an expression of something like the Calvinist doctrine of Predestination. But this angry repudiation of bloody oblations follows (or, to place Cain historically, anticipates) a central prophetic tradition in the Old Testament. One finds throughout the major and minor prophets a recurrent insistence that God himself rejects blood sacrifice in favor of a higher, purer form of religious practice: "To what purpose is the multitude of your sacrifices unto me? saith the Lord: . . . I delight not in the blood of bullocks, or of lambs, or of goats" (Isaiah 1: 11). "I desired mercy, and not sacrifice; and the knowledge of God more than burnt offerings" (Hosea 6: 6). When Adah says of Cain's vegetable sacrifice, "These are a goodly offering to the Lord, / Given with a gentle and contrite spirit" (III, i, 107–8) Byron is nudging his reader to recall Psalm 51, familiar from its use daily in the Prayer Book's "Order for Morning and Evening Prayer": "For thou desirest not sacrifice . . . thou delightest not in burnt offering. The sacrifices of God are a broken spirit: a broken and a contrite heart, O God, thou wilt not despise."[54]

Byron knew enough of the higher criticism of scripture, if only from the Deist writers he read,[55] to understand that the prophets articulated a more sophisticated set of religious sentiments than those attributed to the tribal God of Genesis. And he was familiar enough with the Bible to know that the repudiation of blood offerings was often linked with demands for social justice as an integral part of true religion. The classic statement of this connection came from the prophet Amos, who reports the Lord as warning, "Though ye offer me burnt offerings and your meat offerings, I will not accept them: neither will I regard the peace offerings of your fat beasts . . . But let judgment run down as waters, and righteousness as a mighty stream" (Amos 5: 22–24). Abraham Heschel points out that the Authorized Version's "judgment" would be closer to "justice" in our modern usage, and that "righteousness" is nearer to "compassion" – a sympathetic concern for the unfortunate or the oppressed that goes beyond the obligations of strict justice.[56] Byron thus allows Cain in his final prayer to adumbrate the later Biblical tradition of social protest, a tradition that was still exerting a potent influence on the politics of Byron's own day. Like the other Romantics, Byron's primary objection to the public religion of his time was to the political and economic injustices it countenanced. When he wrote, "I never arraigned [Christ's] creed, but the use – or abuse – made of it," he went on to recall a specific instance of such abuse. "Mr Canning one day quoted Christianity to sanction Negro Slavery, and Mr Wilberforce had little to say in reply. And was Christ crucified, that black men might be scourged? If so, he had better been born a Mulatto, to give both colours an equal chance of freedom, or at least salvation."[57] When Byron attacked the use of Christianity to countenance slavery, he was repeating the prophetic insistence that any true religion must incorporate basic principles of social justice.

Most readers did not find the religious message of *Cain* to be positive or constructive in any sense. Insofar as the drama was perceived to have any reformational effect, it was the one F. D. Maurice later identified as the power to shock people out of a state of religious complacency or indifference. Keats thought that "a mighty providence subdues the mightiest Minds to the service of the time being, whether it be in human Knowledge or Religion."[58] If so, upon Byron was bestowed a special charismatic gift for unsettling, perplexing, and, in his word, "frightening" believers with unusual challenges to the security of their faith. The necessity of theism seemed to engender in the instinctively skeptical Byron a peculiarly strong compulsion to confront head on not only the historical corruptions and failures of religion but also the anomalies and contradictions that are the necessary entailments of belief. It was a kind of metaphysical integrity or stubbornness that drove him to speculate so boldly within the limits of faith and to find and probe so searchingly the religious vulnerabilities of his contemporaries. The first reviewers condemned *Cain* as impious, sacrilegious, and blasphemous, but the more candid and thoughtful of them also acknowledged that the play was deeply, dangerously unsettling. Even while protesting Byron's failure to refute Lucifer's and Cain's indictment of the divine order, a few critics conceded that there are no good answers to questions like those concerning the origin of evil and complained that to raise them at all was mischievous, even cruel. The *Edinburgh Review* foresaw that *Cain* would be "the means of suggesting the most painful doubts and distressing perplexities, to hundreds of minds that might never otherwise have been exposed to such dangerous disturbance." The *Eclectic Review* accused Byron of intentionally imperiling his readers' souls with theological difficulties that they could not overcome: "In the very spirit of the fabled Sphinx, he propounds these dark enigmas, that those who fail to unravel them, may perish." *Blackwood's* too protested the theological embarrassment that Byron's play would generate: "On all occasions throughout this poem his end and aim appears to be to perplex his readers by starting doubts necessarily inexplicable to human understanding, . . . and filling their minds with discontent at the nature which it has pleased Infinite Wisdom to bestow on mankind."[59] The concluding complacency does not invalidate *Cain*'s central argument – that there is something radically wrong with this "nature which it has pleased Infinite Wisdom to bestow on mankind." Byron was condemned because in a non-theological age, one whose pragmatic impatience with theology was compounded with a political fear of it left over from the seventeenth century, he raised hard questions about evil, freedom, and the "politics of paradise." Looking back on the controversy seven years later, the *London University Magazine* concluded that *Cain* was execrated by the religious establishment precisely because it raised questions to which the clergy could provide no easy answers. Byron had challenged their theological authority in a peculiarly embarrassing way, and they "dreaded lest their facile and pleasant mode of journeying through the world might be thereby interrupted."[60] The Pilgrim of Eternity, whose exigent, mistrustful religious sense prevented him from resting long at any shrine, would have little compunction about interrupting the facile and pleasant journeys of others – especially "the scoundrels of priests, who do more harm to religion than all the infidels that ever forgot their catechisms."[61]

The judgment of the *London University Magazine*, delivered after the heat of battle had cooled, makes somewhat more plausible Byron's own self-defence that his object was "only to combat hypocrisy, which I abhor in everything, and particularly in the matter of religion; and which now, unfortunately, appears to me to be prevalent. I seek to unveil the vices, or the vile, interested views which so many cover under a hypocritical mantle, and for this, [they] wish to render me odious, and make me to be believed an impious person, and a monster of incredulity."[62] Convincingly or not, Byron is here claiming the reformer's warrant for his assaults on religion – his desire to make it more worthy of its own ideals.

Prominent among the "vile interested views" that motivated the reaction to *Cain* were political ones. The suggestion of even a Whig publication like the *Edinburgh Review* that works like *Cain* should be banned as a danger to the commonwealth (see p. 38) indicated that Byron's religious missiles were hitting sensitive political targets; so did the response of Richard Carlile, whose long-term strategy of subverting the government by subverting the national religion led him to publish his own pirated edition of *Cain* in 1822, confident that it would assist the work of unhinging the established order. Coming to Carlile's defence at the time of his trial for blasphemy, both Byron and Shelley protested the collusion of religion and politics in this prosecution, which for Shelley was only the latest demonstration of an intimate relationship that had long augmented the evils of oppressive government in England.[63] When the Poet Laureate, Robert Southey, in April 1821 attacked the "Satanic school" of poets, accusing Byron and Shelley of having rebelled "against the holiest ordinances of human society,"[64] he demonstrated how casually and routinely the protective veneer of holiness was applied to political institutions at the time. Southey's accusation was included in the introduction to his poem *A Vision of Judgment*, an especially brazen effort to sacralize the established political order, in which

George III is solemnly welcomed into the courts of heaven while his political enemies are consigned to hell. Those Whigs and republicans whom Southey did not dare to damn were purged of their political errors in heaven – Milton, for example:

> of passion now as of blindness
> Heal'd, and no longer here to Kings and Hierarchs hostile,
> He was assoil'd from taint of the fatal fruit.   (IX)

In their own way, Byron and Shelley might have enjoyed this suggestion that the original sin was political discontent.

Byron's parodic reply to Southey, *The Vision of Judgment,* was written during the same period that produced *Cain* (they were completed within a month of each other). In the *Vision* Byron once again intruded upon holy ground, again carried his protest into the purlieus of divine power, with a change of venue this time from the gates of Eden to the gates of Heaven itself. In turning from tragedy to burlesque, Byron was evidently determined to demonstrate even more audaciously than he had done in *Cain* that nothing is truly sacred except the Divine Being – who is here once again kept offstage, mentioned only when the Archangel Michael is described as "a goodly work of him from whom all glory and good arise," an expression of praise that offers another counter to Cain's assertion that God created nothing but evil.

In the *Vision* Byron once again concedes to God the status of Supreme Ironist. In what could be considered another manifestation of his Calvinist tendencies, he allows George III to be saved by the inscrutable mercy of a God whose ways are past finding out. Amazing grace, indeed, to save a wretch like George, but, as Byron observed, "if [God] will / Be saving, all the better; for not one am I / Of those who think damnation better still" (98–100). And to have denied salvation to the old king would have been playing by Southey's rules. We last glimpse the blind monarch commencing his life in eternity with an effort to learn the hundredth psalm, the one proclaiming that "the Lord is good; his mercy is everlasting; and his truth endureth to all generations" – no matter how that mercy may be abridged and that truth arrogated by transient political and theological systems.

Long before Karl Marx drew his analogy between religion and narcotics, Byron knew that spiritual complacency was a crucial buttress of the established political and economic order. His own encounters with the bench of bishops in the House of Lords showed him that the struggle for human liberty must be fought as strenuously on the religious front as on any other, and his experience of international politics after Waterloo made him see even more clearly how the power structure in Europe secured its legitimacy by wrapping itself in the mantle of the sacred, a strategy exemplified most egregiously by what Byron called "the impious Alliance which insults the world with the name of 'Holy'!" – that anti-liberal conspiracy of monarchs who proclaimed themselves "defenders of the Christian religion, as a united Christian family."[65]

Byron's assault on that kind of "cant," which he considered "the crying sin of this double-dealing and false-speaking time of selfish spoilers," intensified as he himself became increasingly the object of criticism by the religious community. His defence was to counter-attack ever more vociferously:

The hackneyed and lavished title of blasphemer – which, with radical, liberal, Jacobin, reformer, etc., are the changes which the hirelings are daily ringing in the ears of those who will listen – should be welcome to all who recollect on whom it was originally bestowed. Socrates and Jesus Christ were put to death publicly as blasphemers, and so have been and may be many who dare to oppose the most notorious abuses of the name of God and the mind of man.[66]

Byron here boldly positions himself in a great tradition of religious radicalism that began with the irreproachable names of Socrates and Jesus and continued in his own day with prosecuted blasphemers like the publishers of Paine's *Age of Reason* – most recently Richard Carlile, to whom Byron was specifically referring in the passage just quoted. Demonstrating again his understanding of the connection between religious skepticism and political radicalism, Byron said in defence of *Cain*: "I shall not be deterred by any outcry . . . they shall not interrupt the march of my mind – nor prevent me from telling the tyrants who are attempting to trample upon all thought – that their thrones will yet be rocked to their foundation."[67]

Byron's credentials as a religious thinker or reformer are easy enough to challenge. It is not clear that his overall religious policy was any more carefully considered than his political one, and, as Alvin Kernan has pointed out, what distinguishes purposeful satire from mere comedy or burlesque is a specific reformist agenda.[68]

Even a sympathetic critic like Andrew Rutherford conceded Byron's "poverty of religious ideas."

> He had no talent for this kind of thinking – his opinions were confused and contradictory, and his conversations with Dr Kennedy show how far he was from having worked out any real critique of Christianity. He was incapable of ever becoming a philosopher or theologian, and his attempts to write poetry which he himself described as "metaphysical" reveal an ignorance of his own limitations, and a misconception of his true poetic powers.[69]

But power is as power does. Byron frightened and angered the religious establishment more than any other poet of the time. When Shelley, whose credentials as a philosopher and theologian are less easily challenged, read *Cain*, he was startled by the magnitude of the achievement. "What think you of Lord Byron's last volume?" he wrote to John Gisborne. "In my opinion it contains finer poetry than has appeared in England since the publication of *Paradise Regained*. *Cain* is apocalyptic; it is a revelation not before communicated to man."[70] To compare *Cain* with Milton's religious verse was high praise indeed. Milton provided the pattern for poets who enlisted their talents in the service of political and religious change and Shelley was identifying Byron as another of those "bold enquirers into morals and religion" who were continuing the progress of the English Reformation.

Additional testimony to Byron's power as a critic of religion came from another formidable contemporary. In 1821 William Blake, growing old in poverty and obscurity, read *Cain* and immediately wrote a revisionary reply entitled *The Ghost of Abel*, in which a merciful Jehovah repudiates Abel's blood sacrifice and his ghost's demand for vengeful justice. He dedicated the work "To Lord Byron in the Wilderness," and asked, "What doest thou here Elijah? Can a Poet doubt the Visions of Jehovah?"[71] Blake's use of the adverb "here" suggests that he and Byron, so far separated by class and now by geography, are nevertheless companions in intellectual exile, two voices crying in the same cultural wilderness, where the just man rages while "the sneaking serpent walks in mild humility."[72] Whatever Blake might have thought of Byron's metaphysics, to have called the author of *Cain* "Elijah" was an expression of very high esteem. This was the name he gave the union of fideist angel and doubting devil at the end of the *Marriage*, an indication that he may have noticed Byron's oscillation between belief and denial. More seriously it was a title that he gave to Los, the Zoa of imagination and prophecy, whose work was the reformation and purification of religion in human history. The significance of the name becomes clear in *Jerusalem* when the other Zoas give to Los the responsibility of rescuing Albion from his fallen state:

> And feeling the damps of death they with one accord delegated Los
> Conjuring him by the Highest that he should Watch over them
> Till Jesus shall appear: & they gave their power to Los
> Naming him the Spirit of Prophecy, calling him Elijah.[73]

Albion is both cause and victim of a diseased culture characterized by "a pretence of Art, to destroy Art: a pretence of Liberty / To destroy Liberty, a pretence of Religion to destroy Religion" (*J* 38: 35–36). Elijah-Los is the prophetic spirit that works within humanity to substitute reality for pretence in these three interconnected realms of human endeavor. No one understood more clearly than Blake the extent to which true liberty depended on true religion, and no one worked so hard to demonstrate the role that art could play in the religious reformation that must accompany or precede a revival of political freedom. Whatever he may have thought of Byron as an artist, Blake clearly saw him as an important participant in the great work of religious reform to which all poets worthy of the name must be dedicated. Like the Dragon-Man in Hell's printing house, Byron was engaged in the work of "clearing away the rubbish from a cave's mouth," cleansing the doors of perception so that humanity could see reality more clearly. Not as thoughtfully or as deliberately, perhaps, as Blake or Shelley, but more effectively because of his public eminence, Byron was leading an attack on "state religion" that must inevitably contribute to the purification of Christianity by encouraging it to re-examine its theological professions and the nature of its influence in society.

If the prophetic mantle has a somewhat rakish look as modeled by Byron, Blake could still place him in the tradition of those who were sent to rebuke religion in God's name. In the Biblical world, Abraham Heschel observes,

The prophet is an iconoclast, challenging the apparently holy, revered, and awesome. Beliefs cherished as certainties, institutions endowed with supreme sanctity, he exposes as scandalous pretensions . . . The prophet knew that religion could distort what the Lord demanded of man, that priests themselves had committed perjury by bearing false witness, condoning violence, tolerating hatred, calling for ceremonies instead of bursting forth with wrath and indignation at cruelty, deceit, idolatry, and violence . . . To the patriots, they seemed pernicious; to the pious multitude, blasphemous; to the men in authority, seditious.[74]

And the solemnity of the prophetic purpose did not exclude humor, irony, and derision, even in scripture. Jesus himself found those rhetorical weapons useful in his effort to disturb the self-assurance of Scribes and Pharisees.[75]

Still, Byron remains a problematic prophet. For Max Weber, the prophet expresses "a unified view of the world derived from a consciously integrated and meaningful attitude toward life. To the prophet both the life of man and the world, both social and cosmic events, have a certain systematic and coherent meaning. To this meaning the conduct of mankind must be oriented if it is to bring salvation, for only in relation to this meaning does life obtain a unified and significant pattern."[76] Such faith would not seem to leave room for the skepticism that was so central in Byron's religious consciousness. Perhaps that is why in the dedication to *The Ghost of Abel,* in that dramatic moment when one Romantic reformer acknowledged the mission of another, a puzzled William Blake needed to ask, "Can a prophet doubt the visions of Jehovah?" Even the author of the *Marriage of Heaven & Hell* was troubled by the ambiguous stances of this modern Elijah.

"God's ways are odd," Byron shrugged in *Don Juan* (8: 104), acknowledging the anomalies and discordances at the heart of religion. His sense of the transcendent mystery of the divine encouraged him to accept no human formulations of holiness or sacredness as meriting uncritical respect, especially if they were being used as excuses for political corruption, economic oppression, or the large-scale homicide of the war against France. Byron's idea of reform involved the excoriation of hypocrisy, the unsettlement of complacency, and the redemption of the idea of the holy so that it would become less readily available to sanctify bad government. He found it beneficial, politically as well as in religious terms, to disturb the complacency of the clergy and their congregations by reminding them of their ignorance of the ultimate nature of God and man. Undermining the assurance of believers would, he felt certain, make no small contribution to dissolving the old structures of power in Britain.

It was a central premise of Byron's faith that what is true and valuable in religion need not fear, and could only profit from, the closest, most skeptical scrutiny. Near the end of *Don Juan* he speaks with respect of

> Those holier mysteries, which the wise and just
> Receive as gospel, and which grow more rooted,
> As all truths must, the more they are disputed. (16: 6)

As he approached the end of his career as a determined and effective critic of religion he could here still be seen acknowledging the sacredness of what he profaned, oscillating in his characteristic manner between reverent acceptance of the reality of holy mysteries and an unshaken confidence in the utility and probity of disputing them. True religion, as Byron would have been assured by Milton's *Areopagitica*, need not fear the closest critical investigation. To such confidence can be attributed the peculiar blend of belief and skepticism, of reverence and derision that most of his contemporaries found, and many of ours still find, so hard to comprehend. His oscillation was not an expression of indifference, or confusion, or helplessness. It was the intellectual policy of a theist whose goal, sometimes mischievous but most often resolutely serious, was the discomposure and reformation of the national religion of England.

CHAPTER 5

The politics of Greek religion

John Keats understood as clearly as any of his Romantic contemporaries that he was called to continue the work of religious reformation in England, joining Wordsworth in the vanguard of a "grand march of intellect" that would liberate religion from dogmas and superstitions left in place by earlier poet-reformers like John Milton.[1] If the title of reformer seems somehow inappropriate to Keats (by contrast with the more politically attentive Wordsworth, Blake, or Shelley), that is partly the result of a misconstruction of his poetic character by some influential critics, and partly the effect of his own reluctance to use poetry as a medium for political argument. A few occasional pieces address the issue of religious reform directly – most obviously the sonnet "Written in Disgust of Vulgar Superstition," which sees the Christianity of his day "dying like an outburnt lamp" and being replaced by more enlightened forms of faith. But such overt statements are rare in Keats's poetry. His ideal of negative capability, the capability "of being in uncertainties, Mysteries, doubts, without any irritable reaching after fact & reason" (*Letters* 1: 193), discouraged contentiousness in the expression of religious or political opinion as inappropriate to the purposes of art. Nevertheless, it can be argued that the character of Keats's major poetry was profoundly affected by his religious politics.

Despite the intense critical scrutiny given in recent years to Keats's political interests,[2] the most significant impact of these interests on his verse has been largely overlooked – his choice of Greek mythology as the subject matter of his most ambitious poems. This crucial artistic decision has usually been attributed to the complex of aesthetic, psychological, and religious predilections suggested in his expressed admiration for "the Greek spirit, – the Religion of the Beautiful, the Religion of Joy."[3] While there certainly were temperamental and purely aesthetic reasons for Keats's attraction to Greek mythology, the central role it assumed in his poetry and many of the artistic problems it engendered can be accounted for convincingly, I think, in terms of the political significance that classical mythology carried in his time.[4] I will argue here that contemporary politics, specifically religious politics, encouraged his initial interest in Greek mythology and perceptibly influenced the changing attitudes to these myths that are detectable in his mature poetry.

I pointed out earlier that critics of the established political order in Britain often found it expedient, and usually gratifying, to attack the power structure on its more vulnerable religious side, in an effort to discredit the national religion that provided the ideological rationale for subservience to the existing order of power. Some of the most famous political show trials of Keats's day were prosecutions for blasphemy rather than sedition, e.g. those of William Hone in 1817 and Richard Carlile in 1819, both of which Keats followed with close attention and with expressed admiration for the defendants (*Letters* 1: 191, 2: 194). For liberals less eager to risk prosecution and imprisonment, there were subtler ways of impugning the national faith. One prominent strategy devised by disaffected rationalists in the eighteenth century was to display an ostentatious nostalgia for classical civilization in preference to the Christian cultural order that supplanted it.

Edward Gibbon was one widely read enthusiast for what he called "the elegant mythology of the Greeks" and "the cheerful devotion of the pagans" that in his view had been brutally extirpated by intolerant Christian fanatics. *The Decline and Fall of the Roman Empire* did much to encourage the notion that what was lost in the dissolution of paganism was better than, or at least as good as, what replaced it. While more rigorous deists like Thomas Paine scorned polytheism as a corruption of the pure monotheistic religion of nature, and atheists despised it as just another variety of superstition, other critics of Christianity found Greek superstition preferable to the Biblical varieties as being at least more beneficial, or less baneful, in its social and political effects. The ancient Greeks, it was thought, had satisfactorily demonstrated the possibility of creating a happy, humane political and social order without the guidance of Biblical revelation.[5] In David Hume's *The Natural History of Religion* (1757) the polytheism of antiquity is preferred to monotheism as being more tolerant of religious difference, less productive of metaphysical perplexity, and, since it lacked a spirit of submission and self-abasement, more conducive to "activity, spirit, courage, magnanimity, love of liberty, and all the virtues which aggrandize a people. . . To which we may add, that the fables of the pagan religion were, of themselves, light, easy, and familiar; without devils, or seas of brimstone, or any object that could much terrify the imagination. Who could forbear smiling, when he thought of the loves of Mars and Venus, or the amorous frolics of Jupiter and Pan?"[6] It was also understood that Greek religion tolerated freedom of speculation beyond the "vulgar polytheism" of the unlearned, allowing philosophers to indulge privately in rational monotheism. "Thus the religion of the common people was left undisturbed," William Godwin remarked, "and the enlightened were satisfied, while they joined on ordinary occasions in the exteriors of that religion, secretly to worship one God under the emblems of the various manners and forms in which he operates."[7] Combining freedom of speculation with the aesthetic comforts of a beautiful and poetical mythology, the Greeks cultivated a healthier, more natural, and more humane approach to religion than anything the Biblical creeds had generated. My argument here will be that Keats began his poetic career as a devotee of mythology in the Humean and Gibbonesque mode, but that he ended it subscribing to the more critical anti-mythological views of the radical deists. The motivation behind his adoption of both positions was essentially political.

In Keats's time, one of the more ardent public advocates of the superiority of Greek religion over Christian was Leigh Hunt, the man generally recognized, then and now, as Keats's most influential political mentor. Hunt was energetically engaged in the political debates of his time, but his war with established power was fought with equal vigor, and sometimes with apparently greater relish, on the religious front. I have argued elsewhere that Hunt had a profound influence on the poet's radical thinking in religion and on the version of deism that he adopted as his personal faith.[8] Hunt has also been credited with having inspired Keats's adoption of Greek myths as the primary subject matter of his most characteristic verse. In the course of its attack on the "Cockney School of Poetry," *Blackwood's Magazine* asserted: "From his prototype Hunt, John Keats has acquired a sort of vague idea, that the Greeks were a most tasteful people, and that no mythology can be so finely adapted for the purposes of poetry as theirs."[9] Friendlier critics in our own time have awarded Hunt similar credit.[10]

While Hunt ("the Cockney Homer," as *Blackwood's* called him) was illustrating in his own verse the adaptability of Greek myth to modern poetic purposes, he was also demonstrating its utility in the arena of religious polemic. The *Examiner* regularly used "Greek religion" as a touchstone to suggest the moral and theological flaws in England's national religion. An 1815 editorial, for example, introduced a favorite theme of Hunt's – the cheerfulness of the Greek religious spirit as contrasted with the gloom of Christianity:

The very finest and most amiable part of our notions on [religion and morality] comes originally from [Greek] philosophers; – all the rest, the gloom, the bad passions, the favouritism, are the work of other hands . . . Even the absurd parts of the Greek Mythology are less painfully absurd than those of any other; because, generally speaking, they are on the chearful side instead of the gloomy. We would rather have a Deity, who fell in love with the beautiful creatures of his own making, than one, who would consign nine hundred out of a thousand to destruction for not believing ill of him.[11]

In the *Examiner*'s lead editorial for April 27, 1817, Hunt again made invidious comparisons between paganism and Christianity in the matter of tolerance, pointing out that Greek and Roman poets and philosophers were permitted to teach deism and atheism "without the least political molestation" (p. 259). He was still on the subject on May 4, 1817 in an editorial that Keats praised as "a battering ram against Christianity" (*Letters* 1: 137). Granted that all religion is subject to abuses, Hunt wrote, pagan abuses at least tended to be "on the pleasurable side of things. . . They dealt in loves and luxuries, in what resulted from the first laws of nature, and tended to keep humanity alive: – the latter have dealt in angry debates, in intolerance, in gloomy denouncements, in persecutions, in excommunications, in wars and massacres, in what perplexes, outrages, and destroys humanity."[12] For Hunt, Greek faith was more natural and rational than that of the Bible largely because it depended on no professional priesthood, no authoritative theology, and no sacred books apart from the works of poets like Homer and Hesiod, which could be interpreted freely and selectively.

A more coherent formulation of this political-religious-aesthetic critique may be found in Hunt's *Foliage* (1818), specifically in the "Preface, including Cursory Observations on Poetry and Cheerfulness," where Hunt argues that "cheerful" creeds are more conducive to poetry than "unattractive" gloomy ones composed of "opinions which make humanity shudder" – such as some of those recently espoused in William Wordsworth's published verse. As an excellent example of a cheerful creed Hunt points to Greek mythology, a high opinion of which, he observes, characterizes the new generation of poets just emerging on the scene, particularly Keats and Shelley, who are, if only on that account, more poetically appealing than Wordsworth.[13] Hunt goes on to assert that admiration of Greek myth has always been the sign of a true poet. Shakespeare, although "not a scholar," knew by a kind of fine poetical instinct how the Greek stories should be valued and used. In Milton, however, "the beauty of natural and ancient taste" had to struggle with "the Dragon Phantom Calvinism."

Milton, when he was young and happy, wrote Grecian Mythology in his Lycidas and Comus. . . In old age, there is good reason to suspect that he was, at any rate, not bigoted; and in the meantime, allusions to romance and to Greek mythology, which he never could prevail upon himself to give up, are the most refreshing things in his Paradise Lost and Regained, next to the bridal happiness of poor Adam and Eve. They are not merely drops in the desert; – they are escapes from every heart-withering horror, which Eastern storms and tyranny could generate together.[14]

"Eastern," we know from Keats's revision of *Endymion* 4: 10, was a code word for Biblical.[15] The alternatives, then, for an aspiring poet, as Hunt saw them, were the the cheerful Greek religion that graced the work of Shakespeare and Milton, or the "heart-withering horrors," "the swarthy bigotries" that nearly sank *Paradise Lost* and were sinking Wordsworth in a later day. That Keats subscribed generally to Hunt's vision of the cultural struggle is suggested by his sonnet "Written in Disgust of Vulgar Superstition," with its scorn of the "gloominess" and "dreadful cares" of a Christian religion that distracts people from "Lydian airs," and its confidence that contemporary poetry will be efficacious in dispersing the religious darkness. Keats identified himself publically with Hunt's nostalgia for the happier religion of the Greeks in the politically provocative sonnet "To Leigh Hunt, Esq." that dedicated his 1817 *Poems*. I too, the poet says, miss the good old times when nymphs adorned the shrine of Flora in May, but I am consoled for the fact that "Pan is no longer sought" by my ability to please Leigh Hunt with my poems.

It hardly needs to be said that the conception of Greek religion that Keats would have acquired from Hunt was eccentric and inadequate. Hunt frankly acknowledged that he selected from the culture of the ancient Greeks only what coincided with his own happy, eclectic, "religion of the heart." With little real understanding of the actualities of religious practice in the ancient world, Hunt tended vaguely to equate the religion of Greece with its mythology, being always more interested in nymphs and dryads than he was in mystery or sacrifice. One cannot fault him for lacking insights that have since been articulated by modern historians and anthropologists, but even his literary knowledge of the Greek mind was limited by his depreciation of the tragedies, which seemed to him an aberration produced by an unhealthy "melancholy" undercurrent in the predominantly cheerful Greek consciousness.[16] He shared the view of other sentimental deists that the Greeks of the golden age manifested in their religious consciousness some of the purity and freshness of the rational and natural religion that was instilled by the Creator into the nascent human mind. His optimistic version of natural religion left little room for anything dark or disquieting.

This notion that Greek mythology embodied pristine, natural religious truth could have been reinforced, ironically enough, by Keats's reading of *The Excursion* (a poem to which Hunt seems to have introduced him).[17] In Book 4, a book that we know Keats read with special attention, the Greek mythopoeic imagination is presented, along with that of the Persians, Babylonians, and Chaldeans, as exemplary of a universal religious sense that, guided by Providence even when undisciplined by Revelation, developed correct intuitions of divinity from observation of nature. The Greeks were thankful, reverential, moral, and hopeful of immortality; in other words, they professed an approximation of the natural religion accessible to all inquiring minds (4: 729–45, 925–40). While Wordsworth was, as Douglas Bush observed, "glad to find in the origins of myth a traditional and religious sanction for his own natural religion,"[18] the author of *The Excursion* would certainly not have considered Greek mythology an adequate substitute for Christianity, as his poem goes on to make clear, and yet some such extrapolation seems to have been made by Keats at the time. When the older poet dismissed Keats's "Hymn to Pan" as "a very pretty piece of paganism," he had probably detected the subversive agenda of this Greek poem written by one of Leigh Hunt's protégés. In his account of the incident, Benjamin Robert

Haydon recalled that "Wordsworth's puling Christian feelings were annoyed."[19]

The "Hymn to Pan" and its setting provide striking evidence that Keats intended the opening of *Endymion* to illustrate the attractions of Greek worship as an enlightened natural religion with none of the negative features of Christianity. Here is Hunt's religion of joy at full tilt, complete with laughing children, dancing damsels, singing and fluting shepherds, and venerable elders whose relaxed speculations about the afterlife involve only "anticipated bliss" in a heavenly Elysium, with no hint of the dark underworld even of Greek tradition. The sacrifice they offer to Pan is a bloodless one of wine and sweet herbs. Keats would have known from Homer that animal sacrifice was a routine component of Greek worship (Endymion himself later promises to sacrifice a kid to Pan), so this initial insistence on a bloodless oblation is evidently meant to emphasize the cheerful innocence of the Pan festival, as compared with the blood sacrifices that play so large a role in the Bible. Just at the time when he was working on this section of the poem Keats read in the *Examiner* (the "battering ram" issue of May 4, 1817) another of Hunt's editorials on the gloomy, bloodstained religion of the Christians, along with a news item concerning a German religious cult that practiced human sacrifice. Drawing a connection between "the dreadful Petzelians and their expiation by Blood" and the doctrine of the Atonement, Keats remarked, "and do Christians shudder at the same thing in a Newspaper which they attribute to their God in its most aggravated form?" (*Letters* 1: 137).[20]

Keats's Latmians generally demonstrate a purer religious consciousness than one might expect to find in a primitive community. Pan worshippers in ancient Greece were usually rather peremptory in the demands they made of their god, not hesitating to beat and otherwise abuse his effigies to hasten his compliance.[21] Keats's shepherds ask nothing of their divinity beyond his attention, as though aware that enlightened religion does not indulge in prayer of petition, which seems to expect that the sublime order of nature will be changed to meet individual needs.[22] And the Latmians are rather closer to monotheism than Greek shepherds typically ventured in the early stages of Pan worship. After being invoked in his primary identity as the goatlike, playful patron of shepherds, hunters, and farmers, in the hymn's fifth stanza Pan's character suddenly becomes awesomely larger, taking on the dimensions of his later identity as the personification of universal nature, a cosmic rather than a local divinity. And in their prayer to Universal Pan, Keats's shepherds demonstrate a remarkable sophistication of thought and diction:

> Be still the unimaginable lodge
> For solitary thinkings; such as dodge
> Conception to the very bourne of heaven,
> Then leave the naked brain: be still the leaven,
> That spreading in this dull and clodded earth
> Gives it a touch ethereal – a new birth:
> Be still a symbol of immensity;
> A firmament reflected in a sea;
> An element filling the space between;
> An unknown – but no more. (1: 293–302)

To select only one of these striking phrases,[23] the designation of Pan as "a symbol of immensity" suggests that some serious metaphysical thinking has been going on in Latmos. Rational religionists knew that every attempt to conceive a concrete image corresponding to the abstract notion of deity necessarily falls short. Jupiter, Jehovah, Vishnu – all are only symbols pointing to what is essentially ineffable. Keats's philosophical shepherds acknowledge Pan as such a symbol, as useful as any to signify an immensity that cannot be captured by language. Throughout the hymn, even in the early stanzas where he is almost totally anthropomorphized, the worshippers merely guess at Pan's nature and activity; they do not claim to know him. And they seem content that he remain unknown – indeed they prefer it – so long as he is willing to continue his beneficent ministry.

Keats's choice of Pan as tutelary deity of Latmos, although in one sense controlled by tradition,[24] is a quite appropriate one for his political purposes. The cult of Pan had been connected in a particular way with religious apologetics since the fourth century, when Christian commentators seized on Plutarch's strange account in *De Oraculorum Defectu* of a group of mariners who heard a disembodied voice cry out, "Great Pan is dead" – and interpreted it as signifying the dispersal of the pagan gods and oracles by the coming of Christ.[25] The tradition was evidently familiar in Keats's circle of acquaintance. Early in 1818 Leigh Hunt wrote to Shelley's friend, T. J. Hogg:

I hope you paid your devotions as usual to the Religio Loci, and hung up an evergreen. If you all go on so, there will be a hope some day that old Vansittart [the Chancellor of the Exchequer] & others will be struck with a

Panic Terror, and that a voice will be heard along the water saying "The great God Pan is alive again," – upon which the villagers will leave off starving, and singing profane hymns, and fall to dancing again.[26]

Here the resurrected Pan is seen as ushering in a post-Christian age of political and economic renovation. In an ideological milieu where Pan symbolized an alternative social order to the established Christian one, Keats's Pandean festival would inevitably have had a distinctly liberal political resonance. Another member of this circle of "Athenians," Thomas Love Peacock, might have been describing Keats's festival of Pan when he wrote, "I regret the days of antiquity, when the youths and maidens led the choral dance . . . in honor of those elegant and congenial divinities, for whose glory no throats were cut, and no inquisitorial piles were kindled; who were truly the deities of love and harmony, of cheerfulness and peace."[27]

The attempt to use classical mythology to express a modern conception of what religion ought to be (and thus to demonstrate the defects and inadequacies of Christianity) created artistic problems as well as opportunities for Keats. One such problem arose immediately in *Endymion*. After his introductory lesson on the characteristics of an enlightened, purified public religion, Keats had some difficulty characterizing his hero's private relationship with the moon goddess. The attraction between the two was mainly physical, but Keats seemed to feel that the behavior of Greek divinities and their devotees ought to be metaphysically respectable, so he put into Endymion's mouth a long, Neoplatonic-sounding disquisition on love as a "fellowship with essence," introducing it as an account of "the clear religion of heaven" (1: 777–842): How this "clear religion" of love relates to the established, public worship of Pan does not become apparent in the poem. The attempt in *Endymion* to platonize or at least etherealize a sensual relationship in an effort to make it seem more spiritual has confounded interpretation of the poem since its publication. Even a close friend like Benjamin Bailey, who ought to have understood Keats's intention, concluded that the poem was tainted by "that abominable principle of *Shelley's* – that *Sensual Love* is the principle of *things*."[28] That Keats did not subscribe to such a principle in general is suggested by his marginal note to Burton's *Anatomy* which comments sourly on the "horrid relationship" that seemed to exist in the human mind between heavenly and sensual love, between "the abstract adoration of the deity" and "goatish winnyish lustful love."[29] One may conclude that the linkage between religion and sexual passion in *Endymion* was an attempt to add dignity and solemnity to what otherwise might seem a too frivolous and self-indulgent religion of joy.

In Book 3 of the poem one can see another complication arising from Keats's apparent effort to raise Greek myth to a level of moral dignity qualifying it for competition with Christianity. Endymion's humanitarian, even Christ-like redemption of the dead lovers in the cave of Glaucus (the Christian archetype is the harrowing of hell) has generally struck readers as a successful invention, but a curiously inauthentic interpolation into the Greek legend. As Margaret Sherwood put it, "The old myth, which was a simple tale of love, takes on, in [Endymion's] sympathy with age, with suffering, a conception of love unknown to any ancient myth."[30] Jeffrey Baker's more thorough analysis of the poem's conflicting Christian and Greek elements sees the resulting "mythopoeic pastiche" as the chief cause of the failure of the third book, wherein Endymion, says Baker, "performs a Christlike function without in any other way becoming a Christ-like being. His redemptive act is in itself so trivial that it scarcely modifies his characteristic self-pity and absorption. . . Endymion turns away from 'religion' to engage in the pleasures of 'myth.'"[31] Speaking in more general terms, Morris Dickstein observed that the poem "is always aspiring to penetrate mysteries that it never adequately succeeds in defining."[32] It seems that Keats, like Hunt, was not especially skillful at developing the theological ramifications of his use of myth.

Keats's evident dissatisfaction with the Endymion myth on its own terms, his attempt to import a modern humanitarianism as well as a spiritual dimension into it, may indicate the influence of another of the poet's close friends, one whose views on Greek mythology conflicted dramatically with those that Keats would have been hearing from Leigh Hunt, and who saw himself as Hunt's antagonist in a struggle for Keats's salvation as an artist as well as an immortal soul. Just at the time when Keats first became acquainted with Benjamin Robert Haydon, the painter was engaged in a long-running, often heated argument with Hunt on the religious value of Greek mythology.[33] We do not know whether Keats was a witness to all the quarrels that Haydon records in his diary, but he must have known about them; the theme and language of the painter's remarks seem to resonate later in the poet's verse.

"Leigh Hunt says he prefers infinitely the beauties of Pagan Mythology to the gloomy repentance of the Christians," writes Haydon, neatly summarizing what we have seen to be Hunt's basic premise, and goes on to dissect the latter's religion of cheerfulness in a manner that reveals the full religio-political dimension of the debate:

No man feels more acutely than myself the poetical beauties of the Pagan mythology. Apollo, with his fresh cheek & God like beauty, rising like a gossamer from out a laurel grove, heated with love, after having panted on the bosom of some wandering nymph, is rich, beaming, rapturous! But these are beauties fit for those who live in perpetual enjoyment of immortality, without a care or a grief or a want. But what consolation to the poor, what relief to the widow & the orphan, to the sick, or the oppressed? Could the minds of such beings turn for assistance to a thoughtless & beautiful youth, warm with love & wine, just rising from having debauched a girl? Christianity is a religion adapted to give relief to the wretched & hope to the good, and Christ having suffered is a bond of sympathy between man & his Saviour that nothing in any other religion before or after affords. . . Is the association connected with Apollo issuing from a laurel grove in the morning freshness to be put in comparison with "give alms of thy goods" [Luke 11: 41], and never turn thy face from any poor man, and then the face of the Lord shall not be turned from thee.

The political nature of the argument becomes clearer as Haydon develops the theme of Christianity's contribution to society:

When I said "the Ancients had no hospitals," Hunt said, "so much the better – prevent poverty and not encourage it." . . . Prevent poverty! – prevent crime! – take away evil – but how? Evil is in the World; it cannot be rooted out. Alleviate its consequences, give means of mental consolation to those who suffer from it. . . [Christianity] teaches to bear those evils of an imperfect Nature, of a world which will not be altered in system to please us, but being as it is, Xtianity is sent to help us through it. Prevent poverty! – prevent illness, prevent old age or any weakness of the body; prevent vice or any of the aberrations of mind; prevent them you cannot, but alleviate them you may, and shew me before Xtianity such alleviation of misery as since its belief, such a triumph in Philosophy as the abolition of the Slave Trade![34]

Haydon's reference to hospitals was a commonplace of Christian apologetics at the time, traceable to William Paley's *Principles of Moral and Political Philosophy* (1785). "It does not appear," Paley wrote, "that, before the times of Christianity, an infirmary, hospital, or public charity of any kind, existed in the world; whereas, most countries in Christendom have long abounded with these institutions."[35] Paley was participating in a debate on Christianity's social legacy that had been provoked by Gibbon's *Decline and Fall*; Haydon's rhetoric shows that in the intensification of this debate after the French Revolution, the pragmatic argument for Christianity had been reinforced by the activities of the Evangelicals, who were busily and conspicuously alleviating misery and illiteracy wherever their search for souls took them. Their most celebrated effort, as Haydon notes, was the successful campaign waged alongside the Quakers to abolish the British slave trade, but their work in prison and factory reform was widely admired as well.[36]

Arnold Toynbee has written, "The practical test of a religion, always and everywhere, is its success or failure in helping human souls to respond to the challenges of Suffering and Sin."[37] This pragmatic touchstone is as old as the Bible's "By their fruits ye shall know them" (Matt. 7: 20). When Haydon asserted that the cheerful beauties of Greek myth had no humanitarian value to compare with the comforts of Christianity, he challenged his opponent to find a rationale for the Greek "religion of joy" beyond its aesthetic appeal, in other words, to find moral utility in the Greek tales. Hunt's suggestion that poverty should be eliminated rather than encouraged seemed naive and flippant to the painter, revealing an inadequate awareness of economic and social realities, a detachment that contrasted unfavorably with the dedication of those Christian activists who had been responsible, as Haydon reminded his adversaries on many occasions, for "the abolition of African Slavery, the institution of Charities & Hospitals, & all this amelioration of human Conditions."[38]

Haydon's arguments would have probed a sensitive conscience in Keats, who as a medical practitioner knew at first hand the state of public misery in England in 1816 and was poignantly aware that the worst of it could not be eliminated, but only comforted to some degree. He would have been particularly susceptible to arguments concerning the alleviation of suffering, since the medical education he had just completed contained a new emphasis on professional ethics, on the physician's humanitarian responsibilities.[39] To give up medicine for poetry, as he did early in 1817, was not easily defended as a humanitarian act, but Keats hoped that the dual identity of Apollo as poet and healer meant that poetry itself might prove to be a healing art, one whose practitioner could serve the world as "sage, humanist, physician to all men." Having chosen Greek mythology as the primary subject matter for this humanitarian poetry, Keats needed to show that the myths had something to offer mankind beside their beauty. We have seen evidence of this humanitarian concern in *Endymion,* and one can find it earlier in his first attempt to tell the story of the mortal and the moon-goddess, "I Stood Tip-Toe," wherein the wedding of Endymion and Diana results in a general cure of earthly disease. But the cure is left an unanalyzed miracle: Keats is not able to demonstrate what exactly his favorite Greek myth has to do with public health.

It may seem curious that an argument on mythology should have ranged so far, but if Greek religion were seriously to be presented as culturally superior to Christianity, its usefulness in concrete human terms needed to be demonstrated. The political quarrel between Christians and their radical critics focused on the question of which group was best qualified to diagnose and treat mankind's distressed condition. Haydon's strictures on Greek myth challenged Keats to demonstrate that the pagan legends offered something to match the kind of consolation that Christianity provided. Keats's immediate response can be detected in the humanitarian insertions in *Endymion.* But he met the challenge most boldly when he determined to write another Greek poem that would deliberately invite comparison with his country's great Christian epic, a poem that would compete ideologically as well as artistically with *Paradise Lost*'s attempt to justify the ways of God to men. In *Hyperion,* John Barnard has observed, "Milton's epic is divested of its Christianity, and recast as a pagan poem. *Hyperion* has no concept of Sin, no Christian cosmogony, and no Hell or Satan. It depicts an evolutionary struggle between lower and higher kinds of good, and is at root optimistic, with a progressive view of mankind's history."[40]

Such an ideological revision of Milton's epic would have to include something corresponding to what Keats called the "hintings at good and evil in the Paradise Lost" (*Letters* 1: 282) – some explanation of the distressed condition of humanity and a prognosis concerning the possibility of restoration, if not redemption. And, given Haydon's strictures on Greek myth, the poem would need to provide some form of consolation for human suffering. But *Hyperion*'s conception of the worth and meaning of suffering turns out to be oddly ambivalent. One attitude, expressed by the father of the Titans in a passage that demonstrates divine detachment from the concerns of humanity, despises suffering as literally ungodly:

I have seen my sons most unlike Gods.
Divine ye were created, and divine
In sad demeanour, solemn, undisturb'd,
Unruffled, like high Gods, ye liv'd and ruled:
Now I behold in you fear, hope, and wrath;
Actions of rage and passion; even as
I see them, on the mortal world beneath,
In men who die.   (1: 328–35)

This passage articulates what is, in fact, an authentically Greek conception of the gods, whose most characteristic demeanor was supposed to be dispassionate serenity. As Shelley remarked, "The Greeks rarely in their representations of the Divinities (unless we call the poetic enthusiasm of Apollo a mortal passion) expressed the disturbance of human feeling"; he was surprised when he found in a representation of Minerva "deep and impassioned grief, animating a divine countenance."[41]

On the other hand, in formulating his conception of his hero, Apollo, Keats apparently entertained the notion that for him the experience of suffering was a means of attaining the fullness of divinity. Although he told Haydon that he intended to treat *Hyperion* "in a more naked and grecian Manner" than he had achieved in *Endymion* (*Letters* 1: 207), it seems that he found it necessary once again to import non-Grecian elements into his poem. The idea that suffering could be instructive and formative for human beings was a common enough theme in Greek tragedy, but except in fertility myths the Greeks were unable to see much value or logic in a god's agony, as St. Paul once complained to the Corinthians (1 Cor. 1: 23). Even the suffering of Prometheus, which seemed so admirable to the Romantics, was presented by Aeschylus as an embarrassing indignity rather than an act of meritorious self-sacrifice.[42] When Apollo's apotheosis in *Hyperion* is compared to the struggle of "one who should take leave / Of pale immortal death, and with a pang / As hot as death's is chill, with fierce convulse / Die into life," one is reminded inevitably of a quite different resurrection story. Indeed Apollo resembles at moments a kind of Socinian version of Jesus, an apprentice deity who must earn or learn godhood through experience and effort. Insofar as Keats's Apollo is more than a "thoughtless & beautiful youth," he reminds one of the Christian Savior. But once again as in *Endymion* the intrusion of Christian elements into a Greek story seems adventitious, and the final impression one has of Apollo recalls Haydon's indictment: he is "rich, beaming, rapturous," but not especially relevant to the suffering human condition.

The situation of the Titans seems more authentically Greek in that no reward or compensation is promised for their pain and loss. Insofar as there is any consolation at all, it is embodied in the evolutionary optimism of Oceanus's theory "that first in beauty must be first in might" (2: 229). This "radical (and non-Christian) re-reading of human history and its possible future," as John Barnard describes it,[43] was another of Keats's original contributions to the myth. Having positioned himself in the vanguard of a "grand march of intellect" that had left superstitions like those of Milton behind, Keats tried to make his poem express the forward-looking optimism that the Enlightenment had opposed to Christianity's retrospective emphasis on the fall of man. *Hyperion* suggests the possibility of a secular redemption to be wrought in time by human effort or cultural inevitability. But there is a problem in Keats's use of a Greek myth to express a vision of human destiny in the real world – a problem Shelley avoided in *Prometheus Unbound* by detaching his titan's struggle from chronological time and projecting it into some just possible future. Once Oceanus's speculation is thought of as a prophecy made in the past concerning the order of human history whose progress is noticed in the poem (1: 273–80, 333–35), one faces the fact that historically the prophecy was not accomplished, nor has its major premise, that first in beauty must be first in might, normally been an operative principle in human affairs – as a moment's reflection on the Napoleonic wars and the Congress of Vienna would have convinced anyone. Even in the realm of cultural history, the Olympian succession, if such a thing may be said to have "taken place," was followed, as Gibbon eloquently lamented, by the triumph of a quite antithetical mythological system when classical civilization surrendered to Christianity. In a kind of formal or dramatic irony, Keats's Miltonic model continually reminds the reader of the victory of Christianity over the paganism he celebrates, a succession that Milton himself took pleasure in recalling. One wonders if Keats's revision, *The Fall of Hyperion*, could have repeated without irony Oceanus's statement of historic and aesthetic optimism against the setting of the ruined temple "where black gates /Were shut against the sunrise evermore," and where Moneta presided alone as the "pale omega of a withered race."

Whether or not it was loss of faith in the actualization of the poem's optimistic thesis that brought it to a halt, one notes that just at the time his work on *Hyperion* was faltering, Keats's views on the purpose of human suffering were undergoing a change, rejecting the kind of "march of mind" historical optimism to which he had earlier subscribed. In the meditations that culminated in his conception of the world as a "vale of Soul-making" – the theodicy that he devised to help him "bear those evils of an imperfect Nature, of a world which will not be altered in system to please us" (to use Haydon's words), he resigned himself to the realization that even if mankind might be made happy in a better social order, such happiness would only end in death, and one would leave such a world "as Eve left Paradise – But in truth I do not at all believe in this sort of perfectability – the nature of the world will not admit of it" (*Letters* 2: 101). The allusion to *Paradise Lost* is interesting in this context, suggesting that Keats was reconsidering the validity of Milton's "hintings at good and evil." He went on to elaborate the alternative rationale for human suffering and the vision of human potential that underlie his conception of the world as a "vale of Soul-making," where suffering is the means devised by God for the formation of the individual human identity. This long meditation on "systems of salvation" included a striking revision of his conception of classical myth and of its relation to the Christian story – a changed attitude toward the value and utility of all such anthropomorphic religious systems:

It is pretty generally suspected that the christian scheme has been coppied from the ancient persian and greek Philosophers. Why may they not have made this simple thing even more simple for common apprehension by introducing Mediators and Personages in the same manner as in the hethan mythology abstractions are personified – Seriously I think it probable that this System of Soul-making – may have been the Parent of all the more palpable and personal Schemes of Redemption, among the Zoroastrians the Christians and the Hindoos. For as one part of the human species must have their carved Jupiter; so another part must have the palpable and named Mediatior and saviour, their Christ their Oromanes and their Vishnu. (*Letters* 2: 103)

Keats had described the Titans in *Hyperion* as "the first-born of all shap'd and palpable Gods" (2: 153), contrasting them with their "unseen parent" Coelus (2: 159). Now palpability becomes for him a pejorative concept in relation to the divine. Keats's disdain for the "common apprehension" that requires palpable and named divinities and his reductive equation of Christ and Jupiter suggest a significant qualification of his response to what the Preface to *Endymion* called "the beautiful mythology of Greece."

One noteworthy aspect of this altered vision of mythology is the similarity his sentiments and his language bear to the radical critique of pagan mythology that appeared in Thomas Paine's *The Age of Reason*, a book that had achieved new currency in this year 1819 when it was republished by the radical bookseller Richard Carlile – an offense for which Carlile was prosecuted in a trial that attracted international attention and that Keats himself followed with intense interest. For Paine *The Age of Reason* had been a necessary sequel and complement to *The Rights of Man*, the second book intended as a blow against the religious prop of the inequitable social order that he had indicted in the first. He knew there could be no lasting political change without radical religious reform. That meant to Paine the repudiation of all revealed religion, all forms of belief that depended on priests and mediators, who in his view inevitably corrupted religion for their own selfish purposes. "It has been the scheme of the Christian church," he wrote, "and of all the other invented systems of religion, to hold man in ignorance of the Creator, as it is of government to hold him in ignorance of his rights. The systems of the one are as false as those of the other, and are calculated for mutual support."[44] The only way to combat priestcraft, Paine believed, was a "return to the pure, unmixed, and unadulterated belief of one God, and no more." Ancient paganism was as pernicious in this regard as any modern superstition. If anything, "the mythologists pretended to more revealed religion than the christians do. They had their oracles and their priests, who were supposed to receive and deliver the word of God verbally on almost all occasions."[45]

A truly radical political stance demanded rigorous repudiation of all such distractions and props, however charming. By contrast with writers like Gibbon and Hunt, Paine espoused the more radical deist critique of mythology as an irrational corruption of pure monotheism and made no sentimental exception of the Greek tales. Ancient superstitions were as bad as modern ones, since every variety of priestcraft plays into the hands of repressive government:

Every national church or religion has established itself by pretending some special mission from God, communicated to certain individuals. The Jews have their Moses; the Christians their Jesus Christ, their apostles and saints;

and the Turks their Mahomet; as if the way to God was not open to every man alike.[46]

The similarities in content and even syntax between this passage and the one just quoted from Keats's "vale of Soul-making" letter are striking enough to suggest the possibility that Keats had recently been reading Paine's remarks.[47] Indeed, if Keats ever read *The Age of Reason*, he was more likely to have done so at this time than at any other. Richard Carlile had republished the book in December 1818 and put up placards around London announcing its availability. The first edition, 1,000 copies, sold so quickly that another run of 3,000 was ordered. Carlile's indictment in January increased sales of the book, as did his imprisonment in Newgate a month later.[48] (Keats mentions the arrest in a letter to his brother on Febuary 14th [*Letters* 2: 62].) Solely on the basis of his interest in the case and the book's new availability, one can speculate that Keats might well have seen the book in the spring of 1819, when so many copies were in circulation and when the government's attempt to repress it became a *cause célèbre* among liberals.

Keats's letter resembles Paine's thinking in its dismissal of Christianity as another species of mythology, another surrender to the polytheistic impulse, one more corruption of pure theism by those who, whether ancient oracles or modern priests, would interpose palpable mediators between divinity and humanity. To Paine, the "Christian system . . . was only another species of mythology; and the mythology to which it succeeded, was a corruption of an ancient system of theism."

It is curious to observe how the theory of what is called the Christian Church, sprung out of the tail of the heathen mythology. . . The statue of Mary succeeded the statue of Diana of Ephesus. The deification of heroes changed into the canonization of saints. . . The Christian theory is little else than the idolatry of the ancient mythologists, accommodated to the purposes of power and revenue; and it yet remains to reason and philosophy to abolish the amphibious fraud. . . The most effectual means to prevent all such evils and impositions is, not to admit of any other revelation than that which is manifested in the book of Creation, and to contemplate the Creation as the only true and real word of God that ever did or will exist; and every thing else called the word of God is fable and imposition.[49]

Whether directly inspired by Paine, or indirectly by the deistic attitudes that Paine had helped to revitalize among radicals in England, Keats's disdain for the "common apprehension" that requires palpable and named divinities and his syncretic equation of Christ with Jupiter constitute an important qualification of his admiration for Greek mythology. Given this new attitude to myth, it does not seem surprising that he now found it difficult to continue work on *Hyperion* and that the "Greek" poems that followed – the odes to Psyche and on a Grecian Urn, *Lamia*, and the revision of *Hyperion* – show a new detachment from the world of the ancient myths, a new tendency to see "Greek religion" as something remote, transient, and fanciful. In the "Ode to Psyche," which was composed within days of the "Vale of Soul-making" letter, the goddess's tenuous lease on life is made entirely dependent on the poet's imaginative cooperation. Only by a kind of whimsical indulgence is she allowed a continuing existence. In this poem, Paul Sheats remarks, "The balance of power has shifted, as it were, from the mythological past to the modern present, from the 'vigour' of Maia to the 'working brain' of the modern imagination. Despite its classical subject, then, *Psyche* implies a farewell to the 'beautiful mythology of Greece.'"[50] In the "Ode on a Grecian Urn," the little town that worshiped on that "pious morn" long ago is now forever desolate. And in the last of his great odes, "To Autumn," one finds a noticeable absence of the classical and mythological material that was such a significant element in the earlier odes. Autumn is not Ceres; the sun is not Apollo. Indeed, as Helen Vendler has noted, one of Keats's manuscript revisions specifically excludes Apollo from the poem, reducing him to a natural process.[51] Instead of gods, one finds personifications; nature proffers its blessings and its rigors without any need for the costume of mythological mediators. In *Lamia*, written at the same time, the heroine is said to belong to a time when the Greek gods had not yet been succeeded by other, later species of "faery," and the delusive goddess herself is finally dismissed by cold philosophy, which demonstrates the impropriety, indeed the impossibility, of a lasting relationship between gods and mortals.[52] Finally, in the revised version of *Hyperion*, which absorbed Keats's attention as he approached the end of his creative life, the last of the Greek divinities, the "pale omega of a withered race," is "left supreme," officiating at a shrine to which no one ever comes except a rare dreamer. This "Shade of Memory" is all that remains of Greek religion, whose gods, even Apollo himself, are "far flown."

The Fall of Hyperion persistently emphasizes the antiquity and strangeness of what it represents. Even Moneta's Latin name puts her Greek origin in an historical perspective, and the traditional association of that name with Juno and Minerva as well as with Mnemosyne suggests that the reductive process of mythological syncretism has already been at work when the poem begins.[53] Syncretism is also suggested by the appearance of the temple and its furnishings. Noticing that the "strange vessels and large draperies" seem to derive from the Book of Exodus, John Livingston Lowes called attention to "the merging in Keats's mind of the crowded glories of the tabernacle and its service with the majestic simplicity of the Greek, and the vastness of the Egyptian temples."[54] But Moneta's temple is a "domed monument" (1: 70) as Greek and Egyptian shrines were not. It therefore recalls, along with the Parthenon, that other archetypal religious edifice and architectural model, the most famous domed structure in antiquity – the Pantheon in Rome, symbol of polytheism and also, in its later status as a Christian church, of the passing away of superannuated religions.

The dreaming poet brings to his encounter with Moneta an educated sense of history, particularly the history of religion. His allusions indicate knowledge of the Bible (both Testaments) and of other Greek myths beside the one the Titaness recounts. References to the Caliphate and the scarlet conclave show that he knows the history of Islam and of Roman Catholicism. He has evidently read Dante's great Catholic poem and Milton's Protestant epic, and he can compare Moneta's temple with the "grey cathedrals" of his own era. The visionary poet's religious experience tends to relativize Moneta's authority, providing the poet with a rhetorical shield that allows him, for instance, to celebrate his survival of the goddess's death threat with a Biblical allusion whose very impropriety seems to help liberate him from the stagnancy and ruin surrounding him:

> I mounted up
> As once fair angels on a ladder flew
> From the green turf to Heaven   (1: 134–36)

The reference to Jacob's interactions with God, a narrative of dream-visions and physical struggles that culminate in a divine gift and blessing (Gen. 28: 11–17; 32: 24–32) is in stark contrast with the strife between Keats's dreamer and the imperious divinity he confronts. Describing the power struggle between poet and priestess in a different critical vocabulary, Margaret Homans has observed, "Through the poem's carefully orchestrated and undecidable epistemological reversals, Moneta's initial dominance as a reader is subdued, and the very grandeur of Moneta and of the process dignifies the male authority that neutralizes the woman reader."[55] Whatever gender antagonism affects the interaction here, it is undeniable that, having survived the threat to his life, Keats's dreamer quickly regains his equilibrium and begins acting from a position of increased strength in his dealings with the goddess. Critics have tended to look on Moneta as a beneficent character,[56] but in her actions she is hardly the "benign goddess" the poet calls her in an effort at propitiation; she is a threatening figure whose effect is to intimidate and discourage him rather than comfort and inspire. The reader, of course, is always conscious – even when the dreaming poet seems not to be – that the dangerous goddess and her awe-inspiring temple are as much creations of the poet's brain as were the goddess and temple of the "Ode to Psyche," that other belated, vestigial divinity whose existence is so oddly dependent on having been rediscovered by a modern poet. Moneta is an imposing presence, as are all the authoritarian divinities we project. She is able to induce feelings of anguished guilt in the poet for his dreamer's negligence of the world's miseries. But the reader may pose objections where the narrator apparently cannot. What is this priestess doing here ministering in a ruined temple with no congregation in attendance? Why, for all her imposing manner, does she seem powerless to do anything but recall the dead past?

And by what ethic does a Greek goddess criticize the poet's social conscience? What ancient standard of charity or compassion allows her to praise "those to whom the misery of the world are misery and will not let them rest"? "Where," Haydon asked, "were the hospitals in the ancient world?" And Haydon was not alone among Keats's friends in questioning the social conscience of the Greeks. In November 1819, the first of Hazlitt's lectures on the Age of Elizabeth insisted that modern humanitarianism derived not from classical culture but from the revolutionary teachings of Jesus Christ:

The very idea of abstract benevolence, of the desire to do good because another wants our services, and of regarding the human race as one family, the offspring of one common parent, is hardly to be found in any other code or system. . . The Greeks and Romans never thought of considering others, but as they were Greeks or Romans, as they were bound to them by certain positive ties, or, on the other hand, as separated from them by fiercer antipathies. Their virtues were the virtues of political machines, their vices were the vices of demons, ready to inflict or to endure pain with obdurate and remorseless inflexibility of purpose.[57]

We do not know whether Keats ever heard such sentiments from Hazlitt (he did not attend the lecture in question but was given a report on it [*Letters* 2: 230]), or whether he arrived at similar conclusions on his own. At any rate he too had come to realize that Greek religion was, at best, no more conducive to human welfare than the Christianity that replaced it. Moneta's sponsorship of humanitarian endeavor sounds strange coming from this sphinx-like figure who would have watched "with obdurate and remorseless inflexibility" as the poet died and rotted at her feet (1: 107–17).

But if "Greek religion" had lost its political virtue (along with its cheerfulness), there is no sign that Keats was preferring Haydon's Christian alternative. He had firmly closed off that retreat in his "vale of Soul-making" letter, in which Christianity's offer of redemption from this "vale of tears" is dismissed as "a little circumscribed straightened notion." More than one critic has discerned a resemblance to Jesus Christ in Moneta's appearance,[58] and we are probably meant to recall Jesus here along with other "palpable and named mediators" in the history of religion. Ministering before a statue of a supreme divinity whose features are too high, too "cloudy" to be seen clearly, Moneta represents all those surrogates and intermediaries, superfluous at best, pernicious at worst, that the world's religions have interposed between God and man. The poet wonders, "Whose altar this; for whom this incense curls; what image this whose face I cannot see" (1: 212–13), and he has to take Moneta's word as an answer. She carries her arcane knowledge in "the dark secret chambers of her skull" (1: 278) and insists on interpreting for the poet the story of the Titans, whose sorrow, she says, is "too huge for mortal tongue," and she claims the necessity of translating her account if the poet is to understand it properly.

> Mortal, that thou may'st understand aright,
> I humanize my saying to thine ear,
> Making comparisons of earthly things;
> Or thou might'st better listen to the wind,
> Whose language is to thee a barren noise,
> Though it blows legend-laden through the trees.   (2: 1–6)

In thus arrogating to herself the sole right to interpret the history of the gods, she assumes the posture of all priests; indeed, "priestess," a

title she gives herself, is the poet's final name for her (1: 227; 2: 53).
Her condescension is shown to be mere priestcraft when the poet
demonstrates that his own narrative competence is a match for hers,
as is his intellectual grasp of things divine:

> there grew
> A power within me of enormous ken,
> To see as a God sees. . . I set myself
> Upon an eagle's watch, that I might see
> And seeing ne'er forget.   (1: 302–4, 308–10)

Apart from illustrating the questionable credentials of self-proclaimed oracles, in another sense Moneta represents the irrelevance
of religious myths and rituals that operate in temples secluded from
the suffering world. Of the benefactors of humanity, those who "feel
the giant agony of the world, / And more, like slaves to poor
humanity, / Labour for mortal good" she says: "They seek no
wonder but the human face. . . They come not here, they have no
thought to come" (1: 157–9, 163–5). Her accusatory question, "What
benefit canst thou do, or all thy tribe, To the great World?" (1: 167–
68) might, then, be directed back at her. To those with humanity's
best interests at heart, the "giant agony of the world" (1: 157) is of
more compelling interest than the giant agony of the gods which the
poet is invited to witness.[59]

Moneta's ruined Greek temple, then, is emblematic of the decline
of religion as a force in society, of the futility of its attempts to
concretize and control the Divine, and of its detachment from, even
its antagonism to, mankind's temporal welfare. In presenting her
temple as a shrine of dead and irrelevant religions, I think Keats may
have been recalling another ruined sanctuary that had been used in
this way in a celebrated poem by a contemporary. In the induction
to *The Fall of Hyperion*, one catches persistent echoes of the opening
stanzas of Canto 2 of Byron's *Childe Harold* – a poem that Keats read
and admired during the period of his youthful adulation of the noble
poet.[60] The particular stanzas I have in mind attracted more
attention than others at the time because of their impudent skepticism. Whether or not Byron's poem directly inspired Keats's, it
provides an interesting parallel, since it too draws connections
between a ruined temple, an isolated, vestigiary goddess, and the
paradise of which fanatics dream. The Byronic narrator sits in the
ruined temple of the "son of Saturn" looking at the Acropolis – "yon

fane / On high, where Pallas lingered, loth to flee / The latest relic of her ancient reign," and addresses the goddess:

> Ancient of days! august Athena! where,
> Where are thy men of might? thy grand in soul?
> Gone – glimmering through the dream of things that were . . .

> Look on this spot – a nation's sepulchre!
> Abode of gods, whose shrines no longer burn.
> Even gods must yield – religions take their turn:
> 'Twas Jove's – 'tis Mahomet's – and other creeds
> Will rise with other years, till man shall learn
> Vainly his incense soars, his victim bleeds;
> Poor child of Doubt and Death, whose hope is built on reeds.[61]

Like Byron's, Keats's ruined Greek temple symbolizes the declension and the futility of religion. But Byron could look back on the faith of antiquity with something like nostalgia, the response of a person for whom Greek religion does not present an intellectual challenge. For Keats, Moneta's religion is, although an ancient cult, still unaccountably impressive and powerful, even threatening. The imposing priestess must still be struggled with and overcome.

The radicalism of Keats's new attitude to Greek myth, his final response to the argument between Hunt and Haydon, was the poet's plainest reaction in verse to the political crisis that shook England in 1819. Like many of his countrymen, Keats found his liberalism turning to radicalism when, after a summer of social unrest, peaceful protesters in Manchester were massacred by local troops set on by Anglican clergy serving as magistrates. That collusion of civil and ecclesiastical power would have reminded anyone who needed reminding that the struggle for liberty in England was a war on two fronts. While recent examinations of Keats's politics have looked closely at his response to the Peterloo massacre,[62] they have not very carefully considered the religious dimension of that public crisis as it affected Keats and his liberal contemporaries. It was at the height of the angry national debate following Peterloo that Richard Carlile was tried and convicted on a charge of blasphemous libel for having published *The Age of Reason* along with other anti-Christian writings. Carlile had been closely associated in the public mind with Peterloo, since he had himself attended the Manchester meeting and had published eye-witness accounts of the atrocities, accounts that became the basis of the radical version of what had taken place, and for publication of which he became subject to additional indictments for seditious libel.[63] During the period when he was writing *The Fall of Hyperion*, Keats was as absorbed by the blasphemy trial as he was by the political aftershocks of the Peterloo Massacre. The prosecution was in his view an event "of great moment"; he predicted that it "would light a flame [that the government] could not extinguish" (*Letters* 2: 194).

The trial attracted widespread attention among liberals in England and abroad. The publisher's uncompromising skepticism polarized public opinion, forcing his sympathizers toward more radical religious positions than they might otherwise have adopted. For many the choice became one between Christianity and Carlile's brand of radical deism. For the first time, Leigh Hunt used the term "deist" to describe his own position and predicted the eventual triumph of deism as the de facto national religion of England.[64] Byron too predicted that Carlile's suffering for conscience's sake would win new proselytes to deistic beliefs, comparing the publisher to Socrates, Jesus, and "all who dare to oppose the most notorious abuses of the name of God and the mind of man."[65] Shelley, in an open letter from Italy defending Carlile, suggested that there was now no alternative between a discredited, state-sponsored Christianity and the kind of radical religious views articulated by Paine and his publisher. "What men of any rank in society from their talents are *not* Deists whose understandings have been unbiassed by the allurements of worldly interest? Which of our great literary characters not receiving emolument from the advocating a system of religion inseparably connected with the source of that emolument, is not a Deist?"[66] Whereas Leigh Hunt's endorsement of Greek religion as a cheerful alternative to British Christianity had once divided the literary world into Christians and Grecians, Shelley now saw the division lying between salaried Christianity and the kind of radical religious skepticism championed by Carlile. The only answer to repressive superstition was rational religion in its purest, most uncompromising form.

Given the religious revival that Britain was experiencing at this time, it seemed to be an urgent political necessity for liberals to sponsor a radical counterweight to a resurgent and increasingly reactionary Christianity. This new rationalism had as little tolerance for ancient superstition as for more modern kinds. In its account of Carlile's prosecution *The Examiner* quoted from the trial transcript the following example of Paine's blasphemy. *The Age of Reason* said of

Jesus Christ, "So far from his being the Son of God, he did not exist even as a man; that he is merely an imaginary or allegorical character, as Apollo, Hercules, Jupiter, and all the deities of antiquity were."[67] Or, as Keats had put it, "as one part of the human species must have their carved Jupiter; so another part must have the palpable and named Mediator and saviour, their Christ their Oromanes and their Vishnu" (*Letters* 2: 103). Whereas he had once embraced Greek myth as a positive alternative to Christianity, he now, in his last major effort in poetry, appeared determined to renounce it as a surrogate for all religion that is built on mystery and fear and that distracts the attention of humanity from its own intellectual, political, and economic servility.

One sees clearly in *The Fall of Hyperion* signs of the renunciation of the old myths, even those that had been particularly dear to Keats. His beloved legend of Endymion is implicitly denied, along with the Greek mythopoeic imagination that invented it, when the poet says of Moneta's eyes,

> they saw me not,
> But in blank splendour beamed like the mild moon,
> Who comforts those she sees not, who knows not
> What eyes are upward cast.   (1: 268–71)

Such realism makes Keats's first long Greek poem seem naive and credulous, for example in the hero's long, ardent declaration of love for the moon (3: 144–89). And when in *The Fall of Hyperion* Apollo is invited to send his "misty pestilence" to kill all fraudulent and incompetent poets (1: 204–10), we are reminded for the first time in Keats's verse that the poet-healer, who had once symbolized Keats's "entire complex of aesthetic values,"[68] is also traditionally "the author of plagues and contagious diseases" and the god whom Homer describes "shooting his arrows in various directions at the defenceless sons of men."[69] The primary sources of Keats's knowledge of Greek myth – Lempriere, Tooke, and Spence – had all referred to Apollo as the god of disease and poison,[70] but until this point Keats had, in Leigh Hunt's manner, expurgated the "gloomy" aspects of his story. Now, evidently, he no longer saw the need to elide the negative or problematic features of the old tales.

"A post-Christian man is not a Pagan," said C. S. Lewis. "The post-Christian is cut off from the Christian past and doubly from the Pagan past."[71] Keats offered his stringent "system of soul-creation" as an alternative to Christianity, which he characterized as an "affront [to] our reason and humanity." Keats's new system left no room for palpable, personal deities, or mediators, or saviors, and the political crisis of autumn 1819 reinforced for him the necessity of rejecting all religion but the "abstract adoration of the Deity" allowed by the austere piety of Paine's radical faith.[72] He had determined to reason his way toward abstract adoration without the common supports of community or tradition that are usually necessary to the religious life. Of the essential truths of religion, Shelley had written earlier in the year, "each to itself must be the oracle." All other oracles were silent, and no resurrection of Pan to restore their voices was to be expected or desired. The priestcraft of the priestess Moneta had nothing to reveal to a poet but an old story of dying gods. As he relived the last agony of those fated divinities, the poet found that he could now get by without their ambiguous mediation.

> Without stay or prop
> But my own weak mortality, I bore
> The load of this eternal quietude.   (1: 389–91)

CHAPTER 6

The Christian monster

Mary Shelley merits attention in any study of the British Romantic period, not only because of her close personal relationship with many of the poets and political philosophers who exemplified what her husband called "the spirit of the age" but also because she developed her own original critical perspective on the values represented by that spirit, a perspective that has earned increasing attention and respect in recent revaluations of British Romanticism.[1] More importantly, she created the most famous fiction to have emerged from the Romantic context, a book that has had a broader cultural influence than any other literary product of the age. Much of that influence can be attributed to *Frankenstein*'s metaphysical resonance, to the sense readers have had that the book constitutes a disturbing critique of traditional religious accounts of the nature, origin, and purpose of human life. At its publication, the novel was generally understood to be, in a way that was not entirely clear, a contribution to the debate on the national religion that William Godwin, with other radicals and dissenters, had provoked in the 1790s.

Frankenstein was always suspected of being subversive in its religious tendency, even when the precise objectives of its hidden agenda were not clearly discerned. Partly because of the dedication to Godwin, the novel's earliest readers thought they detected immorality and impiety lurking beneath the book's surface. One uneasy reviewer complained of the novel's "incongruity . . . with our established and most sacred notions" and protested that its "dark and gloomy views of nature and of man [bordered] too closely on impiety . . . Some of our highest and most reverential feelings receive a shock from the conception on which it turns, so as to produce a painful and bewildered state of mind while we peruse it. We are accustomed, happily, to look upon the creation of a living and intelligent being as a work that is fitted only to inspire a religious emotion, and there is an impropriety, to say no worse, in placing it in any other light."[2] The common interpretation of *Frankenstein* as a cautionary tale warning against the temptation to usurp the creative power of God began with the early reception of the book.

In more recent criticism, the notion has persisted that there is something ambiguous or oblique in the book's religious disposition. One commonly articulated suspicion is that the novel was meant as a criticism of Genesis, as a "Miltonic travesty" and "a nightmarish parody of patriarchal religion."[3] A quite different suggestion came from Leslie Tannenbaum, who argued that the novel's allusions to *Paradise Lost* work ironically to point up Victor Frankenstein's failures as a creator in contrast with Milton's more loving and responsible Divinity.[4] Tannenbaum's interpretation was part of a general reassessment of the novel carried out during the 1970s, principally by feminist and psychoanalytic critics who found in the novel a subtle but insistent protest against some of the ideas and much of the conduct of the author's father, William Godwin, and of her husband, Godwin's disciple, Percy Bysshe Shelley. This revisionist reading sees Victor Frankenstein as a composite of Godwin and Shelley (and perhaps Byron as well), and the Monster, the novel's most sympathetic character, as a representation of the author herself – the victim, to an extent the product, of Godwinian theory and experimentation. And the novel is therefore interpreted as asking how it is possible that a man like Frankenstein (or like Shelley or Godwin), considered by himself and others to be the benevolent benefactor of his species, can somehow, with the best intentions and the highest principles, bring misery and ruin upon those around him as the result of his experiments with human life.[5]

Since Miltonic religion and Godwinian "philosophy" offer radically antithetical views of human nature and destiny, one is left wondering at which ideology the novel's satiric or parodic intent is primarily directed. That Milton's system is employed to show the inadequacies of Godwin's indicates one answer; that the Miltonic faith is espoused by a homicidal freak suggests another. The religious equivocality is, of course, only one aspect of a larger pattern of ambivalence that has been detected in the novel. The dedication to Godwin of a book now generally perceived as embodying a protest against Godwin's kind of radicalism suggests, as U. C. Knoepflmacher has observed, the "conflicting emotions of allegiance and resentment" that always characterized Mary Shelley's relationship with her father.[6] This conflict is one way of accounting for the opposing tendencies detectable in the novel's metaphysics. By making a monster the exponent of the religious system that stood in radical ideological opposition to her father's views, she set up a curious dialectic by which she was able to call the Godwinian order into question without distinctly affirming the Christian alternative, which functions so ambiguously as to leave its validity in question. What I argue here is that the ineffectual, baffled Christian faith of the Monster, the primary victim and critic of benevolent philosophy in *Frankenstein*, is used by Mary Shelley to call into question both Christianity itself and the ideology that Godwin had offered as an alternative to it.

When one sets out to read *Frankenstein* in search of its religious meaning, what is immediately striking is the total absence of the supernatural as a functioning element in the plot. Judith Wilt has called attention to the rich freight of religious imagery and allusion the novel inherited from the "God-haunted Gothic tradition,"[7] but on inspection these religious elements show themselves to be purely decorative. One need only compare the book with that other great horror myth that originated in Geneva in 1816, which, as it culminated in Bram Stoker's *Dracula*, depends so heavily on powerful sacramentals and effective necromancy, to be reminded how bare of supernatural machinery *Frankenstein* is. Indeed, the very lack of religious content is one of the things that gives the story its peculiar horror. Neither God nor demon has any role to play in this tale of curiosity, pride, and error, in which humanity has only itself to blame and fear. The absence of the supernatural is not surprising in a novel emanating from the Shelley circle. What *is* peculiar is that on those occasions when traditional religion is introduced, it is not subjected to the kind of criticism or derision one might anticipate. On the contrary, Christian belief is almost always depicted in a positive light. Practical concerns about the novel's marketability would have encouraged discretion in religious editorializing, but it would not account for, say, the sympathetic treatment of Justine Moritz's Catholic faith, since in English Gothic fiction Popery was always fair game. Justine's religious beliefs and piety, reported uncritically by Victor Frankenstein, are attractive enough to neutralize the negative impression given by the priest who threatens her with "excommunication and hellfire" for continuing to maintain her innocence. Her faith brings consolation and serenity to "the saintly

sufferer" (Victor's phrase) as she awaits execution, a serenity that is
in striking contrast with Victor's own paralyzing anxiety.[8]

Although Victor Frankenstein's own religious views are never
clearly articulated, it is evident that he is not a Christian. M.
Krempe's joking remark that Victor "believed in Cornelius Agrippa
as firmly as in the gospel" (p. 68) serves only to remind us of the
absence of any other suggestion that he believed in the gospel at all.
In fact, although he refers to himself and Elizabeth as children sent
from heaven and periodically exclaims "Great God!" – and although
he ransacks the Christian maledictory tradition to find terms of
abuse with which to berate his creature, it becomes clear early on
that Victor is not even a theist in any traditional sense. The 1831
revision allows him to indulge in some brief metaphysical meditations
in the ravine of Arve,[9] where, like Percy Shelley, he detects intimations of Omnipotence, but in the 1818 edition, and as a general rule
in 1831, Victor demonstrates a scientist's interest in proximate causes
rather than a philosopher's concern for ultimate ones. At the same
time, he is shown to have more than his quota of superstition, such as
his belief that various good and evil agencies were struggling for
control of his destiny (p. 45). This lack of a coherent metaphysics may
be blamed in part for his irresponsible creation of a living being with
so little forethought given to the meaning or consequences of his act.

By contrast, his creature, from the beginning of his existence,
shows a strong metaphysical curiosity. He subjects himself early on to
a rigorous catechetical inquisition: "Who was I? What was I?
Whence did I come? What was my destination? These questions
continually recurred," he says, "but I was unable to solve them"
(p. 128). The answers come to him unexpectedly when he stumbles
by chance upon a copy of *Paradise Lost*. He receives the poem literally
as a revelation, "a true history" as he calls it (p. 129), not only of the
events recorded in Genesis but of the subsequent unfolding of the
divine redemptive plan and even of the development of Christian
doctrine as presented in Michael's prophecy to Adam in Book 12.
Milton's epic provides the Monster with an organized, identifiable
set of religious beliefs, a quite adequately orthodox creed.[10] He
becomes not only a theist but what one has to call a Christian, since
he accepts as true the central tenets of the Christian faith. And it is
worth noting that his acceptance of Milton's religion is not a case of
vulgar superstition or credulous ignorance seduced by the art of a
persuasive poet. The Monster had already heard the standard

Enlightenment critique of Christianity earlier in the book, when he
eavesdropped as Felix DeLacey read aloud and offered "very minute
explanations" of Volney's *Ruins*, which runs through, in some detail,
the long catalogue of Christian crime and imposture.[11] When, therefore, the monster accepts the religion of *Paradise Lost* he does so
having heard the worst of what was being said against it in his time.
He embraces the Miltonic world-view in preference to the critical
rationalism of modern "philosophy," with which Mary Shelley has
thus taken pains to acquaint him.

The Monster's Christian concepts, attitudes, and language affect
significantly our assessment of him and also of the society that rejects
him. The film director James Whale saw this tendency in the novel
and emphasized it when in *The Bride of Frankenstein* (1935) he depicted
the Monster as a kind of Christ-figure. While that was surely not
Mary Shelley's intent, the Christian frame of reference in which she
placed the Monster accounts for much of our sympathetic response
to him. His religious beliefs and language do not estrange or
gothicize him; on the contrary, they situate him in a familiar universe
in which the reader, even today, feels intellectually more at home
than in the uncharted ontological borderland that Victor Frankenstein inhabits. In addition to providing him with a history and a map
of the cosmos (to guide his and our perception of his place in the
order of things), Milton equips the Monster with an identifiable set of
values, of ethical norms, a standard of right and wrong to which he
appeals with fine rhetorical effect when hurling reproaches at his
negligent creator, reminding him over and over of the Christian
duties of charity and pity for the unfortunate, demanding as his due
not only justice (Godwin would give him that), but also clemency and
even affection, and promising in return mildness and docility.
Victor's own rhetorical borrowings from the Christian tradition, by
contrast, seem histrionic and factitious: "Fiend that thou art!" he
cries out in a typical diatribe, "The tortures of hell are too mild a
vengeance for thy crimes. Wretched devil!" (p. 99).

It would not be a mere flippancy to say that the Monster is a better
Christian than Victor Frankenstein. Some approximation of that
perception contributes in an important way to our assessment of him
as a moral being. The ideal of "benevolence" that Victor claims as
his motivating principle and that is so problematic in its fruits
compares unfavorably with the practical charity (to use a less
"enlightened," traditionally Christian term) demonstrated in the

Monster's humble, anonymous services to the DeLacey family. The word "humble" suggests another Christian virtue that one may justifiably claim for the Monster. The student of *Paradise Lost* seems to have learned a lesson about humanity's place in the order of things that makes him less likely than Victor to succumb to hubris, or – once again to use a more characteristically Christian term – the sin of pride. The Monster's humility is revealed most clearly in an attitude that in 1816 was especially characteristic of a Christian consciousness, a sense of sin. While his Christian beliefs do not prevent the Monster from becoming a criminal, they do lead him to acknowledge his sins (as he calls them) and the apparently sinful nature that has led to their commission. The Monster's acceptance of moral culpability is a refreshing contrast with Victor's nearly invincible innocence. Frankenstein's unwillingness to admit to any serious moral fault is one of the things that make him seem less human than his creature. When the Monster is driven to crime by frustration and rage, he does not justify himself morally. He acknowledges his feelings of revenge and hatred to be wrong and "hellish." Robert Walton calls him "Hypocritical fiend!" but the Monster is not in the least a hypocrite. He freely confesses what he calls "the frightful catalogue of my sins" (pp. 220–21).

And yet, despite his willingness to confess and repent, there is no religious consolation, and there can be no salvation for this believer. The strangest aspect of the Monster's Christianity is his realization that, although he accepts the truth of the Christian faith, the faith is uniquely irrelevant to him. Nowhere in *Paradise Lost* can he find any parallel for his condition:

Like Adam, I was apparently united by no link to any other being in existence; but his state was far different from mine in every other respect. He had come forth from the hands of God a perfect creature, happy and prosperous, guarded by the special care of his Creator; he was allowed to converse with and acquire knowledge from beings of a superior nature: but I was wretched, helpless, and alone. (p. 129)

And when he learns from Victor's notebooks the circumstances of his own special creation, the contrast becomes even more painful. He says to Victor:

God, in pity, made man beautiful and alluring, after his own image; but my form is a filthy type of yours, more horrid even from the very resemblance. Satan had his companions, fellow devils, to admire and encourage him; but I am solitary and abhorred. (130)

Only in fantasy can he live in Milton's cosmos and share its joys and rewards.

I allowed my thoughts, unchecked by reason, to ramble in the fields of Paradise, and dared to fancy amiable and loving creatures sympathizing with my feelings and cheering my gloom; their angelic countenances breathed smiles of consolation. But it was all a dream; no Eve soothed my sorrows nor shared my thoughts; I was alone. I remembered Adam's supplication to his Creator. But where was mine? He had abandoned me, and in the bitterness of my heart I cursed him. (131)

"Adam's supplication to his Creator" in *Paradise Lost* includes the lines used as an epigraph to *Frankenstein*:

> Did I request thee, Maker, from my clay
> To mould me Man, did I solicit thee
> From darkness to promote me?[12]

The Maker's response to this protest is a determination to redeem mankind by sacrificing Himself. In striking contrast is Victor's response to his own creature's complaint: "You reproach me with your creation; come on, then, that I may extinguish the spark which I so negligently bestowed" (p. 95). We are told in scripture that God does not desire the death of the sinner, but Victor from the beginning desires only the Monster's death. Repentance, a change of heart, is never allowed as an option. While one is conscious throughout the novel that the local genius of Rousseau presided over its conception in Switzerland, nothing is ever said of that other Genevan ghost, John Calvin. Yet as often as the Monster's development brings Rousseau to mind, his creator's response to him recalls the stern theology of the reformer. The Monster is treated as a being who is totally depraved: "His soul is as hellish as his form," says Victor, "full of treachery and fiendlike malice" (pp. 198–99). Victor plays the role of punishing divinity despite the Monster's quiet reminder that he too is a creature – had a creator. "You, my creator, abhor me; what hope can I gather from your fellow creatures, who owe me nothing?"

Thus cast out from human society, the Monster is more alone than any being in the Miltonic order that he accepts as real. Having been repudiated by his own creator, he has no relationship to any other. He is metaphysically as well as physically a monster, a surd in the theological system to which he subscribes. While spiritual isolation is not uncommon in English Romantic literature, Frankenstein's

Monster is unique in his peculiar ontological loneliness. He resembles to some degree those other trapped individuals driven to violence by a kind of religious desperation, Byron's Cain and Shelley's Beatrice Cenci. Cain likewise can find no mental refuge in a Biblical milieu from which there is no escape, and Beatrice is entrammeled in a religious power structure she has to accept as inevitable. Each illustrates from his or her own experience the intolerability rather than the invalidity of an orthodox religious system. Their protest involves not heterodoxy so much as what one is tempted to call paradoxy – a feeling that one is somehow outside, set apart from, a religious system whose truth one cannot deny. But the Monster's ontological plight is even worse than that of Cain or Beatrice. Cain is repudiated by a God who is acknowledged, even by Cain himself, as the Supreme Being and he is encouraged in his disaffection by yet another powerful supernatural personage who assures him that if he is to be damned he will have company in his eternal misery. Beatrice can demand, if only rhetorically, vindication in the next world from the same God that her executioners profess to worship. But Frankenstein's creature has no reason to expect divine protection or even attention; there is for him no mercy, no redemption, no heavenly destiny. The most he expects after death is that "My spirit will sleep in peace, or if it thinks, it will not surely think thus" (p. 223). Victor Frankenstein is all the god he has, and the Monster with a logical and desperate kind of piety prays to him continually, wrestling with him like Jacob or Job with their own visions of God, but receiving neither blessing nor insight.

At times *Frankenstein* seems as much a parody of Job as of Genesis, and a comparison with the Old Testament drama serves to illustrate further the Monster's anomalous religious status. When he pleads with Victor, "Listen to me, and then if you can, and if you will, destroy the work of your hands" (p. 96), one hears a distinct echo of Job 10, in which creature says to creator:

Is it good unto thee that thou shouldst oppress, that thou shouldst despise the work of thine hands . . . ?

Thine hands have made me and fashioned me together round about; yet thou dost destroy me.

Remember, I beseech thee, that thou hast made me as the clay; and wilt thou bring me into dust again?

Thou hast clothed me with skin and flesh, and hast fenced me with bones and sinews . . .

The Monster resembles Job in other ways too, such as his inability to understand the reason for the suffering he has endured even when still innocent of any offense. Like Job he attempts to justify himself by defining a rational relationship with his creator: "I am thy creature, and I will be even mild and docile to my natural lord and king if thou wilt also perform thy part, the which thou owest me" (p. 100). He is also like Job in his inability to connect gratuitous suffering with the supposedly benevolent God revealed to him in *Paradise Lost*, preserving his faith intact despite his inability to understand.

But the Monster's intellectual dilemma is curiously more complicated than Job's because he has to reckon with two different creators. Not long after reading Milton's account of the creation of Adam and Eve, the Monster discovers Victor Frankenstein's laboratory notes describing his own creation. As he says to Victor,

Everything is related in them which bears reference to my accursed origin; the whole detail of that series of disgusting circumstances which produced it is set in view; the minutest description of my odious and loathsome person is given, in language which painted your own horrors and rendered mine indelible . . . Why did you form a monster so hideous that even *you* turned from me in disgust? God, in pity, made man beautiful and alluring, after his own image, but my form is a filthy type of yours, more horrid even from the very resemblance. (p. 130)

In the lower ontological context of the Monster's creation by Victor Frankenstein, the creature's sufferings have not even an educational or inspirational value; they are no test of fortitude or faith; they manifest neither his own virtues nor God's inscrutable righteousness. While Job's Creator rejects all claims upon Him by reason of His utter transcendence, the Monster's human creator repudiates the claimant out of something more like human self-righteousness and vanity. By contrast with Job's confrontation with the whirlwind, the Monster's encounter with his human creator only accentuates Victor's diminutive stature, both physical and moral. Having tried humbling himself before this creator and having experienced only rejection, the creature inverts the Jobean archetype by threatening devastation upon his vulnerable maker and all his household. The Monster finally becomes a kind of existentialist criminal, driven to violence by realization of the absurdity of his situation. It is as though Job, taking his wife's advice, had agreed at last to curse his creator and die. The Monster's resemblance to Job finally serves only to accentuate the difference between the two figures, demonstrating

again the creature's peculiar isolation from the sublimities as well as
the consolations of the Judaeo-Christian religious tradition he
accepts as true and from which he has so strangely been precluded.

Why did Mary Shelley create this religious monster, this discon-
nected Christian whose faith brings no hope? The question acquires
particular interest in light of the growing critical consensus that the
reader's sympathetic response to the Monster is an effect of the
author's own identification with him. "Beneath the contorted visage
of Frankenstein's creature," wrote U. C. Knoepflmacher, "lurks a
timorous yet determined female face."[13] In the Monster's spiritual
isolation might not one see a projection of Mary Shelley's own
situation in the Godwinian milieu, living in an ideological order
whose general validity she accepted but whose value, at least for
herself, she could not always clearly see. In relation to this system she
was in the paradoxical situation of her monster with regard to
Christianity – subscribing intellectually to its beliefs but feeling in a
peculiar way excluded from its proclaimed blessings and consolations.

Anne Mellor has recently argued that Shelley's book champions a
counter-revolutionary ideology based on the bourgeois ideal of
family stability. "No revolutionary herself, Mary Shelley clearly
perceived the inherent danger in a Promethean, revolutionary
ideology: commitment to an abstract good can justify an emotional
detachment from present human relationships and family obligations, a willingness to sacrifice the living to a cause whose final
consequences cannot be fully controlled, and an obsession with
realizing a dream that too often masks an egotistical wish for
personal power." Another recent book has likewise detected in
Frankenstein "an uncompromising critique of optimistic myths of
revolutionary change."[14]

Lee Sterrenberg has found in the book a subversion of all
ideology,[15] the result of a profound if not completely articulate
disenchantment with the actualization of her father's and her
husband's moral ideals. There was at this time large room for
disenchantment with "philosophy," "benevolence," and "virtue" as
defined and practiced in the Shelley family circle. Mary Shelley was
hard at work on *Frankenstein* in October of 1816 when Fanny Imlay,
her half-sister, committed suicide, and Godwin, dreading unfavor-
able publicity, refused to claim the body or acknowledge kinship and
allowed the young woman to be buried anonymously in a pauper's
grave. Two months later came the suicide of Harriet Shelley,

pregnant with an illegitimate child, and Shelley's apparent inability to accept responsibility or even express remorse for the fate of his abandoned wife. One month afterward there was the birth of Claire Clairmont's child by Byron, a child dismissed with apparent indifference by a father who refused any further communication with the mother. Much of this behavior Mary Shelley would have heard rationalized according to Godwinian notions of moral pragmatism, the supremacy of the individual conscience, and the triumph of reason over emotion. After Fanny's death, for example, when she wrote to console her father, his cool pedagogical reply was: "I cannot but thank you for your strong expressions of sympathy. I do not see however that sympathy can be of any service to me."[16]

How, among these prophets of universal justice and benevolence, could there have arisen so much misery, and so much obduracy in response to misery? If common sense suggested that something had gone wrong with the Godwinian system, Mary Shelley would have found it difficult to formulate or express an effective critical response, living as she did in an intellectual milieu where Godwinian theory was in control of the premises, where the ideas and actions of her father and his disciples were, almost by definition, morally unassailable. To question the system she would have had to assume a position outside it, and in doing so she would have found herself sharing strategic ideological ground with other philosophical critics of Godwin. Most obviously outside the Godwinian system, and most potently in ideological opposition to it, was Christianity, which had recently been offering intellectual sanctuary to disaffected Godwinians of the caliber of Wordsworth, Coleridge, and Southey. If her book was meant as a subversion of Godwinian-Shelleyan ideology, it would have been nicely subversive to make the victim of philosophic experimentation a partisan of that Biblical faith to which her father and husband were sworn ideological enemies. To have enlisted the intellectual and cultural force of a Christian ideology in which she did not believe as a weapon against another which she was beginning to question was a brilliant bit of dialectical strategy, allowing her to challenge one system without distinctly affirming the other – since the other appears, after all, only as the content of an epic poem naively accepted as true by a creature who is not precisely human.

One might also characterize such sympathy as an appeal from her father's principles to those of her mother. Before she met Godwin, Mary Wollstonecraft's religious views were conventionally, even ardently, Christian, in the "rational" style of doctrine and practice associated with dissenting preachers like Richard Price, who was her spiritual director. One finds throughout her writings passages like the following, written in 1786:

Here we have no resting place nor any stable comfort but what arises from our resignation to the will of Heaven and our firm reliance on those precious promises delivered to us by Him who brought light and immortality into the world – He has told us not only that we *may inherit* Aeternal life but that *we* shall be *changed* if we do not perversely reject the offered Grace.[17]

Although the character and intensity of her religious faith were altered by radical associations, Wollstonecraft remained a theist and in the year of her death could write irritably to Godwin: "How can you blame me for taken [sic] refuge in the idea of a God, when I despair of finding sincerity on earth."[18] In *Frankenstein*, Safie's mother, whom one critic sees as "a cartoon, distorted but recognizable, of the author's mother, Mary Wollstonecraft,"[19] is honored for her Christian faith – or at least for that faith's social effects. Although they were living in an Islamic society, "she instructed her daughter in the tenets of her religion, and taught her to aspire to higher powers of intellect, and an independence of spirit, forbidden to the female followers of Muhammad" (p. 124). Here is yet another of the novel's sympathetic, isolated Christians, cultivating an independent religious perspective amid a community of infidels, and passing her faith on to her daughter as an assurance of intellectual independence.

All this is not to suggest that Mary Shelley herself was some sort of crypto-Christian. All evidence indicates that, while she was more obviously sympathetic toward theism than Shelley or Godwin, she would, at the time of *Frankenstein*, have subscribed generally to the critique of Christianity expressed, for example, in the text and notes of *Queen Mab* – agreeing with Shelley that the Christian religion was dying and that, as he put it, "Milton's poem alone will give permanency to the remembrance of its absurdities."[20] But when she herself selects Milton's poem as the vehicle of revelation to the character with whom she most sympathizes, and when her novel consistently points not to the absurdities and iniquities of Christianity but to its positive qualities and effects, one detects symptoms of a divided mind. This is an ambivalence with which even her husband might have sympathized. I will point out in the next chapter that Percy Shelley's own views on Christianity were complicated by his increasing admiration for the character and teachings of Jesus Christ. It was in 1817, while Mary was hard at work on *Frankenstein*, that he wrote his "Essay on Christianity," which expresses in rhapsodic terms his admiration for the beauty and benevolence of Christ's doctrines. Later he would go so far as to say that the political and social ideals of Jesus were more laudable and even more radical than those of Godwin. In the manner of Shelley's "Essay," *Frankenstein*'s Monster appeals to the Christian ideals of love and compassion, suggesting that in a truly Christian social order the cruelty and injustice he has suffered would not be possible. If only in this sense, Mary Shelley's novel shows its participation in the reformational enterprise of Romanticism.

E. P. Thompson speaks of the imaginatively fruitful transition period that may accompany the breakdown of old ideological allegiances before new ones are taken up. He points out that Wordsworth and Coleridge enjoyed their greatest creative moment in the 1790s when "they were isolated as Jacobins and they abominated Godwinian abstraction. They had broken out of the received culture and they were appalled by some features of the new."[21] Mary Wollstonecraft was another such casualty of transition, in Thompson's view, and I suggest that one can similarly understand her daughter's situation at the end of 1816. It is generally acknowledged that Mary Shelley's political and religious opinions became gradually more conservative as she grew older, and more than one critic sees this detachment from radicalism already at work in *Frankenstein*, with its insistence on the primacy of the domestic affections over all other considerations. Mary Poovey has argued persuasively that Mary Shelley was divided by conflicting impulses, one toward the Romantic ideal of creative independence and the other toward conformity with convention and propriety as dictated by her society. Poovey finds in *Frankenstein* a narrative strategy that "enables Shelley to express and efface herself at the same time and thus, at least partially, to satisfy her conflicting desires for self-assertion and social acceptance."[22]

In allowing the character who is the main focus of sympathy in her novel to express his protest against an unsatisfactory metaphysical order in language borrowed from the rival religious dispensation, Shelley may have been expressing the uneasiness of one fated to live in a transition period when the moral principles and social structures of the old Christian order were giving way to the yet untested ones proclaimed by Godwin, Shelley, and those who shared their vision of the future. In its allusions to Milton, Leslie Tannenbaum remarks, "*Frankenstein* points to the need for the kind of redemptive vision that the world it describes so flagrantly lacks."[23] It is as though, while she knew it was neither possible nor desirable to return to an earlier age of faith, Shelley felt that some counterweight to Godwinian rationalism was needed, something that placed a higher premium on the domestic virtues of tenderness, constancy, and mercy. Not Christianity perhaps, but something to carry forward the best values of Christianity was needed. Mary Shelley, too, was involved in the work of cultural salvage that Abrams speaks of in *Natural Supernaturalism*.

The positive treatment of Christianity in *Frankenstein*, then, seems to have been more an investigatory experiment than an expression of religious advocacy. Shelley was examining for herself the meaning and effect of Christian belief in an intellectual environment that was hostile to it. It appears that her own attitude to the Christian tradition was more sophisticated than her husband's, or at least more detached, in its ability to acknowledge Christianity's cultural value without endorsing its theology. Her creature's Miltonic faith accounts for much that is appealing, even beautiful, in his character; it clothes him with a cultural identity and at times a moral dignity that makes him more than a match for Victor Frankenstein in their competition for the reader's sympathy. But as religion, the Monster's Christianity is comfortless, ineffectual, and finally pointless. It does not prevent his crimes; it cannot forgive his sins; it cannot make him happy. If Mary Shelley was searching for an alternative to Godwinism, her book suggests that the most obvious alternative, Christianity, was not for her a viable one. There is an element of pathos in her handling of this which may suggest regret, or perhaps only nostalgia, for an older kind of spiritual security that was no longer available. Christopher Small observed that *Frankenstein* "deals in uncertainties much more difficult to resolve than any to be found in Godwin or, for that matter, in Milton."[24] In her Monster's strange metaphysical distress we can see a representation of Mary Shelley's own ambivalence, anxiety, and sense of isolation as she searched, independently, for a system of belief and consolation adequate to her own needs and those of the society in which she lived.

CHAPTER 7

The unknown God

The phrase "religious reformer" may sound paradoxical as applied to Percy Bysshe Shelley, whose ideas about reformation usually involved eradication of what most people call religion. Yet Shelley's theological dispositions were always subtler than his polemic stances suggested – a situation that has produced the critical anomaly of a self-proclaimed atheist who has been admired in every generation as a profound religious poet.[1] From the beginning, Shelley's readers have tended to divide into those who take his assertions of atheism as the deepest truth about him and those who find a contrary tendency to religious affirmation present in his poetry from the start.[2] An attempt to mediate these conflicting readings may tempt a critic to qualify or sentimentalize the meaning of religion until the term is broad enough to accommodate atheism – too often the tactic of readers who want their religion and their favorite lyric poet too. A better solution to the problem involves reconsidering the meaning of atheism, a word that in Shelley's time had no precise definition beyond polemical ones formulated by those to the right of the "atheist" on the spectrum of religious opinion.

One hesitates before attempting to mitigate the reality of Shelley's atheism or qualify his contempt for the Christian religion as it was embraced by most of his contemporaries; it is a stance that he maintained with unrelenting passion and vigor, and one for which he willingly suffered considerable personal hardship, beginning with his expulsion from Oxford for publishing and refusing to retract *The Necessity of Atheism*. To diminish its importance would be to betray his memory. But an observation made by James Thrower in connection with ancient religion seems to me appropriate to Shelley's own position: "The majority of thinkers whom later writers designated *atheoi* are found upon closer examination to deny only the notion of the gods as expressed in popular belief, and this more often than not as a prelude to the putting forward of a more sophisticated and developed conception of the divine."[3] Shelley made just such a qualification when he said of himself to Godwin, "I became in the popular sense of the word 'God' an Atheist."[4] As to the word atheist, the poet explained to Trelawny, "I used it to express my abhorrence of superstition; I took up the word, as a knight took up a gauntlet, in defiance of injustice."[5] And another of the poet's contemporaries, Henry Crabb Robinson, also found reason to question the absoluteness of Shelley's atheism. In 1836 Robinson, who was himself a Unitarian, read *Queen Mab* and concluded,

His atheism is very repulsive, but the God he denies seems to be after all but the God of the superstitious . . . He draws in one of his notes a picture of Christianity, or rather he sums up the Christian doctrine, and in such a way that perhaps Wordsworth would say: "This, I disbelieve as much as Shelley, but that is only the caricature and burlesque of Christianity." And yet this is the Christianity most men believe."[6]

Even at his most militantly irreligious, Shelley's expressions of atheism were always carefully qualified. For example, Queen Mab's bold assertion, "There is no God!" is immediately modified in a footnote: "This negation must be understood solely to affect a creative Deity. The hypothesis of a pervading Spirit coeternal with the universe remains unshaken."[7] Shelley was always distinguishing in this manner false conceptions of God from others that he allowed to be true, if only for the sake of argument. The deity whose existence Shelley denied was the one he called "the god of human error,"[8] a god that had little to do with the high conception of divinity that he entertained as an ideal all his life. My argument here is that Shelley himself cultivated such an exalted idea of what a Supreme Being might be that he was intolerant of any inadequate or distorted representation of it. He set himself up as a critic of religion not from a position outside the realm of belief, but from a position of higher authority and insight within that sphere. One of the primary influences on Shelley's "atheism," the Baron d'Holbach, had adopted a similar stance, appealing to a standard of religious purity that made most religions seem impious by contrast. "To be impious," says Holbach, "is to impute to God those crimes which would annihilate his divine perfections."[9] Given the kind of religion embraced by most of the world, Holbach insisted that atheism was the only honorable recourse for a scrupulous mind. In this sense, Shelley's atheism, his intolerance of all religion, can be seen as an expression of respect for a purer conception of divinity than most of the world was able or willing to imagine. Similarly, he made a point of distinguishing the authentic character of Jesus Christ from the misconstructions of it fostered by what he called "the popular religion." The actual teachings of Jesus, he said, "afford an example and an incentive to the attainment of true virtue, whilst the [erroneous interpretation of them] holds out a sanction and apology for every species of mean and cruel vice."[10]

When his angry political sonnet "England in 1819" characterized the religion of his country as "Christless, Godless, a book sealed," the poem was evidently imagining a Christlike, godly religion that British Christianity had failed to approximate, apparently because the national religion did not understand or could not accept the true character of God and Christ. The sonnet also, typically, uses scripture to substantiate its critique of the public religion of the day, recalling the prophet Isaiah's condemnation of the state religion of Israel:

And the vision of all is become unto you as the words of a book sealed, which men deliver to one that is learned, saying, Read this, I pray thee: and he saith, I cannot; for it is sealed . . . Wherefore the Lord said, Forasmuch as this people draw near me with their mouth, and with their lips do honour me, but have removed their heart far from me, and their fear toward me is taught by the precept of men: Therefore, behold, I will proceed to do a marvellous work among this people, even a marvelous work and a wonder: for the wisdom of their wise men shall perish, and the understanding of their prudent men shall be hid (Is. 29: 11–14).

In England, as in ancient Israel, corruption in the religious sphere has wrought disaster in the political order. Shelley uses the Biblical text to devastating effect in suggesting that George III – England's "old, mad, blind, despised, and dying King," his disreputable sons, and the nation's other "rulers who neither see, nor feel, nor know" are victims and portents of God's judgment on an irreligious people. The poem suggests that the state of the nation might be improved by a better religion, one that properly understood the character and will of God as revealed in Christ.

Shelley was more articulate when criticizing religious error than when characterizing the true, godly, Christian faith from which the religion of his country had deviated. In religious discourse he was disabled rhetorically by a philosophical reticence arising from his belief that ultimate reality was beyond the reach of human comprehension and human language. Shelley's skepticism has been traced through William Drummond to the influence of David Hume,[11] but he could have learned a similar epistemology from Plato, of whom Rudolf Otto wrote: "No one has enunciated more definitively than this master-thinker that God transcends all reason, in the sense that He is beyond the powers of our conceiving, not merely beyond our powers of comprehension. Therefore is it an impossible task both to discover the creator and father of this whole universe and to publish the discovery of him in words for all to understand."[12] Either Platonism or Humean skepticism would account for Shelley's insistence that in religion "the deep truth is imageless" (*Prometheus Unbound* II.iv.116). In this world, anything we predicate about God is likely to be an error and very likely a pernicious one. Even using the name God is dangerous, because it carries with it so much historical baggage of erroneous speculation. "The word 'God,' Shelley wrote, has been [and] will continue to be the source of numberless errors until it is erased from the nomenclature of Philosophy" (*Letters* 1: 35).

The safest course for the religious reformer, then, was a *via negativa* that identified religious error rather than affirming religious truth. In his 1819 essay "On Life," Shelley assigned this purgative function to "Philosophy," a word that carried, as it so often did in the polemic vocabulary of the time, the connotation of opposition to superstitious religion:

Philosophy, impatient as it may be to build, has much work yet remaining as pioneer for the overgrowth of ages. It makes one step towards this object; it destroys error, and the roots of error. It leaves, what is too often the duty of the reformer in political and ethical questions to leave, a vacancy. It reduces the mind to that freedom in which it would have acted, but for the misuses of words and signs, the instruments of its own creation.[13]

One can see Shelley using his talent for such reformational purposes in one of the great religious poems of our literature, "Mont Blanc," the central purpose of which is precisely to create such a vacancy in a place where religious error had previously gone unchallenged.

Shelley arrived at Chamounix in the summer of 1816 in the wake of a procession of pilgrims who had come there anticipating a religious experience – the kind of metaphysical *frisson* that the poet Thomas Gray had reported in letters whose publication helped make the valley a fashionable religious resort. "Not a precipice," Gray wrote, "not a torrent, not a cliff, but is pregnant with religion and poetry. There are certain scenes that would awe an atheist into belief

without help of other arguments."[14] A more formidable precursor
than Gray was a poet who had visited Mont Blanc more recently, but
only in imagination – Samuel Taylor Coleridge. His "Hymn Before
Sunrise, in the Vale of Chamouni" (first published in 1803 and
reprinted in *The Friend* in 1809) seems to have been consciously
offered as a contribution to the pious literary fashion inaugurated by
Gray. In an introductory note to the poem as originally published in
the *Morning Post*, Coleridge shows Gray's influence when he writes:
"the whole vale, its every light, its every sound, must needs impress
every mind not utterly callous with the thought – Who *would* be, who
could be an Atheist in this valley of wonders!"[15] It was this kind of
conventional and coercive religiosity that provoked Shelley, when he
arrived in the valley, to register as an atheist in one or more of the
local inns – a prank that, when it was reported in England, did
permanent damage to his reputation.

Shelley probably knew that Coleridge had never in fact seen Mont
Blanc, although he may not have known that much of his response to
Chamounix was borrowed, without acknowledgment, from the
German writer Friederike Brun, and therefore that his pious emotion
was secondhand in more senses than one.[16] Awareness of Coleridge's
plagiarism would only have reinforced his feeling that such confident
piety could not authentically be inspired by a clear vision of that
disquieting landscape. Shelley's poem contains what sound like
deliberate allusions to Coleridge's; gazing upon the same mountain,
the same fierce, ceaselessly raving river, the same black, jagged rocks,
the poets ask similar questions: "Who called you forth from night
and utter death?" "Who gave you your invulnerable life?" The
questions are similar; the answers are strikingly different.[17]

Coleridge/Brun finds positive religious meaning everywhere:

> Ye Ice-falls! ye that from the mountain's brow
> Adown enormous ravines sweep amain –
> Torrents, methinks, that heard a mighty voice,
> And stopped at once amid their maddest plunge!
> Motionless torrents, silent cataracts!
> Who made you glorious as the Gates of Heaven
> Beneath the keen full moon? Who bade the sun
> Clothe you with rainbows? Who, with living flowers
> Of loveliest blue, spread garlands at your feet? –
> God! let the torrents, like a shout of nations,
> Answer! and let the ice-plains echo, God!
> God! sing ye meadow-streams with gladsome voice!

> Ye pine-groves, with your soft and soul-like sounds!
> And they too have a voice, yon piles of snow,
> And in their perilous fall shall thunder, God!

Coleridge's account doesn't notice, as Shelley's does, that the gar-
lands of "living flowers" at the feet of the mountain are being
crushed by the inexorable glacier, which has not been completely
stopped by divine command; and the older poet seems unaware of
any theological ambiguity or irony in his statement that the ruinous
avalanche thunders the name of God. Shelley, by contrast, sees and
laments the relentless "flood of ruin . . . that from the boundaries of
the sky / Rolls its perpetual stream":

> The dwelling-place
> Of insect, beasts, and birds, becomes its spoil;
> Their food and their retreat forever gone,
> So much of life and joy is lost. The race
> Of man flies far in dread; his work and dwelling
> Vanish, like smoke before the tempest's stream,
> And their place is not known.

Shelley details the brutal, destructive side of the natural phenomena
that Coleridge's absent-minded piety attributes placidly to a benevolent deity. Although Coleridge sees the ruin too, he cannot
accommodate it to his preconceptions about God. Only the "adverting mind," Shelley says, can be taught by Mont Blanc that
whatever created this flood of ruin is not the comforting, mentally
domesticated divinity of Coleridge's poem.

He had himself been impressed by the "magnificence" and
"radiant beauty" of the glaciers (*Letters* 1: 496–99) but his poem, as
though in refutation of the argument from design, insists on the
deformity and menace of the landscape and on its inability to
proclaim any religious truth distinctly. Indeed, his description raises
religious questions, in both a mythopoeic and a scientific manner,
only to refrain from answering them:

> Is this the scene
> Where the old Earthquake-demon taught her young
> Ruin? Were these their toys? or did a sea
> Of fire envelop once this silent snow?
> None can reply – all seems eternal now.
> The wilderness has a mysterious tongue
> Which teaches awful doubt, or faith so mild,
> So solemn, so serene, that man may be,

But for such faith, with nature reconciled;
Thou hast a voice, great Mountain, to repeal
Large codes of fraud and woe; not understood
By all, but which the wise, and great, and good
Interpret, or make felt, or deeply feel.

The doubt (it would have been "awful" even to the author of *Queen Mab*, who liked to imagine the creative power as a nurturing principle) is the inability to believe in the existence of a benevolent creator. The mild faith that keeps mankind from being reconciled with nature is that of observers like Gray and Coleridge, who cannot see nature for what it really is because it would disturb their religious security.[18]

Commentators struggling with Shelley's syntax in lines 77–79, which speak of "awful doubt, or faith so mild, / So solemn, so serene, that man may be, / But for such faith, with nature reconciled," have attempted to eliminate his precise equivocality,[19] not seeing that the point of the poem is its two-edged skepticism, its genuine agnosticism. Shelley is deliberately asserting that humanity may become reconciled with nature *except for* a too serene faith. Faith in general was suspect in Shelley's eyes. In the "Hymn to Intellectual Beauty," written at the same time as "Mont Blanc," he substituted "self-esteem" for faith among his three primary virtues (line 37), and he later spoke of faith as a creation of hell, coeval with fear (*Prometheus Unbound* III.i.10). Even the mild, undogmatic faith of natural religion prevents a proper accommodation with nature. This is an insight he could have found in the work of Baron d'Holbach, who warns that attributing sponsorship of nature to a transcendent benevolent deity must end in theological difficulties whenever one observes apparent cruelty and disorder in the natural world:

Man has ceased to study nature, that he might recur by thought to a substance which possesses nothing in common with her; this substance he has made the mover of nature, without which she would not be capable of any thing; to whom every thing that takes place in her system must be attributed; the conduct of this being has appeared mysterious, has been held up as marvellous, because he seemed to be a continual contradiction; when if man had but recurred to the immutability of the laws of nature, to the invariable system she pursues, all would have appeared intelligible; every thing would have been reconciled; the apparent contrariety would have vanished. By thus taking a wrong view of things, wisdom and intelligence appeared to be opposed by confusion and disorder; goodness to be rendered nugatory by evil; while all is only just what it must inevitably be under the given circumstances.[20]

Religious preconceptions distort our vision of nature. The "mild faith" of natural religion selects only what can be accommodated to its serene confidence in the benevolent God it likes to worship. This complacent assurance, based on selective perception of reality, is what allows us to create gods in our own image and subscribe to those "large codes of fraud and woe" that have ravaged history. Another mountain far from Mont Blanc casts its long shadow over Shelley's poem – Mount Sinai, with its restrictive codes that began the coercive history of Judaeo-Christian religion. For Shelley, as for Holbach, perceiving nature without theological preconceptions would foster a less comforting and therefore more intensely inquisitive, even skeptical religious sense. Looking without preconceptions at a landscape like the one surrounding Mont Blanc, what can one say with certainty of its Creator? What moral attitudes can one predicate of the Maker of that conflict of beauty and ruin? How can we invoke such a Being to sanction or sanctify our religious and political systems?

Shelley is not underwriting either the awful doubt or the mild faith of "Mont Blanc." What the mountain "says" to the adverting mind is that the Power present in nature is incomprehensible and that surrender to intellectual uncertainty might help to repeal the codes of fraud and woe that have resulted from the anthropomorphizing tendency that leads people, in Leigh Hunt's words, to "palm their bad and vindictive passions on Heaven."[21] Shelley was to illustrate this kind of fraud and woe at its most brutal in *The Cenci*, in which the worst crimes are justified (whether by Count Cenci or the Pope or Beatrice) by a presumption of divine authorization.

Coleridge illustrated Shelley's principle that "where indefiniteness ends idolatry and anthropomorphism begin"[22] when he concluded his "Hymn" with an apostrophe personifying the mountain, and he demonstrated the political consequences of this kind of projection by falling into the language of monarchy and hierarchy:

> Thou kingly Spirit throned among the hills,
> Thou dread ambassador from Earth to Heaven,
> Great Hierarch! tell thou the silent sky,
> And tell the stars, and tell yon rising sun
> Earth, with her thousand voices, praises God.

To this kind of political projection Shelley had already responded in a note to *Queen Mab*: "It is probable that the word God was originally only an expression denoting the unknown cause of the known events which men perceived in the universe. By the vulgar mistake of a metaphor for a real being, of a word for a thing, it became a man, endowed with human qualities and governing the universe as an earthly monarch governs his kingdom."[23] It was this monarchical conception of the Christian God that Shelley especially reprobated – this "paternal Monarch" whom he described in the *Essay on Christianity* as "seated in gorgeous & tyrannic majesty . . . upon the throne of infinitude."[24] The conception of God as a royal divinity assisted the sacralization of the power structure in Europe and inspired Shelley's lifelong association of priestcraft with kingcraft.

As Coleridge's poem was bold enough to command the "Great Hierarch," to obey his will, Shelley also assumes a position of authority in his confrontation with the Power of the mountain. From the start of the poem he has insisted in a Berkeleyan manner that his own mind substantiates whatever he seems to perceive in this landscape, and at the end, having spoken of Mont Blanc as the symbol of ultimate power dwelling apart in its tranquillity, "remote, serene, and inaccessible," and after conceding even that "The secret Strength of things / Which governs thought, and to the infinite dome / Of heaven is as a law, inhabits thee!" he turns upon the Power and reminds it that his own mind determines their relationship, insofar as any relationship exists. He has attributed religious significance to the mountain by an act, by a gift, of his imagination. The human mind, ultimately, is where religion is made, as "it peoples with its wishes vacancy & oblivion" (*Letters* 2: 60). "And what were thou," he finally asks, "If to the human mind's imaginings / Silence and solitude were vacancy?" The mind infuses with significance what would otherwise be mere vacancy. The kind of significance it attaches to its projections depends on its preconceptions and its psychic needs. We can create regal, authoritarian gods, like Coleridge's, or we can imagine more liberating and loving divinities if we so choose. The suggestion that silence and solitude may be mere vacancy – that the Coleridge who "worshipped the Invisible" was worshiping a nonentity (a "sovran Blanc," as Coleridge wrote, apparently without any sense of irony) contributes to the ambiguity of the poem's attribution to a transcendent power of "the secret strength of things / Which governs thought, and to the infinite dome / Of heaven is as a law." Evidently belief in a transcendent order is possible, but it must be tendered carefully, indeed skeptically. As Blake suggested in the *Marriage of Heaven & Hell*, a believer must continually hold open the option of atheism. Faith must always be on guard against the complacencies of religion, struggling to purify theology of perversions and accretions that are too readily accepted as intrinsic and inevitable.

In "Mont Blanc" Shelley emphasized the absolute otherness of supreme power in order to rescue the concept of divinity from anthropomorphisms that, in his view, have corrupted religion from the start. His insistence on the unknowable otherness of God did not abate as he grew older, but he became increasingly willing to risk the dangers of anthropomorphism in order to imagine a Divine Being whose essence is love and whose creative power is directed toward the enhancement of human life in a manner concordant with our own highest ideals. His earlier, stricter metaphysics, scrupulous in its avoidance of anthropomorphic indulgence, may be seen in *Queen Mab* when the Fairy speaks of the "Spirit of Nature":

> the caprice
> Of man's weak will belongs no more to thee
> Than do the changeful passions of his breast
> To thy unvarying harmony: the slave,
> Whose horrible lusts spread misery o'er the world,
> And the good man, who lifts, with virtuous pride,
> His being, in the sight of happiness,
> That springs from his own works; the poison-tree,
> Beneath whose shade all life is withered up,
> And the fair oak, whose leafy dome affords
> A temple where the vows of happy love
> Are registered, are equal in thy sight:
> No love, no hate thou cherishest; revenge
> And favoritism, and worst desire of fame
> Thou knowst not: all that the wide world contains
> Are but thy passive instruments, and thou
> Regardst them all with an impartial eye,
> Whose joy or pain thy nature cannot feel,
> > Because thou hast not human sense,
> > Because thou art not human mind.   (6: 200–19)

This is admirably guarded speculation, but a moralist with a social conscience as sensitive as Shelley's, whose metaphysics, as Kenneth Neill Cameron observed, were always subordinate to his ethics,[25] could not long remain content with the restrained religiosity of *Queen*

Mab, or with a deity that is unable to choose between an upas and an oak, that is too detached from human values to prefer a good man over a sensual slave, love over hate, or joy over pain. As alert as he was to the danger of anthropomorphizing God, he finally could accept, even in theory, only a divinity that was humane in sympathy and purpose, one who promoted the ethical and political ideals to which Shelley himself subscribed. As it endorsed positive human emotions like love and justice, such a Being must also be understood to sponsor the human champions of love and compassion – such as Jesus Christ, for whom Shelley's admiration increased as he grew older.

The younger Shelley was not likely to attribute any enlightened thinking to Jesus, against whom he harbored a fierce personal grudge because the Galilean had, among other offenses, alienated the affections of Harriet Grove, the poet's first love. "Oh how I wish I *were* the Antichrist," he wrote in 1810, "that it were *mine* to crush the Demon, to hurl him to his native Hell never to rise again – I expect to gratify some of this insatiable feeling in Poetry. You shall see, you shall hear" (*Letters* 1: 35). By 1814, his feelings about Jesus had become ambivalent, if not contradictory. In *Queen Mab* while Ahasuerus is describing Jesus as a malignant being who promoted intolerance and persecution, Shelley's notes speak of him as "a man of pure life, who desired to rescue his countrymen from the tyranny of their barbarous and degrading superstitions" and acknowledge the importance of distinguishing "between the pretended character of this being as the Son of God and the Saviour of the world, and his real character as a man who, for a vain attempt to reform the world, paid the forfeit of his life to that overbearing tyranny which has since so long desolated the universe in his name."[26] As the years went by, the "malignant soul" scorned by Ahasuerus began to assume the appearance of the "youth with patient looks nailed to a crucifix" who is honored and pitied in *Prometheus Unbound*. For Shelley, it was a case of one misunderstood benefactor of mankind coming to discover how much he had in common with another.

In the *Essay on Christianity*, which most scholars agree was written between 1816 and 1817,[27] Jesus begins to sound remarkably like Shelley:

We discover that he is the enemy of oppression and of falsehood; that he is the advocate of equal justice; that he is neither disposed to sanction bloodshed nor deceit, under whatsoever pretences their practise may be vindicated. We discover that he was a man of meek and majestic demeanour, calm in danger, of natural and simple thoughts and habits, beloved to adoration by his adherents, unmoved and solemn and serene . . . He tramples upon all received opinions, on all the cherished luxuries and superstitions of mankind. He bids them cast aside the chains of custom and blind faith by which they have been encompassed from the very cradle of their being, and become the imitators and ministers of the Universal God.[28]

Given his increasing identification with Jesus, he found, not surprisingly, that the Galilean shared some of his own theological opinions – including even the Shelleyan version of atheism.

It is important to observe that the author of the Christian system had a conception widely differing from the gross imaginations of the vulgar relatively to the ruling Power of the universe. He every where represents this Power as something mysteriously and illimitably pervading the frame of things . . . the overruling Spirit of the collective energy of the moral and material world.[29]

But Jesus, like Shelley, could not be content with an entirely impersonal God: "Jesus Christ represented God as the principle of all good, the source of all happiness, the wise and benevolent creator and preserver of all living things."[30]

As Shelley's esteem for Jesus increased, his attitude toward Christianity inevitably underwent a corresponding transformation. What started as standard rationalist disgust for vulgar superstition modulated to disappointment and impatience with a religion that was unworthy of its origins, and he began attacking Christianity as a betrayal and a cruel mockery of its founder's admirable ideals. The final development in the evolution of his opinions was an even more sympathetic acknowledgment that this betrayal of Christ's ideals was inevitable, since the ideals transcended any possibility of application in reality. *A Philosophical View of Reform* (1819) sees Jesus as having envisioned a social order so perfect that it could not be realized in this recalcitrant world, but could only provide an ideal "toward which with whatever hope of ultimate success, it is our duty to tend. We may and ought to advert to it as to the elementary principle, as to the goal, unattainable perhaps by us, but which, as it were, we revive in our posterity to pursue."[31] Realizing that to put the teachings of Jesus into effect would require or precipitate a social revolution, Shelley's Godwinian cautiousness led him to conclude that the world at present could not tolerate any serious application of true Christianity. "That equality in possessions which Jesus Christ so passionately taught is a moral rather than a political truth and is such as social institutions cannot without mischief inflexibly secure . . . Equality in possessions must be the last result of the utmost refinements of civilization."[32]

As he grew older, Shelley thus displayed two conflicting dispositions toward Christianity, one that "burned toward heaven with fierce reproach and doubt" (*Prometheus Unbound* iii.i.6), waging relentless mental warfare against the religion he considered the archenemy of human liberty and progress, and another that searched for what was originally and truly beneficial in this faith that now dominated the European mind. It seemed necessary for one part of Shelley's consciousness to resist and repudiate "impious" conceptions of God while another part strove to articulate a worthier theology. His most ambitious poem, *Prometheus Unbound*, might be read as as an allegory of these two responses.

Prometheus's role is to defy and resist a repressive, authoritarian image of God until it is finally abandoned by mankind. Yet while Prometheus may be "the type of the highest perfection of moral and intellectual nature, impelled by the purest and the truest motives to the best and noblest ends" (Preface), he evidently lacks certain important mental qualities that one may observe in his female counterpart, Asia. While Prometheus, bound, is resisting and scorning Jupiter, Asia sets out on a journey of discovery and uses her sensitive metaphysical intuition to discern an alternative theology to the one Jupiter personifies. She learns to distinguish (or to make her interlocutor, Demogorgon, distinguish) the God "who reigns" from an "almighty" and "merciful" God who is "eternal Love" (ii. iv. 120). Asia brings about the downfall of Jupiter not by challenging his power directly but by imagining and then appealing to a worthier conception of Deity that makes it impossible for the inferior one to endure.[33] Prometheus himself seems unable to see beyond the Jupiter who reigns as "God and Lord" (i. 282), and he remains imprisoned in his own defiance. His very hatred of his conception of God is debilitating and self-destructive. This helps to explain why Shelley prefaces his drama with a rejection of what we have learned to call Romantic Satanism. Rebellious defiance of God, he says, may be admirable but ultimately it has deleterious effects on the rebel's character. Prometheus's hatred of God inhibits his imagination; only when the hero adopts a more magnanimous attitude to Jupiter does Asia become free to set out on her quest for a clearer understanding of what Divinity ought to be.

Evidently, incessant reproach and doubt and insurrection cannot by itself bring down the empire of Jupiter, so securely is that empire pillared on faith and fear (3: 1–17). Change in theology is brought about most effectively not by mere denial but by the articulation of alternative beliefs. In the *Defence of Poetry* Shelley suggests that "dispersing the grosser delusions of superstition" is the accomplishment of an inferior mental power. While the rational faculty is useful for discrediting erroneous conceptions of God, the imaginative faculty is the one that intuits more authentic conceptions as it sifts "the evidence of things unseen" for fresh insight. In his early life Shelley had insisted that conceptions of ultimate reality must be reasonable and logical; he was always on guard against his own propensity to believe what his reason could not countenance, conscious that "belief is but desire."[34] Later, he came to trust desire as an expression of imagination and, as such, an avenue to truth. In religious matters he would have agreed with Keats that "what the Imagination seizes as Beauty must be truth."[35]

As Shelley's idealistic politics eventually accommodated themselves to the realities of history, one can see his religious principles likewise acquiring an alloy of pragmatism as he grew older. His ultimate goal might continue to be the radical purification or, failing that, the eradication of Christianity, but he was coming to see that the Christian religion even in its present state could generate beneficial effects in society, serving as a kind of homeopathic antidote to belief systems with worse social consequences. For example, he suggests in *A Philosophical View of Reform* that Christian missionary activity in India might assist in extricating the native population from what he saw as less enlightened, less progressive creeds, providing a kind of half-way house on the road to more complete intellectual emancipation. "It cannot be doubted but the zeal of the missionaries of what is called the Christian faith will produce beneficial innovation there, even by the application of dogmas and forms of what is here an outworn incumbrance."[36] Events in Europe in 1821 seem to have encouraged Shelley in this new optimism regarding the social utility of Christianity. In April he could have read a letter in the *Examiner* which reported the presence of priests among the Carbonari: "This society is at once political and religious. Its principles have their foundation in the purest maxims of the Gospel, from which they derive eternal hatred to political and religious tyranny."[37] When later in that year revolution broke out in Greece, Leigh Hunt, laboring under the mistaken impression that the Greeks were treating the Turks with "generosity of spirit," attributed this forbearance to their Christian principles. "The noble spirit which the Greeks have evinced . . . is evidently the same as that which has actuated the Reformers in Spain and Portugal, and proceeds from the same causes. It is the growth of the philosophical part of Christianity, as distinguished from the dogmas that have hitherto been confounded with and perverted it."[38] While Shelley does not seem to have joined fully in this effort to transmogrify the Greeks into Unitarians, he was able to convince himself that "the chiefs of the Greeks are almost all men of comprehension and enlightened views on religion and politics."[39] Like other Philhellenes he understood the usefulness for fund-raising purposes of accentuating the Greeks' Christianity, a rhetorical strategy that is reflected in the preface to *Hellas* when it describes the Turks as "the enemies of domestic happiness, of Christianity and civilization."[40]

Shelley welcomed the Greek rebellion of 1821 as signaling the revival of the spirit of freedom in the post-Napoleonic world. As the Greeks with their ancient democratic heritage provided a suitable embodiment of the libertarian spirit, their antagonists in the Ottoman Empire offered an especially appropriate incarnation of the principle of repression.[41] The Turkish Sultan was a monarch more absolute than any European king, and his power had a sacred dimension that offered a single focus for Shelley's contempt of kingcraft and priestcraft. Four years earlier he had located an imaginary popular revolution in "Islam" and named his tyrant "Othman" – a word that is used in *Hellas* as an alternate spelling for "Ottoman" (l. 1019). Now current events had transformed his visionary revolution into historical reality – the revolt of Islam had begun in the real world and had begun with satisfying poetic propriety in the very birthplace of democracy.

The challenge posed to the Ottoman Empire by the Greek uprising took on a larger, apocalyptic resonance from the millenarian consciousness that pervaded every level of Western society at that time, when even well educated people believed that they were living in the last phase of human history. A tradition of prophecy more than six centuries old predicted that the end of time would come only after a great battle had been fought against the Turkish Empire, whose downfall would permit the Jews to return to their homeland, a generally acknowledged precondition for the Second Coming of Christ. The prophecy regarding the Ottoman Empire was repeated often during the 1790s by popular revivalists,[42] as well as by intellectuals like Joseph Priestley, who wrote in 1796: "I fully expect the personal appearance of Jesus . . . but this will hardly be before the restoration of the Jews, of which there are no symptoms at present. The Turkish empire must fall before that event."[43] A more secular-minded prophet, the Comte de Volney, predicted in his popular book, *The Ruins*, the impending dissolution of the Ottoman Empire. Following a detailed enumeration of "the evils of this tyrannical system of government," Volney uttered an apocalyptic prophecy: "The decree is gone forth; the day approaches when this colosus [sic] of power shall be dashed to pieces, and fall, crushed by its own weight . . . The result of this fall will be a complete change of the political system, as far as it relates to the coast of the Mediterranean."[44]

Shelley obviously thought of his drama as a contribution to the millenarian discourse of his time, calling attention to the apocalyptic tenor of his work in a note alluding to the twenty-fourth chapter of Matthew's gospel: "Prophecies of wars, and rumours of wars, etc. may safely be made by poet or prophet in any age, but to anticipate however darkly a period of regeneration and happiness is a more hazardous exercise of the faculty which bards possess or feign."[45] *Hellas* is an extended meditation on the possibility that the Greek rising might inaugurate such a "period of regeneration and happiness," and it anticipates this millennium in language borrowed from the apocalyptic literature of the Bible. When the Sultan, Mahmud, says:

> take this signet,
> Unlock the seventh chamber in which lie
> An Empire's spoil stored for a day of ruin.
> O spirit of my sires, is it not come?

any contemporary reader would have instantly recognized that conjunction of a signet, the opening of a seventh chamber, and the prophecy of a day of ruin as an allusion to the opening of the seventh seal which precipitates the destruction of the earth in the Book of Revelation.[46]

As an account of a final decisive struggle between Islam and the forces striving to effect a religious and political revolution in Greece, *Hellas* is charged with apocalyptic urgency. A dying Greek Christian becomes possessed by the spirit of prophecy and cries out to the Turks:

> Time has found ye light as foam.
> The Earth rebels; and Good and Evil stake
> Their empire o'er the unborn world of men
> On this one cast; – but ere the die be thrown,
> The renovated genius of our race,
> Proud umpire of the impious game, descends,
> A seraph-winged Victory, bestriding
> The tempest of the Omnipotence of God,
> Which sweeps all things to their appointed doom,
> And you to oblivion! (442–451)

The Sultan himself becomes obsessed with reading the portents of impending apocalypse, finding signs in the heavens and the earth of the fall of Islam and the triumph of Christianity.

> Look, Hassan, on yon crescent moon emblazoned
> Upon that shattered flag of fiery cloud
> Which leads the rear of the departing day,
> Wan emblem of an empire fading now.
> See! How it trembles in the blood-red air
> And like a mighty lamp whose oil is spent
> Shrinks on the horizon's edge while from above
> One star with insolent and victorious light
> Hovers above its fall, and with keen beams
> Like arrows through a fainting antelope
> Strikes its weak form to death. (337–47)

The star of freedom that rises against the Turkish crescent, and in which Mahmud finds an "insolent" emblem of universal insubordination (351–55), is elsewhere identified as the "folding star of Bethlehem" (231). It may be surprising, even disconcerting, to find Shelley thus representing Christianity as an ideology of liberation, but in the religio-political order established in the play, and in Shelley's maturing vision of history, the teaching of Christ had come to represent a truly revolutionary vision, advocating "doctrines of reform" far more radical than any which had been advanced by others – more daring than those of Plato before him or Godwin after him.[47]

The struggle for Greek freedom is called in *Hellas* "the Christian cause" (l. 554), and the drama becomes as much a meditation on religion as on politics, on the rebels as Christians as on the rebels as Greeks. The revolution was in fact a religious war, its passion and its rhetoric (whether in battle cries or in official proclamations) deriving special intensity from the centuries-old antagonism between a Christian people and their Islamic rulers. The conflict provided Shelley with an occasion to give imaginative expression to his theory that Christianity was, or ought to be, fundamentally antithetical to political and religious tyranny. As the modern Greeks in his drama incarnated the spirit of the eternal Hellas even in their present degraded condition, he allowed Greek Christianity, in all its superstition and corruption, to serve as a representation of the liberating faith originally taught by Jesus, that pure religion that Shelley acknowledged might never be realizable on earth but which could still serve as an enduring inspirational ideal. The Christianity of the Greek rebels thus functions in the play as a kind of Coleridgean symbol representing what it cannot itself adequately express.

By the time he wrote *Hellas*, Shelley was in the habit of treating earthly realities as emblematic of higher things; he had done so most strikingly in *Epipsychidion*, written earlier in 1821, wherein a chance female acquaintance became, as "Emilia," an embodiment or symbol of the ideal beauty and perfection that the poet had been seeking all his life and had despaired of finding on earth – "an image of some bright Eternity, / A shadow of some golden dream" (lines 115–16). Shelley hinted that he was pursuing a similar strategy in *Hellas* when he remarked in the Preface, "The modern Greek is the descendant of those glorious beings whom the imagination almost refuses to figure to itself as belonging to our Kind." While acknowledging that we have idealized the ancient Greeks beyond what any reality could warrant, Shelley nevertheless understood that such "beautiful idealisms of moral excellence" were useful for enriching humanity's sense of its own potential dignity.

But even the glorious Greeks did not represent the highest ideals that humanity was capable of conceiving. Ancient Greek society, with all its magnificent intellectual and cultural achievements, was a radically flawed civilization, contaminated by some deadly Shelleyan sins:

The desire of revenge for the aggression of Persia outlived among the Greeks that love of liberty which had been their most glorious distinction among the nations of mankind, and Alexander became the instrument of its completion. The mischiefs attendant on this consummation of fruitless ruin are too manifold and too tremendous to be related. If all the thought which had been expended on the construction of engines of agony and death . . . had been employed to promote the true welfare, and extend the real empire of man how different would have been the present situation of human society.[48]

The decline of Greek civilization into autocracy and militarism indicated that something was lacking in the Hellenic spirit, an inadequacy that jeopardized and finally vitiated their great achievements in art and philosophy. What was missing, *Hellas* suggests, was the nobler vision of human potential that was later articulated by Jesus.

The poet who once lamented Christianity as "those events and opinions which put an end to the graceful religion of the Greeks" (*Letters* 2: 230) had come to see the religion of Jesus, in its ideal form, as representing important values lacking in ancient Greece. In *A Defence of Poetry* he concedes that even at its best "the scheme of Athenian society was deformed by many imperfections" and credits Christianity with "the abolition of personal and domestic slavery" and "the emancipation of women from a great part of the degrading restraints of antiquity."[49] More generally, the Christian gospel made available to people on all levels of society the moral and political wisdom that had been confined to elite groups in the classical world.

Plato, following the doctrines of Timaeus and Pythagoras, taught also a moral and intellectual system of doctrine comprehending at once the past, the present, and the future condition of man. Jesus Christ divulged the sacred and eternal truths contained in these views to mankind, and Christianity, in its abstract purity, became the exoteric expression of the esoteric doctrines of the poetry and wisdom of antiquity.[50]

The most important contribution to civilization of the religion of Jesus was its central emphasis on charity, mercy, and forgiveness. Warning against the brutality and bloodshed that the Greek rebellion would inevitably provoke, the chorus in *Hellas* sings,

> In sacred Athens, near the fane
> Of Wisdom, Pity's altar stood:
> Serve not the unknown God in vain,
> But pay that broken shrine again,
> Love for hate and tears for blood.   (733–37)

Shelley is alluding here to the passage in *Acts of the Apostles* (17: 16–23)
narrating the disturbance caused in Athens when the apostle Paul
"preached unto them Jesus, and the resurrection."

Then Paul stood in the midst of Mars' hill, and said, Ye men of Athens, I
perceive that in all things ye are too superstitious. For as I passed by, and
beheld your devotions, I found an altar with the inscription, TO THE
UNKNOWN GOD. Whom therefore ye ignorantly worship, him I declare unto
you.

Shelley was nearly paraphrasing the last sentence of Paul's address
when he called Christianity "the exoteric expression of the esoteric
doctrines of the poetry and wisdom of antiquity." But his assertion is
qualified: only in its "abstract purity" does Christianity surpass the
Greek achievement. This pure Christianity was a religion that had
never yet existed on earth and perhaps never could. The chorus's
reference to the "unknown God" expresses Shelley's painful consciousness that the God who joins wisdom and pity, who prefers love
to hate and tears to blood, is a God whom humanity seems incapable
of serving, incapable even of knowing. This is the "almighty, merciful
God" of *Prometheus Unbound* whose existence is veiled by the reign of
the usurping Jupiter.

Shelley's understanding of the Greek revolution as a critical
moment in the perpetual struggle between liberty and tyranny,
between ideals of freedom and justice on one hand and on the other
a persistent antithetical tendency in mankind to deny or despair of
those ideals is expressed most clearly in what is called the "Prologue
to *Hellas*," a fragment that seems to have been intended to introduce
the drama but which was not published with it in 1821. This cosmic
dialogue between Christ and Satan might have carried the scriptural
epigraph that Blake used to introduce the *Four Zoas*: "For we wrestle
not against flesh and blood, but against principalities, against
powers, against the rulers of the darkness of this world, against
spiritual wickedness in high places." In this debate Satan (showing
little resemblance here to a Romantic hero) advocates slavery or,
more broadly, fatalism. He represents the old tyrannies and what
sustained them – the pessimistic assumption that human society is
incapable of radical improvement, whether moral or political. Jesus
is more optimistic about the human condition, and Shelley leaves no
doubt where his own sympathies lie when Christ condemns the

"miscreeds" of the Holy Alliance and identifies himself with the
Greek rebels, for whose triumph he pleads with his heavenly Father,

> by Plato's sacred light,
> Of which my spirit was a burning morrow –
> By Greece and all she cannot cease to be,
> Her quenchless words, sparks of immortal truth,
> Stars of all night – her harmonies and forms,
> Echoes and shadows of what Love adores
> In thee.[51]

Calling his own spirit a "burning morrow" of Plato's, Jesus here
identifies himself as the fulfillment of all the highest aspirations of
ancient Greek civilization, recalling Shelley's argument in *A Philosophical View of Reform* that Jesus incorporated in his teaching the best
elements of the poetry and philosophy of antiquity. The debate
between Christ and Satan in the "Prologue to *Hellas*" restates the
question at issue in *Prometheus Unbound*: can humanity free itself from
the mental habits and assumptions that bind it to the past and create
a new order of justice, love, and peace?

Within the drama itself, advocacy of the pessimistic, Satanic
viewpoint is provided by the somewhat surprising appearance of
Ahasuerus, the Wandering Jew who had figured so prominently in
Shelley's early poetry. Most interpreters have assumed that the
Ahasuerus of *Hellas* is the same sympathetic figure who is called to
testify against religion in *Queen Mab*, that he is still in 1821, as Neville
Rogers put it, the "incarnation of accumulated Shelleyan philosophy."[52] But as Shelley's attitude to Jesus Christ had altered since
Queen Mab, one might also expect a change in his opinion of this
ancient scorner and repudiator of Christ – whom he would now see
as one of the multitude that misunderstood his character and his
mission. When Jesus came, as the chorus sings in *Hellas*, "a Power
from the unknown God," treading "the thorns of death and shame"
(lines 211–14) he was mocked by Ahasuerus, very much as Christ is
mocked by Satan in the "Prologue to *Hellas*." In fact, in the terms of
the Prologue Ahasuerus has to be seen as a Satanic figure.[53] When
he says to Mahmud: "The Past / Now stands before thee like an
Incarnation / Of the To-come" (lines 852–54), he aligns himself with
the Satan of the Prologue, to whom Christ says: "Obdurate spirit!
Thou seest but the Past in the To-come."[54] Ahasuerus denies any
real distinction between past and future:

> All is contained in each.
> Dodona's forest to an acorn's cup
> Is that which has been, or will be, to that
> Which is – the absent to the present.[55]

In the running debate in *Hellas* between fate and freedom, Ahasuerus denies the possibility of any real progress in human affairs. He represents in his own history the inability to change or conclude, "condemned to behold for millenniums that yawning monster Sameness, and Time, that hungry hyaena, ever bearing children, and ever devouring again her offspring."[56] His primary dramatic action in *Hellas* involves raising the phantom of Mahomet II, the sultan who conquered Constantinople in 1453. Mahomet II's return from the dead reinforces the pessimistic theme that the present and future are fated to repeat the past. When Ahasuerus says, "The Future and the Past are idle shadows / Of thought's eternal flight – they have no being," his denial of humanity's potential and of its responsibility for creating its own future reinforces the resigned fatalism articulated by Satan and the Sultan.

The central struggle in *Hellas*, then, is between two competing religious ideologies, one redemptive, insisting on the possibility of radical alteration in mankind's situation, the other fatalistic, denying the possibility of any significant change for the better in the human condition. Inadequate attention to this conflict accounts for some of the difficulty critics have had in interpreting the best known lines in the drama – the great concluding chorus, "The world's great age begins anew" – a lyric that encapsulates the tension in the drama between its longing for a "brighter Hellas" that will revive the spirit of Athens in her prime and its dread of a return of the kind of violence that has been an integral part of Greek history and literature from the beginning. Even if a brighter Hellas were to emerge from the present political struggle, the chorus acknowledges that the Greek story could once again end in hatred, brutality, and "fruitless ruin," for want of an ideal that goes beyond the ethics of revenge.

> The world's great age begins anew
>   The golden years return,
> The earth doth like a snake renew
>   Her winter weeds outworn;
> Heaven smiles, and faiths and empires gleam
> Like wrecks of a dissolving dream.

A brighter Hellas rears its mountains
　　From waves serener far,
A new Peneus rolls his fountains
　　Against the morning-star,
Where fairer Tempes bloom, there sleep
Young Cyclads on a summer deep.

A loftier Argo cleaves the main,
　　Fraught with a later prize;
Another Orpheus sings again,
　　And loves and weeps and dies;
A new Ulysses leaves once more
Calypso for his native shore.

O, write no more the tale of Troy,
　　If earth Death's scroll must be!
Nor mix, with Laian rage the joy
　　Which dawns upon the free;
Although a subtler Sphinx renew
Riddles of death Thebes never knew.

Another Athens shall arise,
　　And to remoter time
Bequeath, like sunset to the skies,
　　The splendour of its prime,
And leave, if nought so bright may live,
All earth can take or Heaven can give.

Saturn and Love their long repose
　　Shall burst, more bright and good
Than all who fell, than One who rose,
　　Than many unsubdued;
Not gold, not blood their altar dowers
But votive tears and symbol flowers.

O cease! must hate and death return?
　　Cease! must men kill and die?
Cease! drain not to its dregs the urn
　　Of bitter prophecy.
The world is weary of the past,
O might it die or rest at last!

The last stanza has caused consternation among some critics
because it has seemed to them an abrupt auctorial intrusion rather
than an organic, dramatically appropriate development in the poem.
Jerome McGann, for example, called the last lines a repudiation, a
"strangling" of what went before: "He overturns and denies the

whole of *Hellas* in the last six lines."[57] A less self-assured reader might have hesitated before attributing such an inconsistency to such an artist. McGann does not see that the pessimism of the last stanza is an undercurrent in the chorus as it is in the drama as a whole. He is not alone in missing the moral anxiety that pervades the poem. Carl Woodring heard the chorus proclaiming that "Empire and all else that mutability rules must pass. Hellenism, which is freedom of the human spirit, breaks out of this cycle of time, space, and material nothingness."[58] But Shelley's complaint is precisely that Hellenism itself seems to be imprisoned within that cycle. The central stanza of the poem expresses awareness that revenge, brutality, and warfare were a major, indeed a central, part of ancient Greek history. Greece rose on the ruins of Troy and other defeated rivals; the Golden Age of Pericles was preceded and followed by centuries of cruelty and bloodshed. Even Plato's *Republic* required universal military training. Can one recreate the glory that was Greece in isolation from the brutality and misery that was Greece? Can one separate the battle of Marathon from the seige of Troy, the courage of Leonidas from that of Agamemnon and Alexander? We see in Shelley's chorus an ironic acknowledgement that idealizing ancient Greece requires a selective memory. The central stanza introduces a fear that the anticipated new Hellas will be unable to avoid the carnage that characterized ancient Greek history and literature. The penultimate stanza, hailing a renewal of the Greek golden age presided over by a resurrected Saturn and Aphrodite, serves only to remind the poet that the renewal of a past age is likely to be followed, in a cycle controlled by a mysterious, implacable, Sphinx-like power, by another fall into war and imperialism leading to moral and political self-destruction.

The problem of interpretation has arisen, in short, because critics want to read the chorus as an optimistic poem, then object to it because it is not sufficiently or consistently optimistic. But what sounds like optimism in the poem is really a kind of wishful thinking that is then undercut by the ironic historical consciousness of the Greek women who sing the chorus – a captive people and, as women, doubly enslaved by the Turks. Misreading tends to begin with an interpretation of the word "great" in the first line as celebratory, paralleling "golden" in the next line, when it actually means great in length or duration. Shelley is referring to Plato's sense of earthly time as a cycle eternally returning upon itself. In his book *The Myth of the Eternal Return*, Mircea Eliade includes a quotation from Henri-Charles Puech that illuminates Shelley's meaning:

According to the celebrated Platonic definition, time, which is determined and measured by the revolution of the celestial spheres, is the moving image of unmoving eternity, which it imitates by revolving in a circle. Consequently all cosmic becoming, and, in the same manner, the duration of this world of generation and corruption in which we live, will progress in a circle or in accordance with an indefinite succession of cycles in the course of which the same reality is made, unmade, and remade in conformity with an immutable law and immutable alternations. Not only is the same sum of existence preserved in it, with nothing being lost and nothing created, but in addition certain thinkers of declining Antiquity – Pythagoreans, Stoics, Platonists – reached the point of admitting that within each of these cycles of duration, of these *aiones*, of these *aeva*, the same situations are reproduced that have already been produced in previous cycles and will be reproduced in subsequent cycles – *ad infinitum*.[59]

In each of these "great years," the past is only a prophecy of the "to-come." From the beginning, then, Shelley's chorus expresses as much dread of historical recurrence as optimism about renewal. Mahmud had earlier suggested that cycles of loveliness come accompanied by cycles of desolation (lines 746–47) and predicted, "Come what may, / The Future must become the Past." This grim suggestion of an equation between past and future, with the possibility that the terms of the equation are reversible, is what the chorus's final stanza protests. The Sultan and Ahasuerus, like Satan in the Prologue, have been saying, in the language of the chorus, that hate and death must return, that men must continue to kill and die. It is fear of that fatality – fear that the absence of pity and forgiveness will make a revival of "the tale of Troy" just as likely as a resurrection of Periclean Athens – that inspires the chorus's weary exclamation, "Oh Cease!"

But it is too much to say with John Hodgson that "*Hellas* ends, despairingly, with a lamentation over all cyclicity."[60] To lament cyclicity is not necessarily to despair. To demand an end to recurrent, predictable evil is to reject the fatalist vision of Satan in the "Prologue" for the optimistic ideal articulated by Jesus Christ. What Jesus offers is the possibility of escape from historical determinism. If Shelley indulged in a longing for such a redemption from history, it would not necessarily have been a betrayal of radical principles. That there will be a final conflict, a war to end all wars, has been the dream of political visionaries for centuries. William

Blake understood that the primary responsibility of the prophetic imagination was to discover a means of escape from the natural cycles in which humanity is imprisoned, like the cycle of revolution and repression that was repeating itself in Greece at the time. Blake's horror of the endlessly revolving Satanic mills led him finally to accept the need for intervention by a transcendent Redeemer who would in mercy put an end to the cyclical fatality of life in the fallen world. ("Then wondrously the Starry Wheels felt the divine hand. Limit was put to Eternal Death."[61]) Commenting on the debt Shelley's chorus seems to owe to Virgil's Fourth Eclogue, M. H. Abrams says of Blake and Shelley, "these poets cry out for a transformation of history from the shape of eternal recurrence to the shape of apocalyptic prophecy, in which history reaches its highest point and then stops."[62]

A recent book by Bryan Shelley draws a helpful distinction between prophetic eschatology, which foresees gradual improvement in the human condition, and apocalyptic eschatology, which envisions a future perfection that can only result from a radical break with the present unpromising order of history. Whereas prophets anticipate progress, apocalyptists expect transcendence.[63] *Hellas* concludes with this latter kind of eschatological yearning for a way out, a final, absolute redemption. Multiple allusions to the Biblical apocalypse suggest a hope that the Greek rebellion might prove to be a kind of Armageddon in which "Good and Evil [would] stake / Their empire o'er the unborn world of men / On this one cast." If the Greeks could embrace the Hellenic ideal, if the Christian rebels could accept as their program the genuine ethical and political teachings of Jesus, then Greece might be changed forever and provide a pattern of revolution for the rest of the world to follow. But as Shelley's drama ends, the chorus of Greek women is still enslaved and the world stands waiting for a redemption, an apocalyptic revelation, that does not come. To serve the unknown God of pity and forgiveness apparently remains beyond the capacity of the Greek revolutionaries, whose imaginations have apparently surrendered to the fatalist vision of Satan and the ethic of revenge that it justifies.

Christian eschatology offers an alternative to historical fatalism, but it offers such hope on terms that Shelley evidently could not bring himself to accept, even in a visionary work like *Hellas*. He could take no comfort from the prospect of a glorified Christ coming to transform the world. In his drama Shelley alludes specifically to the prophecies of the second coming in Matthew 24: 29–30; and Mark 13: 24–26 ("they shall see the Son of man coming in the clouds of heaven with power and great glory") and revises them:

> The Greeks expect a Saviour from the West
> Who shall not come, men say, in clouds and glory:
> But in the omnipresence of that spirit
> In which all live and are. (598–601)

Here the image of the returning Christ fades into a universal transformative power like the one in *Adonais* that "sweeps through the dull dense world, compelling there / All new successions to the forms they wear" and "wields the world with never-wearied love." This universal renovation of the human spirit, Shelley suggests, should be the object of the Greeks' messianic hope, not the Christ who is worshiped in the Christian churches and invoked as the sponsor of half the atrocities generated by the war in Greece. This Christ, Shelley insists, represents no improvement over the old gods of Greece.

> Saturn and Love their long repose
>   Shall burst, more bright and good
> Than all who fell, than One who rose,
>   Than many unsubdued;
> Not gold, not blood their altar dowers
> But votive tears and symbol flowers.

This apparent repudiation of the Christianity he has been celebrating, and even of Jesus Christ himself, is at first confusing, but Shelley here is insisting once again on his distinction between the Jesus of history and the Christ of faith. When he says that the revived Saturn and Love would be more bright and good "than One who rose," he is referring not to Jesus as he actually lived but as he was revised by those who fabricated the story of his resurrection – the primary fiction on which the religion called Christianity was founded. Shelley would have agreed with Thomas Paine's description of the resurrection account as a "wretched contrivance . . . with every mark of fraud and imposition stamped upon the face of it."[64] The poet is insisting here at the end of *Hellas*, as he had always done, that historical Christianity was a betrayal of the teaching and example of Jesus Christ. In the "Essay on Christianity" he had written:

The doctrines [of Jesus] indeed, in my judgment, are excellent and strike at the root of moral evil. If acted upon, no political or religious institution could subsist a moment . . . This alone would be a demonstration of the falsehood of Christianity, that the religion so called is the strongest ally and bulwark of that system of successful force and fraud and of the selfish passions from which it has derived its origin and permanence, against which Jesus Christ declared the most uncompromising war, and the extinction of which appears to have been the great motive of his life.[65]

We see here clearly expressed Shelley's continuing ambivalence about Christianity. The doctrines of Jesus are at enmity with repressive political systems; the religion of Jesus serves as a chief bulwark of those systems. His admiration of the ideals of Jesus left him no choice but to excoriate their corruption and repudiate the ecclesiastical perpetuations of that corruption. The painful ambivalence at which Shelley had arrived in his effort to imagine a properly reformed Christianity is expressed in a note to *Hellas*:

The sublime human character of Jesus Christ was deformed by an imputed identification with a Power, who tempted, betrayed, and punished the innocent beings who were called into existence by His sole will; and for the period of a thousand years, the spirit of this most just, wise, and benevolent of men has been propitiated with myriads of hecatombs of those who approached the nearest to His innocence and wisdom, sacrificed under every aggravation of atrocity and variety of torture.[66]

By the fatality that distills the worst from the corruption of the best, Christianity has become one of the most baneful of those large codes of fraud and woe by which humanity is deluded and oppressed. And yet the political and religious ideals of its founder hold out a unique hope for human salvation. The ambivalence of *Hellas*, its inability to realize its own optimistic vision, stems from the conflict between his dream of what Christianity might be ideally and his awareness of what it actually was in Europe in 1821.

If Shelley had ever thought that he might live to see a reformation of England's national religion that would bring it more into line with the ideals of its founder (and his own), he appears to have abandoned that hope as he approached the end of his life, along with his hope for a general amelioration of society's ills. For a moment he had been able to find in the Christianity of *Hellas* a symbol of an ideal faith that might triumph in some ideal future as the result of a progressive reformation. The *Defence of Poetry* had expressed the hope that the great writers of his own time were "the companions and forerunners of some unimagined change in our social condition or the opinions which cement it." But the opinions that cemented society had recently been moving perceptibly in the other direction. By late 1821 the strength and the conservative nature of the Evangelical revival in Britain had become apparent to him, and he now saw that the real spirit of the age was inimical to his principles and to the poetry that articulated them: "I write nothing, and probably shall write no more . . . If I cannot be something better, I had rather be nothing, and the accursed cause to the downfall of which I dedicated what powers I may have had – flourishes like a cedar and covers England with its boughs" (*Letters* 2: 331). The scriptural allusion (Ps. 92: 12–14 and Hos. 14: 5–6) leaves little doubt that the "accursed cause" whose triumph he lamented was, or included, British Christianity, and his final judgments on that religion reveal his bitterness and disappointment. Three months before he died he wrote to Horace Smith:

I differ with [Thomas] Moore in thinking Christianity useful to the world; no man of sense can think it true; and the alliance of the monstrous superstitions of the popular worship with the pure doctrines of the Theism of such a man as Moore, turns to the profit of the former, and makes the latter the foundation of his own pollution. I agree with him that the doctrines of the French, and Material Philosophy, are as false as they are pernicious; but still they are better than Christianity, inasmuch as anarchy is better than despotism; for this reason, that the former is for a season, and the latter is eternal. (*Letters* 2: 412)

Yet even this explicit repudiation of Christianity contains its quota of Shelleyan qualifications, suggesting the tension between rational suspicion and imaginative intuition I have been pointing out. He employs, for example, the common Enlightenment distinction between popular superstition and pure theism, and he also distinguishes between the falseness of French materialism and its usefulness as a corrosive of oppressive belief systems. He rejects the despotism of dogma for the anarchy of a system of denial that affords the freedom to believe differently. Employing a kind of Blakean dialectic, Shelley expresses the paradox that atheism allows religious speculation a kind of spontaneity and freedom that would be denied by any formal creed. The continuing ambivalence of his attitude can be seen in another letter to Horace Smith written two months later, less than a month before his death: "The destiny of man can scarcely be so degraded that he was born only to die: and if such should be the case, delusions, especially the gross & preposterous ones of the existing religion, can scarcely be supposed to exalt it" (*Letters* 2: 442). He wants to believe in the soul's immortality, but not on the terms offered by Christian belief.

The bitterness of these final repudiations of Christianity in 1822 recalls his remark to John Gisborne in the same year confessing his disenchantment with Teresa Viviani, the "Emilia" of *Epipsychidion*: "The error, and I confess it is not easy for spirits cased in flesh and blood to avoid it, consists in seeking in a mortal image the likeness of what is perhaps eternal" (*Letters* 2: 434). No religion on earth can be an adequate expression of the eternal truth it purports to represent; the higher the truth, the more odious and treacherous the counterfeit. Shelley could not accept, as Blake did, the "religion of generation" as "Jerusalem's covering until the time of the End." He understood that the corruption of Christianity was unavoidable, but unlike Blake, he concluded that its chronic deficiencies were incurable.

Shelley's conviction that Christ's teachings were beyond application in this world was restated in *The Triumph of Life*, that grim vision of the surrender of almost everyone to the dehumanizing compulsions that constitute "life." A year earlier in *Adonais* he had been able to express some degree of optimism about the struggle that takes place "when lofty thought / Lifts a young heart above its mortal lair, / And love and life contend in it, for what / Shall be its earthly doom" (lines 392–95). In *Adonais* the outcome of this contention between life and love was susceptible to positive influence by the Power that "wields the world with never wearied love" (line 377). No such power operates in *The Triumph of Life*, which lists Jesus and Socrates among the few who were exempt from the confusion and corruption of earthly life, but does not offer them as models for imitation. Not even their own disciples, those who had lived in their luminous presence, had been able to follow their example. Stuart Sperry comments that, for Shelley, unique individuals like Socrates and Jesus "represent no practical course for dealing with life's evils but only dramatize through their revulsion the hopelessness they perceive."[67] With Jesus died his unique understanding of the Unknown God, and his followers "rose like shadows between Man and god / Till that eclipse, still hanging under Heaven, / Was worshipped by the world o'er which they strode / For the true Sun it quenched" (*Triumph*, lines 289–92).

The true Sun, the "burning fountain" that received the spirit of Adonais, the "Unknown God" of Love and Pity spoken of in *Hellas*, the "almighty, merciful God" of *Prometheus Unbound*, whose reality has always been concealed or distorted by

> those foul shapes, abhorred by God and man –
> Which under many a name and many a form
> Strange, savage, ghastly, dark and execrable
> Were Jupiter, the tyrant of the world;
> And which the nations panic-stricken served
> With blood, and hearts broken by long hope　　(III.iv.180–85)

– that transcendent ineffable Being who haunts Shelley's imagination but whom he seems hesitant even to name, remains the Unknown God, forever eclipsed by religion. Knowledge of that God could save mankind, but the knowledge seems unattainable. In its place there is only the "religion, Christless, Godless, a book sealed" that was so dramatically increasing its influence in England at the time of Shelley's death. That the Unknown God will never be known, that those who labor for the welfare of mankind must deny the very idea of God to prevent its corruption, was, in Shelley's view, close to the heart of the human tragedy. The necessity of atheism ensured the triumph of life.

Conclusion: Romantic Reformation

Having examined the evidence that the literary artists who constituted the Romantic Movement in England took as one of their primary social goals the reformation of the national religion, it becomes necessary finally, however briefly, to consider the question of their achievement. Can one speak of a Romantic Reformation in any sense that goes beyond the realm of intentionality? To what extent was their confidence in the efficacy of literature as a means of national reform justified? Did they succeed demonstrably in altering the religious consciousness and behavior of their contemporaries or of later generations?

In my first chapter I suggested that Romanticism in Britain emerged in close relationship with a national religious revival that reached its peak intensity during the years in which the literary movement flourished. There is no doubt that the religious revival brought about a remarkable transformation of British society; much of what we understand as "Victorianism" in the British as well as the international context is the product of that revival, which wrought a change in national religious consciousness affecting every sphere of life including the political. And when the new religious enthusiasm was channeled into foreign missionary activity, it contributed importantly to the expansion of British influence overseas by providing an essential ideological rationale for imperialism and colonialism. When one considers the nature and scope of the reformation accomplished by the various Christian denominations, the effect of Romanticism on the nation's religious consciousness seems inconsequential by comparison. Even when one narrows one's focus to the sphere of the fine arts, the Romantics cannot claim to have made an impact on the national culture comparable to some developments for which the revivalists could claim responsibility, for example the discrediting of the drama as a respectable art form or the creation of a new audience for religious poetry, an audience whose taste was sophisticated enough to admire works such as *The Excursion* and *In Memoriam*.

Even in their own day, in their appeal to the "more select classes of poetical readers" whom Shelley imagined as the audience of works like *Prometheus Unbound*, the Romantics were unable to compete successfully for readership with their chief rivals, the Evangelicals. Computing the results of that rivalry purely in economic terms, the Evangelicals must be said to have won handily. The most widely read essayist of the time was not Hazlitt, Hunt, or Lamb, but John Foster, a Calvinist Baptist whose collected essays, published in 1804, ran to eighteen editions in his lifetime. Hannah More's pious novel *Coelebs in Search of a Wife* went through ten editions in one year and outsold Scott's *Waverley* during the first quarter of the century.[1] The best-selling poet throughout the Romantic period was not one of those I have discussed in this book but rather the "Evangelical Laureate," William Cowper, of whose verse more than ninety collected editions were published between 1782 and 1837 (not including American editions), bringing his publisher profits in excess of £10,000. Hannah More expressed the consensus of middle-class readers when she said of Cowper, "I have found what I have been looking for all my life, a poet whom I can read on a Sunday, and whose whole writings I can recommend to my young and my female friends, without restriction or exception."[2] Byron, who was emphatically not safe for Sunday reading and who scorned Cowper as a "maniacal Calvinist and coddled poet" was the only Romantic who competed with the Evangelicals in sales figures, which may account for some of the special rancor that was directed at him by the religious community. Their control of the middle-class market actually imposed a measure of censorship upon the Romantics themselves. When Leigh Hunt's *Examiner* ran a series of editorials against religious intolerance (including the one Keats described as "a Battering Ram against Christianity," John Hunt, who handled the periodical's business interests, cautioned his brother: "I fear those Articles on Religious topics – every way sound and true and admirable as they were, – have assisted to lower our sale."[3] Even poetry showed its susceptibility to such pressures when Keats was persuaded to alter "The Eve of St. Agnes" in accord with new standards of public propriety – standards that had been documented convincingly a year earlier by the publication and reception of Thomas Bowdler's *The Family Shakespeare*.[4]

Since their impact cannot be measured in souls saved or in books sold, is there any sense in which the English Romantics can be said to have had a significant effect on the religious state of the nation? A distinction made by Max Weber in his *Sociology of Religion* may be helpful here. Weber distinguishes between the "ethical prophet" who presents himself as the agent of God's will and demands conformity to a particular set of beliefs and practices and the "exemplary prophet" who, "by his personal example, demonstrates to others the way to religious salvation, as in the case of the Buddha. The preaching of this type of prophet says nothing about a divine mission or an ethical duty of obedience, but rather directs itself to the self-interest of those who crave salvation, recommending to them the same path as he himself traversed."[5] When Wordsworth in *The Prelude* describes himself and Coleridge as "Prophets of Nature" and predicts, "What we have loved / Others will love, and we may teach them how,"[6] he is presenting himself and his friend as what Weber would call exemplary prophets, teaching not a body of doctrine but a way of looking at and conducting oneself in the world.

Apart from Coleridge, the Romantics offered no specific program of religious reform, however much they insisted on the need for it. Keats's sonnet expressed "disgust of vulgar superstition" and predicted its eventual disappearance from the world, but he did not suggest in detail how the work of enlightenment would be accomplished. The Romantics were not interested in organizing groups of disciples and certainly not in founding churches, but they did, all of them, clearly hope to affect the religious disposition of their readers and they achieved some exemplary success in individual cases. Shelley's poetry, for example, exerted a major formative influence on the young Robert Browning, an influence whose most dramatic manifestation was a sudden, if temporary, conversion to atheism. I have argued elsewhere that Shelley's thought and example also helped form the independent religious vision that found expression in Tennyson's *In Memoriam*, a poem whose impact on the religious attitudes of the Victorian reading public was itself enormous.[7] It is difficult to calculate but also to underestimate the extent of Byron's religious influence on Emily Bronte, whose last poem, "No coward soul is mine," suggests a larger spiritual debt to that poet than to her father the vicar. In his *Defence of Poetry*, Shelley wrote: "it exceeds all imagination to conceive what would have been the moral condition of the world if neither Dante, Petrarch, Boccaccio, Chaucer,

Shakespeare, Calderon, Lord Bacon, nor Milton, had ever existed."[8] One might say the same about the religious condition of the English-speaking world during the nineteenth century if Wordsworth, Byron, Keats, and Shelley had not lived to inspire the likes of Tennyson, Browning, Mill, Arnold, Morris, and Shaw.

One can observe and document the power of this essential influence most clearly in the first generation of earnest young Victorians who tended to look back upon their Romantic predecessors as having made as important a contribution in the religious as in the literary sphere. Stephen Prickett's valuable study of the Victorian Church, *Religion and Romanticism*, credited Wordsworth and Coleridge with effecting a broad transformation of religious sensibility that substituted an aesthetic conception of religious experience for the rational one that had earlier been dominant, profoundly affecting the way the Church of England came to think about itself in the nineteenth century. Prickett finds especially clear expressions of what he calls "the Romantic theological tradition" in F. D. Maurice's *The Kingdom of Christ* (1838) and John Henry Newman's *A Grammar of Assent* (1870).[9]

Maurice's name has appeared several times earlier in this study; on his way to becoming the most eminent Protestant theologian of the Victorian period, he began in the 1820s to predict that "social regeneration would come not through political change but through the spiritual influence of modern literature, specifically the writings of Coleridge, Wordsworth, Shelley, and Keats."[10] For Maurice, the Romantic poets were not merely "literary" in their significance; they were philosophers of great power, askers and answerers of ultimate questions, who had purified and enriched the religious consciousness of the nation. As Shelley had done before him, Maurice noted the coincidence of great periods of literature in Britain and periods of religious reformation and identified the Romantic period as "the second miraculous descent upon English literature of the purifying and kindling fire from heaven" – the first such literary Pentecost having occurred at the time of the Reformation.[11]

That other preeminent religious leader of nineteenth-century England, John Henry Newman, also attributed a crucial religious influence to the Romantics. In an 1839 essay whose continuing relevance he emphasized by quoting liberally from it in 1864 in *Apologia Pro Vita Sua*, Newman credited the Romantics with having created a cultural environment that allowed the Oxford Movement to flourish. Speaking in particular of Walter Scott, but including Coleridge, Wordsworth, and Southey in his frame of reference, he said that Romantic writing had been responsible for "the spiritual awakening of spiritual wants," having the effect on readers of "stimulating their mental thirst, feeding their hopes, setting before them visions, which, when once seen, are not easily forgotten, and silently indoctrinating them with nobler ideas, which might afterwards be appealed to as first principles."[12]

The nineteenth century reverberates with individual voices similarly crediting the Romantic poets with the amendment, the refinement, and even the preservation of religion in Britain. William Hale White, when he attributed to Wordsworth a central, critical influence on his own religious life, was one of those who used the word reformation to characterize the impact of Romantic poetry: "Wordsworth unconsciously did for me what every religious reformer has done, – he re-created my Supreme Divinity; substituting a new and living spirit for the old deity, once alive, but gradually hardened into an idol." While studying theology at a Dissenting college, White read *Lyrical Ballads* and experienced a radical alteration in his religious disposition. Attempting to define more precisely how his mode of religious thinking had been transformed, White recalled that Wordsworth's poetry

conveyed to me no new doctrine, and yet the change it wrought in me could only be compared with that which is said to have been wrought on Paul himself by the Divine apparition . . . It encited a movement and a growth which went on till, by degrees, all the systems which enveloped me like a body gradually decayed from me and fell away into nothing. Of more importance, too, than the decay of systems was the birth of a habit of inner reference and a dislike to occupy myself with anything which did not in some way or other touch the soul, or was not the illustration or embodiment of some spiritual law.[13]

At about the age when White was experiencing his Pauline conversion under the influence of Wordsworth, George Bernard Shaw was being similarly unhorsed by another Romantic poet. "The saint who called me to the religious life when I was eighteen was Shelley," the playwright reported to a Roman Catholic abbess. He spoke with some irony in this instance, but he generally tended to recall Shelley's impact as that of "a religious force." "I had read much poetry; but only one poet was sacred to me: Shelley. I had read his works piously from end to end, and was in my negations atheist and republican to the backbone. I say in my negations, for I had not reached any affirmative position."[14] Shaw spent the rest of his life working out his affirmative position in religion, as though to validate the assertion of Sir Andrew Undershaft in *Major Barbara* that "Religion is the only thing capable people really care about." And he consistently credited Shelley with being an essential formative influence on his thought, a thinker from whom he learned not only atheism but a searching, exacting sense of what a humane religion ought to be – what Christianity ought to be, in fact, and had failed to become. Attesting to the continuing vitality of the poet's impact on the culture of the English-speaking world, Shaw said in 1892, "Shelley became a Power – a Power that is still growing. He made and is still making men and women join political societies, Secular societies, Vegetarian societies, societies for the loosening of the marriage contract, and Humanitarian societies of all sorts."[15]

Of many similar testimonies, let another Irish one suffice. In James Joyce's *A Portrait of the Artist as a Young Man*, Stephen Dedalus is accused of heresy and roughed up by schoolmates for insisting that Byron was "the greatest poet."[16] Joyce's biographer, Richard Ellman, records that the author had himself experienced such an assault when he was a student at Belvedere College, and points out that his devotion to Byron persisted throughout his life (he later worked on the libretto for an operatic adaptation of *Cain* – conscious of the "bad manners" involved in endeavoring "to rewrite the text of a great English poet."[17] In *A Portrait*, Byron is used to represent a symbolic alternative to the life in which young Stephen Dedalus feels trapped, providing the pattern for his escape into artistic exile. In Chapter 4, in an interlude between Stephen's conversation with the Jesuit retreat director who has invited him to consider a priestly vocation and the grand epiphany of a girl wading in the water who becomes an emblem of the beauty of mortal flesh, between those two defining moments Stephen is depicted waiting impatiently for his father:

From the door of Byron's publichouse to the gate of Clontarf Chapel, from the gate of Clontarf Chapel to the door of Byron's publichouse and then back again to the chapel and then back again to the publichouse he had paced slowly at first, planting his steps scrupulously in the spaces of the patchwork of the footpath, then timing their fall to the fall of verses . . . For a full hour he had paced up and down, waiting: but he could wait no longer.[18]

Of all the pubs in Dublin Joyce chose the one with Byron's name (such a pub actually existed) to represent the direction away from the equally emblematic chapel. Stephen's Byronism is presented with considerable irony, as Hugh Kenner has observed,[19] but it is clear that Byron provided a working model and an inspiration for the young James Joyce as he forged his own character, rejecting the religious vocation planned for him by his parents and teachers and preparing for a self-imposed exile in Italy. Helene Cixous remarks that "Byron, as Stephen's spiritual ally, presides over his entry into literature as he had over the boy's first steps in heresy."[20]

All the instances I have cited thus far involved an individual who was detached from orthodoxy by the Romantic influence and set adrift in the direction of skepticism or at any rate encouraged to adopt a more critical approach to religion. But the influence of the Romantics could operate in the other direction as well. Not long after Wordsworth's death, Aubrey De Vere visited a Roman Catholic monastery "and was surprised to find a portrait of Wordsworth in the Abbot's room, among those of the Catholic Saints. The Abbot told him that as a young man it was Wordsworth's poetry which had first turned his thoughts to the contemplative life."[21] In our own century another monastic voice has testified to the impact of Romantic poetry on his vocation. In *The Seven Storey Mountain*, Thomas Merton recalls that his conversion to Christianity in 1938 occurred while he was writing a Master's thesis at Columbia University on William Blake.

As Blake worked himself into my system, I became more and more conscious of the necessity of a vital faith, and the total unreality of the dead, selfish rationalism which had been freezing my mind and will for the last seven years. By the time the summer was over, I was to become conscious of the fact that the only way to live was to live in a world that was charged with the presence and reality of God . . . Through Blake I would one day come, in a round-about way, to the only true Church, and to the One Living God, through his Son, Jesus Christ.[22]

It will seem ironic that Blake led Merton on the path to "the only true Church," but Merton's orthodoxy resembled Blake's in the powerful witness it bore against war, injustice, and the arrogance of power, including ecclesiastical power. No official of the Catholic Church ever accused Thomas Merton of erring on the conservative side in doctrine or discipline. Having had his own mind stirred out of "selfish rationalism" by Blake, the cloistered activist spent the rest of his life trying to stir his coreligionists out of lifeless dogmatism and pietism and to open the American Catholic mind to a new range of theological and political experience. His outspoken opposition to nuclear weapons and to the war in Vietnam, his critique of American racism and materialism, and his broad indictment of "the delusion of a culture where man has first been completely alienated from himself by economic individualism, and then precipitated into the morass of mass-technological society,"[23] were impressive updatings of Blake's critique of the social ills of his own time. To give credit to the full range of Blake's religious influence, I should note also that while Merton was being inspired by Blake to embrace the life of a Trappist monk, another American religious thinker, Thomas Altizer, was claiming Blake as the chief influence on his radical theology of the death of God, a theology that he called Christian Atheism.[24]

When William Hale White said that as a result of reading Wordsworth, "all the systems which enveloped me like a body gradually decayed from me and fell away into nothing," he may have come close to defining the precise nature of the religious impact that the British Romantic writers have had on their readers. In Blake's *Jerusalem*, Los devotes himself to the work of "Striving with Systems to deliver Individuals from those Systems" (*J* 11:5). For Blake the solvent of systems is the imagination, the faculty that, in Coleridge's famous definition, "dissolves, diffuses, dissipates, in order to re-create." What the religious imagination recreates from the dissolution of abandoned belief-systems depends on the individual's psychic make-up and historical environment. He might align himself by choice with an established church, as Wordsworth did, reimagining that church differently from what it had become in history. He might repudiate all church structures while privately cultivating his own radically refashioned Christian faith, in the Blakean manner. He might preserve a suspicious distance from all religions in the style of Byron, reduce belief to a bare minimum of intellectual and cultural content as Keats did, or challenge the conception of religion itself as inimical to humanity's best interests, in imitation of Shelley. Or the individual might, in Mary Shelley's way, set one system of religious ideology against another in a search for a synthesis combining the best values of both. In each case, what remained after the process of dissolution and recreation was a still vital religious vision or at least a sense of the importance of religion's claims in human life. What was sacred was not any particular religion but the liberty of the individual believer to inquire freely until he or she found a religion that would suffice. "I know of no other Christianity," Blake insisted, "and of no other Gospel than the liberty both of body & mind to exercise the Divine Arts of Imagination."

What Shelley did for Browning, Tennyson, and Shaw, what Wordsworth did for White and the Abbot of Grace Dieu, what Blake did for Merton and Altizer, and Byron for Joyce, was to serve in this way as a solvent of systems, setting them free from old forms of religious thinking and sending them forth in search of new ones. However radically they altered their readers' religious views, their primary effect was not to reconvert them to specific sets of alternate beliefs but to launch them on Byronic pilgrimages toward indefinite intellectual destinations. As Larry Swingle has observed, "Rather than raising questions in order to move toward a presentation of doctrine, Romantic poetry tends to do quite the opposite: it employs doctrine in order to generate an atmosphere of the open question . . . The Romantic poet's basic concern is not to indoctrinate . . . rather it is to advance the case of whatever is antithetical to commonly accepted belief, thus to keep alive the possibility of an opposite belief."[25] A poetry that questions inevitably has a different religious impact from a poetry that teaches. Its reformational effect will be to dislodge rather than fix an individual in a particular system.

When the religious revival that had coincided with the birth of Romanticism lost its early exuberance and began to chill and harden into the bleak, oppressive public religiosity we associate with the Victorian period, when even the term "Nonconformity" came into ironic conflict with itself, the Romantics preserved what much of the religious community abandoned, the ideal of freshness of experience, of individual freedom, of imaginative autonomy in matters of the spirit. As the revival lapsed into institutional conservatism, the Romantic tradition, true to its dissenting inspiration, continued to foster a hunger for religious freedom. Those who had been most profoundly influenced by the Romantics tended, even when they joined organized churches, to remain nonconformists within their new ecclesial communities. In 1858, the Reverend F. D. Maurice was deprived of his professorship at King's College, London after being charged with heresy for repudiating the doctrine of eternal punishment on the grounds that it was unscriptural. Even after

Newman went over to Rome he preserved in that most authoritarian religious environment a stubborn independence and integrity that continually discomposed the clerical bureaucrats who were his superiors until he became in their eyes "the most dangerous man in England."[26] Thomas Merton lived as a self-described "Christian anarchist" within the equally repressive American Catholic Church of the mid-twentieth century, thriving as poet and polemicist and unaccountably free man despite efforts by Church officials to suppress his activities.[27] The institutional Church in its most authoritarian moods proved remarkably unable to break such individuals to its mold; even as believers they showed evidence of their kinship with the atheists, agnostics, and honest doubters of the nineteenth century who also claimed a Romantic inheritance – Tennyson, Ruskin, Arnold, Emerson, Whitman, Swinburne, Shaw, and the others.

There seems to be a special religious vitality in the work of the Romantic writers that continues to serve a kind of scriptural function, teaching and inspiring individual readers generation after generation. Whether believers or skeptics, those who have acknowledged the Romantic influence have attributed a unique efficacy to their writings. Perhaps it was only that good poetry adds intensified rhetorical power to religious insights. Bernard Shaw, who was often said to have derived his unconventional ideas from European intellectual traditions, himself gave most of the credit to English poetry – Shelley's especially: "I am always asked how it is that my opinions have changed so little since my youth. It is because I got to them by poetry. As I always say, the aesthetic is the most convincing and permanent. Shelley made his ideas sing; I made them dance."[28] Shelley himself had argued that poetry was more efficacious than philosophy in finding truth and in employing that truth for the welfare of humanity. Wordsworth spoke as explicitly and confidently of the profound vitality present in poetry, a life he descibed as praeternatural in its origin and effects. "Visionary power," he wrote, "Attends the motions of the viewless winds,/ Embodied in the mystery of words." Honoring in *The Prelude* the "memory of all books which lay / Their sure foundations in the heart of man," he paid reverent tribute to the power of the written word, a power second only to Sacred Scripture in its ability to bless, inspire, and save. In celebration of all such nurturing books, he wrote:

> 'Tis just that in behalf of these, the works,
> And of the men that framed them, whether known,
> Or sleeping nameless in their scattered graves,
> That I should here assert their rights, attest
> Their honours, and should, once for all, pronounce
> Their benediction; speak of them as Powers
> For ever to be hallowed; only less,
> For what we are and what we may become,
> Than Nature's self, which is the breath of God,
> Or his pure Word by miracle revealed.[29]

Apart from that last line, added later in his life, Wordsworth's tribute could have been endorsed by all the Romantics. Shelley, with whom this book began, may be permitted to have the final word in the matter. In the writings of his fellow Romantics he found that same mysterious vitality that Wordsworth detected in all great poetry – "an electric life," he called it, "which burns within their words." And in another of his prophecies of the new Reformation that he believed was coming upon England, he hailed his contemporaries as natural leaders of the religious renovation:

We live among such philosophers and poets as surpass beyond comparison any who have appeared since the last great struggle for civil and religious liberty. The most unfailing herald, companion, and follower of the awakening of a great people to work a beneficial change in opinion or institution, is Poetry.[30]

Notes

INTRODUCTION

1 *The Romantic Ideology: A Critical Investigation* (University of Chicago Press, 1983), p. 26.
2 *The Critical Twilight: Explorations in the Ideology of Anglo-American Literary Theory from Eliot to McLuhan* (Boston: Routledge, 1977), p. 4.
3 "Fictions and Freedom: Wordsworth and the Ideology of Romanticism" in *New Historical Literary Study: Essays on Reproducing Texts, Representing History*, ed. Jeffrey N. Cox (Princeton University Press, 1993), pp. 178, 180.
4 *On Revolution* (New York: Viking, 1963), p. 19. Sociologists and cultural historians, reconsidering the relationship between religion and political activism in the light of the Iranian revolution, have lately become more willing to acknowledge that religious belief can act as a powerful stimulus to social change. See *Religion, Rebellion, Revolution: An Interdisciplinary and Cross-Cultural Collection of Essays*, ed. Bruce Lincoln (London: Macmillan, 1985).
5 My understanding of the religious character of English politics has been influenced by J. C. D. Clark's *English Society 1688–1832: Ideology, Social Structure and Political Practice during the Ancien Regime* (Cambridge University Press, 1985), which emphasizes the critical role religion played in the politics of the period leading up to the Reform Bill. Other church historians on whom I have depended include R. A. Soloway, *Prelates and People: Ecclesiastical Social Thought in England 1783–1852* (London: Routledge & Kegan Paul, 1969); E. R. Norman, *Church and Society in England 1770–1970* (Oxford: Clarendon Press, 1976); Robert Hole, *Pulpits, Politics, and Public Order in England 1760–1832* (Cambridge University Press, 1989); James Bradley, *Religion, Revolution, and English Radicalism: Nonconformity in Eighteenth-Century Politics and Society* (Cambridge University Press, 1990), and various others whom I will cite in the course of this study.
6 *The Letters of Percy Bysshe Shelley*, ed. Frederick L. Jones (Oxford: Clarendon Press, 1964), I: 143.
7 Richard Carlile, *The Report of the Proceedings of the Court of Kings Bench* . . .

being the mock trial of Richard Carlile for alledged blasphemous libel, etc. (London: Carlile, 1822), p. 5.

8 *On the Constitution of the Church and State,* ed. John Colmer, in *The Collected Works of Samuel Taylor Coleridge,* vol. 10 (Princeton University Press, 1976), p. 70.

9 Fekete, *Critical Twilight,* p. 5.

10 What Frederic Jameson said of Milton's society is applicable to the Romantic cultural milieu as well: "The religious community serves as a concrete mediation between the public and the private and as a space in which problems of institution and power meet problems of personal relationships and ethics or private life." "Religion and Ideology: A Political Reading of *Paradise Lost*" in *Literature, Politics and Theory: Papers from the Essex Conference 1976–1984,* ed. Francis Barker, et al. (New York: Methuen, 1986), p. 53.

11 "English Romanticism, The Spirit of the Age" in *Romanticism Reconsidered: Selected Papers from the English Institute,* ed. Northrop Frye (Columbia University Press, 1963), p. 53.

12 Keats's Marginalia to *Paradise Lost* in *John Keats,* ed. Elizabeth Cook (Oxford University Press, 1990), p. 339.

13 Malcolm Miles Kelsall, *Byron's Politics* (Totowa, NJ: Barnes and Noble, 1987), p. 2.

14 *The Radical Triumvirate; or Infidel Paine, Lord Byron, and Surgeon Lawrence colleaguing with the patriotic Radicals to emancipate Mankind from all Laws, human and divine. A Letter to John Bull* by "Oxonian" (1820), pp. 46–47. For William Lawrence, see my *Keats: The Religious Sense* (Princeton University Press, 1976), pp. 54–59, 62–63, 66–67.

15 *Radical Triumvirate,* p. 49.

16 *The Republican,* February 15, 1822, p. 212.

17 In *The Social Contract: Essays by Locke, Hume, and Rousseau,* ed. Ernest Barker (London: Oxford University Press, 1947), p. 305. The concept of a "public religion" is discussed by Robert N. Bellah in "Civil Religion in America," *Daedalus* 96 (1967): 1–21, and by J. F. Maclear in "Isaac Watts and the Idea of Public Religion," *Journal of the History of Ideas* 53 (1992): 25–45.

18 See, for example, James Benziger, *Images of Eternity: Studies in the Poetry of Religious Vision from Wordsworth to T. S. Eliot* (Southern Illinois University Press, 1962) and John Middleton Murry, *Keats and Shakespeare* (1935; rpt. London: Oxford University Press, 1958), pp. 141–44. Scholarship has not yet produced an entirely satisfactory study of the religious beliefs of the Romantic poets as expressed in the poetry. There have been useful investigations of individual poets, but few scholars have attempted a comprehensive survey of the major authors as participants in a common religious enterprise. The most ambitious attempts at such a summary have tended to overlook or oversimplify the complex issues involved. In the third volume of *Religious Trends in English Poetry* (Columbia University

Press, 1949), H. N. Fairchild measured the poets against his own standard of Anglican orthodoxy and found them all wanting in good religious sense. M. H. Abrams's *Natural Supernaturalism: Tradition and Revolution in Romantic Literature* (New York: Norton, 1971) uses modern secularism as its standard of metaphysical authenticity and tends to underestimate the traditional nature, as well as the peculiar contemporary resonance, of Romantic religious attitudes. Counter-arguments to Fairchild and Abrams can be found in *English Romanticism: The Grounds of Belief* (Northern Illinois University Press, 1983) by John Clubbe and Ernest Lovell and in *Locke, Wesley, and the Method of English Romanticism* (University of Florida Press, 1984) by Richard Brantley.

19 *Speculations: Essays on Humanism and the Philosophy of Art*, ed. Herbert Read (1924; rpt. London: Routledge & Kegan Paul, 1949), p. 118.

20 Coleridge's religious politics are examined by Cyril Kennan Gloyn, *The Church in the Social Order: Study of Anglican Social Theory from Coleridge to Maurice* (Forest Grove, Oregon: Pacific University Press, 1942); Charles R. Sanders, *Coleridge and the Broad Church Movement* (Duke University Press, 1942); Carl Woodring, *Politics in the Poetry of Coleridge* (University of Wisconsin Press, 1961); Leonard W. Deen, "Coleridge and the Radicalism of Religious Dissent," *JEGP* 61 (1962): 496–510; Morton D. Paley, "'These promised Years': Coleridge's 'Religious Musings' and the Millenarianism of the 1790s" in *Revolution and English Romanticism: Politics and Rhetoric*, ed. Keith Hanley and Raman Selden (New York: St. Martin's, 1990), pp. 49–65. See also the introduction and notes to various volumes in *The Collected Coleridge*, published by the Bollingen Foundation and Princeton University Press, especially volume 1: *Lectures 1795: On Politics and Religion*, ed. Lewis Patton and Peter Manning (1971), and volume 10: *On the Constitution of the Church and State*, ed. John Colmer (1976).

21 For Blake, see Harold Bloom, *Blake's Apocalypse: A Study in Poetic Argument* (New York: Doubleday, 1963) and J. G. Davies, *The Theology of William Blake* (Oxford: Clarendon, 1948). For Wordsworth, see Edith C. Batho, *The Later Wordsworth* (1933; rpt. New York: Russell & Russell, 1963), pp. 237–41, 251–2, and Richard E. Brantley, *Wordsworth's "Natural Methodism"* (Yale University Press, 1975). For Byron, see Anne K. Mellor, *English Romantic Irony* (Harvard University Press, 1980) and G. Wilson Knight, *Lord Byron: Christian Virtues* (London: Routledge and Kegan Paul, 1952). Finally, for Keats see Robert M. Ryan, *Keats: The Religious Sense*, and Ronald A. Sharp, *Keats, Skepticism, and the Religion of Beauty* (University of Georgia Press, 1979).

22 D. G. James, *The Romantic Comedy: An Essay on English Romanticism* (New York: Oxford University Press, 1948); Harold Bloom, *The Visionary Company: A Reading of English Romantic Poetry* (New York: Doubleday, 1963); Edward E. Bostetter, *The Romantic Ventriloquists: Wordsworth, Coleridge, Keats, Shelley, Byron* (University of Washington Press, 1963); Carl Woodring, *Politics in English Romantic Poetry* (Harvard University Press,

1970); Marilyn Butler, *Romantics, Rebels, and Reactionaries: English Literature and its Background 1760–1830* (New York: Oxford University Press, 1982).

1 "A SECT OF DISSENTERS"

1 *Shelley's Poetry and Prose*, ed. Donald H. Reiman and Sharon B. Powers (New York: Norton, 1977), p. 134.

2 *The Excursion* 7: 1009–12. In *The Poetical Works of William Wordsworth*, ed. Ernest de Selincourt and Helen Darbishire (Oxford: Clarendon Press, 1949), 5: 263.

3 On this "religion of the heart" that, unlike Christianity, did not "affront our reason and humanity," see *The Letters of John Keats*, ed. H. E. Rollins (Harvard University Press, 1958), 2: 103, and my *Keats: The Religious Sense* (Princeton University Press, 1976), pp. 171–72, 202–5.

4 *Letters* 1: 281–82.

5 *Complete Prose Works of John Milton*, vol. 1: *1624–1642*, ed. Don M. Wolfe (Yale University Press, 1953), p. 598.

6 *Complete Prose*, vol. 2: *1643–1648*, ed. Ernest Sirluck (Yale University Press, 1959), pp. 549–50.

7 *Complete Prose* 1: 853, 2: 553.

8 Arthur E. Barker, *Milton and the Puritan Dilemma 1641–1660* (University of Toronto Press, 1942), p.19.

9 *Complete Prose* 1: 820–21, 816.

10 *Letters* 1: 255.

11 *Complete Prose* 2: 566.

12 *The Age of Reason*, ed. Moncure Daniel Conway (New York: Putnam, 1896), p. 23.

13 "Everyone talked of it, everyone was attracted by its eloquence, everyone admitted the benevolence and talents and sincerity of the author." Introduction to *A Practical View* (1797 rpt. New York: American Bible Society, 1830), pp. 18–19.

14 *A Practical View*, p. 313.

15 "Evangelical" was a name of broad signification that was used originally to designate those who claimed to take the gospels as a rule of life, irrespective of their denominational affiliation. There were Evangelicals among the Dissenters as well as in the Church, but the word came to be applied more particularly to the party within the Anglican Establishment whose piety and conduct marked them as spiritual heirs of John Wesley and George Whitefield, although they did not follow the Methodists out of the Church.

16 *Complete Prose* 2: 554.

17 See Joseph Nicholes, "Revolutions Compared: The English Civil War as Political Touchstone in Romantic Literature" in *Revolution and English Romanticism: Politics and Rhetoric*, ed. Keith Hanley and Raman Selden (New York: St. Martin's, 1990), pp. 261–76.

18 J. C. D. Clark provides a most coherent account of the unsettling impact of the Catholic Question on British politics in this period.

19 The most thorough recent study of the history of Dissent in England is Michael R. Watts, *The Dissenters*, vol. 1: *From the Reformation to the French Revolution* (Oxford: Clarendon Press, 1978).

20 Detailed accounts of the repeal campaign may be found in Anthony Lincoln, *Some Political and Social Ideas of English Dissent 1763–1800* (1938; rpt. New York: Octagon, 1971); Richard Burgess Barlow, *Citizenship and Conscience: A Study in the Theory and Practice of Religious Toleration in England During the Eighteenth Century* (University of Pennsylvania Press, 1962); and Ursula Henriques, *Religious Toleration in England 1787–1833* (University of Toronto Press, 1961).

21 Thomas W. Davis, ed., *Committees for Repeal of the Test and Corporation Acts, Minutes, 1788–90 and 1827–28* (London Record Society, 1978), pp. 19, 43.

22 G. M. Ditchfield, "Anti-trinitarianism and Toleration in Late Eighteenth Century British Politics: The Unitarian Petition of 1792," *Journal of Ecclesiastical History* 42 (1991): 31–67. For the continual pressure for reform brought by the Unitarians throughout the Romantic period, see Frida Knight, *University Rebel: The Life of William Frend, 1757–1841* (London: Gollancz, 1971).

23 Lincoln, *Political and Social Ideas of Dissent*, p. 249.

24 See G. M. Ditchfield, "The Parliamentary Struggle over the Repeal of the Test and Corporation Acts, 1787–1790," *English Historical Review* 89 (1974): 563.

25 Richard Price, *Political Writings*, ed. D. O. Thomas (Cambridge University Press, 1991), pp. 183, 195–96.

26 H. N. Brailsford, *Shelley, Godwin and Their Circle* (New York: Holt, 1920), p. 1.

27 *The Writings and Speeches of Edmund Burke*, vol. 8: *The French Revolution 1790–1794*, ed. L. G. Mitchell (Oxford: Clarendon Press, 1989), pp. 61–62, 64, 66, 76, 116–17.

28 "Perhaps no single action of the revolutionary governments caused greater resentment among Frenchmen than the policy toward the Church." Charles Breunig, *The Age of Revolution and Reaction, 1789–1850* (New York: Norton, 1970), p. 22.

29 [Anonymous], *Temperate Comments upon Intemperate Reflections or, A Review of Mr. Burke's Letter* (London: J. Walter, 1791), p. 47.

30 See, for example, *Writings and Speeches* 8: 117.

31 "Remarks on the Policy of the Allies" (1793) in *Writings and Speeches* 8: 485.

32 *Writings and Speeches* 8: 141, 149.

33 See, for example, *Letter to Richard Burke, Esq.* (1792), in *Writings and Speeches* 9: 647–48.

34 Harold Perkin, *Origins of Modern English Society* (1969; rpt. London: Routledge, 1991), p. 203.

35 W. R. Ward, "The French Revolution and the English Churches," *Miscellanea Historiae Ecclesiasticae* 4 (1970): 75–76. On cooperation among Dissenters see also J. E. Cookson, *The Friends of Peace: Anti-War Liberalism in England, 1793–1815* (Cambridge University Press, 1982) and Barlow, *Citizenship and Conscience*, pp. 256, 259, 272.

36 Some recent studies include Gordon Rupp, *Religion in England 1688–1791* (Oxford: Clarendon Press, 1986), pp. 325–485; Boyd Hilton, *The Age of Atonement: The Influence of Evangelicalism on Social and Economic Thought, 1795–1865* (Oxford: Clarendon Press, 1988); and David Bebbington, *Evangelicalism in Modern Britain: A History from the 1730s to the 1980s* (Winchester, MA: Allen & Unwin, 1989).

37 *The Miscellaneous Works and Remains of the Rev. Robert Hall, with a Memoir of his Life, by Olinthus Gregory and a Critical Estimate of His Character and Writings by John Foster* (London: Bohn, 1846), p. 476.

38 See Alan D. Gilbert, *Religion and Society in Industrial England: Church, Chapel and Social Change, 1740–1914* (London: Longmans, 1976); Deryck W. Lovegrove, *Established Church, Sectarian People: Itinerancy and the Transformation of English Dissent, 1780–1830* (Cambridge University Press, 1988); W. R. Ward, *Religion and Society in England 1790–1850* (London: Batsford, 1972) and "The Baptists and the Transformation of the Church, 1780–1830," *Baptist Quarterly* 25, no. 4 (Oct. 1973): 167–84.

39 The historian Elie Halévy is usually credited with establishing the notion that religion acted as a counter-revolutionary force in Britain. For a review of responses to Halévy, see Elissa S. Itzkin, "The Halévy Thesis – A Working Hypothesis? English Revivalism: Antidote for Revolution and Radicalism 1789–1815," *Church History* 44 (1975): 47–56. The argument has received more careful scrutiny in E. P. Thompson, *The Making of the English Working Class* (1963; New York: Pantheon, 1964), Bernard Semmel, *The Methodist Revolution* (New York: Basic Books, 1973), and A. D. Gilbert, "Methodism, Dissent and Political Stability in Early Industrial England," *Journal of Religious History* 10 (1979): 381–99. A sophisticated analysis of the political impact of evangelical religion, particularly Methodism, may also be found in Perkin, *Origins of Modern English Society*, pp. 196–207, 347–62.

40 *Religion and Culture* (London: Sheed and Ward, 1948), p. 59. In Bruce Lincoln's terms, the "religion of the status quo" was apparently becoming a "religion of resistance," which could too easily become a "religion of revolution." See Bruce Lincoln, "Notes toward a Theory of Religion and Revolution" in *Religion, Rebellion, Revolution* (London: Macmillan, 1985), pp. 266–92.

41 *The Second Coming: Popular Millenarianism 1780–1850* (Rutgers University Press, 1979), p. 222.

42 *English Society 1688–1832*, p. 277. Coleridge noticed the political significance of a ubiquitous clergy as a "germ of civilization" transplanted "to every parish throughout the kingdom," a situation which patriots

"cannot estimate at too high a price." *Biographia Literaria*, ed. James Engell and W. J. Bate (Princeton University Press, 1983), 1: 227.

43 The number of clerical magistrates increased markedly from the 1790s to the 1820s. Anthony Russell, *The Clerical Profession* (London, SPCK, 1981), pp. 32–41, 146–67.

44 Quoted by Ward, *Religion and Society*, p. 54

45 *The Charge of Samuel Lord Bishop of Rochester to the Clergy of His Diocese, Delivered at his Second General Visitation in the Year 1800* (London: Robson, 1800), pp. 19–20.

46 Two recent books that have demonstrated convincingly the relationship between religious and political radicalism in the 1790s are Iain McCalman's *Radical Underworld: Prophets, Revolutionaries and Pornographers in London, 1795–1840* (Cambridge University Press, 1988) and Jon Mee's *Dangerous Enthusiasm: William Blake and the Culture of Radicalism in the 1790s* (Oxford: Clarendon Press, 1992). See also C. B. Jewson, *The Jacobin City: A Portrait of Norwich in its Reaction to the French Revolution 1788–1802* (London: Blackie, 1975), 52, 87, 138.

47 See Perkin, *Origins of Modern English Society*, pp. 196, 203, 353–64.

48 *Religion and Society in Industrial England*, pp. 145–46. See also McCalman, *Radical underworld*, p. 57; R. F. Wearmouth, *Methodism and the Working-Class Movements of England, 1800–1850* (2nd edn., London: Epworth press, 1947), pp. 7–8; and Gerhard Lenski, *The Religious Factor: A Sociological Study of Religion's Impact on Politics, Economics, and Family Life* (Garden City, NY: Doubleday, 1961), pp. 300–1.

49 Leslie Chard observed that, except for his brother Richard, "all of [Wordsworth's] known associates in the spring of 1793 were Dissenters, and his thought of that time has many striking similarities to Dissenting ideas." *Dissenting Republican; Wordsworth's Early Life and Thought in Their Political Context* (The Hague: Mouton, 1972), p. 122.

50 *Miscellaneous Works*, pp. 153–55.

51 Coleridge, "Dejection: An Ode," lines 69–70, in *The Poems of Samuel Taylor Coleridge*, ed. Ernest Hartley Coleridge (Oxford University Press, 1961), p. 366.

52 "Prospectus" to *The Excursion*, lines 60–62. The temperamental affinities between British Romanticism and the Evangelical Revival have been examined by other scholars, most recently Richard Brantley in *Wordsworth's "Natural Methodism"* (Yale University Press, 1975) and *Locke, Wesley, and the Method of English Romanticism* (University of Florida Press, 1984).

53 *Edinburgh Review* 1 (Oct. 1802), p. 66. *The Romantics Reviewed: Contemporary Reviews of British Romantic Writers*, ed. Donald H, Reiman (New York: Garland Press, 1972), Part A, vol. 2, pp. 415–17.

54 See William Haller, *The Early Life of Robert Southey 1774–1803* (1917; rpt. New York: Octagon, 1966), pp. 268–75.

55 *Sermon on the Evidence of a Future Period of Improvement in the State of Mankind* (London, 1787), p. 27.

56 John Randolph, *A Charge Delivered to the Clergy of the Diocese of Oxford* (Oxford, 1802), p. 11.
57 *Complete Prose* 2: 256.
58 David Erdman identifies the papal eminence as George III in *The Illuminated Blake* (Garden City, NY: Doubleday/Anchor, 1974), p. 169.
59 *Milton* 18: 51–19: 3–14, in *The Complete Poetry and Prose of William Blake*, ed. David V. Erdman (revised edn., New York: Doubleday/Anchor, 1988), p. 112.
60 "Prospectus" to *The Excursion*, 1814 edition, ed. Jonathan Wordsworth (New York: Woodstock Books, 1991).
61 E.g. by Harold Bloom in *The Visionary Company: A Reading of English Romantic Poetry* (New York: Doubleday, 1963), pp. 132–36.
62 *The Excursion* Book 4, p. 169.
63 Essay, Supplementary to the Preface to *Poems* (1815). *The Prose Works of William Wordsworth*, ed. W. J. B. Owen and Jane Worthington Smyser (Oxford: Clarendon, 1974), 3: 65, 34–35.
64 *Letters* 1: 281, 2: 103. See also *The Complete Works of John Keats*, ed. H. B. Forman, 5 vols. (1901; rpt. New York: AMS, 1970), 3: 268, for Keats's remarks on "the abstract adoration of the Deity."
65 Stuart Curran, "Blake and the Gnostic Hyle: A Double Negative," *Blake Studies* 4 (1972): 117–33.
66 See Walter Jackson Bate, *The Burden of the Past and the English Poet* (Belknap Press of Harvard University Press, 1970) and Harold Bloom, *The Anxiety of Influence: A Theory of Poetry* (New York: Oxford University Press, 1973). For rebuttals to Bloom, see Joseph A. Wittreich, *Angel of Apocalypse: Blake's Idea of Milton* (University of Wisconsin Press, 1975), and Lucy Newlyn, *Paradise Lost and the Romantic Reader* (Oxford: Clarendon, 1993).
67 *Prose Works* 3: 64.
68 *The Prelude* (1805) 1: 59–63.
69 *Milton* 2: 25. In Erdman, *The Illuminated Blake*, p. 96.
70 "Aird's Religious Characteristics," *Blackwood's* (June 1827), p. 677.
71 *His Very Self and Voice: Collected Conversations of Lord Byron*, ed. Ernest J. Lovell (New York: Macmillan, 1954), p. 444.
72 *Edinburgh Review* 36 (Feb. 1822), p. 438. In *The Romantics Reviewed*, B-2: 931.
73 *The Autobiography of Leigh Hunt*, ed. J. E. Morpurgo (London: Cresset, 1949), p. 451.
74 The first volume of the periodical ran a series of articles attacking "the intolerant disciples of the merciless Calvin, the gloomy Methodists." *Examiner*, May 15, 1808, p. 301. For an overview of Hunt's struggle against the religious establishment see my *Keats: The Religious Sense*, pp. 40, 51–53, 71–78, 86–94.
75 *Foliage* (London, 1818), p. cxxii.
76 *The Complete Works of William Hazlitt*, ed. P. P. Howe (London: Dent, 1930–34), 11: 124.

77 *Complete Works* 16: 105–6.

78 *The Defence of Poetry*, in *Shelley's Poetry and Prose*, ed. Reiman and Powers, pp. 485, 488. Shelley's *Defence* provides most of the material for the discussion that follows; to simplify documentation I have included page references to the Reiman–Powers edition within in the text.

79 *A Philosophical View of Reform* in *The Complete Works of Percy Bysshe Shelley*, ed. Roger Ingpen and W. E. Peck (New York: Scribner's, 1926–1930), 7: 20.

80 Ibid., 7: 7.

81 Ibid., 7: 9.

2 BLAKE'S ORTHODOXY

1 For a brief analysis of the Church's condition, see my *Keats: The Religious Sense* (Princeton University Press, 1976), pp. 12–22, and recent works by Peter Virgin, *The Church in an Age of Negligence: Ecclesiastical Structure and the Problem of Church Reform 1700–1840* (Cambridge University Press, 1989) and F.C. Mather, *High Church Prophet: Bishop Samuel Horsley (1733–1806) and the Caroline Tradition in the Later Georgian Church* (New York: Oxford University Press, 1992), the eighth chapter of which discusses some limited efforts at church reform in the 1790s and early 1800s.

2 For a recent discussion of contemporary conceptions of Druidism, see Jon Mee, *Dangerous Enthusiasm: William Blake and the Culture of Radicalism in the 1790s* (Oxford: Clarendon Press, 1992), pp. 90–104.

3 Annotations to *An Apology for the Bible* by R. Watson, Bishop of Llandaff. *The Complete Poetry and Prose of William Blake*, ed. David V. Erdman (revised edn. New York: Doubleday/Anchor, 1988), p. 618. All quotations from Blake's writings will be taken from this edition and will be cited in the text.

4 *The Theology of William Blake* (Oxford: Clarendon Press, 1947), p. 1.

5 Northrop Frye, "William Blake" in *The English Romantic Poets and Essayists*, ed. Lawrence and Carolyn Houtchens (New York: Modern Language Association, 1957), p. 18.

6 *Blake's Apocalypse: A Study in Poetic Argument* (Garden City, NY: Doubleday, 1963), p. 411.

7 J. G. Davies found Blake's Christology "in the main a rephrasing of orthodox doctrine in the terms of his own idiom" (p. 110), but still had difficulty organizing Blake's religious ideas into a coherent system that coincided comfortably with Anglican orthodoxy and worried about Blake's lack of ecclesiastical affiliation. A few critics have argued persuasively for Blake's orthodoxy, most notably Margaret Bottrall, who found that "no English poet can compare with [Blake] as an interpreter of the religion of Jesus." *The Divine Image: A Study of Blake's Interpretation of Christianity* (Rome: Edizioni di Storia e Letteratura, 1950), p. 7.

8 G. E. Bentley, Jr., ed. *William Blake's Writings* (Oxford: Clarendon Press,

1963), p. 175. In a recent book on Blake E. P. Thompson, locating the poet within "the obscure traditions of London dissent," concluded that his Christian faith was "highly unorthodox and idiosyncratic." *Witness Against the Beast: William Blake and the Moral Law* (New York: The New Press, 1993), pp. xv, 20.

9 " 'The Wrath of the Lamb': A Study of William Blake's Conversions," in *From Sensibility to Romanticism*, ed. Frederick W. Hilles and Harold Bloom (Oxford University Press, 1965), p. 325.

10 Jon Mee, who understands as well as anyone the subversive character of Christian fringe groups in Blake's time, nevertheless feels obliged to detach Blake from "the hegemonic Christian tradition" (*Dangerous Enthusiasm*, p. 83).

11 *Letter to Hercules Langrishe* (1792), *Edmund Burke: The Works, Twelve Volumes in Six (1887)* (Hildesheim and New York: Georg Olms, 1975), 4: 263.

12 To Thomas Butts, November 22, 1802; E 720.

13 To Thomas Butts, November 1, 1803; E 724.

14 See Nancy Bogen, "The Problem of Blake's Early Religion," *The Personalist* 49 (1968): 510.

15 *Quarterly Review* 39 (Jan. 1829): 132.

16 *The Eighteenth Century Background: Studies on the Idea of Nature in the Thought of the Period* (1940; Boston: Beacon Press, 1961), p. 169.

17 *Charge to Clergy of the Diocese of Chester* (1825), pp. 11, 14.

18 *The Life and Correspondence of Thomas Arnold D.D.*, ed. Arthur Penrhyn Stanley, 2 vols. (Boston: Osgood, 1873), 1: 231.

19 *Collected Letters of Samuel Taylor Coleridge*, ed. E. L. Griggs (Oxford: Clarendon Press, 1956–71), 6: 622.

20 Leopold Damrosch, Jr., *Symbol and Truth in Blake's Myth* (Princeton University Press, 1980), p. 246. Although Damrosch recognizes that there is nothing necessarily unorthodox in the Swedenborgian emphasis on Jesus Christ as the only God, he still insists on the peculiarity of Blake's doctrine in this matter (p. 284).

21 Robert Hindmarsh, *Rise and Progress of the New Jerusalem Church, in England, America, and Other Parts*, ed. E. Madeley (London: 1861), p. 101.

22 *True Christian Religion*, p. 538, quoted by Davies, *The Theology of William Blake*, p. 35. A detailed account of the doctrine of the Divine Humanity as it was articulated by various English Swedenborgians in Blake's time can be found in Thompson, *Witness Against the Beast*, pp. 146–52.

23 Morton Paley, " 'A New Heaven is Begun': William Blake and Swedenborgianism," *Blake: An Illustrated Quarterly* 13 (Fall 1979): 82. Paley says that Blake's interest in Swedenborg revived around 1800. In "An Audience for *The Marriage of Heaven and Hell*," *Blake Studies* 3 (1970): 19–52, John Howard argues that *Marriage* was an attack on the political conservatism of Hindmarsh's church, written to amuse Joseph Johnson's circle. Michael Scrivener quarrels with this reading in "A Swedenborgian Visionary and the *Marriage of Heaven and Hell*" in *Blake: An Illustrated*

Quarterly 21 (1989): 102–3. The most thorough study of Blake's Sweden-borgian doctrine is still J. G. Davies, *The Theology of William Blake.*

24 See Hindmarsh, *Rise and Progress*, pp. 27, 40.

25 For a discussion of the two, see Donald John, "Blake and Forgiveness," *The Wordsworth Circle* 17 (Spring 1986): 75.

26 *A Memoir of the Late Rev. John Clowes, A.M. . . . Written by Himself* (2nd. edn. London, 1849), p. 29.

27 Robert Hodgson, *The Life of the Right Reverend Beilby Porteus D. D., Late Bishop of London* (2nd edn. London: Cadell & Davies, 1811), pp. 270–76.

28 J. Robert Barth has said of Coleridge, "However daring he may have been in his speculation, in his doctrinal commitment he was extremely orthodox." "Waiting for the Palfreys: The Great Prelude Debate," *The Wordsworth Circle* 17 (Winter 1986): 21.

29 *Collected Letters*, 6: 583–4, 5: 87–89. Coleridge's comments on Luther and Calvin were written on the flyleaf of a copy of vol. 2 of Swedenborg's *True Christian Religion*, now in the British Library.

30 Coleridge professed to have no belief one way or another on the Virgin Birth. See "Notes on Donne" in "Literary Remains," *Complete Works of Samuel Taylor Coleridge*, ed. W. G. T. Shedd (New York: Harper, 1884), 5: 79. Given Blake's dialectic manner, one is not surprised to find in *Milton* what appears to be casual acceptance of Mary's virginity in a line like "Christ took on Sin in the Virgins Womb, & put it off on the Cross" (5: 3), while in *Jerusalem* the doctrine is considered at length and repudiated (*J* 61).

31 *Complete Works* 1: 229–30.

32 Swinburne was one of the earliest critics to notice the effect of this. "Blake uses the current terms of religion, now as types of his own faith, now in the sense of ordinary preachers: impugning therefore at one time what at another he will seem to vindicate." *William Blake: A Critical Essay* (1869; rpt. London: Hotten, 1968), p. 212.

33 I myself will no doubt be accused of selecting one set of texts to support my own preunderstanding of Blake, while slighting those that conflict with it. But since I am arguing for an orthodox Blake, the atypicality of my position will at least have the virtue of serving as a Blakean contrary to the preponderance of critical argument on the other side.

34 John Beer, *Blake's Humanism* (Manchester University Press, 1968), pp. 12–13 and 13n., and Margaret Bottrall, *The Divine Image*, pp. 22–26.

35 *The Awakening of Albion: The Renovation of the Body in the Poetry of William Blake* (Cornell University Press, 1974), p. 142. David Erdman also refers to the hybrid Los–Jesus in *The Illuminated Blake* (New York: Doubleday, 1974), p. 312.

36 *Prophecy and the Philosophy of Mind: Traditions of Blake and Shelley* (University of Alabama Press, 1985), p. 76. This reduction is in the tradition of Harold Bloom, who asserts that "Blake's God possesses no powers that differ in kind from the highest human gifts." *The Visionary Company: A*

Reading of English Romantic Poetry (New York: Doubleday, 1963), pp. 5–6. Denial of the transcendence of Jesus constitutes a basic premise of Michael Ferber's *The Social Vision of William Blake* (Princeton University Press, 1985), which asserts, "Jesus and Adam are states of our own soul, and there is no 'outside' from which salvation might come" (p. 77).

37 *Conversing in Paradise: Poetic Genius and Identity-as-Community in Blake's Los* (University of Missouri Press, 1983), p. 256.

38 *Witness Against the Beast*, p. 216.

39 "William Blake" in *The Norton Anthology of English Literature*. Major Authors Edition (New York: Norton, 1975), pp. 1298–99.

40 For a discussion of dialectical theology, in which religious truth is looked for in the tension or balance between conflicting statements about the divine, see John Macquarrie, *Twentieth-Century Religious Thought: The Frontiers of Philosophy and Theology, 1900–1970* (London: SCM Press, 1971), p. 323.

41 *Blake's Apocalypse*, pp. 256–7.

42 Jon Mee, for example, detects heterodoxy in the way "Blake's Saviour disrupts one of the most basic biblical paradigms: the opposition between Christ's inspiration and Satan's energy." *Dangerous Enthusiasm*, p. 70.

43 See John Sutherland, "Blake and Urizen" in *Blake's Visionary Forms Dramatic*, ed. David V. Erdman and John E. Grant (Princeton University Press, 1970), pp. 244–62.

44 One can watch Blake functioning like Los as he mediates between Tom Paine and the Bishop of Llandaff in his Annotations to Watson. See Florence Sandler, " 'Defending the Bible': Blake, Paine, and the Bishop on the Atonement" in *Blake and His Bibles*, ed. David V. Erdman (West Cornwall, CY: Locust Hill Press), p. 66.

45 My understanding of the poem's central allegory has been influenced primarily by Northrop Frye, *Fearful Symmetry* (Princeton University Press, 1947) and to a lesser degree by Harold Bloom, *Blake's Apocalypse* and Morton Paley, *The Continuing City: William Blake's "Jerusalem"* (Oxford: Clarendon Press, 1983).

46 *The Illuminated Blake* (Garden City, NY: Doubleday, 1974), p. 284.

47 For a recent account of deism see Peter Harrison, *"Religion" and the Religions in the English Enlightenment* (Cambridge University Press, 1990), pp. 61–98.

48 George Every, *The High Church Party 1688–1718* (London: SPCK, 1956), p. 67.

49 Recent studies have attempted to rescue the Latitudinarians from accusations, originating with contemporary Calvinist critics, that they abandoned orthodoxy for rationalism and even deism. See, for example, W. M. Spellman, *The Latitudinarians and the Church of England, 1660–1700* (University of Georgia Press, 1993).

50 Quoted by John Gascoigne, *Cambridge in the Age of the Enlightenment: Science,*

Religion, and Politics from the Restoration to the French Revolution (Cambridge University Press, 1989), p. 115.

51 Margaret C. Jacob, *The Newtonians and the English Revolution 1689–1720* (Cornell University Press, 1976), p. 144. See also James R. Jacob and Margaret C. Jacob. "The Anglican Origins of Modern Science: The Metaphysical Foundations of the Whig Constitution," *Isis* 71 (1980): 251–67; and Margaret C. Jacob, *The Radical Enlightenment: Pantheists, Freemasons and Republicans* (Boston: Allen & Unwin, 1981).

52 Spellman, *The Latitudinarians*, p. 159. A detailed analysis of the Latitudinarians' connection with Newton may be found in Gascoigne, *Cambridge in the Age of the Enlightenment.*

53 Defenders of the Latitudinarians argue that they were actually attempting to moderate the brutal economics of Hobbesian self-interest. They hoped, as Jacob puts it, that "natural religion would curb rapacious greed and render its practitioners into godly men." *The Newtonians*, p. 35–36.

54 Jacob, *The Newtonians*, p. 51.

55 Jacob, "Anglican Origins," p. 258.

56 *The Writings and Speeches of Edmund Burke*, ed. Paul Langford (Oxford: Clarendon Press, 1991), 9: 137.

57 Quoted by Robert Hole, *Pulpits, Politics and Public Order in England 1760–1832* (Cambridge University Press, 1989), p. 128.

58 Adam Smith, *Wealth of Nations* (London: Liberty Press, 1981), IV, ii, p. 456. Smith had earlier written a history of astronomy that expressed his admiration for Newton's accomplishment. See "Invisible Hand," *The New Palgrave: A Dictionary of Economics*, ed. John Eatwell et al. (New York: Stockton, 1987), 2: 997–99.

59 Abraham J. Heschel, *The Prophets* (New York: Harper, 1969), p. 219.

60 See Hole, *Pulpits, Politics and Public Order*, pp. 119, 128–9. For a closer analysis of the Church's views on political economy, see R. A. Soloway, *Prelates and People: Ecclesiastical Social Thought in England 1783–1852* (London: Routledge & Kegan Paul, 1969), especially pp. 107–26. As Soloway reports, the clergy found "no essential conflict between the new laws of political economy and the inspired regulations of revelation" (p. 107).

61 *A Sermon Preached Before the Stewards of the Westminster Dispensary . . . April 1785. With an Appendix* (London: Cadell, 1793), pp. 6, 18.

62 *A Sermon on His Majesty's Call for the United Exertions of His People Against the Threatened Invasion. Preached at Christ's Church, Bath, Sunday, July 31st, 1803* (London 1803), p. 15.

63 Quoted by Hole, *Pulpits, Politics and Public Order*, p. 232.

64 "The Moral Teaching of Jesus Christ" in *The Complete Works of Percy Bysshe Shelley*, ed. Roger Ingpen and W. E. Peck (New York: Scribner, 1926–30), 6: 255.

65 In 1822 Francis Place observed that many important members of the London Corresponding Society had since become "all in business all

flourishing men, some of them were rich." David A. Wilson, *Paine and Cobbett: The Transatlantic Connection* (Kingston and Montreal: McGill–Queen's University Press, 1988), p. 187.

66 "Speech on a Motion . . . to Repeal and Alter Certain Acts Respecting Religious Opinions, Upon the Occasion of a Petition from the Unitarian Society, May 11, 1792," *Works* 7: 43.

67 Karl Barth, *Church Dogmatics*, trans. G. T. Thomson and Harold Knight, vol. 1, Part 2 (New York: Scribner, 1956), p. 280. Further references to this work will be abbreviated *CD* and included in the text.

68 See Robert P. Ericksen, "The Barmen Synod and Its Declaration: A Historical Synopsis" in *The Church Confronts the Nazis: Barmen Then and Now*, ed. Hubert G. Locke (Toronto Studies in Theology, 16) (New York and Toronto: Edward Mellen Press, 1984).

69 *Systematic and Philosophical Theology* (vol. 1 of *The Pelican Guide to Modern Theology*) (Baltimore: Penguin, 1969), p. 129.

70 *The Word of God and the Word of Man* (New York: Harper, 1957), p. 70.

71 Blake had punned on Lamb and Lambeth before. See *Jerusalem* 12: 41.

72 Erdman sees lines 71–73 as a reference to Hunt's imprisonment for libeling the Prince Regent in 1812. *Prophet Against Empire* (rev. edn. Princeton University Press, 1969), pp. 454–57.

73 Bogen, "The Problem of Blake's Early Religion," p. 511.

74 *A Vision of the Last Judgment*, E 551; *A Descriptive Catalogue*, V. E 545.

3 NATURE'S PRIEST

1 John Keble, *Lectures on Poetry, 1832–1841*, trans. Edward Kershaw Francis, 2 vols. (Oxford: Clarendon Press, 1912).

2 *Letters and Memories of His Life* (London: King, 1877), 1: 120.

3 W. J. B. Owen, "Costs, Sales, and Profits of Longman's Editions of Wordsworth," *Library*, 5th Series, 12 (1957): 107.

4 See Arnold, "Wordsworth" [1879] in *English Literature and Irish Politics*, ed. R. H. Super. *The Complete Prose Works of Matthew Arnold*, vol. 9 (University of Michigan Press, 1973), pp. 48–49. See also David Pym, "William Wordsworth: From Matthew Arnold to A. C. Bradley: A Study in Victorian Belief and Wordsworth's Poetry," *Durham University Journal*, n.s. 51 (Jan. 1990): 191–97. A useful, comprehensive survey of criticism has been compiled by Dan Kenneth Crosby in "Wordsworth's *Excursion*: An Annotated Bibliography of Criticism," *Bulletin of Bibliography* 48 (1991): 33–49.

5 See, for instance, V. G. Kiernan, "Wordsworth and the People" in *Democracy and the Labour Movement*, ed. John Saville (1956), reprinted with a new postscript in *Marxists on Literature: An Anthology*, ed. David Craig (Penguin, 1975), pp. 161–206. The charge was taken up and given new currency by Jerome McGann in *The Romantic Ideology: A Critical Investigation* (University of Chicago Press, 1983).

6 References to *The Prelude* are to the 1805 version, unless otherwise indicated, and are cited from *The Prelude: 1799, 1805, 1850*, ed. Jonathan Wordsworth, M. H. Abrams, and Stephen Gill (New York: Norton, 1979).

7 E. P. Thompson, "Disenchantment or Default? A Lay Sermon" in *Power & Consciousness* ed. Conor Cruise O'Brien (New York University Press, 1969), p. 153. Another normally careful critic, David Perkins, has through a popular anthology put in the minds of generations of undergraduates the vague idea that "with the growth of [Wordsworth's] later faith his genius as a poet declined, and there is probably a causal connection." *English Romantic Writers* (Harvard University Press, 1969), p. 175. The probable connection is not further examined. In another work likely to reach a wide audience, Stephen Gill has written: "What can be said with confidence is that all of Wordsworth's greatest poetry pre-dates the period [of his commitment to the Anglican Church]." *Wordsworth: The Prelude* (Cambridge University Press, 1991), pp. 40–41.

8 The process of Wordsworth's turn to conservatism, when examined carefully, has proven recalcitrant to precise analysis, so that the word apostasy in the sense of a dramatic recantation now seems hardly useful. In *Wordsworth's Second Nature: A Study of the Poetry and Politics* (University of Chicago Press, 1984), James Chandler locates the truly "pivotal point" of Wordsworth's political evolution in early 1797, at the start rather than at the end of his "great decade" (p. 235).

9 *The Letters of William and Dorothy Wordsworth: The Early Years, 1787–1805*, ed. E. de Selincourt, rev. Chester Shaver, 2nd edn. (Oxford: Clarendon Press, 1967), 1: 76, 87–88.

10 Wordsworth's memory of such desecrations seems to have been colored over time by his evolving politics, but a denunciation as "blasphemy" of the attack on the Grande Chartreuse can be found as early as *Descriptive Sketches* (1792). See Carl Woodring, *Politics in English Romantic Poetry* (Harvard University Press, 1970), pp. 103–4.

11 *The Prose Works of William Wordsworth*, ed. W. J. B. Owen and Jane Worthington Smyser (Oxford: Clarendon Press, 1974) 1: 52, 62; reminiscence (1849) of Ellis Yarnall in *The Prose Works of William Wordsworth*, ed. A. B. Grosart (London: Macmillan, 1896), 3: 478. For Wordsworth's possible acquaintance with Gregoire, see Nicholas Roe, *Wordsworth and Coleridge: The Radical Years* (New York: Oxford University Press, 1988), pp. 66–70.

12 *Letters, Early Years*, p. 76.

13 Lines 792–93, 806–9, *"Descriptive Sketches" by William Wordsworth*, ed. Eric Birdsall (Cornell University Press, 1984), pp. 116, 118.

14 Paine, Thomas, *The Rights of Man*, intro. Eric Foner (New York: Penguin Books, 1984), p. 272.

15 *Prose Works* 1: 31.

16 *The Social Contract: Essays by Locke, Hume, and Rousseau*, ed. Ernest Barker

(London: Oxford University Press, 1947), p. 304. For Rousseau's influence on the *Letter* see *Prose Works* 1: 23.

17 John McManners, *The French Revolution and the Church* (New York: Harper & Row, 1969), p. 98.

18 The text is taken from *The Excursion*, 1814, ed. Jonathan Wordsworth (New York: Woodstock Books, 1991). Hereafter all quotations of the poem will be taken from this facsimile edition. Since the facsimile does not number lines, I have included references to the poem as it appears in volume 5 of *The Poetical Works of William Wordsworth, Edited from the Manuscripts, with Textual and Critical Notes*, ed. Ernest de Selincourt and Helen Darbishire (Oxford: Clarendon Press, 1940–49; rev. 1952–59).

19 *The Salisbury Plain Poems of William Wordsworth*, ed. Stephen Gill (Cornell University Press, 1975), p. 38. Quotation from "The Convict" taken from Jonathan Wordsworth, *The Music of Humanity* (New York: Harper & Row, 1969), p. 58. *Imitation of Juvenal* is included in Wordsworth's *Poems*, ed. John O. Hayden (New York: Penguin, 1977) 1: 142–43.

20 *Collected Letters of Samuel Taylor Coleridge*, ed. E. L. Griggs (Oxford: Clarendon Press, 1956–71), 1: 206.

21 See, for example, Paul D. Sheats, *The Making of Wordsworth's Poetry, 1795–1798* (Harvard University Press, 1973); Alan Grob, *The Philosophic Mind: A Study of Wordsworth's Poetry and Thought 1797–1805* (1973); and Kenneth R. Johnston, "Wordsworth's Revolutions, 1793–1798" in *Revolution and English Romanticism: Politics and Rhetoric*, ed. Keith Hanley and Raman Selden (New York: St. Martin's, 1990), pp. 169–204.

22 *Romantic Ideology*, p. 87.

23 *The Making of Wordsworth's Poetry*, p. 161.

24 *Collected Letters* 1: 410.

25 McManners, *The French Revolution and the Church*, p. 99.

26 William Hamilton Reid, *The Rise and Dissolution of the Infidel Societies in the Metropolis: including, the origin of modern deism and atheism . . . from the Publication of Paine's Age of Reason till the Present Period* (London: J. Hatchard, 1800), p. 22.

27 *The Age of Reason*, ed. Moncure Daniel Conway (New York: G. P. Putnam's Sons, 1896), pp. 85, 45.

28 *Daniel O' Connell: His Early Life and Journal, 1795–1802*, ed. A. Houston (London: Isaac Pitman, 1906), p. 116.

29 H. W. Piper, *The Active Universe* (London: Athlone, 1962), p. 73 ff. John O. Hayden, "The Dating of the '1794' Version of Wordsworth's *An Evening Walk*," *Studies in Bibliography* 42 (1989): 265–71.

30 *The Music of Humanity*, pp. 184–212; see also *William Wordsworth: The Borders of Vision* (Oxford: Clarendon Press, 1982), p. 22.

31 "The Pedlar," lines 190–208. *The Ruined Cottage and The Pedlar by William Wordsworth*, ed. James Butler (Cornell University Press, 1979), pp. 398, 400.

32 *Peter Bell*, ed. John Jordan (Cornell University Press, 1985), p. 146.

33 *The Romantic Ideology*, p. 88.

34 Lines 337–39, "The Pedlar," ed. Butler, p. 410.

35 The bias is clear in the influential Norton edition of *The Prelude*, where the notes carry on a campaign against "pietistic" additions to the 1850 poem (e.g., p. 47 n.6).

36 *Music of Humanity*, p. 202.

37 Lines 209–17, "The Pedlar," ed. Butler, p. 400.

38 *The Calvinist Temper in English Poetry* (The Hague: Mouton, 1980), p. 390. Among the admirable scholarly efforts to trace the slow metaphysical progression by which Wordsworth arrived at an orthodox faith in a transcendent Deity, perhaps the most impressively painstaking is John A. Hodgson's *Wordsworth's Philosophical Poetry, 1797–1814* (University of Nebraska Press, 1980).

39 *Collected Letters* 5: 95.

40 "Thanksgiving after Childbirth," *Ecclesiastical Sonnets* 3:27 in *Poetical Works* 3: 397.

41 *Letters, Early Years*, pp. 396, 418, 493.

42 *The Letters of William and Dorothy Wordsworth: The Middle Years*, ed. E. de Selincourt, Part II, *1812–1820*, rev. Mary Moorman and Alan G. Hill (Oxford: Clarendon Press, 1970), 1: 487. Dorothy had reported earlier, in 1807, that the family had become regular churchgoers (1: 136).

43 *Poetical Works* 5: 474–75.

44 The idea of Anglicanism as a comprehensive religion "natural" to Britain is developed in *Ecclesiastical Sketches*.

45 *Letters, Early Years*, p. 556.

46 *Letters, Early Years*, p. 355.

47 *The Music of Humanity*, p. 167. *Excursion* 1:397–400.

48 See a thoughtful discussion by Robert Barth of the significance of Wordsworth's naming of Divinity in the *Prelude* in *The Wordsworth Circle* 17 (1986): 19–20.

49 *Letters, Early Years*, p. 1004.

50 *Letters, Middle Years* 2: 146.

51 *The Letters of John Keats*, ed. H. E. Rollins (Harvard University Press, 1958), 1: 281–82.

52 *The British Critic*, 2nd series, 3 (Jan. 1815): 444–67; rpt. in *The Romantics Reviewed*, ed. Donald H. Reiman (New York: Garland, 1972), A:1, 138–47. On the enraptured bishop, see *Letters, Middle Years*, 2: 181–82.

53 *Eclectic Review*, 2nd Series, III (Jan. 1815), 20; rpt. in *The Romantics Reviewed*, A:1, 352–65. Judson Lyon included a detailed discussion of the poem's orthodoxy in *The Excursion: A Study* (Yale University Press, 1950), concluding that in Wordsworth's poem "the highest religious act is still communion with nature" (p. 138).

54 *Examiner*, August 21, 1814, p. 542; rpt. in *Romantics Reviewed* A:2, 523. Alan G. Hill has examined the poem as a conscious imitation of the traditional philosophical dialogues that Hazlitt scorned. See his "New

Light on *The Excursion*," *Ariel* 5 (1974): 37–47. David Q. Smith in "The Wanderer's Silence: A Strange Reticence in Book IX of *The Excursion*" in *The Wordsworth Circle* 9 (1978): 162–72, argues that there is more real drama in the poem than has hitherto been noticed.

55 *Letters, Middle Years*, 3: 165.

56 *The Letters of Charles and Mary Lamb*, ed. Edwin M. Marrs, Jr. (Cornell University Press, 1978), vol. 3. 1809–1817, p. 112.

57 "Panentheism" seems a more precise word than pantheism to denote the kind of natural religion Wordsworth articulated, as Carl Woodring has observed in *Wordsworth* (Boston: Houghton Mifflin, 1965), p. 106. For a more thorough philosophical analysis, see Daniel Dombrowski, "Wordsworth's Panentheism," *The Wordsworth Circle* 16 (1985): 136–42 and "Panpsychism," *The Wordsworth Circle* 19 (1988): 38–45.

58 *Letters, Middle Years* 2: 188.

59 See George Stephens Spinks, *Psychology and Religion: An Introduction to Contemporary Views* (London: Methuen, 1964), pp. 98–99.

60 Lyon, *The Excursion: A Study*, p. 91.

61 Ibid., pp. 69–70.

62 *Wordsworth's Poetry 1787–1814* (New Haven: Yale University Press, 1964), p. 307.

63 "The Politics of 'Tintern Abbey,'" *The Wordsworth Circle* 14 (1983), 9.

64 *First Essay on Population, 1798* (1926; rpt. New York, St. Martin's Press, 1966), p. 351.

65 See R. A. Soloway, *Prelates and People: Ecclesiastical Social Thought in England 1783–1852* (London: Routledge & Kegan Paul, 1969), pp. 107ff.

66 Bernard Semmel, *John Stuart Mill and the Pursuit of Virtue* (Yale University Press, 1984), p. 28.

67 *The Romantic Ventriloquists: Wordsworth, Coleridge, Keats, Shelley, Byron* (University of Washington Press 1963), p. 81.

68 Lyon, *The Excursion: A Study*, p. 45. See also *Letters, Middle Years* 2: 26, 29, 33, 62, 75, 81–85.

69 Anne L. Rylestone finds that in the *Ecclesiastical Sonnets* the Church of England "serves as a unifier, a source of stability, and a peacemaker . . . interrelating human experience and psychic life, combatting alienation in a fallen world, and encouraging harmony and a sense of belonging in humanity and between humanity and the natural world." *Prophetic Memory in Wordsworth's Ecclesiastical Sonnets* (Southern Illinois University Press, 1991), p. 63.

70 "Church Going," in *Collected Poems*, ed. Anthony Thwaite (New York: Farrar Straus Giroux, 1989), p. 98.

71 *Ecclesiastical Sonnets*, 2: 30, in *Poetical Works*, 3: 376.

72 Susan Wolfson sees the "play of questioning as a central preoccupation of the imagination in Romantic poetry" and finds even *The Excursion* to be "an interrogative drama that is not entirely legislated by the poem's sententious voices." *The Questioning Presence: Wordsworth, Keats, and the*

Interrogative Mode in Romantic Poetry (Cornell University Press, 1986), pp. 28, 96. William Galperin considers the Solitary only "a foil for the Wanderer's conventional wisdom," and finds the Pastor's views "virtually identical to the Wanderer's" but acknowledges the reader's "prerogative of rejecting *all* of the poem's viewpoints for the sake of something better." "'Imperfect While Unshared': The Role of the Implied Reader in Wordsworth's 'Excursion,'" *Criticism* 22 (1980): 194, 199, 202. This argument is taken farther in Galperin's *Revision and Authority in Wordsworth: The Interpretation of a Career* (University of Pennsylvania Press, 1989).

73 *Wordsworth and the Empirical Dilemma* (New York: Peter Lang, 1990) and "Church Building as Political Strategy in Wordsworth's *Ecclesiastical Sonnets*," *Mosaic* 25/3 (1992): 31–46.

74 "Mr. Southey," *Athenaeum*, Jan. 29, 1828; "Mr. Wordsworth" February 2, 1828.

75 *Athenaeum*, rev. of Barton, 1828.

76 Robinson, *Henry Crabb Robinson on Books and Their Writers*, ed. Edith J. Morley (London: Dent, 1938), 2: 314.

77 *The Letters of William and Dorothy Wordsworth: The Later Years* ed. E. de Selincourt, rev. Alan G. Hill (Oxford: Clarendon Press, 1978–88), 3: 249.

78 *Peter Bell III*, 566–68, in *Shelley's Poetry and Prose*, ed. Donald H. Reiman and Sharon B. Powers (New York: Norton, 1977), p. 341. Crabb Robinson remarked in 1836 that "Wordsworth's own religion, by the bye, would not satisfy either a religionist or a sceptic." *On Books and Their Writers*, 2: 461.

4 THE IRONIES OF BELIEF

1 Samuel C. Chew, *Byron in England* (London: John Murray, 1924), pp. 221–22.

2 "Lord Byron's Monument," *Athenaeum*, Sept. 24, 1828, p. 751.

3 "Lord Byron's Monument," *Athenaeum*, October 1, 1828, p. 767.

4 Byron's note to *Don Juan* 15: 18; in *Lord Byron: The Complete Poetical Works*, ed. Jerome J. McGann, vol. 5: *Don Juan* (Oxford: Clarendon Press, 1986), p. 1067. Further references to *Don Juan* will be cited from this edition and included in the text.

5 *The Letters of Percy Bysshe Shelley*, ed. Frederick L. Jones (Oxford: Clarendon Press, 1964), 2: 412.

6 *Lord Byron's Works Viewed in Connexion with Christianity and the Obligations of Social Life: A Sermon* (London: 1824), p. 6.

7 *The Romantics Reviewed: Contemporary Reviews of British Romantic Writers* (New York: Garland, 1972), B-1: 315; *British Critic*, April 1831, p. 324.

8 *Childe Harold's Pilgrimage* 2: 3–4 in *Lord Byron: The Complete Poetical Works*, ed. Jerome J. McGann (Oxford: Clarendon Press, 1980–93), vol. 2, p. 45. All subsequent references to Byron's poetry will be cited from this edition and included parenthetically in the text.

9 *Self, Text, and Romantic Irony* (Princeton University Press, 1988), p. 125.

10 *His Very Self and Voice: The Collected Conversations of Lord Byron*, ed. Ernest J. Lovell, Jr. (New York: Macmillan, 1954), p. 195.

11 Hume's dialectical mode of argument has left large room for debate on his ultimate religious position. Perhaps Richard Wollheim's phrase "non-atheist" comes closest to describing his minimalist metaphysics. *Hume on Religion* (New York: Meridian Books, 1969), p. 28.

12 *Byron as Skeptic and Believer* (Princeton University Press, 1938), pp. 23–24. James Boulger agreed that Byron's "religious uncertainty was a constant source of inward distress and suffering to him." *The Calvinist Temper in English Poetry* (The Hague: Mouton, 1980), p. 439.

13 *Byron: The Record of a Quest* (1949; rpt. Hamden, CT: Archon Books, 1966), p. 22. Lovell allows Byron a choice between a deist Prime Mover and a Calvinistic deity that he inevitably calls "cruel and capricious" (pp. 192, 201), "a God of wrath and vengeance" (p. 227). This caricature divinity with His limited emotional repertoire is not Calvin's God and there is no evidence that it was ever Byron's.

14 *The Idea of the Holy*, pp. 58–59.

15 Boulger, *The Calvinist Temper*, pp. 430–32.

16 Col. Leicester Stanhope, *Greece in 1823 and 1824* (London, 1825); in Lovell, ed., *His Very Self*, p. 545.

17 *The Works of Lord Byron*, ed. E. H. Coleridge and R. E. Prothero (London: Murray, 1922), 6: 261–62, n. 2.

18 James Kennedy's reminiscences, in Lovell, ed., *His Very Self*, p. 447.

19 Frida Knight, *University Rebel: The Life of William Frend, 1757–1841* (London: Gollancz, 1971), pp. 238–39.

20 "Lord Byron's Theology," *Monthly Repository*, 2nd series, 4 (1830): 611.

21 *Byron: A Biography* (New York: Knopf, 1957), 1: 35–38.

22 *Byron's Letters and Journals*, 12 vols., ed. Leslie Marchand (Harvard University Press, 1973–82), 3: 64.

23 *Journals of Claire Clairmont*, ed. Marion Kingston Stocking (Harvard University Press, 1968), p. 226.

24 *Christianity as Old as the Creation* (1730); quoted in "Deism" article, *Encyclopedia of Religion and Ethics*, ed. James Hastings (New York: Scribner's, 1925–27), 5: 536.

25 D. C. Muecke, *The Compass of Irony* (London: Methuen, 1969), p. 121.

26 George M. Ridenour, *The Style of "Don Juan"* (Yale University Press, 1960); Andrew Rutherford, *Byron: A Critical Study* (Stanford University Press, 1961).

27 *English Romantic Irony* (Harvard University Press, 1980), vii, 4. Peter Thorslev Jr. offers a more informed and incisive analysis of Romantic irony in *Romantic Contraries: Freedom versus Desire* (Yale University Press, 1984), pp. 156–75 – an admirable effort to "demystify Romantic irony, liberate it from the entanglements of German metaphysics, and restore

it to its rightful paternity [in the eighteenth century Enlightenment]"
(p. 166).

28 *Dark Interpreter: The Discourse of Romanticism* (Cornell University Press, 1980), p. 265.

29 Quoted by Garber, *Self, Text, and Romantic Irony*, p. 168.

30 See Jerome McGann's thoughtful discussion of the ending of *Childe Harold* in *Fiery Dust: Byron's Poetic Development* (University of Chicago Press, 1968), pp. 36–40.

31 See Mircea Eliade's discussion of the religious significance that aquatic symbolism has had in all cultures, in *The Sacred and the Profane*, trans. Willard Trask (New York: Harcourt, Brace & World, 1959), p. 131.

32 It was originally the next stanza, but Byron later inserted two others at this point. See Jerome McGann, *Fiery Dust*, pp. 124, 313–14.

33 *Romantic Contraries*, p. 168.

34 *The Keats Circle: Letters and Papers, 1816–1878*, ed. Hyder Edward Rollins (Harvard University Press, 1965), 2: 134.

35 *The Letters of Percy Bysshe Shelley*, 2 vols., ed. Frederick L. Jones (Oxford: Clarendon Press, 1964), 2: 198.

36 *The Romantic Ventriloquists: Wordsworth, Coleridge, Keats, Shelley, Byron* (University of Washington Press, 1963), p. 282.

37 *His Very Self*, p. 441. The first published defense of the play's orthodoxy appeared in 1822: *A Letter to Sir Walter Scott, Bart., in Answer to the Remonstrance of Oxoniensis on the Publication of Cain, a Mystery, by Lord Byron*, written by the still unidentified "Harroviensis." Byron was so impressed that he wanted the essay included as an appendix in any future edition of *Cain*. In our own day a plausible argument for the play's fundamental orthodoxy has been offered by Wolf Z. Hirst, who finds Lucifer's and Cain's critique consistently subverted by the drama's "artistic pattern of conflict, irony, reversal, and recognition" ("Byron's Lapse into Orthodoxy: An Unorthodox Reading of *Cain*," *Keats–Shelley Journal* 29 [1980], p. 152). Recent criticism has been inclined to agree with Jerome McGann that "the moral norm in *Cain* is not embodied in any single character, but is implied in the dramatic relationships that develop between the various people." *Fiery Dust*, p. 255. See John P. Farrell, *Revolution as Tragedy: The Dilemma of the Moderate from Scott to Arnold* (Cornell University Press, 1980) and Martyn Corbett, *Byron and Tragedy* (New York: St. Martin's Press, 1988).

38 *Lord Byron, The Complete Miscellaneous Prose*, ed. Andrew Nicholson (Oxford: Clarendon Press, 1991), pp. 150, 158.

39 *The Poems of Alexander Pope* (Yale University Press, 1947), III, pt. 1, p. lviii.

40 *Letters and Journals*, 8: 36, 43.

41 Ibid., 9: 54.

42 Ibid., 9: 118–19, 123.

43 Stanley Eugene Fish, *Surprised by Sin: The Reader in Paradise Lost* (New York: St. Martin's Press, 1967).

44 Ibid., p. 38.
45 Leslie Marchand, *Byron's Poetry: A Critical Introduction* (Boston: Houghton Mifflin, 1965), p. 86; Jerome McGann, *Don Juan in Context* (University of Chicago Press, 1976), p. 24.
46 *Cain*, Act II, scene II, 459–66. Lord Byron, *The Complete Poetical Works*, vol. 6, ed. Jerome J. McGann and Barry Weller (Oxford: Clarendon Press, 1991), p. 275.
47 Preface to *Prometheus Unbound*, in *Shelley's Poetry and Prose*, ed. Reiman and Powers, p. 133.
48 *The Romantic Ventriloquists*, p. 288.
49 Byron's stage direction leaves ambiguous the question of whether the fire that burns Abel's offering is sent or assisted by God, or is only the natural product of the fat that is feeding it.
50 *Byron's Fictions* (Wayne State University Press, 1978), p. 156.
51 In "Byron's Lapse into Orthodoxy," Wolf Z. Hirst draws a number of illuminating parallels between *Job* and *Cain* but, curiously, fails to mention the whirlwind with which Byron seems to invite the comparison.
52 *Works of Lord Byron* 6: 261–62, n. 2.
53 "Byron's Lapse into Orthodoxy," p. 168.
54 As he read *Cain*, William Blake was evidently reminded of this psalm. In his reply to Byron, *The Ghost of Abel*, the dead victim asks, "Are these the Sacrifices of Eternity O Jehovah, a Broken Spirit / And a contrite Heart?" *The Complete Poetry & Prose of William Blake*, ed. David V. Erdman (rev. edn. New York: Doubleday/Anchor, 1988), p. 272.
55 See Elinor S. Shaffer, *"Kubla Khan" and The Fall of Jerusalem: The Mythological School in Biblical Criticism and Secular Literature, 1770–1880* (Cambridge University Press, 1975).
56 See Abraham Heschel, *An Introduction to the Prophets* (New York: Harper & Row, 1969), pp. 200–1.
57 Byron's note to *Don Juan* 15: 18.
58 *The Letters of John Keats*, ed. H. E. Rollins, 2 vols. (Harvard University Press, 1958), 1: 282.
59 *Romantics Reviewed*, B-2: 930; B-2: 773; B-1: 184–85.
60 *London University Magazine*. "The Poetry of Thought, No. 1. – Lord Byron's *Cain*," 1 (Oct.–Jan. 1829): 146.
61 *Letters & Journals* 9: 111.
62 Pietro Gamba's reminiscence, in Lovell, ed., *His Very Self*, p. 373.
63 See above, pp. 3–4 and *Letters of Percy Bysshe Shelley*, 1: 125.
64 *The Poetical Works of Robert Southey* (Boston: Osgood, 1875), 10: 196.
65 *Examiner*, Feb. 11, 1816, p. 83.
66 Preface to Cantos 6–8 of *Don Juan*.
67 *Letters and Journals* 9: 152.
68 *The Plot of Satire* (Yale University Press, 1965), pp. 171–222.
69 *Byron: A Critical Study*, p. 91.
70 *Letters* 2: 376.

71 *Complete Poetry & Prose of William Blake*, p. 270.
72 *Marriage of Heaven & Hell* E 33. Blake had been calling himself "a voice crying in the wilderness" since the start of his career; see *All Religions Are One* E 1. For Elijah in the wilderness, see 1 Kings 19.
73 *Jerusalem* 39: 28–31. E 187.
74 Heschel, *The Prophets*, pp. 10, 11, 19.
75 See Edwin M. Good, *Irony in the Old Testament* (Philadelphia: Westminster, 1965), and Conrad M. Hyers, ed., *Holy Laughter: Essays on Religion in the Comic Perspective* (New York: Seabury, 1969).
76 Max Weber, *The Sociology of Religion*, trans. Ephraim Fischoff (Boston: Beacon Press, 1963), p. 59.

5 THE POLITICS OF GREEK RELIGION

1 *The Letters of John Keats*, ed. H. E. Rollins (2 vols. Harvard University Press, 1958), 1: 281–82. All quotations from Keats's letters will be taken from this edition and cited hereafter as *Letters* in the text. I have discussed this 1818 letter and the larger question of Keats's religious beliefs at greater length in my book *Keats: The Religious Sense* (Princeton University Press, 1976).
2 The new phase of political analysis seems to have been provoked by Jerome McGann ("Keats and the Historical Method in Literary Criticism," *MLN* 94 [1979], 988–1032); the topic was pursued by scholars like Morris Dickstein in "Keats and Politics," *Studies in Romanticism* 25 (1986), 175–81, Marilyn Butler in *Romantics, Rebels and Reactionaries* (New York: Oxford University Press, 1982), and Susan Wolfson in "Keats's *Isabella* and the 'Digressions' of 'Romance,'" *Criticism* 27 (1985), 247–61. See also the stimulating forum on Keats's politics that Wolfson edited for *Studies in Romanticism* 25 (Summer 1986): 171–229. More recent studies of Keats's political dimension include Marjorie Levinson's *Keats's Life of Allegory: The Origins of a Style* (Oxford: Blackwell, 1988), and Paul Hamilton, "Keats and Critique" in *Rethinking Romanticism: Critical Readings in Romantic History* (Oxford: Blackwell, 1989).
3 William Sharp, *The Life and Letters of Joseph Severn* (New York: Scribner, 1892), p. 29.
4 Others who have found political significance in Keats's use of myth include Carl Woodring, who saw in the poet's Hellenism "a degree of reaction against the Latinate moral statesmanship promoted in the rhetoric of the Augustans." *Politics in English Romantic Poetry* (Harvard University Press, 1970), p. 77. For John Barnard, Keats's "reanimation of Greek myth is neither antiquarian nor decorative in intention, but a means of exploring beliefs and propositions counter to, or subversive of, conventional religious and political beliefs." *John Keats* (Cambridge University Press, 1987), p. 59.
5 For a wide-ranging discussion of this development, see Frank E.

Manuel, *The Eighteenth Century Confronts the Gods* (Harvard University Press, 1959).

6 David Hume, *The Natural History of Religion*, ed. A. Wayne Colver (Oxford: Clarendon Press, 1976), p. 75.

7 William Godwin, ["Edward Baldwin"], *The Pantheon, or, Ancient History of the Gods of Greece and Rome* (1814; rpt. New York: Garland, 1984), p. 24.

8 In *Keats: The Religious Sense*, pp. 71–113.

9 "Cockney School of Poetry, No. iv," *Blackwood's Edinburgh Magazine* 3 (August 1818), p. 522. In *The Romantics Reviewed: Contemporary Reviews of British Romantic Writers*, 9 vols. (New York: Garland, 1972), C-1: 93.

10 See, for example, Aileen Ward, *John Keats: The Making of a Poet* (1963; rev. edn., New York: Farrar, Straus and Giroux, 1986), pp. 80–81, 423n.

11 *Examiner*, November 12, 1815, pp. 731–32.

12 Ibid., May 4, 1817, p. 274.

13 Leigh Hunt, *Foliage; or Poems Original and Translated* (London: Ollier, 1818).

14 *Foliage*, pp. 25–26.

15 *The Poems of John Keats*, ed. Jack Stillinger (Harvard University Press, 1978), 192n. All further references to Keats's verse will be to this edition and will be included in the text.

16 *Foliage*, pp. 35–39.

17 Robert Gittings, *John Keats* (London: Heinemann, 1968), pp. 88, 92.

18 Douglas Bush, *Mythology and the Romantic Tradition in English Poetry* (Harvard University Press, 1937), p. 85.

19 *The Keats Circle: Letters and Papers, 1816–1878*, ed. H. E. Rollins (2 vols., Harvard University Press, 1965), 2: 144.

20 Keats's ceremony reminds one too of the public festivals of nature organized by the French Revolutionary government as a substitute for the outlawed Catholic liturgies. It seems also reminiscent of the description of primitive natural religion in Pope's *Essay on Man* 3: 155–58, 263–64.

21 Jane Ellen Harrison, *Prolegomena to the Study of Greek Religion* (1903: rpt. Princeton University Press, 1991), p. 101.

22 A concise statement of the standard rationalist objection to such prayer, and of the political dimension of the objection, is given by Shelley in his note to *Queen Mab* 7: 135–6.

23 I have discussed the others in "Keats's 'Hymn to Pan': A Debt to Shaftesbury?" *Keats–Shelley Journal* 26 (1977): 31–34.

24 The goat-god was traditionally associated with a pastoral economy, and Michael Drayton's *The Man in the Moon*, which Keats seems to have read, also begins with a ceremony in honor of Pan. Drayton's ten-line introduction to his Endymion story does not describe the ritual in any detail; its brevity accentuates by contrast the elaborateness of Keats's liturgy.

25 Plutarch, *Selected Essays and Dialogues*, trans. Donald Russell (New York:

Oxford University Press, 1993), p. 28. See also Patricia Merivale, *Pan the Goat-God: His Myth in Modern Times* (Harvard University Press, 1969), pp. 12–16.

26 W. S. Scott, *The Athenians* (London: Golden Cockerel Press, 1943), p. 44.

27 Nicholas A. Joukovsky, "The Lost Greek Anapests of Thomas Love Peacock," *Modern Philology* 89 (Feb. 1992): 372.

28 *The Keats Circle*, 1:35. Keats's attempt to link religion and sexual passion in *Endymion* may reflect a common tendency in the Hunt circle. Marilyn Butler discusses some ways in which Shelley and Thomas Love Peacock employed Greek myth tactically to argue a liberated, non-ascetic sexual ethic in contrast with Christianity's "false and inadequate religion of love" in Marilyn Butler, "Myth and Mythmaking in the Shelley Circle," *ELH* 49 (1982): 50–72.

29 *The Complete Works of John Keats*, ed. H. B. Forman (1901; New York: AMS, 1970), 3: 268.

30 Margaret Sherwood, *Undercurrents of Influence in English Romantic Poetry* (1934; rpt. New York: AMS, 1971), p. 234.

31 Jeffrey Baker, *John Keats and Symbolism* (New York: St. Martin's Press, 1986), p. 75.

32 Morris Dickstein, *Keats and His Poetry: A Study in Development* (Chicago University Press, 1971), p. 74, n.17.

33 I examine this conflict in detail in *Keats: The Religious Sense*, pp. 78–80, 86–93.

34 *The Diary of Benjamin Robert Haydon*, ed. Willard B. Pope, 5 vols. (Harvard University Press, 1961–1963), 2:67–69.

35 *The Works of William Paley, D.D.*, introd. D. S. Wayland (London: George Cowie, 1837), 1: 153.

36 Ernest Marshall Howse, *Saints in Politics: The "Clapham Sect" and the Growth of Freedom* (Toronto: University of Toronto Press, 1952), 130–31. The Quakers were attracting especially admiring attention at this time because of Mrs. Elizabeth Fry's reform work in prisons, a glowing report on which (by Robert Owen) appeared in the *Examiner* as Keats was beginning Book 3 of *Endymion*.

37 Arnold Toynbee, *An Historian's Approach to Religion* (New York: Oxford University Press, 1956), p. 298.

38 *Diary* 2: 165.

39 In *Romantic Medicine and John Keats* (New York: Oxford University Press, 1990), Hermione de Almeida offers convincing evidence of the period's "growing preoccupation with defining who knew most of life and pain and so deserved best the accolade of physician" (p. 36). She cites Michel Foucault's *The Birth of the Clinic* on "the secularization of the priest's role into the humanitarian practice of medicine" (p. 330, n.6).

40 *John Keats*, p. 58.

41 "Notes on Sculptures" no. 34. *The Complete Works of Percy Bysshe Shelley*,

ed. Roger Ingpen and W. E. Peck, 10 vols. (New York: Scribner's, 1926–30), 6: 322.

42 See *Greek Tragedies*, ed. David Grene and Richard Lattimore (University of Chicago Press, 1960), 1: 71, 81.

43 *John Keats*, p. 63.

44 *The Age of Reason*, ed. Moncure Daniel Conway (New York: G. Putnam's Sons, 1896), p. 191.

45 Ibid., p. 61n.

46 Ibid., p. 23.

47 In "Keats's Skepticism and Voltaire," *Keats–Shelley Journal* 12 (1963): 75–93, Stuart Sperry has suggested Voltaire as the source of many of these ideas, but Paine seems to me just as likely a stimulus and a more immediate one.

48 *Report of the Proceedings of the Court of King's Bench, etc.* (London: Carlile, 1822).

49 *Age of Reason*, pp. 25, 60, 61n.

50 "Keats, the Greater Ode, and the Trial of Imagination" in *Coleridge, Keats, and the Imagination: Romanticism and Adam's Dream*, ed. J. Robert Barth and John L. Mahoney (Columbia: University of Missouri Press, 1990), 188.

51 Helen Vendler, "The Living Hand of Keats" in *John Keats: – Poetry Manuscripts at Harvard, A Facsimile Edition*, ed. Jack Stillinger (The Belknap Press of Harvard University Press, 1990), p. xxi. In her earlier book Vendler presented Autumn as a goddess, by analogy with those she found presiding in the preceding odes. *The Odes of John Keats* (The Belknap Press of Harvard University Press, 1983), pp. 262–64. John Creaser has demonstrated even more clearly Keats's effort to demythologize this last of his odes, pointing out how Keats's use of personification reduces the quasi-divine Autumn to a merely natural terrestrial phenomenon. "From 'Autumn' to Autumn in Keats's Ode," *Essays in Criticism* 38 (1988): 190–214.

52 George C. Gross reads the poem as expressing "deliberate denial of the possibility of lasting happiness in a mortal's love for an immortal." "*Lamia* and the Cupid-Psyche Myth," *Keats–Shelley Journal* 39 (1990): 165.

53 Anne K. Mellor, "Keats's Face of Moneta," *Keats–Shelley Journal* 25 (1976), 66.

54 John Livingston Lowes, "Moneta's Temple," *PMLA* 51 (1936): 1112.

55 Margaret Homans, "Keats Reading Women, Women Reading Keats," *Studies in Romanticism* 29 (1990): 368.

56 Among those who have been able to overlook the menacing aspects of Moneta are Aileen Ward, who sees in her face "infinite compassion" (p. 340) and R. S. White, who is reminded of Cordelia (*Keats as a Reader of Shakespeare* (University of Oklahoma Press, 1987), pp. 214–18). In a less positive response, Daniel Watkins calls Moneta "a goddess of consu-

merism and self-interest." *Keats's Poetry and the Politics of the Imagination* (Cranbury, NJ: Associated University Presses, 1989), p. 172.

57 *Complete Works of William Hazlitt*, ed. P. P. Howe, 21 vols. (London: Dent, 1930–34), 6: 184.

58 D. G. James, *The Romantic Comedy* (Oxford University Press, 1948), p. 150; Stuart M. Sperry, *Keats the Poet* (Princeton University Press, 1973), 330–31; Robert M. Ryan, "Christ and Moneta," *English Language Notes* 13 (March 1976): 190–92.

59 See Leon Waldoff, *Keats and the Silent Work of Imagination* (University of Illinois Press, 1985), pp. 202–3.

60 Beth Lau's useful survey of Keats's allusions to Byron makes no mention of this apparent reference. *Keats's Reading of the Romantic Poets* (University of Michigan Press, 1991), pp. 115–46.

61 *Lord Byron: The Complete Poetical Works*, ed. Jerome J. McGann (Oxford: Clarendon Press, 1980), 2: 44–45, 47.

62 For example, David Bromwich, "Keats's Radicalism," *Studies in Romanticism* 25 (1986): 197–210.

63 Joel H. Wiener, *Radicalism and Freethought in Nineteenth-Century Britain: The Life of Richard Carlile* (Westport, CT: Greenwood Press, 1983), p. 42.

64 *Examiner*, October 24, 1819, p. 675.

65 Preface to *Don Juan*, Cantos 5–8.

66 *Letters of Percy Bysshe Shelley* 2: 242.

67 *Examiner*, October 17, 1819, p. 668.

68 Walter Evert, *Aesthetic and Myth in the Poetry of Keats* (Princeton University Press, 1965), p. 39.

69 Godwin, *The Pantheon*, p. 47.

70 De Almeida, *Romantic Medicine*, p. 19.

71 C. S. Lewis, "De Descriptione Temporum" in *They Asked for a Paper* (London: G. Bles, 1962), p. 20.

72 In his last will and testament Paine described himself as "reposing confidence in my Creator God, and in no other being, for I know of no other." These words were quoted in the *Examiner* for September 12, 1819, p. 586.

6 THE CHRISTIAN MONSTER

1 See, for example, Anne K. Mellor, "Why Women Didn't Like Romanticism: The Views of Jane Austen and Mary Shelley" in *The Romantics and Us: Essays on Literature and Culture*, ed. Gene W. Ruoff (Rutgers University Press, 1990), pp. 274–87, which detects in *Frankenstein* "profound disillusionment with the central philosophical, poetic, and political tenets of romanticism."

2 *Edinburgh [Scots] Magazine*, in *The Romantics Reviewed* C-1, pp. 819, 823.

3 The phrases are those of Chris Baldick (pp. 4–5, 40, 43), who sees the story as "impiously secular," an exploration of "the godless world of

specifically modern freedoms and responsibilites." In *Frankenstein's Shadow: Myth, Monstrosity, and Nineteenth-Century Writers* (Oxford: Clarendon Press, 1987), pp. 4–5, 40, 43, 58–61.

4 Leslie Tannenbaum, "From Filthy Type to Truth: Miltonic Myth in *Frankenstein*," *Keats–Shelley Journal* 26 (1977): 101–13.

5 Muriel Spark is credited with initiating this revisionary reading in "Mary Shelley: A Prophetic Novelist," *Listener*, Feb. 22, 1951: 305–6. How quickly this interpretation became critical commonplace is illustrated in a collection of articles called *The Endurance of Frankenstein*, ed. George Levine and U. C. Knoepflmacher (University of California Press, 1979), in which essay after essay takes for granted the polemic against Mary Shelley's father and husband, disagreeing only as to how deliberate or specific the criticism is. This critical tradition continued in the 1980s in such works as Anne K. Mellor's *Mary Shelley: Her Life, Her Fiction, Her Monsters* (New York: Routledge, 1989), in which Victor Frankenstein becomes "the image of all that Mary Shelley most feared in both her husband and in the Romantic project he served" (p. 75).

6 "Thoughts on the Aggression of Daughters" in *The Endurance of Frankenstein*, p. 92.

7 "*Frankenstein* as Mystery Play" in *The Endurance of Frankenstein*, p. 32.

8 *Frankenstein, or, The Modern Prometheus*, ed. M. K. Joseph (London: Oxford University Press, 1969). All further references to Shelley's novel will be to this edition, unless otherwise indicated, and will be cited by page number in the text.

9 *Frankenstein, or, The Modern Prometheus*, ed. James Rieger (Indianapolis: Bobbs-Merrill, 1974), p. 248. Rieger's edition is useful in showing the revisions that Mary Shelley made in her 1831 edition.

10 Most readers of the time considered the poem to be basically orthodox in its doctrinal content – an adequate compendium of what Christians believed. The main source for our modern knowledge of Milton's heresies – e.g. his Arianism and Materialism – is the *De Doctrina Christiana*, which was not published until 1825, at which time orthodox readers were astonished and dismayed to discover the heretical tendencies they had not previously noticed in *Paradise Lost*. As wary a reader as Samuel Johnson had declared the poem "untainted with any heretical peculiarity of opinion." See Francis E. Mineka, "The Religious Press vs. John Milton, Heretic" in *The Dissidence of Dissent: The Monthly Repository, 1806–1838* (1944; rpt. New York: Octagon, 1972), pp. 85–86.

11 *The Ruins, or, A Survey of the Revolutions of Empires* (1792; London, 1836), pp. 178–81.

12 *Paradise Lost* 10:743–45.

13 "Mary Shelley's Monster: Politics and Psyche in *Frankenstein*" in *Endurance of Frankenstein*, p. 144.

14 Mellor, *Mary Shelley: Her Life, Her Fiction, Her Monsters*, p. 86; Pamela

Clemit, *The Godwinian Novel: The Rational Fictions of Godwin, Brockden Brown, Mary Shelley* (New York: Oxford University Press, 1993), p. 155.

15 "Mary Shelley's Monster: Politics and Psyche in *Frankenstein*," p. 144.

16 Quoted by Don Locke in *A Fantasy of Reason: The Life and Thought of William Godwin* (London: Routledge & Kegan Paul, 1980), p. 273.

17 *Collected Letters of Mary Wollstonecraft*, ed. Ralph Wardle (Cornell University Press, 1979), p. 110.

18 Ibid., p. 404.

19 Marc Rubenstein, " 'My Accursed Origin': The Search for the Mother in *Frankenstein*," *Studies in Romanticism* 15 (1976): 169.

20 *Poetical Works*, ed. Thomas Hutchinson, 2nd edn., corrected by G. M. Matthews (London: Oxford University Press, 1971), p. 821.

21 "Disenchantment or Default – A Lay Sermon," in *Power and Consciousness*, ed. Conor Cruise O'Brien (New York University Press, 1969), p. 152.

22 *The Proper Lady and the Woman Writer: Ideology as Style in the Works of Mary Wollstonecraft, Mary Shelley, and Jane Austen* (University of Chicago Press, 1984), p. 131.

23 Tannenbaum, "From Filthy Type to Truth," p. 113.

24 *Ariel Like a Harpy: Shelley, Mary, and "Frankenstein"* (London: Gollancz, 1972), p. 64.

7 THE UNKNOWN GOD

1 In 1828, F. D. Maurice declared Shelley to have been the preeminent religious poet of his generation, and, in our own day, Stuart Curran has called him "the greatest religious poet in the English language between Blake and Yeats." *Shelley's Annus Mirabilis: The Maturing of an Epic Vision* (San Marino, CA: Huntington Library, 1975), p. 205.

2 Maurice wrote "Apart from Queen Mab . . . in all his avowed productions that we have seen, there is no denial of the existence of a Supreme Perfection; but there is, on the other hand, a constant inculcation of the doctrine of an all-informing Power, an Essential Wisdom and Benevolence. The utmost that can be justly and positively asserted against Shelley's religious opinions, is, that he was not a Christian" (*Athenaeum*, March 7, 1828). In our own century Ellsworth Barnard, in *Shelley's Religion* (University of Minnesota Press, 1936), argued that Shelley was, in fact, essentially Christian, and Richard Brantley has even ushered him into the camp of the Wesleyans (*Locke, Wesley, and the Method of English Romanticism* (University of Florida Press, 1984)). Those other readers who from Shelley's time to our own have characterized his religious position as unmitigated atheism may be represented here by Kenneth Neill Cameron, who wrote, "He was not skeptical about the existence of God; he was sure there was none." *Shelley: The Golden Years* (Harvard University Press, 1974), p. 157.

3 *The Alternative Tradition: Religion and the Rejection of Religion in the Ancient World* (The Hague: Mouton, 1980), p. 17.
4 *The Letters of Percy Bysshe Shelley*, ed. Frederick L. Jones, 2 vols. (Oxford: Clarendon Press, 1964), 1: 228. All further references to this edition will be included in the text.
5 Edward John Trelawny, *Records of Shelley, Byron, and the Author*, 2 vols. (London: Pickering, 1878), 1: 92–93.
6 *Henry Crabb Robinson on Books and Their Writers*, ed. Edith J. Morley (London: Dent, 1938), 2: 479.
7 *Shelley: Poetical Works*, ed. Thomas Hutchinson, 2nd edn., corrected by G. M. Matthews (London: Oxford University Press, 1971), p. 812. The most careful and helpful analysis to date of Shelley's shifting conceptions of this transcendent "Spirit" as they were influenced by his reading of Berkeley, Hume, Holbach, Spinoza, Drummond, and others, is offered by Jerrold E. Hogle in *Shelley's Process: Radical Transference and the Development of His Major Works* (New York: Oxford University Press, 1988). It will be evident that I do not concur with Hogle's central thesis – that Shelley's apparent theism is only a metaphor for an unceasing process of linguistic transference.
8 *Queen Mab* 6: 199, in *Shelley's Poetry and Prose*, ed. Donald H. Reiman and Sharon B. Powers (New York: Norton, 1977), p. 50. Unless otherwise indicated, all quotations from Shelley's poetry are taken from this edition and references will be cited in the text.
9 Paul Henry Thiry, Baron d'Holbach. *The System of Nature, or the Laws of the Moral and Physical World. From the original French of M. Mirabaud*, trans. Samuel Wilkinson (London: B. D. Cousins, 1839), 2:11, p. 459.
10 "Essay on Christianity" in *The Complete Works of Percy Bysshe Shelley*, ed. Roger Ingpen and Walter E. Peck, 10 vols. (New York: Scribner, 1926–30), 6: 240.
11 C. E. Pulos, *The Deep Truth: A Study of Shelley's Skepticism* (University of Nebraska Press, 1954), pp. 24–41.
12 *The Idea of the Holy* (New York: Oxford University Press, 1958), p. 95.
13 *Shelley's Poetry and Prose*, ed. Reiman and Powers, p. 477.
14 *The Correspondence of Thomas Gray*, ed. P. Toynbee and L. Whibley (Oxford: Clarendon Press, 1935), 1: 125.
15 *The Poems of Samuel Taylor Coleridge*, ed. Ernest Hartley Coleridge (London: Oxford University Press, 1912), p. 377n.
16 See Norman Fruman, *Coleridge: The Damaged Archangel* (New York: Braziller, 1971), pp. 26–30. See also Keith G. Thomas, "Coleridge, Wordsworth, and the New Historicism: 'Chamouny; The Hour Before Sunrise. A Hymn' and Book 6 of *The Prelude*," *Studies in Romanticism* 33 (Spring 1994): 81–117.
17 He wrote at this time from Geneva, "Coleridge is in my thoughts" (*Letters* 1: 490). Harold Bloom offers a provocative examination of the contrasts between these two poems in *Shelley's Mythmaking* (Cornell

University Press, 1959), pp. 11–19. See also Hogle, *Shelley's Process*, pp. 79–86.

18 Shelley evidently had Wordsworth as well as Coleridge in mind throughout this poem. The account of the glacier's destruction of animal habitats could be a deliberate denial of the nurturing benignity attributed to Providence in *Excursion* 4: 427–38. Shelley's concluding remarks on "Silence and Solitude" seem to echo *Excursion* 4: 1029–34.

19 Timothy Webb says that the standard reading "But for such faith" "can only be justified by the most tortuous explanations." *Shelley: A Voice Not Understood* (Atlantic Highlands, NJ: Humanities Press, 1977), p. 137. See *Shelley's Poetry and Prose*, ed. Reiman and Powers, p. 91, n. 6, for an example of what Webb means. Other helpful recent discussions include Michael Erkkelenz, "Shelley's Draft of 'Mont Blanc' and the Conflict of 'Faith,'" *Review of English Studies* 40 (1989): 98–103 and Robert Brinkley, "Spaces Between Words: Writing *Mont Blanc*" in *Romantic Revisions*, ed. Robert Brinkley and Keith Hanley (Cambridge University Press, 1992), p. 262.

20 Holbach, *The System of Nature*, p. 370.

21 *Examiner*, Sept. 6, 1818, p. 563.

22 *Complete Works* 6: 232.

23 *Poetical Works*, ed. Hutchinson/Matthews, p. 811.

24 *Complete Works* 6: 230.

25 *Shelley: The Golden Years*, p. 115.

26 *Poetical Works*, ed. Hutchinson/Matthews, p. 820.

27 On the basis of external evidence, Andre Koszul argues for a date no later than 1818, but thinks that 1817 is more likely. *Shelley's Prose: The Bodleian Manuscripts* (London: Henry Frowde, 1910). Michael Scrivener makes a thoughtful case for dating the essay between summer 1816 and Autumn 1817. *Radical Shelley: The Philosophical Anarchism and Utopian Thought of Percy Bysshe Shelley* (Princeton University Press, 1982), p. 89.

28 *Complete Works* 6: 240–41, 243.

29 Ibid. 6: 230–31.

30 Ibid. 6: 239.

31 Ibid. 7: 43.

32 Ibid. 7: 42–43.

33 I am particularly indebted here to F. A. Pottle, "The Role of Asia in the Dramatic Action of Shelley's *Prometheus Unbound*" reprinted in *Shelley: A Collection of Critical Essays*, ed. George M. Ridenour (Englewood Cliffs, NJ: Prentice-Hall, 1965), pp. 133–43.

34 The phrase is Jerrold Hogle's in *Shelley's Process*, p. 29.

35 *The Letters of John Keats*, ed. H. E. Rollins (Harvard University Press, 1958), 1: 184.

36 *Complete Works* 7: 17–18.

37 *Examiner*, April 1, 1821, p. 195.

38 *Examiner*, October 7, 1821, p. 631.

39 Shelley's note to *Hellas*, in *Poetical Works*, ed. Hutchinson/Matthews, p. 458.
40 *Shelley's Poetry and Prose*, ed. Reiman and Powers, p. 409.
41 In *British Romantic Writers and the East: Anxieties of Empire* (Cambridge University Press, 1992), Nigel Leask notes that the "binary opposition of Hellenism and Asiatic despotism" was a recurrent theme in the literature of the time. See also Mohammed Sharafuddin, *Islam and Romantic Orientalism: Literary Encounters with the Orient* (New York: Tauris, 1994), who challenges the argument of Edward Said's *Orientalism* (New York: Pantheon, 1978).
42 Clarke Garrett, *Respectable Folly: Millenarians and the French Revolution in France and England* (Johns Hopkins University Press, 1975), pp. 112, 116, 136, 177.
43 *The Theological and Miscellaneous Works of Joseph Priestley*, ed. John Towell Butt (London: Smallfield, 1817–32), vol. I, part 2, p. 401. Even the most secular-minded people thought about contemporary political events in apocalyptic terms. Godwin wrote to Shelley in 1812 expressing his own optimism about the progressive liberalization and enlightenment of public opinion and concluded his remarks with a quotation from the gospels: "In the hour that ye think not, the Son of Man cometh." *Letters of P. B. Shelley*, 1: 279n.
44 Constantine Francois Chasseboeuf de Volney, *The Ruins, or, A Survey of the Revolutions of Empires* (1792; London: 1836), pp. 56, 57n.
45 *Poetical Works*, ed. Hutchinson/Matthews, p. 479.
46 As early as 1810 Shelley was copying out passages from Revelation 6, which introduces the narrative of the breaking of the seals. Considering the reappearance of Ahasuerus in the apocalyptic setting of *Hellas*, it is interesting that he copied these passages under the heading "Wandering Jew." See Desmond Hawkins, "A Newly Discovered Shelley Diary," *Contemporary Review* 261 (July 1992): 35.
47 "On the Moral Teaching of Christ," *Complete Works* 6: 255.
48 *Complete Works* 6: 237–38. Despite such evidence, critics of Shelley still routinely assert that Greece represented the poet's highest vision of human achievement and potential. See, for example, Timothy Webb, *Shelley: A Voice Not Understood* (Manchester University Press, 1977).
49 *Shelley's Poetry and Prose*, ed. Reiman and Powers, pp. 488, 496.
50 Ibid., p. 496.
51 *Poetical Works*, ed. Hutchinson/Matthews, p. 450.
52 *Shelley at Work* (Oxford: Clarendon, 1967), p. 293. In his discussion of *Hellas* Michael Scrivener presents Ahasuerus as articulating "the poem's libertarian vision." *Radical Shelley: The Philosophical Anarchism and Utopian Thought of Percy Bysshe Shelley* (Princeton University Press, 1982), p. 296.
53 Carlos Baker points out the similarities between Ahasuerus and Milton's Satan in *Shelley's Major Poetry: The Fabric of a Vision* (Princeton University Press, 1948), pp. 277–78. It is worth noting that the other great Satan

that materialized in Pisa in 1821, *Cain*'s Lucifer, is also a fatalist who claims to see in the future only an inevitable repetition of the past.

54 *Poetical Works*, ed. Hutchinson/Matthews, 452.
55 A perceptive analysis of these lines is offered by William A. Ulmer in *"Hellas* and the Historical Uncanny." *ELH* 58 (1991): 618–19.
56 Note to *Queen Mab* 7: 67. *Poetical Works*, ed. Hutchinson/Matthews, p. 819.
57 Jerome J. McGann, "The Secrets of an Elder Day: Shelley after *Hellas*," *Keats–Shelley Journal* 15 (1966), p. 26.
58 *Politics in English Romantic Poetry* (Harvard University Press, 1970), p. 317.
59 Henri-Charles Puech, quoted in *Myth of the Eternal Return* (New York: Pantheon, 1954), p. 89n.
60 *Coleridge, Shelley, and Transcendental Inquiry: Rhetoric, Argument, Metapsychology* (University of Nebraska Press, 1989), p. 90.
61 *The Four Zoas*, IV, 56: 23–24. *The Complete Poetry and Prose of William Blake*, ed. David V. Erdman (rev. edn. New York: Doubleday/Anchor, 1988), p. 338.
62 *Natural Supernaturalism: Tradition and Revolution in Romantic Literature* (New York: Norton, 1971), p. 488, n. 79.
63 Bryan Shelley, *Shelley and Scripture: The Interpreting Angel* (Oxford: Clarendon Press, 1994), pp. 149–50.
64 *The Age of Reason*, ed. Moncure Daniel Conway (New York: Putnam, 1896), p. 27.
65 *Complete Works*, 6: 255.
66 *Poetical Works*, ed. Hutchinson/Matthews, p. 480.
67 *Shelley's Major Verse: The Narrative and Dramatic Poetry* (Harvard University Press, 1988), p. 196.

CONCLUSION

1 Ford K. Brown, *Fathers of the Victorians: The Age of Wilberforce* (Cambridge University Press, 1961), p. 395.
2 See Lodwick Hartley, *William Cowper: The Continuing Revaluation: An Essay and a Bibliography of Cowperian Studies from 1895 to 1960* (University of North Carolina Press, 1960), pp. 5–8.
3 *The Letters of John Keats*, 1: 137. For John Hunt, see *Keats–Shelley Journal* 33 (1964): p. 36.
4 See *The Poems of John Keats*, ed. Jack Stillinger, pp. 628–29, and *Letters* 2:162–63, 182–83.
5 *The Sociology of Religion*, trans. Ephraim Fischoff (Boston: Beacon Press, 1963), p. 55.
6 *The Prelude*, 1805, 13: 444–45. In *The Prelude 1799, 1805, 1850*, ed. Jonathan Wordsworth, M. H. Abrams, and Stephen Gill (New York: Norton, 1979).
7 "The Genealogy of Honest Doubt: F. D. Maurice and *In Memoriam*" in

The Critical Spirit and the Will to Believe: Essays in Nineteenth-Century Literature and Religion, ed. D. Jasper (London: Macmillan, 1989), pp. 120–30.

8 *Shelley's Poetry and Prose*, ed. Reiman and Powers, p. 502.

9 *Romanticism and Religion: The Tradition of Coleridge and Wordsworth in the Victorian Church* (Cambridge University Press, 1976). Another very useful work in this area is C. R. Sanders, *Coleridge and the Broad Church Movement* (Duke University Press, 1942).

10 Peter Allen, *The Cambridge Apostles, the Early Years* (Cambridge University Press, 1978), p. 36.

11 "Mr.Wordsworth," *Athenaeum*, February 19, 1828.

12 *Apologia Pro Vita Sua*, ed. Martin J. Svaglic (Oxford: Clarendon Press, 1967), pp. 93–94.

13 *The Autobiography of Mark Rutherford*, ed. Reuben Shapcott, 3rd edn. (London: Trubner, 1889), pp. 18–19.

14 Quotations taken from Charles A. Berst, "In the Beginning: The Poetic Genesis of Shaw's God," *Shaw* 1 (1981): 20; and Roland A. Duerksen, "Shelley and Shaw," *PMLA* 78 (1963): 114–27.

15 "Shaming the Devil about Shelley" in *Selected Non-Dramatic Writings of Bernard Shaw*, ed. Dan H. Laurence (Boston: Houghton Mifflin, 1965), p. 321.

16 *A Portrait of the Artist as a Young Man*, ed. Chester G. Anderson (New York: Viking, 1964), pp. 80–82.

17 Ellman, *James Joyce* (New York: Oxford University Press, 1959), pp. 40, 640–41, 681.

18 *A Portrait*, p. 164.

19 "The 'priest of the eternal imagination' turns out to be indigestibly Byronic," *Dublin's Joyce* (Indiana University Press, 1956), p. 132.

20 *The Exile of James Joyce*, trans. Sally A. J. Purcell (New York: D. Lewis, 1972), p. 401.

21 *Letters of William and Dorothy Wordsworth*, ed. E. De Selincourt and Mary Moorman. *Middle Years*, 1: 519n.

22 *The Seven Storey Mountain* (New York: Harcourt Brace, 1948), pp. 88, 190–91.

23 *Disputed Questions* (1960; rpt. New York: Harcourt Brace, 1985), p. xi.

24 See Altizer's once influential book, *The New Apocalypse: The Radical Christian Vision of William Blake* (Michigan State University Press, 1967).

25 "On Reading Romantic Poetry," *PMLA* 86 (1971), pp. 975, 979. Susan Wolfson has also characterized English Romanticism as "fundamentally interrogative," a literature based on "perceptions that provoke inquiry, experiences that elude or thwart stable organization, events that challenge previous certainties and require new terms of interpretation." *The Questioning Presence: Wordsworth, Keats, and the Interrogative Mode in Romantic Poetry* (Cornell University Press, 1986), pp. 17–18.

26 Monsignor George Talbot to Cardinal Manning, 1867. Wilfrid Ward,

The Life of John Henry Cardinal Newman (London: Longman's, 1921), 2:147.

27 David D. Cooper, *Thomas Merton's Art of Denial: The Evolution of a Radical Humanist* (University of Georgia Press, 1989), p. 219.

28 For this insight, and the quotation, I am indebted to Charles Berst, "In the Beginning," p. 12.

29 *The Prelude*, 1850, 5: 198–99, 213–22.

30 "A Defence of Poetry," in *Shelley's Poetry and Prose*, ed. Reiman and Powers, p. 508.

Bibliography

Abrams, M. H. "English Romanticism: The Spirit of the Age." In *Romanticism Reconsidered: Selected Papers from the English Institute,* ed. Northrop Frye. New York: Columbia University Press, 1963, pp. 26–72.

Natural Supernaturalism: Tradition and Revolution in Romantic Literature. New York: Norton, 1971.

Allen, Peter. *The Cambridge Apostles, the Early Years.* Cambridge University Press, 1978.

Altizer, Thomas. *The New Apocalypse: The Radical Christian Vision of William Blake.* Michigan State University Press, 1967.

Arendt, Hannah. *On Revolution.* New York: Viking, 1963.

Armstrong, Anthony. *The Church of England, the Methodists and Society 1700–1850.* University of London Press, 1973.

Arnold, Matthew. "Wordsworth" in *English Literature and Irish Politics,* ed. R. H. Super. *The Complete Prose Works of Matthew Arnold,* vol. 9. University of Michigan Press, 1973.

Arnold, Thomas. *The Life and Correspondence of Thomas Arnold, D. D.,* ed. Arthur Penrhyn Stanley. 2 vols. Boston: Osgood, 1873.

Baker, Carlos. *Shelley's Major Poetry: The Fabric of a Vision.* Princeton University Press, 1948.

Baker, Jeffrey. *John Keats and Symbolism.* New York: St. Martin's Press, 1986.

Baldick, Chris. *In Frankenstein's Shadow: Myth, Monstrosity, and Nineteenth-Century Writers.* Oxford: Clarendon Press, 1987.

Barker, Arthur E. *Milton and the Puritan Dilemma 1641–1660.* University of Toronto Press, 1942.

Barker, Ernest, ed. *The Social Contract: Essays by Locke, Hume, and Rousseau.* London: Oxford University Press, 1947.

Barlow, Richard Burgess. *Citizenship and Conscience: A Study in the Theory and Practice of Religious Toleration in England During the Eighteenth Century.* University of Pennsylvania Press, 1962.

Barnard, Ellsworth. *Shelley's Religion.* University of Minnesota Press, 1936.

Barnard, John. *John Keats.* Cambridge University Press, 1987.

Barth, Karl. *Church Dogmatics,* trans. G. T. Thomson and Harold Knight. New York: Scribner, 1955–56.

The Word of God and the Word of Man. New York: Harper, 1957.

Bate, Walter Jackson. *The Burden of the Past and the English Poet.* Belknap Press of Harvard University Press, 1970.

John Keats. Harvard University Press, 1963.

Batho, Edith C. *The Later Wordsworth.* 1933; rpt. New York: Russell & Russell, 1963.

Bebbington, David. *Evangelicalism in Modern Britain: A History from the 1730s to the 1980s.* Winchester, MA: Allen & Unwin, 1989.

Beer, John. *Blake's Humanism.* Manchester University Press, 1968.

Bellah, Robert N. "Civil Religion in America," *Daedalus* 96 (1967), 1–21.

Benziger, James. *Images of Eternity: Studies in the Poetry of Religious Vision from Wordsworth to T. S. Eliot.* Southern Illinois University Press, 1962.

Berst, Charles A. "In the Beginning: The Poetic Genesis of Shaw's God." *Shaw* 1 (1981).

Best, G. F. A. *Temporal Pillars: Queen Anne's Bounty, the Ecclesiastical Commissioners, and the Church of England.* Cambridge University Press, 1964.

Blake, William. *Blake's Poetry and Designs,* ed. John E. Grant and Mary Lynn Johnson. New York: Norton, 1979.

The Complete Poetry and Prose of William Blake, ed. David V. Erdman. Rev. edn., New York: Doubleday/Anchor, 1988.

William Blake's Writings, ed. G. E. Bentley, Jr. Oxford: Clarendon Press, 1963.

Blomfield, Charles. *Charge to Clergy of the Diocese of Chester.* Chester, 1825.

Bloom, Harold. *The Anxiety of Influence: A Theory of Poetry.* New York: Oxford University Press, 1973.

Blake's Apocalypse: A Study in Poetic Argument. New York: Doubleday, 1963.

Shelley's Mythmaking. Cornell University Press, 1959.

The Visionary Company: A Reading of English Romantic Poetry. New York: Doubleday, 1963.

Bogen, Nancy. "The Problem of Blake's Early Religion," *The Personalist* 49 (1968).

[Bogue, David.] *Reasons for Seeking a Repeal of the Corporation and Test Acts . . . By a Dissenter.* London: Buckland and Dilly, 1790.

Booth, Wayne C. *A Rhetoric of Irony.* University of Chicago Press, 1974.

Bostetter, Edward E. *The Romantic Ventriloquists: Wordsworth, Coleridge, Keats, Shelley, Byron.* University of Washington Press, 1963.

Bottrall, Margaret. *The Divine Image: A Study of Blake's Interpretation of Christianity.* Rome: Edizioni di Storia e Letteratura, 1950.

Boulger, James. *The Calvinist Temper in English Poetry.* The Hague: Mouton, 1980.

Bouyer, Louis. *Newman, His Life and Spirituality.* New York: Meridian Books, 1960.

Bradley, James E. *Religion, Revolution, and English Radicalism: Nonconformity in Eighteenth-Century Politics and Society.* Cambridge University Press, 1990.

Brailsford, H. N. *Shelley, Godwin and Their Circle.* New York: Holt, 1920.

Brantley, Richard E. *Locke, Wesley, and the Method of English Romanticism.* University of Florida Press, 1984.

Wordsworth's "Natural Methodism." Yale University Press, 1975.

Breunig, Charles. *The Age of Revolution and Reaction, 1789–1850.* New York: Norton, 1970.

Brinkley, Robert. "Spaces Between Words: Writing *Mont Blanc*" in *Romantic Revisions*, ed. Robert Brinkley and Keith Hanley. Cambridge University Press, 1992, pp. 243–67.

Bromwich, David. "Keats's Radicalism," *Studies in Romanticism* 25 (1986), 197–210.

Brown, Ford K. *Fathers of the Victorians: The Age of Wilberforce.* Cambridge University Press, 1961.

Burke, Edmund. *The Writings and Speeches of Edmund Burke.* ed. Paul Langford. 9 vols. Oxford: Clarendon Press, 1981–89.

Edmund Burke: The Works, Twelve Volumes in Six. 1887; New York: Georg Olms, 1975.

Burns, R. Arthur. "A Hanoverian legacy? Diocesan Reform in the Church of England c. 1800–1833" in *The Church of England c. 1689–c. 1833: From Toleration to Tractarianism*, ed. John Walsh et al. Cambridge University Press, 1993, pp. 265–82.

Bush, Douglas. *Mythology and the Romantic Tradition in English Poetry.* Harvard University Press, 1937.

Butler, Marilyn. "Myth and Mythmaking in the Shelley Circle," *ELH* 49 (1982), 50–72.

Romantics, Rebels and Reactionaries: English Literature and its Background 1760–1830. New York: Oxford University Press, 1982.

Byron, George Gordon, Baron. *Byron's Letters and Journals*, ed. Leslie Marchand. 12 vols. Harvard University Press, 1973–82.

His Very Self and Voice: The Collected Conversations of Lord Byron, ed. Ernest J. Lovell, Jr. New York: Macmillan, 1954.

Lord Byron, The Complete Miscellaneous Prose, ed. Andrew Nicholson. Oxford: Clarendon Press, 1991.

Lord Byron: The Complete Poetical Works, ed. Jerome J. McGann. 7 vols. Oxford: Clarendon Press, 1980–93.

The Works of Lord Byron, ed. E. H. Coleridge and R. E. Prothero. 13 vols. London: Murray, 1922.

Cameron, Kenneth Neill Cameron. *Shelley: The Golden Years.* Harvard University Press, 1974.

The Young Shelley: The Genesis of a Radical. New York: Macmillan, 1950.

[Carlile, Richard]. *The Report of the Proceedings of the Court of Kings Bench . . . being the mock trial of Richard Carlile for alledged blasphemous libel, etc.* London: Carlile, 1822.

Chandler, James K. *Wordsworth's Second Nature: A Study of the Poetry and Politics.* University of Chicago Press, 1984.

Chard, Leslie. *Dissenting Republican; Wordsworth's Early Life and Thought in Their Political Context.* The Hague: Mouton, 1972.

Chew, Samuel C. *Byron in England.* London: Murray, 1924.

Cixous, Hélène. *The Exile of James Joyce,* trans. Sally A. J. Purcell. New York: D. Lewis, 1972.

Clairmont, Clara Mary Jane. *Journals of Claire Clairmont,* ed. Marion Kingston Stocking. Harvard University Press, 1968.

Clark, J. C. D. *English Society 1688–1832: Ideology, Social Structure and Political Practice during the Ancien Regime.* Cambridge University Press, 1985.

Clemit, Pamela. *The Godwinian Novel: The Rational Fictions of Godwin, Brockden Brown, Mary Shelley.* New York: Oxford University Press, 1993.

Clowes, John. *A Memoir of the Late Rev. John Clowes, A.M. . . . Written by Himself.* London, 1849.

Clubbe, John, and Ernest Lovell. *English Romanticism: The Grounds of Belief.* Northern Illinois University Press, 1983.

Coleridge, Samuel Taylor. *Biographia Literia,* ed. James Ensell and W. J. Bate. Princeton University Press, 1983.

Collected Letters of Samuel Taylor Coleridge, ed. E. L. Griggs. Oxford: Clarendon Press, 1956–71.

Complete Works of Samuel Taylor Coleridge, ed. W. G. T. Shedd. 6 vols. New York: Harper, 1884.

Lectures 1795: On Politics and Religion, eds. Lewis Patton and Peter Manning. (*The Collected Works of Samuel Taylor Coleridge,* vol. 1.) Princeton University Press, 1971.

On the Constitution of the Church and State, ed. John Colmer. (*The Collected Works of Samuel Taylor Coleridge,* vol. 10.) Princeton University Press, 1976.

The Poems of Samuel Taylor Coleridge, ed. Ernest Hartley Coleridge. Oxford University Press, 1961.

Cook, Elizabeth, ed. *John Keats.* Oxford University Press, 1990.

Cookson, J. E. *The Friends of Peace: Anti-War Liberalism in England, 1793–1815.* Cambridge University Press, 1982.

Cooper, David. D. *Thomas Merton's Art of Denial: The Evolution of a Radical Humanist.* University of Georgia Press, 1989.

Corbett, Martyn. *Byron and Tragedy.* New York: St. Martin's Press, 1988.

Creaser, John. "From 'Autumn' to Autumn in Keats's Ode." *Essays in Criticism* 38 (1988), 190–214.

Crosby, Dan Kenneth. "Wordsworth's *Excursion*: An Annotated Bibliography of Criticism," *Bulletin of Bibliography* 48 (1991), 33–49.

Curran, Stuart. "Blake and the Gnostic Hyle: A Double Negative," *Blake Studies* 4 (1972), 117–33.

Curran, Stuart. *Shelley's Annus Mirabilis: The Maturing of an Epic Vision.* San Marino, CA: Huntington Library, 1975.

Damrosch, Leopold, Jr. *Symbol and Truth in Blake's Myth.* Princeton University Press, 1980.

Daubeny, Charles. *A Sermon on His Majesty's Call for the United Exertions of His People Against the Threatened Invasion. Preached at Christ's Church, Bath, Sunday, July 31st, 1803.* London 1803.

Davies, J. G. *The Theology of William Blake.* Oxford: Clarendon Press, 1948.

Davis, Thomas W. ed. *Committees for Repeal of the Test and Corporation Acts, Minutes, 1788–90 and 1827–28.* London Record Society, 1978.

De Almeida, Hermione. *Romantic Medicine and John Keats.* Oxford University Press, 1990.

Deen, Leonard W. "Coleridge and the Radicalism of Religious Dissent," *JEGP* 61 (1962), 496–510.

Conversing in Paradise: Poetic Genius and Identity-as-Community in Blake's Los. University of Missouri Press, 1983.

Dickstein, Morris. *Keats and His Poetry: A Study in Development.* University of Chicago Press, 1971.

"Keats and Politics". *Studies in Romanticism* 25 (1986), 175–81.

Dinwiddy, John. "Interpretations of Anti-Jacobinism" in *The French Revolution and British Popular Politics,* ed. Mark Philp. Cambridge University Press, 1991.

Ditchfield, G. M. "Anti-trinitarianism and Toleration in Late Eighteenth Century British Politics: The Unitarian Petition of 1792," *Journal of Ecclesiastical History* 42 (1991), 31–67.

"The Parliamentary Struggle over the Repeal of the Test and Corporation Acts, 1787–1790," *English Historical Review* 89 (1974).

Dombrowski, Daniel. "Panpsychism," *The Wordsworth Circle* 19 (1988), 38–45.

"Wordsworth's Panentheism," *The Wordsworth Circle* 16 (1985), 136–42.

Duerksen, Roland A. "Shelley and Shaw," *Publications of the Modern Language Society* 78 (1963), 114–27.

Eatwell, John, ed. *The New Palgrave: A Dictionary of Economics.* New York: Stockton, 1987.

Eliade, Mircea. *The Myth of the Eternal Return,* trans. Willard Trask. New York: Pantheon, 1954.

The Sacred and the Profane, trans. Willard Trask. New York: Harcourt, Brace & World, 1959.

Ellman, Richard. *James Joyce.* New York: Oxford University Press, 1959.

Erdman, David V. *The Illuminated Blake.* Garden City, NY: Doubleday, 1974.

Blake: Prophet Against Empire: A Poet's Interpretation of the History of His Own Times. Garden City, NY: Doubleday, 1969.

Ericksen, Robert P. "The Barmen Synod and Its Declaration: A Historical Synopsis" in *The Church Confronts the Nazis: Barmen Then and Now,* ed. Hubert G. Locke. New York: Edward Mellen Press, 1984.

Erkkelenz, Michael. "Shelley's Draft of 'Mont Blanc' and the Conflict of 'Faith,' " *Review of English Studies* 40 (1989), 98–103.

Evert, Walter. *Aesthetic and Myth in the Poetry of Keats.* Princeton University Press, 1965.

Every, George. *The High Church Party 1688–1718.* London: SPCK, 1956.

Examiner, The: *A Weekly Paper on Politics, Literature, Music and the Fine Arts.* London, 1808–1881.

Fairchild, H. N. *Religious Trends in English Poetry,* vol. 3: *1780–1830, Romantic Faith.* Columbia University Press, 1949.

Farrell, John P. *Revolution as Tragedy: The Dilemma of the Moderate from Scott to Arnold.* Cornell University Press, 1980.

Fekete, John. *The Critical Twilight: Explorations in the Ideology of Anglo-American Literary Theory from Eliot to McLuhan.* Boston: Routledge, 1977.

Ferber, Michael. *The Social Vision of William Blake.* Princeton University Press, 1985.

Fish, Stanley Eugene. *Surprised by Sin: The Reader in Paradise Lost.* New York: St. Martin's Press, 1967.

Frosch, Thomas. *The Awakening of Albion: The Renovation of the Body in the Poetry of William Blake.* Cornell University Press, 1974.

Fruman, Norman. *Coleridge: The Damaged Archangel.* New York: Braziller, 1971.

Frye, Northrop. *Fearful Symmetry: A Study of William Blake.* Princeton University Press, 1947.

"William Blake" in *The English Romantic Poets and Essayists,* ed. Lawrence and Caroline Houtchens. New York: Modern Language Association, 1957.

Galperin, William. " 'Imperfect While Unshared': The Role of the Implied Reader in Wordsworth's 'Excursion,' " *Criticism* 22 (1980).

Revision and Authority in Wordsworth: The Interpretation of a Career. University of Pennsylvania Press, 1989.

Garber, Frederick. *Self, Text, and Romantic Irony.* Princeton University Press, 1988.

Garrett, Clarke. *Respectable Folly: Millenarians and the French Revolution in France and England.* Johns Hopkins University Press, 1975.

Gascoigne, John. *Cambridge in the Age of the Enlightenment: Science, Religion, and Politics from the Restoration to the French Revolution.* Cambridge University Press, 1989.

Gibbon, Edward. *The Decline and Fall of the Roman Empire.* 6 vols. New York: Dutton, 1978–81.

Gilbert, Alan D. "Methodism, Dissent and Political Stability in Early Industrial England," *Journal of Religious History* 10 (1979), 381–99.

Religion and Society in Industrial England: Church, Chapel and Social Change, 1740–1914. London: Longmans, 1976.

Gill, Frederick C. *The Romantic Movement and Methodism: A Study of English Romanticism and the Evangelical Revival.* London: Epworth, 1937.

Gill, Stephen. *Wordsworth: The Prelude.* (Landmarks of World Literature.) Cambridge University Press, 1991.

Gittings, Robert. *John Keats.* London: Heinemann, 1968.

Gloyn, Cyril Kennan. *The Church in the Social Order: Study of Anglican Social*

Theory from Coleridge to Maurice. Forest Grove, Oregon: Pacific University Press, 1942.

Godwin, William ("Edward Baldwin"). *The Pantheon, or, Ancient History of the Gods of Greece and Rome*. 1814; New York: Garland, 1984.

Good, Edwin M. *Irony in the Old Testament*. Philadelphia: Westminster, 1965.

Goodwin, Albert. *The Friends of Liberty: The English Democratic Movement in the Age of the French Revolution*. Harvard University Press, 1979.

Grant, Jack and Mary Lynn Johnson, eds. *Blake's Poetry and Designs*. New York: Norton, 1979.

Gray, Thomas. *The Correspondence of Thomas Gray*, ed. P. Toynbee and L. Whibley. Oxford: Clarendon Press, 1935.

Grob, Alan. *The Philosophic Mind: A Study of Wordsworth's Poetry and Thought 1797–1805*. Ohio State University Press, 1973.

Gross, George C. "*Lamia* and the Cupid-Psyche Myth," *Keats–Shelley Journal* 39 (1990).

Hagstrum, Jean H. " 'The Wrath of the Lamb': A Study of William Blake's Conversions" in *From Sensibility to Romanticism*, ed. Frederick W. Hilles and Harold Bloom. Oxford University Press, 1965.

Hales, Leslie-Ann. "The Figure of Jesus Christ in William Blake's *Jerusalem*," *Heythrop Journal* 24 (1983).

Hall, Robert. *The Miscellaneous Works and Remains of the Rev. Robert Hall, with a Memoir of his Life, by Olinthus Gregory and a Critical Estimate of His Character and Writings by John Foster*. London: Bohn, 1846.

Haller, William. *The Early Life of Robert Southey 1774–1803*. 1917; rpt. New York: Octagon, 1966.

Hamilton, Paul. "Keats and Critique" in *Rethinking Romanticism: Critical Readings in Romantic History*. Oxford: Blackwell, 1989.

Hanley, Keith, and Raman Selden, eds. *Revolution and English Romanticism: Politics and Rhetoric*. New York: St. Martin's Press, 1990.

Harrison, J. F. C. *The Second Coming: Popular Millenarianism 1780–1850*. Rutgers University Press, 1979.

Harrison, Jane Ellen. *Prolegomena to the Study of Greek Religion*. 1903; rpt. Princeton University Press, 1991.

Harrison, Peter. *"Religion" and the Religions of the English Enlightenment*. Cambridge University Press, 1990.

"Harroviensis." *A Letter to Sir Walter Scott, Bart., in Answer to the Remonstrance of Oxoniensis on the Publication of Cain, a Mystery, by Lord Byron*. London, 1822.

Hartley, Lodwick. *William Cowper: The Continuing Revaluation: An Essay and a Bibliography of Cowperian Studies from 1895 to 1960*. University of North Carolina Press, 1960.

Hartman, Geoffrey H. *Wordsworth's Poetry 1787–1814*. Yale University Press, 1964.

Hastings, James, ed. *Encyclopedia of Religion and Ethics*. New York: Scribner, 1925–27.

Hawkins, Desmond. "A Newly Discovered Shelley Diary," *Contemporary Review* 261 (July 1992).

Hayden, John O. "The Dating of the '1794' Version of Wordsworth's *An Evening Walk*," *Studies in Bibliography* 42 (1989), 265–71.

Haydon, Benjamin Robert. *The Diary of Benjamin Robert Haydon*, ed. Willard B. Pope. 5 vols. Harvard University Press, 1961–63.

Hazlitt, William. *Complete Works of William Hazlitt*, ed. P. P. Howe. 21 vols. London: Dent, 1930–34.

Hempton, David. *Methodism and Politics in British Society 1750–1850*. Stanford University Press, 1984.

Henriques, Ursula. *Religious Toleration in England 1787–1833*. University of Toronto Press, 1961.

Heschel, Abraham J. *The Prophets*. New York: Harper, 1969.

Hewitt, Regina. *Wordsworth and the Empirical Dilemma*. New York: Peter Lang, 1990.

"Church Building as Political Strategy in Wordsworth's *Ecclesiastical Sonnets*," *Mosaic* 25/3 (1992), 31–46.

Hill, Alan. "New Light on *The Excursion*," *Ariel* 5 (1974), 37–47.

Hilton, Boyd. *The Age of Atonement: The Influence of Evangelicalism on Social and Economic Thought, 1795–1865* Oxford: Clarendon Press, 1988.

Hindmarsh, Robert. *Rise and Progress of the New Jerusalem Church, in England, America, and Other Parts*, ed. E. Madeley. London: 1861.

Hirsch, E. D., Jr. "Byron and the Terrestrial Paradise" in *From Sensibility to Romanticism*, ed. Frederick W. Hilles and Harold Bloom. New York: Oxford University Press, 1965, pp. 467–86.

Hirst, Wolf Z. "Byron's Lapse into Orthodoxy: An Unorthodox Reading of *Cain*" *Keats–Shelley Journal* 29 (1980), 151–72.

Hoagwood, Terence Allan. "Fictions and Freedom: Wordsworth and the Ideology of Romanticism" in *New Historical Literary Study: Essays on Reproducing Texts, Representing History*, ed. Jeffrey N. Cox. Princeton University Press, 1993.

Prophecy and the Philosophy of Mind: Traditions of Blake and Shelley. University of Alabama Press, 1985.

Hobsbawm, E. J. "Methodism and the Threat of Revolution in Britain," *History Today* 7 (1957), 115–24.

Hodgson, John. *Coleridge, Shelley, and Transcendental Inquiry: Rhetoric, Argument, Metapsychology*. University of Nebraska Press, 1989.

Wordsworth's Philosophical Poetry, 1797–1814. University of Nebraska Press, 1980.

Hodgson, Robert. *The Life of the Right Reverend Beilby Porteus D. D., Late Bishop of London*. 2nd edn. London: Cadell & Davies, 1811.

Hogle, Jerrold E. *Shelley's Process: Radical Transference and the Development of His Major Works*. New York: Oxford University Press, 1988.

Holbach, Paul Henry Thiry, Baron. *The System of Nature, or the Laws of the*

Moral and Physical World. From the original French of M. Mirabaud. trans. Samuel Wilkinson. London: Cousins, 1839.

Hole, Robert. *Pulpits, Politics, and Public Order in England 1760–1832.* Cambridge University Press, 1989.

Homans, Margaret. "Keats Reading Women, Women Reading Keats," *Studies in Romanticism* 29 (1990), 341–70.

Horsley, Samuel. *Sermons by Samuel Horsley.* 3rd edn. 3 vols. Dundee: Chalmers, 1812.

Howard, John. "An Audience for *The Marriage of Heaven and Hell,*" *Blake Studies* 3 (1970), 19–52.

Howse, Ernest Marshall. *Saints in Politics: The "Clapham Sect" and the Growth of Freedom.* University of Toronto Press, 1952.

Hulme, T. E. *Speculations: Essays on Humanism and the Philosophy of Art,* ed. Herbert Read. 1924; rpt. London: Routledge & Kegan Paul, 1949.

Hume, David. *Hume on Religion,* ed. Richard Wollheim. New York: Meridian Books, 1969.

The Natural History of Religion, ed. A. Wayne Colver. Oxford: Clarendon Press, 1976.

Hunt, Leigh. *The Autobiography of Leigh Hunt,* ed. J. E. Morpurgo. London: Cresset, 1949.

Foliage; or Poems Original and Translated. London: Ollier, 1818.

Hyers, Conrad M., ed. *Holy Laughter: Essays on Religion in the Comic Perspective.* New York: Seabury, 1969.

Itzkin, Elissa S. "The Halévy Thesis – A Working Hypothesis? English Revivalism: Antidote for Revolution and Radicalism 1789–1815" *Church History* 44 (1975), 47–56.

Jacob, James R., and Margaret C. Jacob. "The Anglican Origins of Modern Science: The Metaphysical Foundations of the Whig Constitution." *Isis* 71 (1980), 251–67.

Jacob, Margaret C. *The Newtonians and the English Revolution 1689–1720.* Cornell University Press, 1976.

The Radical Enlightenment: Pantheists, Freemasons and Republicans. Boston: Allen & Unwin, 1981.

James, D. G. *The Romantic Comedy: An Essay on English Romanticism.* New York: Oxford University Press, 1948.

Jameson, Frederic. "Religion and Ideology: A Political Reading of *Paradise Lost*" in *Literature, Politics and Theory: Papers from the Essex Conference 1976–1984,* ed. Francis Barker et al. New York: Methuen, 1986, pp. 35–56.

Jewson, C. B. *The Jacobin City: A Portrait of Norwich in its Reaction to the French Revolution 1788–1802.* London: Blackie, 1975.

John, Donald. "Blake and Forgiveness," *The Wordsworth Circle,* 17 (Spring 1986).

Johnston, Kenneth R. "The Politics of 'Tintern Abbey,'" *The Wordsworth Circle* 14 (1983).

Joukovsky, Nicholas A. "The Lost Greek Anapests of Thomas Love Peacock," *Modern Philology* 89 (Feb. 1992).

Keats, John. *The Complete Works of John Keats*, ed. H. B. Forman, 5 vols. 1901; rpt. New York: AMS, 1970.

The Letters of John Keats, ed. H. E. Rollins. 2 vols. Harvard University Press, 1958.

The Poems of John Keats, ed. Jack Stillinger. Harvard University Press, 1978.

Keble, John. *Lectures on Poetry, 1832–1841*, trans. Edward Kershaw Francis. 2 vols. Oxford: Clarendon Press, 1912.

Kelsall, Malcolm Miles. *Byron's Politics*. Totowa, NJ: Barnes and Noble, 1987.

Kenner, Hugh. *Dublin's Joyce*. Indiana University Press, 1956.

Kernan, Alvin B. *The Plot of Satire*. Yale University Press, 1965.

Kiernan, V. G. "Wordsworth and the People" (1956), reprinted with a new postscript in *Marxists on Literature: An Anthology*, ed. David Craig. Harmondsworth: Penguin, 1975, pp. 161–206.

Kingsley, Charles. *Letters and Memories of His Life*. London: King, 1877.

Knight, Frida. *University Rebel: The Life of William Frend, 1757–1841*. London: Gollancz, 1971.

Knight, G. Wilson. *Lord Byron: Christian Virtues*. London: Routledge & Kegan Paul, 1952.

Koszul, André Henri. *Shelley's Prose: The Bodleian Manuscripts*. London: Henry Frowde, 1910.

Lamb, Charles. *The Letters of Charles and Mary Lamb*, ed. Edwin M. Marrs, Jr. 3 vols. Cornell University Press, 1978.

Larkin, Philip. *Collected Poems*, ed. Anthony Thwaite. New York: Farrar Strauss Giroux, 1989.

Lau, Beth. *Keats's Reading of the Romantic Poets*. University of Michigan Press, 1991.

Leask, Nigel. *British Romantic Writers and the East: Anxieties of Empire*. Cambridge University Press, 1992.

Lenski, Gerhard. *The Religious Factor: A Sociological Study of Religion's Impact on Politics, Economics, and Family Life*. Garden City, NY: Doubleday, 1961.

Levine, George, and U. C. Knoepflmacher, eds. *The Endurance of Frankenstein*. University of California Press, 1979.

Levinson, Marjorie. *Keats's Life of Allegory: The Origins of a Style*. Oxford: Blackwell, 1988.

Lewis, Clive Staples. "De Descriptione Temporum" in *They Asked for a Paper: Papers and Addresses*. London: G. Bles, 1962.

Lincoln, Anthony. *Some Political and Social Ideas of English Dissent 1763–1800*. 1938; rpt. New York: Octagon, 1971.

Lincoln, Bruce. "Notes toward a Theory of Religion and Revolution" in *Religion, Rebellion, Revolution: An Inter-disciplinary and Cross-Cultural Collection of Essays*, ed. Bruce Lincoln. London: Macmillan, 1985, pp. 266–92.

Liu, Alan. *Wordsworth: The Sense of History*. Stanford University Press, 1989.

Locke, Don. *A Fantasy of Reason: The Life and Thought of William Godwin*. London: Routledge & Kegan Paul, 1980.

Lovegrove, Deryck W. *Established Church, Sectarian People: Itinerancy and the Transformation of English Dissent, 1780–1830*. Cambridge University Press, 1988.

Lovell, Ernest J., Jr. *Byron: The Record of a Quest*. 1949; rpt. Hamden, CT: Archon Books, 1966.

Lowes, John Livingston. "Moneta's Temple," *PMLA* 51 (1936), 1098–1113.

Lyon, Judson. *The Excursion: A Study*. Yale University Press, 1950.

Machin, G. I. T. *Politics and the Churches in Great Britain 1832–1866*. Oxford: Clarendon, 1977.

Maclear, J. F. "Isaac Watts and the Idea of Public Religion," *Journal of the History of Ideas* 53 (1992), 25–45.

Macquarrie, John. *Twentieth-Century Religious Thought: The Frontiers of Philosophy and Theology, 1900–1970*. London: SCM Press, 1971.

Malthus, Thomas Robert. *First Essay on Population, 1798*. 1926; rpt. New York: St. Martin's Press, 1966.

Manning, Peter. *Byron's Fictions*. Wayne State University Press, 1978.

Manuel, Frank E. *The Eighteenth Century Confronts the Gods*. Harvard University Press, 1959.

Marchand, Leslie. *Byron: A Biography*. 3 vols. New York: Knopf, 1957.

   Byron's Poetry: A Critical Introduction. Boston: Houghton Mifflin, 1965.

Marjarum, E. W. *Byron as Skeptic and Believer*. Princeton University Press, 1938.

Mather, F. C. *High Church Prophet: Bishop Samuel Horsley (1733–1806) and the Caroline Tradition in the Later Georgian Church*. New York: Oxford University Press, 1992.

Mathews, Lawrence. "Jesus as Saviour in Blake's *Jerusalem*," *English Studies in Canada* 6 (Summer 1980), 154–75.

Maynard, Theodore. *Religion and Culture*. London: Sheed and Ward, 1948.

McCalman, Iain. *Radical Underworld: Prophets, Revolutionaries and Pornographers in London, 1795–1840*. Cambridge University Press, 1988.

McGann, Jerome. *Don Juan in Context*. University of Chicago Press, 1976.

   Fiery Dust: Byron's Poetic Development. University of Chicago Press, 1968.

   "Keats and the Historical Method in Literary Criticism," *MLN* 94 (1979), 988–1032.

   The Romantic Ideology: A Critical Investigation. University of Chicago Press, 1983.

   "The Secrets of an Elder Day: Shelley after *Hellas*," *Keats–Shelley Journal* 15 (1966), 25–41.

McManners, John. *The French Revolution and the Church*. New York: Harper & Row, 1969.

Mee, Jon. *Dangerous Enthusiasm: William Blake and the Culture of Radicalism in the 1790s*. Oxford: Clarendon Press, 1992.

Mellor, Anne. *English Romantic Irony*. Harvard University Press, 1980.

"Keats's Face of Moneta," *Keats–Shelley Journal* 25 (1976).

Mary Shelley: Her Life, Her Fiction, Her Monsters. New York: Routledge, 1989.

"Why Women Didn't Like Romanticism: The Views of Jane Austen and Mary Shelley" in *The Romantics and Us: Essays on Literature and Culture,* ed. Gene W. Ruoff. Rutgers University Press, 1990, pp. 274–87.

Merivale, Patricia. *Pan the Goat-God: His Myth in Modern Times.* Harvard University Press, 1969.

Merton, Thomas. *Disputed Questions.* 1960; rpt. New York: Harcourt Brace, 1985.

The Seven Storey Mountain. New York: Harcourt Brace, 1948.

Milton, John. *Complete Prose Works of John Milton.* Yale University Press, vol. 1: *1624–1642,* ed. Don M. Wolfe (1953), vol. 2: *1643–1648,* ed. Ernest Sirluck (1959).

Mineka, Francis E. *The Dissidence of Dissent: The Monthly Repository, 1806–1838.* 1944; rpt. New York: Octagon, 1972.

Muecke, D. C. *The Compass of Irony.* London: Methuen, 1969.

Murry, John Middleton. *Keats and Shakespeare.* 1935; rpt. London: Oxford University Press, 1958.

Newlyn, Lucy. *Paradise Lost and the Romantic Reader.* Oxford: Clarendon Press, 1993.

Newman, John Henry. *Apologia Pro Vita Sua,* ed. Martin J. Svaglic. Oxford: Clarendon, 1967.

Nicholls, William. *Systematic and Philosophical Theology.* Baltimore: Penguin, 1969.

Norman, E. R. *Church and Society in England 1770–1970.* Oxford: Clarendon Press, 1976.

O'Connell, Daniel. *Daniel O' Connell: His Early Life and Journal, 1795–1802,* ed. A. Houston. London: Pitman, 1906.

Otto, Rudolf. *The Idea of the Holy.* New York: Oxford University Press, 1958.

Owen, W. J. B. "Costs, Sales, and Profits of Longman's Editions of Wordsworth," *Library,* 5th Series, 12 (1957), 107.

["Oxonian"]. *The Radical Triumvirate; or Infidel Paine, Lord Byron, and Surgeon Lawrence colleaguing with the patriotic Radicals to emancipate Mankind from all Laws, human and divine. A Letter to John Bull.* London, 1820.

Paine, Thomas. *The Age of Reason,* ed. Moncure Daniel Conway. New York: G. P. Putnam's Sons, 1896.

The Rights of Man, introd. Eric Foner. New York: Penguin Books, 1984.

Paley, Morton D. *The Continuing City: William Blake's "Jerusalem."* Oxford: Clarendon, 1983.

"'A New Heaven is Begun': William Blake and Swedenborgianism," *Blake: An Illustrated Quarterly* 13 (Fall 1979).

Paley. William. *The Works of William Paley, D.D.,* introd. D. S. Wayland. London: George Cowie, 1837.

Perkin, Harold. *Origins of Modern English Society.* 1969; rpt. London: Routledge, 1991.

Perkins, David, ed. *English Romantic Writers*. Harvard University Press, 1969.

Piper, H. W. *The Active Universe*. London: Athlone, 1962.

Plutarch. *Selected Essays and Dialogues*. trans. Donald Russell. New York: Oxford University Press, 1993.

Poovey, Mary. *The Proper Lady and the Woman Writer: Ideology as Style in the Works of Mary Wollstonecraft, Mary Shelley, and Jane Austen*. University of Chicago Press, 1984.

Pottle, F. A. "The Role of Asia in the Dramatic Action of Shelley's *Prometheus Unbound*" in *Shelley: A Collection of Critical Essays*, ed. George M. Ridenour. Englewood Cliffs, NJ: Prentice-Hall, 1965.

Price, Richard. *Political Writings*, ed. D. O. Thomas. Cambridge University Press, 1991.

Sermon on the Evidence of a Future Period of Improvement in the State of Mankind. London, 1787.

Prickett, Stephen. *Romanticism and Religion: The Tradition of Coleridge and Wordsworth in the Victorian Church*. Cambridge University Press, 1976.

Priestley, Joseph. *The Theological and Miscellaneous Works of Joseph Priestley*, ed. John Towell Butt. London: Smallfield, 1817–32.

Pulos, C. E. *The Deep Truth: A Study of Shelley's Skepticism*. University of Nebraska Press, 1954.

Pym, David. "William Wordsworth: From Matthew Arnold to A. C. Bradley: A Study in Victorian Belief and Wordsworth's Poetry," *Durham University Journal*, n.s. 51 (Jan. 1990), 191–97.

Quinones, Richard. "Byron's *Cain*: Between History and Theology," in *Byron, the Bible, and Religion*, ed. Wolf Z. Hirst. University of Delaware Press, 1991.

Rajan, Tilottama. *Dark Interpreter: The Discourse of Romanticism*. Cornell University Press, 1980.

Randolph, John. *A Change Delivered to the clergy of the Diocese of Oxford*. Oxford, 1802.

Reid, William Hamilton. *The Rise and Dissolution of the Infidel Societies in the Metropolis: including, the origin of modern deism and atheism . . . from the Publication of Paine's Age of Reason till the Present Period*. London: J. Hatchard, 1800.

Reiman, Donald H. *Percy Bysshe Shelley*. New York: St. Martin's Press, 1969.

ed. *The Romantics Reviewed: Contemporary Reviews of British Romantic Writers*. 9 vols. New York: Garland, 1972.

Ridenour, George M. *The Style of "Don Juan."* Yale University Press, 1960.

Robinson, Henry Crabb. *Henry Crabb Robinson on Books and Their Writers*, ed. Edith J. Morley. London: Dent, 1938.

Rodgers, Neville. *Shelley at Work*. Oxford: Clarendon, 1967.

Roe, Nicholas. *Wordsworth and Coleridge: The Radical Years*. New York: Oxford University Press, 1988.

Rollins, Hyder Edward, ed. *The Keats Circle: Letters and Papers, 1816–1878*. 2 vols. Harvard University Press, 1965.

Roston, Murray. *Prophet and Poet: The Bible and the Growth of Romanticism.* Northwestern University Press, 1965.

Royle, Edward. *Victorian Infidels: The Origins of the British Secularist Movement 1791–1866.* University of Manchester Press, 1974.

Rubenstein, Marc. "'My Accursed Origin': The Search for the Mother in *Frankenstein,*" *Studies in Romanticism* 15 (1976).

Rupp, Gordon. *Religion in England 1688–1791.* Oxford: Clarendon, 1986.

Russell, Anthony. *The Clerical Profession.* London: S.P.C.K., 1980.

Rutherford, Andrew. *Byron: A Critical Study.* Stanford University Press, 1961.

Ryan, Robert M. "Christ and Moneta." *English Language Notes* 13 (March 1976), 190–92.

"The Genealogy of Honest Doubt: F. D. Maurice and *In Memoriam*" in *The Critical Spirit and the Will to Believe: Essays in Nineteenth-Century Literature and Religion,* ed. D. Jasper. London: Macmillan, 1989, pp. 120–130.

Keats: The Religious Sense. Princeton University Press, 1976.

"Keats's 'Hymn to Pan': A Debt to Shaftesbury?" *Keats–Shelley Journal* 26 (1977), 31–34.

Rylestone, Anne L. *Prophetic Memory in Wordsworth's Ecclesiastical Sonnets.* Southern Illinois University Press, 1991.

Said, Edward. *Orientalism.* New York: Pantheon, 1978.

Sanders, Charles R. *Coleridge and the Broad Church Movement.* Duke University Press, 1942.

Sandler, Florence. "'Defending the Bible': Blake, Paine, and the Bishop on the Atonement" in *Blake and His Bibles,* ed. David V. Erdman. West Cornwall, CT: Locust Hill Press, 1990.

Schorer, Mark. *William Blake: the Politics of Vision.* New York: Holt, 1946.

Scott, W. S. *The Athenians.* London: Golden Cockerel Press, 1943.

Scrivener, Michael. *Radical Shelley: The Philosophical Anarchism and Utopian Thought of Percy Bysshe Shelley.* Princeton University Press, 1982.

"A Swedenborgian Visionary and the Marriage of Heaven and Hell," Blake: An Illustrated Quarterly 21 (1989): 102–3.

Semmel, Bernard. *John Stuart Mill and the Pursuit of Virtue.* Yale University Press, 1984.

The Methodist Revolution. New York: Basic Books, 1973.

Shaffer, Elinor S. *"Kubla Khan" and the Fall of Jerusalem: The Mythological School in Biblical Criticism and Secular Literature, 1770–1880.* Cambridge University Press, 1975.

Sharafuddin, Mohammed. *Islam and Romantic Orientalism: Literary Encounters with the Orient.* New York: Tauris, 1994.

Sharp, Ronald A. *Keats, Skepticism, and the Religion of Beauty.* Athens, University of Georgia Press, 1979.

Sharp, William. *The Life and Letters of Joseph Severn.* New York: Scribner, 1892.

Shaw, George Bernard. "Shaming the Devil about Shelley" in *Selected Non-Dramatic Writings of Bernard Shaw*, ed. Dan H. Laurence. Boston: Houghton Mifflin, 1965.

Sheats, Paul D. "Keats, the Greater Ode, and the Trial of Imagination," in *Coleridge, Keats, and the Imagination Romanticism and Adam's Dream*, ed. J. Robert Barth and John L. Mahoney. University of Missouri Press, 1990.

   The Making of Wordsworth's Poetry, 1795–1798. Harvard University Press, 1973.

Shelley, Bryan. *Shelley and Scripture: The Interpreting Angel*. Oxford: Clarendon Press, 1994.

Shelley, Mary. *Frankenstein, or, The Modern Prometheus*, ed. M. K. Joseph. London: Oxford University Press, 1969.

   Frankenstein, or, The Modern Prometheus, the 1818 Text, ed. James Rieger. Indianapolis: Bobbs-Merrill, 1974.

Shelley, Percy Bysshe. *The Complete Poetical Works of Percy Bysshe Shelley*, ed. Thomas Hutchinson; rev. G. M. Matthews. London: Oxford University Press, 1970.

   The Complete Works of Percy Bysshe Shelley, ed. Roger Ingpen and W. E. Peck. 10 vols. New York: Scribner, 1926–30.

   The Letters of Percy Bysshe Shelley, ed. Frederick L. Jones, 2 vols. Oxford: Clarendon Press, 1964.

   The Prose Works of Percy Bysshe Shelley, ed. E. B. Murray, vol. 1. Oxford: Clarendon Press, 1993.

   Shelley's Poetry and Prose, ed. Donald H. Reiman and Sharon B. Powers. New York: Norton, 1977.

Shepherd, T[homas] B[oswell]. *Methodism and the Literature of the Eighteenth Century*. 1940; rpt. New York: Haskell House, 1966.

Sherwood, Margaret. *Undercurrents of Influence in English Romantic Poetry*. 1934; rpt. New York: AMS, 1971.

Small, Christopher. *Ariel Like a Harpy: Shelley, Mary, and "Frankenstein."*. London: Gollancz, 1972.

Smith, Adam. *Wealth of Nations*. London: Liberty Press, 1981.

Smith, David Q. "The Wanderer's Silence: A Strange Reticence in Book IX of *The Excursion*," *The Wordsworth Circle* 9 (1978), 162–72.

Soloway, R. A. *Prelates and People: Ecclesiastical Social Thought in England 1783–1852*. London: Routledge & Kegan Paul, 1969.

Southey, Robert. *The Poetical Works*. Boston: Osgood, 1875.

Spark, Muriel. "Mary Shelley: A Prophetic Novelist," *Listener*, Feb. 22, 1951, pp. 305–6.

Spellman, W. M. *The Latitudinarians and the Church of England, 1660–1700*. University of Georgia Press, 1993.

Sperry, Stuart M. *Keats the Poet*. Princeton University Press, 1973.

   "Keats's Skepticism and Voltaire," *Keats–Shelley Journal* 12 (1963), 75–93.

Shelley's Major Verse: The Narrative and Dramatic Poetry. Harvard University Press, 1988.

Spinks, George Stephens. *Psychology and Religion: An Introduction to Contemporary Views*. London: Methuen, 1964.

Stanley, Arthur Penrhyn. *The Life and Correspondence of Thomas Arnold D.D.* 2 vols. Boston: Osgood, 1873.

Steffan, Truman Guy, ed. *Lord Byron's Cain: Twelve Essays and a Text with Variants and Annotations*. University of Texas Press, 1968.

Styles, John. *Lord Byron's Works Viewed in Connexion with Christianity and the Obligations of Social Life: A Sermon*. London: 1824.

Sugnet, Charles. "The Role of Christ in Blake's *The Four Zoas*," *Essays in Literature* (1976).

Summerfield, H. "Blake and the Names Divine," *Blake: An Illustrated Quarterly* 15: 1 (1981), 14–22.

Sutherland, D. M. G. *France 1789–1815*. New York: Oxford University Press, 1986.

Sutherland, John. "Blake and Urizen" in *Blake's Visionary Forms Dramatic*, ed. David V. Erdman and John E. Grant. Princeton University Press, 1970, pp. 244–62.

Swinburne, *William Blake: A Critical Essay*. 1869; rpt. London: Hotten, 1968.

Swingle, Larry. "On Reading Romantic Poetry," *PMLA* 86 (1971).

Tannenbaum, Leslie. "From Filthy Type to Truth: Miltonic Myth in *Frankenstein*," *Keats–Shelley Journal* 26 (1977), 101–13.

Thomas, Keith G. "Coleridge, Wordsworth, and the New Historicism: 'Chamouny; The Hour Before Sunrise. A Hymn' and Book 6 of *The Prelude*." *Studies in Romanticism* 33 (Spring 1994), 81–117.

Thompson, Edward P. "Disenchantment or Default? A Lay Sermon" in *Power & Consciousness*, ed. Conor Cruise O'Brien. New York University Press, 1969, pp. 149–81.

The Making of the English Working Class. 1963; New York: Pantheon, 1964.

William Morris: Romantic to Revolutionary. London: Lawrence and Wishart, 1955.

Witness Against the Beast: William Blake and the Moral Law. New York: The New Press, 1993.

Thorslev, Peter, Jr. *Romantic Contraries: Freedom versus Desire*. Yale University Press, 1984.

Thrower, James. *The Alternative Tradition: Religion and the Rejection of Religion in the Ancient World*. The Hague: Mouton, 1980.

Toynbee, Arnold. *An Historian's Approach to Religion*. New York: Oxford University Press, 1956.

Trelawny, Edward John. *Records of Shelley, Byron, and the Author*. 2 vols. London: Pickering, 1878.

Ulmer, William A. "*Hellas* and the Historical Uncanny," *ELH* 58 (1991), 611–32.

Vendler, Helen. "The Living Hand of Keats" in *John Keats: Poetry Manuscripts at Harvard, A Facsimile Edition*, ed. Jack Stillinger. The Belknap Press of Harvard University Press, 1990.
  The Odes of John Keats. The Belknap Press of Harvard University Press, 1983.
Virgin, Peter. *The Church in an Age of Negligence: Ecclesiastical Structure and the Problem of Church Reform 1700–1840*. Cambridge University Press, 1989.
Volney, Constantine Francois Chasseboeuf de. *The Ruins, or, A Survey of the Revolutions of Empires*. 5th English edition. London: Thomas Tegg, 1811.
Waldoff, Leon. *Keats and the Silent Work of Imagination*. University of Illinois Press, 1985.
Walling, William. *Mary Shelley*. New York: Twayne, 1972.
Ward, Aileen. *John Keats: The Making of a Poet*. Rev. edn, New York: Farrar, Straus and Giroux, 1986.
Ward, W. R. "The Baptists and the Transformation of the Church, 1780–1830," *Baptist Quarterly* 25, no. 4 (Oct. 1973), 167–84.
  "The French Revolution and the English Churches," *Miscellanea Historiae Ecclesiasticae* 4 (1970), 55–84.
  Religion and Society in England 1790–1850. London: B. T. Batsford, 1972.
Ward, Wilfrid. *The Life of John Henry Cardinal Newman*. 2 vols. London: Longmans, 1921.
Wasserman, Earl. *Shelley: A Critical Reading*. Johns Hopkins University Press, 1971.
Waterman, A. M. C. "The Ideological Alliance of Political Economy and Christian Theology, 1798–1833," *Journal of Ecclesiastical History* 34 (April 1983), 231–44.
Watkins, Daniel P. *Keats's Poetry and the Politics of the Imagination*. Cranbury, NJ: Associated University Presses, 1989.
Watson, Richard. *A Sermon Preached Before the Stewards of the Westminster Dispensary. . . April 1785. With an Appendix*. London: Cadell, 1793.
Watts, Michael R. *The Dissenters*; vol. 1: *From the Reformation to the French Revolution*. Oxford: Clarendon, 1978.
Wearmouth, R. F. *Methodism and the Working-Class Movements of England, 1800–1850*. 2nd edn. London: Epworth, 1947.
Webb, Timothy. "Shelley and the Religion of Joy," *Studies in Romanticism* 15 (1976), 357–82.
  Shelley: A Voice Not Understood. Manchester University Press, 1977.
Weber, Max. *The Sociology of Religion*. trans. Ephraim Fischoff. Boston: Beacon Press, 1963.
White, William Hale. *The Autobiography of Mark Rutherford*. ed. Reuben Shapcott. 3rd edn., London: Trubner, 1889.
  An Examination of the Charge of Apostasy Against Wordsworth. London: Longmans, 1898.
White, R.S. *Keats as a Reader of Shakespeare*. University of Oklahoma Press, 1987.

Wiener, Joel H. *Radicalism and Freethought in Nineteenth-Century Britain: The Life of Richard Carlile.* Westport, CT: Greenwood Press, 1983.

Wilberforce, William. *A Practical View of the Prevailing Religious Systems of Professed Christians.* 1797; rpt. New York: American Bible Society, 1830.

Wilkie, Brian, and Mary Lynn Johnson. *Blake's "Four Zoas": The Design of a Dream.* Harvard University Press, 1978.

Willey, Basil. *The Eighteenth Century Background: Studies on the Idea of Nature in the Thought of the Period.* 1940; rpt. Boston: Beacon Press, 1961.

Wilson, David, A. *Paine and Cobbett: The Transatlantic Connection.* Kingston and Montreal: McGill–Queen's University Press, 1988.

Wittreich, Joseph A. *Angel of Apocalypse: Blake's Idea of Milton.* University of Wisconsin Press, 1975.

Wolfson, Susan, ed. "Keats and Politics: A Forum," *Studies in Romanticism* 25 (1986), 171–229.

The Questioning Presence: Wordsworth, Keats, and the Interrogative Mode in Romantic Poetry. Cornell University Press, 1986.

Wollstonecraft, Mary. *Collected Letters of Mary Wollstonecraft,* ed. Ralph Wardle. Cornell University Press, 1979.

Woodring, Carl. *Politics in the Poetry of Coleridge.* University of Wisconsin Press, 1961.

Politics in English Romantic Poetry. Harvard University Press, 1970.

Wordsworth. Boston: Houghton Mifflin, 1965.

Wordsworth, Jonathan, et al., eds. *William Wordsworth and the Age of English Romanticism.* Rutgers University Press, 1987.

William Wordsworth: The Borders of Vision. Oxford: Clarendon Press, 1982.

The Music of Humanity. New York: Harper & Row, 1969.

ed. "Waiting for the Palfreys: The Great *Prelude* Debate," *The Wordsworth Circle* 17 (Winter 1986), 1–38.

Wordsworth, William. *"Descriptive Sketches" by William Wordsworth.,* ed. Eric Birdsall. Cornell University Press, 1984.

The Excursion, 1814 Edition, ed. Jonathan Wordsworth. New York: Woodstock Books, 1991.

The Letters of William and Dorothy Wordsworth: The Early Years, 1787–1805, ed. E. de Selincourt, rev. Chester Shaver, 2nd edn. Oxford: Clarendon Press, 1967.

The Letters of William and Dorothy Wordsworth: The Later Years, ed. Ernest de Selincourt, rev. Alan G. Hill. 5 vols. Oxford: Clarendon Press, 1978–88.

The Letters of William and Dorothy Wordsworth: The Middle Years, ed. Ernest de Selincourt, rev. Mary Moorman and Alan G. Hill. Oxford: Clarendon, 1969–70.

Peter Bell, ed. John Jordan. Cornell University Press, 1985.

The Poetical Works of William Wordsworth, Edited from the Manuscripts, with Textual and Critical Notes, ed. Ernest de Selincourt and Helen Darbishire. 5 vols. Oxford: Clarendon Press, 1949.

Poems, ed. John O. Hayden. 2 vols. New York: Penguin, 1977.

The Prelude: 1799, 1805, 1850, ed. Jonathan Wordsworth, M. H. Abrams, and Stephen Gill. New York: Norton, 1979.

The Prose Works of William Wordsworth, ed. A. B. Grosart. London: Macmillan, 1896.

The Prose Works of William Wordsworth, ed. W. J. B. Owen and Jane Worthington Smyser. Oxford: Clarendon Press, 1974.

The Ruined Cottage and The Pedlar by William Wordsworth, ed. James Butler. Cornell University Press, 1979.

The Salisbury Plain Poems of William Wordsworth, ed. Stephen Gill. Cornell University Press, 1975.

Index

CAMBRIDGE STUDIES IN ROMANTICISM

General editors
MARILYN BUTLER, *University of Oxford*
JAMES CHANDLER, *University of Chicago*